Communications in Computer and Information Science   1678

More information about this series at https://link.springer.com/bookseries/7899

Alfonso González-Briones · Ana Almeida ·
Alberto Fernandez · Alia El Bolock ·
Dalila Durães · Jaume Jordán ·
Fernando Lopes (Eds.)

Highlights in Practical Applications of Agents, Multi-Agent Systems, and Complex Systems Simulation

The PAAMS Collection

International Workshops of PAAMS 2022
L'Aquila, Italy, July 13–15, 2022
Proceedings

 Springer

Editors
Alfonso González-Briones 🆔
University of Salamanca
Salamanca, Spain

Ana Almeida
Institute of Engineering - Polytechnic of Porto
Porto, Portugal

Alberto Fernandez 🆔
Universidad Rey Juan Carlos
Madrid, Spain

Alia El Bolock
German International University
Cairo, Egypt

Dalila Durães 🆔
University of Minho
Braga, Portugal

Jaume Jordán 🆔
Universitat Politècnica de València
Valencia, Spain

Fernando Lopes 🆔
National Laboratory of Energy and Geology
Amadora, Portugal

ISSN 1865-0929   ISSN 1865-0937 (electronic)
Communications in Computer and Information Science
ISBN 978-3-031-18696-7   ISBN 978-3-031-18697-4 (eBook)
https://doi.org/10.1007/978-3-031-18697-4

This Springer imprint is published by the registered company Springer Nature Switzerland AG
The registered company address is: Gewerbestrasse 11, 6330 Cham, Switzerland

Preface

The PAAMS Workshops complemented the regular program with new or emerging trends of particular interest connected to multi-agent systems. PAAMS, the International Conference on Practical Applications of Agents and Multi-Agent Systems, is an evolution of the International Workshop on Practical Applications of Agents and Multi-Agent Systems. PAAMS is an international yearly tribune for presenting, discussing, and disseminating the latest developments and the most important outcomes related to real-world applications. It provides a unique opportunity to bring multi-disciplinary experts, academics, and practitioners together to exchange their experience in the development of agents and multi-agent systems.

This volume presents the papers that were accepted in the workshops during the 2022 edition of PAAMS:

- Workshop on Artificial Intelligence for Industry (AI4Industry)
- Workshop on Adaptive Smart areaS and Intelligent Agents (ASSIA)
- Workshop on Character Computing (C2)
- Workshop on Deep Learning Applications (DeLA)
- Workshop on Decision Support, Recommendation, and Persuasion in Artificial Intelligence (DeRePAI)
- Workshop on Multi-agent based Applications for Modern Energy Markets, Smart Grids and Future Power Systems (MASGES)

Each paper submitted to PAAMS went through a stringent peer review by three members of the Program Committee of each workshop. From the 39 submissions received, 25 were selected for presentation at the conference.

We would like to thank all the contributing authors, the members of the Program Committees, the sponsors (IBM, AEPIA, APPIA, and AIR Institute) and the Organizing Committee for their hard and highly valuable work. We thank the funding supporting the project "XAI: Sistemas inteligentes auto-explicativos creados con modelos de mezcla de expertos" (Id. SA082P20) from the Regional Government of Castilla y León and FEDER funds.

Thanks for your help – PAAMS 2022 would not exist without your contribution.

Alfonso González-Briones
Ana Almeida
Alberto Fernandez
Alia El Bolock
Dalila Durães
Jaume Jordán
Fernando Lopes

Organization

General Co-chairs

Frank Dignum   Umeå University, Sweden
Philippe Mathieu   University of Lille, France
Juan Manuel Corchado   University of Salamanca and AIR Institute, Spain
Fernando De la Prieta   University of Salamanca, Spain

Workshop Chair

Alfonso González Briones   University of Salamanca, Spain

Advisory Board

Bo An   Nanyang Technological University, Singapore
Paul Davidsson   Malmö University, Sweden
Keith Decker   University of Delaware, USA
Yves Demazeau   Centre National de la Recherche Scientifique,
                                France
Tom Holvoet   KU Leuven, Belgium
Toru Ishida   Kyoto University, Japan
Takayuki Ito   Nagoya Institute of Technology, Japan
Eric Matson   Purdue University, USA
Jörg P. Müller   Clausthal Technical University, Germany
Michal Pěchouček   Czech Technical University in Prague,
                                Czech Republic
Franco Zambonelli   University of Modena and Reggio Emilia, Italy

Organizing Committee

Juan M. Corchado Rodríguez   University of Salamanca and AIR Institute, Spain
Fernando De la Prieta   University of Salamanca, Spain
Sara Rodríguez González   University of Salamanca, Spain
Javier Prieto Tejedor   University of Salamanca and AIR Institute, Spain
Pablo Chamoso Santos   University of Salamanca, Spain
Liliana Durón   University of Salamanca, Spain
Belén Pérez Lancho   University of Salamanca, Spain
Ana Belén Gil González   University of Salamanca, Spain
Ana De Luis Reboredo   University of Salamanca, Spain

Angélica González Arrieta	University of Salamanca, Spain
Emilio S. Corchado Rodríguez	University of Salamanca, Spain
Alfonso González Briones	University of Salamanca, Spain
Yeray Mezquita Martín	University of Salamanca, Spain
Beatriz Bellido	University of Salamanca, Spain
María Alonso	University of Salamanca, Spain
Sergio Márquez	University of Salamanca, Spain
Marta Plaza Hernández	University of Salamanca, Spain
Guillermo Hernández González	University of Salamanca, Spain
Ricardo S. Alonso Rincón	AIR Institute, Spain
Raúl López	University of Salamanca, Spain
Sergio Alonso	University of Salamanca, Spain
Andrea Gil	University of Salamanca, Spain
Javier Parra	University of Salamanca, Spain

Local Organizing Committee

Pierpaolo Vittorini (Co-chair)	University of L'Aquila, Italy
Tania Di Mascio (Co-chair)	University of L'Aquila, Italy
Federica Caruso	University of L'Aquila, Italy
Anna Maria Angelone	University of L'Aquila, Italy

PAAMS 2022 Organizers and Sponsors

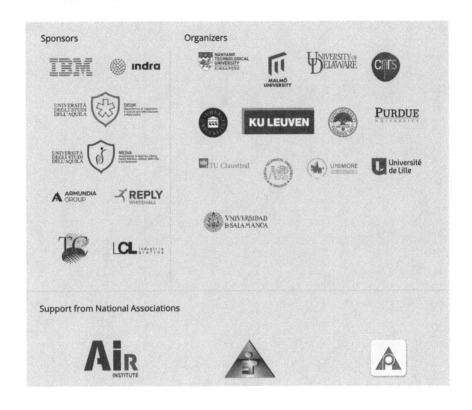

Contents

Workshop on Decision Support, Recommendation, and Persuasion in Artificial Intelligence (DeRePAI)

Workshop on Multi-Agent Based Applications for Modern Energy Markets, Smart Grids and Future Power Systems (MASGES)

Workshop on Artificial Intelligence for Industry (AI4Industry)

Workshop on Artificial Intelligence for Industry (AI4Industry)

The world is witnessing a digitization of most businesses that proliferate in the public and private area. Particularly in industry, the rapid adoption of physical IoT systems culminates in huge amounts of raw data, so industrial organizations are accumulating massive volumes of data which, if explored with adequate artificial intelligence techniques, will allow enhanced decision support, thereby offering new opportunities for industrial organizations to significantly reduce costs, improve efficiency, and transform their operations for the better.

This workshop aims to be a discussion forum on the latest trends and ongoing challenges in the application of artificial intelligence technologies to the area of industry. It intends to link professionals and AI researchers, opening the floor to knowledge dissemination and, in particular, showing how artificial intelligence approaches can be applied in the industry domain.

Organization

Organizing Committee

Ana Almeida   Polytechnic Institute of Porto, Portugal
Ramón J. Durán Barroso   Universidad de Valladolid, Spain
Paulo Leitão   Instituto Politécnico de Bragança, Portugal
Goreti Marreiros   Polytechnic Institute of Porto, Portugal

Program Committee

Baris Bulut   Enforma, Turkey
Dalila Duraes   Univeristy of Minho, Portugal
Héctor Alaiz Moretón   University of Leon, Spain
Honghao Gao   Shanghai University, China
Ignacio de Miguel   Universidad de Valladolid, Spain
Isabel Praça   Polytechnic Institute of Porto, Portugal
José Barata   New University of Lisbon, Portugal
Lino Figueiredo   Polytechnic Institute of Porto, Portugal
Gonçalo Marques   Polytechnic Institute of Coimbra, Portugal
Diogo Martinho   Polytechnic Institute of Porto, Portugal
Jorge Meira   Polytechnic of Institute Porto, Portugal
Peter Mikulecký   University of Hradec Kralove, Czech Republic
Ricardo Santos   Polytechnic Institute of Porto, Portugal
Sara Rodríguez   University of Salamanca, Spain
Serkan Tosun   Kok Digital, Turkey
Stamatis Karnoukos   SAP, Germany
Teresa Pereira   Polytechnic Institute of Porto, Portugal

Towards the Application of Multi-Agent Task Allocation to Hygiene Tasks in the Food Production Industry

Amie Owen[1(✉)], Helen Harman[2], and Elizabeth I. Sklar[2]

[1] School of Computer Science, University of Lincoln, Lincoln LN6 7TS, UK
25388370@students.lincoln.ac.uk
[2] Lincoln Institute for Agri-Food Technology, University of Lincoln,
Lincoln LN2 2LF, UK
{hharman,esklar}@lincoln.ac.uk

Abstract. The food production industry faces the complex challenge of scheduling both production and hygiene tasks. Scheduling is typically done manually. Inefficiencies in scheduling can be costly, adding to challenges already faced due to increasing costs of raw materials/energy and the increasingly strict regulations that factories must adhere to. This paper presents the initial findings of a survey, conducted to learn more about the hygiene tasks within the industry and to inform research on how multi-agent task allocation (MATA) methodologies could automate and improve the scheduling of hygiene tasks. A simulation of a heterogeneous human workforce within a factory environment is presented. This work evaluates experimentally strategies for applying market-based mechanisms, in particular Sequential Single Item (SSI) auctions, to the problem of allocation hygiene tasks to a heterogeneous workforce.

Keywords: Multi Agent Task Allocation · Food hygiene · Multi agent system · Agent based simulation

1 Introduction

A large proportion of time is devoted to hygiene tasks within a food factory environment. Cleaning and sanitizing equipment is fundamental to protecting public health by eliminating the spread of foodborne diseases. If biofilms (thin but robust layers of a collection of microorganisms) are allowed to gain purchase, their resistance to detergents and disinfectants can cause serious issues. Due to the quantity of time devoted to cleaning, and the importance of these cleaning tasks, it is desirable to optimise cleaning operations.

The work presented here proposes that the application of a *Multi-Agent Task Allocation (MATA)* approach to the optimising the scheduling of cleaning tasks within a food production environment. To inform this approach, we conducted a survey of in-practise employees in the UK food industry. Survey participants included Sustainability, Quality, Hygiene and Technical managers, as well as

A. González-Briones et al. (Eds.): PAAMS Workshops 2022, CCIS 1678, pp. 5–16, 2022.
https://doi.org/10.1007/978-3-031-18697-4_1

members of senior management teams within food businesses. The products they handle cover a broad range, including ambient products (products stored at ambient temperature such as dry and tinned food and food stored in glass jars), fresh salads, salmon, cheese, soft drinks, pasta, bread, sandwiches and microwaveable snacks. The intention of conducting the survey was to gain a more in-depth understanding of cleaning within the food industry, the procedures undertaken and the problems faced. We wanted to understand the nature of the cleaning teams and the mechanisms for allocating cleaning tasks to cleaning operatives who conduct cleaning tasks. We were also interested in understanding which tasks are particularly disliked by or dangerous to operatives. An overview of the survey results told us that generally hygiene operatives work in small teams of less than five, and most teams are heterogeneous (only some operatives are trained to carry out certain cleaning tasks). Half of respondents said that tasks were allocated on a flexible basis (rather than weekly or monthly rota). It appears that there is potentially a lack of formalisation of task allocation in some instances, with scope for improvements in efficiency.

A MATA approach is appropriate for situations where a set of tasks must be completed and there exist a team of actors to complete them. It is desirable for tasks to be allocated according to a given objective; this may be to minimise energy usage, or to maximise reward. There are many methodologies employed to solve MATA problems and the research presented here focuses on auction-based methodologies similar to [10] and strategies tailored to heterogeneous teams [22]. Auctions have been proven to be a relatively simple, low (computational) cost method to achieving close-to-optimal solutions in relatively complex scenarios. Auction mechanisms scale well and can adapt dynamically to changes in the problem or scenario. Here we propose MATA as an approach to job scheduling for hygiene tasks within the food production industry, introducing this domain to the multi-agent systems community as a compelling and complex environment for research and development. Two contributions are presented: first, the results of our survey, which illustrates specific features of this task domain; and second, a simulation that demonstrates these features. The simulation draws on feedback from the survey, and offers a first step towards providing a valid and appropriate digital twin of food hygiene teams working in factories, and as a platform for future experimentation with task allocation methodologies.

This paper is structured as follows: Sect. 2 gives background information on hygiene in the food industry. Section 3 details our survey results. Section 4 provides the methodology used for experimentation within the simulation. Section 5 explains our experiment design and Sect. 6 details the results obtained through experimentation. Section 7 closes with a summary and overview of next steps.

2   Background

Food businesses follow standard hygiene protocols and processes. This section provides an introduction to these and Multi-Agent Task Allocation (MATA) methods, which could improve the efficiency of how these processes are scheduled.

2.1   Food Safety and Hazard Analysis and Critical Control Point (HACCP)

In the UK (where this research was conducted), all food businesses must, by law, have a food safety management plan based on Hazard Analysis and Critical Control Point (HACCP) principles. The plan keeps food produced safe from biological, chemical and physical food safety hazards [1]. The plan must identify hazards and methods for controlling these hazards, as well as setting limits and putting things right if a problem is detected. Monitoring of the plan must be maintained and records kept.

Cleaning falls under "preparatory stage A", a *prerequisite* for HACCP [3] as the basic hygiene measures that should be put in place within a business prior to undertaking a HACCP study. There can be a tendency, due to cleaning being a prerequisite and not a core component of the HACCP, for cleaning processes to be less formalised.

Two main practices for cleaning production equipment exist: *cleaning-in-place (CIP)* involves equipment being cleaned by an automated system that runs cleaning chemicals through the equipment without the need for dismantling it, and *cleaning-out-of-place (COP)* where cleaning operatives dismantle equipment before cleaning by hand, e.g. using hand-held water jets. *Open Plant Cleaning (OPC)* involves cleaning walls, ceilings, floors and drain gullies etc. Guided by our survey results (as detailed in Sect. 3), we focus here on COP processes.

2.2   COP Process Steps

In essence, COP processes are simple, with the main backbone following these steps: pre-rinse; wash; post-cleaning rinse; disinfection and final rinse [15].

- **Pre-rinse:** use of water to remove coarse debris and food residues from the surface of equipment. Factors include the type of soiling, applied force necessary to remove the soil and the rinse water temperature.
- **Wash:** use of detergent to scour or scrub equipment in order to remove odors, residual food or other extraneous materials. Critical factors include surface finish, detergent type, concentration and exposure time.
- **Post-cleaning rinse:** for preventing the re-deposit of food soils or foreign matter onto the cleaned surface.
- **Disinfection:** the reduction of undesirable microorganisms to specified and acceptable levels. Identification and characterization of expected microorganisms must be conducted in order to properly target them—inability to do this may include loss in product shelf-life, or life-threatening foodborne illness outbreaks.
- **Final rinse:** removal of the chemicals used in disinfecting in the previous step, due to their toxicity. Many governments globally have maximum residue levels (MRLs) specified for such chemicals.

2.3 Adaption of MATA Methodologies to Food Factory Hygiene Tasks

Our work explores the application of multi-agent and multi-agent task allocation (*MATA*) strategies to the problem of allocating the hygiene tasks performed within the food factories to members of the cleaning teams. In particular, we focus on auction-based mechanisms, which are a popular technique within the MATA and multi-robot task allocation (MRTA) literature. As described by [8, 10, 12, 13, 20], auctions are executed in *rounds* that are typically composed of three phases: (i) announce tasks—an *auction manager* advertises one or more tasks to the agents; (ii) compute *bids*—each agent determines its individual valuation (cost or utility) for one or more of the announced tasks and offers a *bid* for any relevant tasks; and (iii) determine winner—the auction manager decides which agent(s) are awarded which task(s).

The approach explored here draws specifically on two prior works in the literature: [10], where auctions are used to efficiently manage a human fruit harvesting workforce, and [22], where improvements to standard auction mechanisms have been made to tailor allocation to heterogeneous robot teams. In [10], tasks are allocated to *pickers*, who pick the ripe fruits, and *runners*, who collect the fruit from the pickers and transport it to a packing station. *Round Robin, Ordered Single Item* and *Sequential Single Item* methods are employed.

Round Robin (RR) differs from standard auction mechanisms in that only the winner determination phase occurs. The winner is assigned by cycling though ordered lists of agents and tasks, assigning each agent a task in turn. The process concludes when all tasks have been assigned. RR benefits from low computation costs and results in (roughly) even distribution of tasks (i.e. the number of tasks each agent is assigned differs at most by 1 when any agent is capable of performing any of the tasks on offer). Nevertheless, the cost of a task is not considered, synergies between tasks are not exploited and the result is highly dependent on the order in which tasks and agents are matched. As a result, RR alone can result in inefficient task allocations.

In the Sequential Single-Item (SSI) [14], all unassigned tasks are announced to the agents, who place bids on all tasks. The auction manager determines the winner by picking the bidder with the 'best' bid for any task (where the definition of 'best' is domain dependent). The auction repeats in rounds until all tasks have been allocated. SSI is fast (the auction runs in polynomial time in the worst case) and efficient, while also being able to produce an allocation that is close to or within a guaranteed factor away from optimal [14]. SSI has been a popular choice for multi-robot task allocation, and many variants have been studied (e.g. [11, 16–19, 21, 22]).

The work of [22] seeks to improve the performance of SSI when used to assign tasks to heterogeneous robot teams, minimising energy usage and time required to complete all tasks within an experimental domain. The authors state that their algorithms provided consistent and significant improvements for both objectives for a number of scenarios, up to 20% improvement. They developed methods for changing the order in which tasks are allocated to avoid the 'hill-climbing' (building a path in one direction before later being required to complete a task in a different direction) behaviour that SSI can generate. They seek to first allocate tasks that have low levels of competition by employing the *least contested bid*. In addition, using a 'relative expertise' parameter, agents can determine whether or not to bid on a particular task (based on whether they have a relatively high expertise or not).

Other methods documented in relevant research consider defining an allocation problem as a flow-shop model, as in [7] where optimal job scheduling is desired for n jobs of varying processing times on m machines of varying processing power. Biologically-inspired solutions to these types of problems include *Ant Colony Optimization (ACO)* and *Modified Genetic Algorithm (MGA)* for optimization. The work of [6] uses *Mixed-Integer Linear Programming (MILP)* to schedule product runs on a number of different production lines. While we focus here on auctions, our future work may consider other optimization methods.

3   Survey Results

Our survey was administered to volunteers recruited from a pool of in-practice professionals working in the UK food industry. Results are presented from 10 respondents. We provide the survey questions asked to participants and analysis of the responses. Where questions were presented as multiple choice, analysis has been given as the percentage of participants giving each of the possible answers. Where questions required a text description, we have conducted thematic analysis to understand the underlying themes [4].

1. What is your role within the business?
   - *Technical Manager, Sustainability Manager, Quality Manager, QA Technologist, Site Quality Manager, Site Hygiene Manager, Head of Technical, QA Manager, Senior Management, Technical Manager*
2. What does your business manufacture?
   - *Ambient products, vertically farmed salad, salmon processing, cheese, soft drinks, pre-packed salad mixes and whole-head salad vegetables, pasta, packers, sandwiches and microwaveable snacks, sourdough*
3. What determines when cleaning occurs (clean-as-you-go, in-between production runs, deep cleaning etc.)?
   - *All responses describe a variety of combinations including clean-as-you-go, periodic deep clean, shut downs, between product types*
4. Do employees have different skills for cleaning particular equipment?
   - *Yes, individuals often have different training to carry out cleaning of different equipment (60%); no, all members of the team are trained to carry out all cleaning tasks (40%)*
5. Who allocates cleaning tasks?
   - *Team leader (60%); Hygiene manager (30%); Other (10%)*
6. How are tasks allocated?
   - *Flexible each day/shift (50%); Other (30%); Weekly rota (20%)*
7. What data or metrics are collected regarding hygiene?

- *Strong themes were swabbing—micro and instant ATP (detection of adenosine triphosphate, a molecule found in all living things); also mentioned were taking water samples, visual inspections for hygiene audits, staff attendance, production downtime, TVC (Total Viable Counts of microorganisms)/Listeria/Pseudomonas swab pass rates, chemical concentrations and pH levels*

8. Do any data or metrics inform cleaning task allocation?
   - *Mainly participants answered no, although other answers were based on determining the level of the frequency of cleaning, swab results and sign off sheets*

9. Do employees work together when carrying out cleaning of the ceilings, walls, floor and exterior surfaces of equipment?
   - *Small teams of less than 5 people (70%); Individual employees work alone on a task (20%); Other (10%)*

10. How is the team organised during the task?
    - *Everyone knows exactly which sub-tasks they will complete (50%); not structured—anyone can do any sub-task (37.5%); Other (12.5%)*

11. Are there factors that could delay the cleaning of ceilings, walls, floor and exterior surfaces of equipment?
    - *Almost all responses mentioned access to rooms and equipment, especially at high levels or if equipment (such as electrical cables) block the way. Also mentioned was production seasons or growing cycles (for fresh produce).*

12. What are the most time consuming aspects of the cleaning schedule?
    - *Manual cleaning; taking equipment apart; removing gross debris and organising which staff can do what.*

13. What are the most time consuming aspects of the hygiene monitoring schedule?
    - *Swabbing and waiting for results. Other responses mentioned monthly hygiene audits and water sampling.*

14. What aspects of the cleaning and monitoring schedules are inefficient?
    - *A variety of responses without one clear theme. Several participants responded 'not sure' or 'nothing', and one responded 'lacking a clear plan for who does what and when'.*

15. What are the main hazards to employees during cleaning?
    - *Exposure to harsh cleaning chemicals and risk of slips and trips were the main themes and other responses included using sharp equipment, working at height or in confined spaces.*

16. Which jobs do employees dislike or feel uncomfortable doing?
    - *Working at height, working in cold, confined spaces, although generally, cleaning in any environment is disliked.*

17. Which jobs do employees tend to make mistakes and why?
    - *Employees can miss hard to reach areas, trap points or undersides and interiors of surfaces. Other responses mentioned lack of understanding of training, rushing and strict time pressures with the possibility for cross-contamination between not-cleaned and cleaned areas.*

18. Which parts of the factory are the most demanding for maintaining hygiene levels and why?
    – *High care areas due to a lot of equipment (with poor hygienic design) being present in a small floor space. Hard to reach areas and confined spaces like a spiral freezer were also a challenge.*

We understand from responses that allocation of cleaning tasks can be carried out in a flexible manner and generally, data is not used to guide allocation. Operatives usually work in small, heterogeneous teams and a variety of different cleaning practices occur (clean-as-you-go, in-between production/product types, deep clean and shut-downs). Generally the team knows which tasks they will complete, but almost 38% of the time, the process of deciding who will do which task is not structured.

Regarding disliked and dangerous tasks, generally tasks at heights, in cold or constricted areas are disliked and hazardous, in addition to exposure to cleaning chemicals and danger from sharp equipment. Dismantling equipment and manual cleaning are time consuming and, generally, operatives do not enjoy cleaning. Future introduction of robots into cleaning teams has the potential to reduce human exposure to cleaning chemicals and to dangerous conditions. The methodology presented here applies to human workforces of today but also has relevance to hybrid human-robot workforces of the future.

4 Methodology

In order to explore optimisation of cleaning task allocation, a multi-agent based simulation has been created using Mesa [2]. The simulation employs a variety of auction mechanisms to allocate cleaning tasks. Definition of cleaning tasks is based on the five clean-out-of-place (COP) process steps (detailed in Sect. 2.2).

For this iteration of the simulation, the 'pre-rinse' (the first step of the COP process) of a piece of equipment is defined as one task within the simulation. In later work we will include all COP steps.

4.1 Agents

Each agent has a specified 'expertise' for cleaning each type of equipment ('tray washer', 'cheese grater', and 'bottle washer'). In addition, within the simulation, it is possible to vary the agent start positions.

4.2 Task Allocation Mechanisms

For the work presented here, we consider the following mechanisms:

– *Round Robin* (RR) to be used as a baseline for other mechanisms. This involves the first task being assigned to the first agent, the second to the second agent and so forth until each agent has been assigned one task or the list of tasks has been exhausted. If there are more tasks than agents, then the process repeats until all the tasks have been assigned.

- *Sequential Single Item - Lowest Bid* (SSI-LB) whereby in each round of bidding, all unassigned tasks are bid on by all agents. The task with the lowest bid is assigned to the agent who places that bid.
- *Sequential Single Item - Least Contested Bid* (SSI-LCB) similar to SSI-LB, but the bid that is assigned is the one with the maximum difference between the lowest and second-lowest costing bids. If there is a tie between two or more tasks, then the task with the lowest costing bid is assigned.

4.3   Allocation of Cleaning Tasks

For pre-rinse tasks, each task is defined as a list of the perimeter squares for one piece of equipment. In order for agents to bid for tasks, they must calculate the minimum distance to any of the grid squares contained within that task. The bid is made up of the sum of the minimum travel time to the task (calculated using a *Jump Point Search (JPS)* algorithm [5,9]), the time taken to complete the task (to travel the perimeter of the equipment) as well as the time taken to complete all of the tasks already within the agent's schedule. If an agent does not have expertise in carrying out a certain task, it cannot bid on that task—therefore agents bid only on tasks which they are able to complete.

4.4   Execution of Simulation

During execution of agent schedules within the simulation visual environment, operatives move to pieces of equipment in the order in which they appear in their schedules and travel around the perimeter of each equipment. They move through the following states: 'awaiting task assignment', 'waiting to start task', 'navigating', 'cleaning', 'finished task', finally to 'finished all tasks' if they have completed their final task, or back to 'waiting to start task' if there are more tasks to complete.

5   Experiments

Within the simulation, a grid world environment has been created. The dimensions of the room are based on a real pilot plant. Within the plant environment, a randomly generated layout of factory equipment is activated each time a new experiment is begun. Figure 1 shows one example of a randomly generated equipment layout. The amount of equipment, between 15 and 20 pieces, is generated at randomly selected locations (based on a grid structure). Sizes of surfaces are generated, between 5 and 10 grid squares for each piece of equipment. Equipment is randomly allocated as being a 'tray washer' (shown in green), 'cheese grater' (shown in red), or 'bottle washer' (shown in blue), each with their own COP requirements. Three agents are shown as orange grid squares.

We developed a scheduler to run a number of experiments. Experimental conditions compared: *heterogenous* (agents with different values for expertise for different pieces of equipment) vs *homogeneous* (all agents have expertise in all

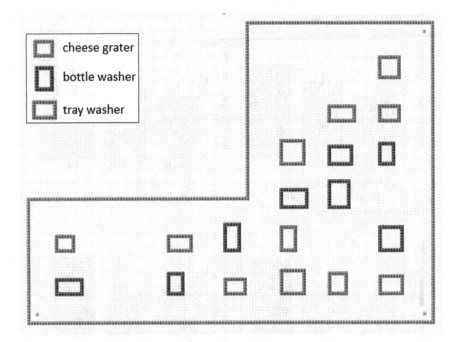

Fig. 1. One configuration of the randomly generated factory layout.

pieces of equipment) agents and for agent starting positions *together* (in the bottom left hand corner of the simulated environment) vs *spread out* at the corners of the factory. Thus we had $\{het|hom\} \times \{tog|spread\} = 4$ combinations of configuration parameters. Each was run 10 times, on 10 different factory layouts, so the results are analysed over 40 runs. For each of the 40 runs, we collected results for each method of allocation (RR, SSI-LB, SSI-LCB). For all runs we used 3 agents and the number of tasks ranged between 15 and 20 (according to the number of equipment generated by the simulation).

6   Results

We analyse our results by looking at the average agent execution time for each of our four scenarios. We define average agent execution time as the average time taken for all agents to complete all of the allocated tasks within their schedule. By optimising performance, we look to minimise the average agent execution time. Results gained using RR act as a baseline from which to evaluate other more effective methods. Figure 2 shows results for heterogeneous and homogeneous agents. We analysed the statistical significance of the results using the Kruskal-Wallis tests and associated H and p values are shown for all scenarios. We use the Kruskal-Wallis test, rather than an Anova t test as the data for all scenarios has been calculated as not being of a normal distribution by the Shapiro-Wilk test.

Heterogeneous agents

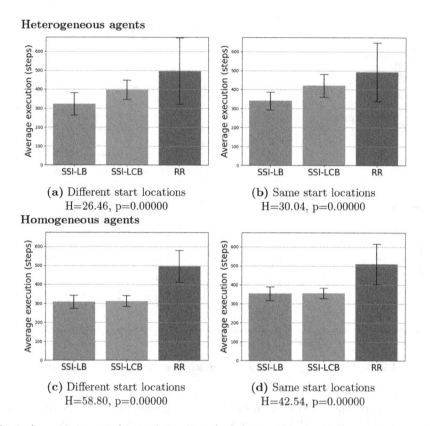

(a) Different start locations
H=26.46, p=0.00000

(b) Same start locations
H=30.04, p=0.00000

Homogeneous agents

(c) Different start locations
H=58.80, p=0.00000

(d) Same start locations
H=42.54, p=0.00000

Fig. 2. Average agent task completion time for heterogeneous and homogeneous agents.

For all four scenarios, SSI-LB achieved a lower average execution time than RR and SSI-LCB; the difference is statistically significant. Scenarios where agents started at spread out locations achieved lower average execution time than when agents started together. For both SSI-LB and SSI-LCB, homogeneous agents achieved a lower average execution time than for heterogeneous agents. Average execution times for SSI-LB and SSI-LCB were more similar for homogeneous agents than for heterogeneous agents.

7   Summary

This paper made steps towards investigating the application of market-based task-allocation mechanisms to the problem of allocating hygiene tasks to operatives in a food factory. A survey is presented and results analysed, giving a greater understanding of the sector. The survey helped to shape the creation of a simulation both to act as a valid and appropriate digital twin and to provide a platform in which to carry out experimentation of task allocation methodologies. Sample results using this simulation were shared.

Future work will look to build upon the work presented here by including all stages of COP processes for each type of equipment, using relevant cleaning schedules. In order to do this, we must look at task durations (which may vary with expertise) as well as the cleaning equipment required. This will lead us to build different types of tasks into the simulation, such as 'collect detergent solution from store', or 'bring hose to another employee' or even 'clean the cleaning equipment'. An understanding of task dependencies will be required at this stage. We will look to investigate non-binary values for expertise for agents. Another avenue that we plan to explore is hygiene monitoring which could result in more dynamic behaviour within the simulation, for example if tasks need to be repeated if cleaning has failed inspection. The complexity of these scheduling challenges makes this domain a compelling area for employing MATA.

References

1. Make an HACCP food plan. https://www.gov.uk/food-safety-hazard-analysis. Accessed 12 Mar 2022
2. Mesa overview. https://mesa.readthedocs.io/en/latest/overview.html. Accessed 11 Mar 2022
3. My HACCP preparatory stage a: Prerequisite food hygiene requirements. https://myhaccp.food.gov.uk/help/guidance/preparatory-stage-a-prerequisite-food-hygiene-requirements. Accessed 08 Mar 2022
4. Doing reflexive ta (2022). https://www.thematicanalysis.net/doing-reflexive-ta/. Accessed 25 Apr 2022
5. Pathfinding (jump point search) (2022). https://discourse.panda3d.org/t/pathfinding-jump-point-search/15149. Accessed 20 Apr 2022
6. Angizeh, F., Montero, H., Vedpathak, A., Parvania, M.: Optimal production scheduling for smart manufacturers with application to food production planning. Comput. Electr. Eng. **84**, 106609 (2020)
7. Berruto, R., et al.: EIT food-EU PRO4BAKE project: improve artigianal bakeries performances considering both demand forecast and process optimisation: the EIT food PRO4BAKE approach. Proceed. Food Syst. Dyn. 126–132 (2021)
8. Dias, M.B., Zlot, R., Kalra, N., Stentz, A.: Market-based multirobot coordination: a survey and analysis. Proc. IEEE **94**(7), 1257–1270 (2006). https://doi.org/10.1109/JPROC.2006.876939
9. Harabor, D., Grastien, A.: Online graph pruning for pathfinding on grid maps. In: Proceedings of AAAI (2011)
10. Harman, H., Sklar, E.I.: A practical application of market-based mechanisms for allocating harvesting tasks. In: Dignum, F., Corchado, J.M., De La Prieta, F. (eds.) PAAMS 2021. LNCS (LNAI), vol. 12946, pp. 114–126. Springer, Cham (2021). https://doi.org/10.1007/978-3-030-85739-4_10
11. Heap, B., Pagnucco, M.: Repeated sequential single-cluster auctions with dynamic tasks for multi-robot task allocation with pickup and delivery. In: Klusch, M., Thimm, M., Paprzycki, M. (eds.) MATES 2013. LNCS (LNAI), vol. 8076, pp. 87–100. Springer, Heidelberg (2013). https://doi.org/10.1007/978-3-642-40776-5_10
12. Heap, B., Pagnucco, M.: Sequential single-cluster auctions for robot task allocation. In: Wang, D., Reynolds, M. (eds.) AI 2011. LNCS (LNAI), vol. 7106, pp. 412–421. Springer, Heidelberg (2011). https://doi.org/10.1007/978-3-642-25832-9_42

13. Kalra, N., Zlot, R., Dias, M.B., Stentz, A.: Market-based multirobot coordination: a comprehensive survey and analysis (2005)
14. Koenig, S., et al.: The power of sequential single-item auctions for agent coordination. In: Proceedings of AAAI, vol. 2 (2006)
15. Lelieveld, H., Gabric, D., Holah, J.: Handbook of Hygiene Control in the Food Industry. Woodhead Publishing (2016)
16. McIntire, M., Nunes, E., Gini, M.: Iterated multi-robot auctions for precedence-constrained task scheduling. In: Proceedings of AAMAS (2016)
17. Nunes, E., Gini, M.: Multi-robot auctions for allocation of tasks with temporal constraints. In: Proceedings of AAAI (2015)
18. Nunes, E., McIntire, M., Gini, M.: Decentralized allocation of tasks with temporal and precedence constraints to a team of robots. In: IEEE International Conference on Simulation, Modeling and Programming for Autonomous Robots (SIMPAR) (2016)
19. Schneider, E., Sklar, E.I., Parsons, S.: Evaluating multi-robot teamwork in parameterised environments. In: Alboul, L., Damian, D., Aitken, J.M.M. (eds.) TAROS 2016. LNCS (LNAI), vol. 9716, pp. 301–313. Springer, Cham (2016). https://doi.org/10.1007/978-3-319-40379-3_32
20. Schneider, E.: Mechanism selection for multi-robot task allocation. Ph.D. thesis, University of Liverpool (2018)
21. Schneider, E., Sklar, E.I., Parsons, S., Özgelen, A.T.: Auction-based task allocation for multi-robot teams in dynamic environments. In: Dixon, C., Tuyls, K. (eds.) TAROS 2015. LNCS (LNAI), vol. 9287, pp. 246–257. Springer, Cham (2015). https://doi.org/10.1007/978-3-319-22416-9_29
22. Sullivan, N., Grainger, S., Cazzolato, B.: Sequential single-item auction improvements for heterogeneous multi-robot routing. Robot. Auton. Syst. **115**, 130–142 (2019)

David – A Novel Approach to an Industrial Recommender System

Rui Marques[1]([⊠]) [iD], Constantino Martins[1] [iD], and María N. Moreno-García[2] [iD]

[1] GECAD - Research Group on Intelligent Engineering and Computing for Advanced Innovation and Development, ISEP – Instituto Superior de Engenharia do Porto, Porto, Portugal
{rfm,acm}@isep.ipp.pt
[2] USAL - Universidad de Salamanca, Salamanca, Spain
mmg@usal.es

Abstract. A conceptual approach to a recommender system that is industrial oriented and optimized for business-to-business. With particular needs, industrial datasets seek assertiveness and contextualization to capitalize on recommender systems. Muscle memory must be implanted on business users, enabling them to harvest the benefits of such technologies. These types of users, which differ from standard ones, are fuzzy and vague in their choices, avoiding explicit forms of feedback. This paper addresses state-of-the-art of such industrial systems, its users and explores a potential solution.

Keyword: Intelligent recommender systems b2b industry

1 Introduction

Recommender Systems (RS) have been in development since 1990's, first as an independent research area, afterword's, focusing on recommendation problems that explicitly rely on the ratings structure. The first papers on the subject by Resnick et al., Hill et al. and Shardanand and Maes, date from 1994 to 1995 [1]. Older proposals already used collaborative filtering (CF) approaches, which are still the basis of a large majority of methods. CF methods predict the ratings that the user would assign to items not rated by them, calculated from other user ratings, using different similarity coefficients. Currently, approaches involving ratings based on other user's experience are among the most successful techniques, where other kinds of similarity coefficients are key factors [2]. In e-commerce, the incorporation of these systems would also mean that they can now deeply understand shopping behavior, increase customer loyalty, excavate potential of each customer, and improve the ability to cross-selling [3].

However, in some real systems, the most relevant item found, may not be the most suitable item to recommend, as rating should be dependent on other factors as stock restriction and coexisting similarity coefficients [2]. Also, some items are easily rated (movies or experiences), while others are too generic. On personal learning environments, where user/student chooses topics, RS's help solve a critical problem of information overload, allowing for fitted contents, while supplying teachers with student profiling, aiding in creating tailored courses, where content quality does not correlate with

A. González-Briones et al. (Eds.): PAAMS Workshops 2022, CCIS 1678, pp. 17–28, 2022.
https://doi.org/10.1007/978-3-031-18697-4_2

high-recommendation accuracy. RS applicability and success rate, largely depends on field of knowledge, underlying strategy on merging item-user information, RS techniques and innovation [4].

While evolved, RSs are still adapting to a multitude of different operational environments and user's profiles. This document reflects such efforts in a business-to-business (B2B) ecommerce for Jewelry and Home Décor products (J + HD). The present document purposes a concept approach to an industrial B2B e-commerce-based Recommender System. In Sect. 2, a brief state of the art of Recommender Systems in Industry and B2B is presented, followed by requisites and specificities of this field of knowledge. Section 3 includes a description of user modelling and different types of rating. Also, a distinct user type named – B2B user – is introduced. In Sect. 4, we also discuss context of operations of *David* while discussing problems and possible solutions. The work projects itself in the advent of one of the biggest trends in web personalization, which is to provide a tailored user experience, matching user preferences, enabling navigation support and linking users to appropriate items [5].

2   Recommender Systems for Industry – Performance and Pitfalls

Many systems use RS as a basis for recommendation, some popular examples are: Amazon.com – the well-known business-to-consumer (B2C) ecommerce, LinkedIn and Facebook – professional and personal space networks, MovieLens – collaborative filtering for movies, GroupLens – identification of interesting articles for users, Netflix and Youtube – notorious video streaming platforms, Grundy – arguably the first RS ever made which recommended books to users [2, 6–9].

RS are comprised of a linear 3 tier architecture: Representation of information, neighborhood formation and recommendation generation [10] and commonly use five types of classification for filtering [6, 8, 11]:

- Collaborative Filtering (CF), compares user's ratings on items, offering recommendation on new items not yet known to a user.
- Content Based Filtering (CBF), suggest items similar to ones previously liked by users, takes into consideration similarity and user preferences.
- Demographic (DM), based on user's personal characteristics.
- Utility-based (UT) and Knowledge-based (KB), requires a utility function that compares items, comparison does not take in consideration statistical content so no common CF and CBF problems, however they require knowledge acquisition for item compare, something like delivery date or other kind of meta-information.

Tables 1 and 2 detail and classify systems by its each RSs type, detailing their pros and cons, providing an overlay of functionality for each type of RS [1, 6, 8, 11–13].

This study shows quite clearly that every system has its drawbacks, where at least one system has 2 or more "Cons" (-). CF and CBF summarize key features better than other methods, supported by options like "Domain knowledge unnecessary", "Adaptative features", while permitting "Implicit feedback" strategies to be used. Another conclusion that can be drawn is that only Utility-based and Knowledge-based RS are immune to

Table 1. Pros and cons on recommender systems

Pros	Cons
A. Allows niche identification;	I. New user scalability problem;
B. Domain knowledge unnecessary;	J. New item scalability problem;
C. Adaptative features, as quality improves over time;	K. Grey sheep problem;
D. Implicit feedback sufficient;	L. Dependent on large historical data set;
E. No Cold Start scalability problems;	M. Stability vs. plasticity problem;
F. Sensitive to preference changes;	N. Requires demographic information gathering;
G. May include external features;	O. Requires utility function user input;
H. Mapping from user to items possible;	P. Not adaptative, suggestion is static;

Table 2. Types of recommender system by Pros (+) and Cons (-)

Classification	A	B	C	D	E	F	G	H	I	J	K	L	M	N	O	P	Q
Collaborative Filtering	+	+	+	+					-	-	-	-	-				
Content Based Filtering		+	+	+					-			-	-				
Demographic	+	+	+						-		-	-	-	-			
Utility-based					+	+	+								-	-	
Knowledge-based					+	+	+	+								-	-

I, J (item and user scalability) and K (Grey Sheep) "Cons". Finally, N - demographic information gathering may suffer a strong limitation in a General Data Protection Regulation (GDPR) compliant operation, including B2C or consumer-to-consumer (C2C) ecommerce's, which limits access and distribution of private user unique identifiable tokens.

Performance is critical in recommendation. RS's must have a methodology directed to evaluating performance. There are 5 key factors of performance that should be tuned, i.e., for measuring accuracy, recommended results should be compared to real user actions, high similarity would yield comparable accuracy. Performance measures are: confidence (if computable, may limit recommendations to a given or user configured confidence interval, however, may limit novelty), coverage (which defines the exact number of items for which recommendations can be generated), diversity (is a way of raising RS usefulness, this can be done by including diverse items on top n results), novelty (when a user tends to respond to something new rather than something that is only popular), and serendipity (measures unexpectedness and acts on diversity and novelty) [8, 10].

Shortcomings are part of any system; RSs are not different. The most impactful limitations are Cold Start (User and Item) and Sparsity as they affect recommendation output. Scalability is often a problem for big inventories and should be accounted for in design stage. The limitation aspect of a RS should allow opportunity for improvement while using a different filtering technique or a hybrid solution. Common and impactful limitations and operational detail are described as Cold Start for User and Items, Sparsity, Over-specialization, Scalability and User comparison [1, 8, 10–12].

Other issues include trust relations between users and similarity of tastes, affecting the "word-of-mouth" aspect of the RS system [8]. Also, grey sheep and popularity bias are also a known problem of modern RS. Users with unusual tastes may struggle to find similarities, while growing popularity of segments of population may infer bias results of RS, affecting accuracy and long tail distribution in output data, which in some cases may be mitigated. In the case of niche users, studies found that these are usually more engaged (rate more items). In order to democratize recommendations, these users should be considered as relevant stakeholders [13].

3   User Modelling and Ratings

A key aspect of RS is to understand the User, while suggesting relevant items. The identification of user's objectives and needs, associated to personality traits and tastes are key aspects in User Modelling (UM) [14]. In a RS where CF is a key factor, adequate user profiling is paramount in building the CF matrix. Building comprehensive and meaningful connections between users will provide also meaningful insights on relevant recommendations. The opposite also applies.

Ratings are divided into two macro groups, explicit and implicit feedback. Explicit ratings can be considered as regular ratings, as they depend on user prompt to classify and rate a given item. Implicit rating depends solely on application domain and can be viewed as a set of inferences on user behavior, obtained by measurable and observable sets of parameters [15]. Given the different strategies, some authors recommend a hybrid approach as the way to go as both types of feedback suffer from noise and are extremely sensitive to user's context [15]. Other authors argue that explicit rating is the best way for information availability in the least amount of time, explicit ratings may not be the best solution for long term information availability, on the other hand inferred implicit methods, while error prone, are much more frequent [8].

To provide a clear view of differences and similarities, Table 3 shows a set of key features for both implicit and explicit ratings. Exactness and abundancy of ratings are key factors for rating to be meaningful. Explicit ratings are useful, only if relevant in count and the user is willing to cooperate. On the opposite, abundant low accuracy ratings, may be repeatedly used, with little to none impact to the user activity. Expressivity of the user is also a relevant factor (i.e., 1 through 5 stars, yes or no) where explicit ratings may provide helpful, even negative ratings, which can be useful to other users. Implicit feedback does not provide such content and has serious limitations on expressivity (measurability) of rating. In the context of continuity, in terms like "interest over time" and "cognitive cost for the user", implicit rating tends to behave better in recommendation system sustainability. A hybrid rating system can be considered a suitable solution as rating types complement each other [8, 15].

Conclusions by some authors show that, however different, datasets of both ratings produce similar performances, also that the rate of providing explicit feedback decreases over time and that overall providing of explicit feedback has a negative impact on the user's behavior also, some users are reluctant to provide explicit feedback, that can be partially explained by the cognitive effort required. Finally, implicit ratings show appreciation towards items, just in a different way as explicit feedback [15].

Table 3. Key features of explicit and implicit ratings – a,b and c [15], d [8]

Feature	Implicit Rating	Explicit Rating
Accuracy [a]	Low	High
Abundance [a]	High	Low
Context-sensitive [a]	Yes	Yes
Expressivity of the user [a,b]	Positive	Positive/Negative
Measurement reference [a]	Relative	Absolute
Interest decays over time [b]	No	Yes
Cognitive effort b / Cost to the user [d]	No	Yes
User impact on repeated request for feedback [c]	None	Negative
Information availability (amount of time) [d]	Low	High

The computational cost of matrixes of users and items are high. Depending on the method, (i.e., a hybrid solution with CF and CBF methods, requires two sets of matrices of users and items) computational cost may be a serious constraint. Several solutions such as clustering, filtering, top n, or even, merging models prior to similarity calculation, have been proposed as valid techniques on how to diminish task complexity [16]. The concepts of implicit rating later developed other areas as web usage mining – which is a set of logs and/or activity tracking of the user, that may include clicks, views, and transactions [17].

In conclusion, rating is a key element in obtaining information. Distinct audiences are prone to a type of feedback given their usability context, a mixed approach in rating could offer an optimized way of collecting rating. While user data collection may be supervised, data anonymization strategies should provide systems viability while fulfilling regulations. UM – User Modelling, elevates rating to content personalization, bringing user context to product ranks, which is a critical factor for success in a RS.

4   Concept of David - An Intelligent Recommender System

4.1   Industrial and B2B Context of Application

B2B is a specialized type of trade between commercial parties, that usually represent industrial backbones. B2B platforms facilitate interactions between buyers and suppliers (B2B partners), by providing a quick, easy, and cheap mean of access to each other industrial or commercial inventory [18] - the range of items that may include raw materials, equipment, and finished products. Such transactions are in a higher number and volume when compared to B2C operations, explained by the repeated transaction of the same good or service in the value chain. B2C, usually, fits in a single transaction model of the same good or service (i.e., Amazon.com) [19].

Scenario for Recommender Systems in such context. B2B E-commerce in the United States of America (USA) is growing rapidly and expected to top 1.8 trillion US Dollars by 2023, accounting for 17% of all B2B sales [18]. In Gross Domestic Product (GDP) terms, a study [20] shows relevant data from a range of business types. The study mentions that B2C is estimated from 2.7% to 4.5% GDP (2017 to 2025) worldwide and in Europe (EU) from 3% to 4.9% GDP (2017 to 2025). Numbers detailing B2B e-commerce are significantly different. GDP on the same study shows that worldwide is estimated from 32.6% to 54.2% GDP, and in EU from 42.4% to 69.2% GDP. Exposing B2B trade relevance in global e-interactions in commerce [20].

In industrial RS datasets, where merged user/item features and interactions are pertinent, datasets often follow a power law distribution, where the scale of dense and sparse features are in numbers of hundreds to thousands [7]. The same author concludes that categories of items can go to 100 M + entries. While acknowledging that every industrial case has its own requirements, and simpler use cases also exist. In particularly large datasets, specific actions must be considered in support systems, technologies, and strategies (i.e., Machine Learning (ML) vocabulary) [7].

Sheer application of RS in B2B and industry, supported by e-commerce, is limited due to its inherent structural complexity. For this reason, these types of systems have been overlooked or merely disregarded, while B2C and C2C have been on active development. RS main challenge for "real-world" B2B is the complicated tree-structures of items and user profiles, imposed by companies' business and industrial applications, that are not manageable by current similarity measures. This may be a reflex of great focus on B2C rather than B2B by corporate brands [21, 22].

B2B business and industrial processes, workloads and datasets can also be an easy target of "information overload". Abundance of information can empower connections between business partners but can also impose limitations where overly complex or indeterministic information structure is used to map B2B business [22].

Business User. Are distinct from common end-users, in a sense that they search for different things. This does not mean they must be different persons, only on different models of requirement fitting, that need to be addressed, to find a suited solution for a given problem, showcasing on how complexity can exacerbate the differences between B2B and B2C users.

A clear distinction is displayed in type of interaction through the online channel, B2B users are often vague and fuzzy and cannot be dealt with by existing recommendation methods [22]. Usually face bigger uncertainty in e-marketplaces, when compared to traditional channels, as it is more difficult to access quality and commitment of participants. They also tend to manage multiple layers of partners, such as manufacturers and suppliers, that involve heavy procurement [21]. In this business scenario, operations depend mostly on intermediaries, shifting a bigger relevance into the B2B e-commerce platform itself, that should provide a role of quality assurance. This effect is also known as "information asymmetry" and mitigated through a diversity of signals such as brand, reputation, service quality, online references, word-of-mouth (WOM) recommendations, legal status, and location [18].

4.2 An Example from the Jewelry and Home Decor Business Area

A B2B product is distinct from a B2C product. This distinction comes from the industrial backend supporting B2B, which may comprehend different specifications (size, color, feature, personalization's, add-ons, etc.), and may even deliver Original Equipment Manufacturer (OEM) product for rebranding. B2B e-services supply further complex, and diverse tree-structure of "item", and may contain warranty, specification assurance, delivery quantity and date, lot control, creation and expiration dates, heavy logistics and transport, and so on. B2B customer may opt for drop shipping, if available, which is a commercial contract where supplier handles storing and shipment of their client's stock, adding single items warehouse handling and logistics to the mix.

Field of Application. Data used from an industrial unit [23], that implements several B2B e-commerce's specialized in Jewelry and Home Décor (J + HD), in a multi-brand, multi-user environment. Significant properties differentiate to B2C, as listed:

- User Controlled Access - B2B is conditioned to pre-enrolled or registry-based users,
- E-commerce user defined personalization's in "Product Customization" - provide complete control to the e-commerce user (drawings, pictures, different fonts, etc.),
- Product aggregations – gross product kits, collections, and quantity discounts,
- JIT pricing in "Pricing Policy" - where materials used depend on market prices or external control indicators (gold and silver prices),
- "Other Features" - tools in B2B intended for B2B User to support their own clients,
- Dataset cardinality – quantity of items is between 4 and 10 times as much as in their B2C counterparts,
- Logistic factors – Item availability, deliverability, and shipment policies.

While inheriting fundamental features, some businesses have concerns that drive B2B e-services context of operations. In J + HD, precious metals take part in characterizing even further such industrial and e-commerce specificities. Gold, Silver or derivates depend on open exchanges and price is affected directly by markets, harmonized with local and global events, directly affecting product price and/or availability.

Similarity. Another frequent issue of J + HD is the concept of similar products, while some are gold, others are golden. This can influence customer as the price tend to be radically different while the overall aspect may not be as distinct. These kinds of products offer the same benefits and intent as the original product, with slight intrinsic differences between them.

For instance, a "ring", may be used in a diversity of situations, from simple relationship celebration, bought for self or even a wedding celebration. The purpose is usually important for an effective suggestion. In a "buy-for-self", a Stainless-Steel ring, may be a wise choice, due to its durability, engraving options, and low price, however in a weeding celebration a gold ring is more suitable, due to its intrinsic value, durability, and engraving options, even with the high price, it can easily be included in the event budget. Choices may even include lower gold percentage rings, that offer the same exterior visual effect, with lower price and less durability. Of course, any of the choices could be the right one, depends on taste, personal values, and budget. For a RS, it would be hard to suggest the right item, if not oriented properly.

Extreme cold-start. Other factors affect recommendation like seasonality, special event dates, novelty, and high product refresh rate. Generating repeated item cold-start. J + HD is prone to commercialize certain products in specific dates. Novelty is a critical success factor, and new products are created according to demand or trend. Product removal is also frequent (end of stock – products have usually low quantities, slow sales of expensive items – intrinsic value due to precious metal, causes higher stock rotation). This creates a problem of product follow-up (product A is replaced by product B) where product B may be a result of a trend, a mix between features of products A and C, a derivation of a best seller A- > B1 and A- > B2, and so on. This process occurs in each season or special event date. The result, the new item, that is not affiliated to the old one in any way, nor does it have any rating due to novelty state, creates systematic cold-start - extreme cold-start - in items that should be most pertinent to audiences.

4.3 A Potentially Good Solution

The actual work embodies a set of novelties that springs into reality an innovative B2B RS, named – *David* – an intelligent RS, fit for B2B e-commerce within industrial datasets, optimized for J + HD. The solution comprehends critical improvements on the areas of popularity bias, implicit rating, and business user modelling on the way to create a new type of Hybrid RS.

The conceptual solution implements a CBF adjusted to J + HD similarity model, based on characteristics, specifications, and attributes with major emphasis on visual similarity. Paralleled with a Hybrid CF with CBF for B2B users, in a way that clicks, add-to-cart's, product visits, category visits, filters and search queries are compiled with orders and sales history, aggregated with geographical data.

The engine must include two critical factors of success in J + HD, which are "novelty detector/enhancer" and "popularity bias mitigation". Novelty should provide a way of showcasing relevant new products, that inherit key characteristics of products once bought/liked by user, that are now available with a new *elan* – solving extreme cold-start. Novelty should also be date and geographic aware (some special dates are local dates). Popularity bias mitigation should provide a way for overly popular items, not to contaminate regional and contextual novelty pertinence (Fig. 1).

Engine strategy for concept purposes a race condition between CBF and Hybrid CF + CBF, where both models are complemented with auxiliary models (for novelty and popularity bias). The objective is to recommend an item, ranked by result confidence. Best result wins and is returned to user.

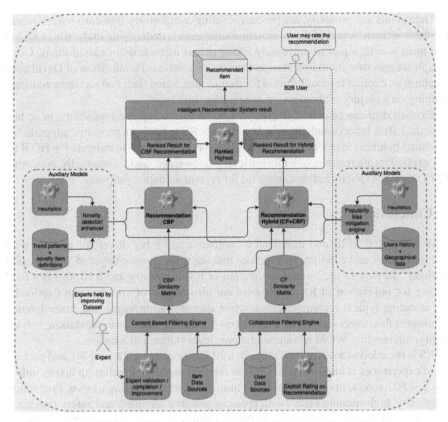

Fig. 1. Exemplifies *David*, an intelligent RS conceptual solution

The output weights higher ranked response as the race condition aims to mitigate low CF results on a given item. CBF should rank higher on off-topic searches and novelty detection while Hybrid CF + CBF should rank higher when historical and geographical patterns emerge. Expert evaluation of CBF model is also possible and considered an important enhancement.

Actual work is placed in implicit rating data retrieval and processing, based on following data-points:

- searches - free text searches made by the user, partial and complete results,
- logins - registers timestamp and approximate location for B2B consumer ecommerce's, useful for regional interest tuning,
- visualizations - click or mouse-overs in products, categories and wish lists, scroll percentage is also measured where the objective is to rate interest,
- filters - activated filters in a view (category or search),
- actions - previously not included actions, like add-to-cart, checkout, express-checkout, add-to-wishlist and product customization selection.

Data points are, presently, in a process of rating composition, that must reflect overall interest in an item. A process of information validation is undergoing study, where a rated item must also be a part of previously added to cart items and/or ordered items. Good enough success rate should yield assertiveness of solution. Planification of David contemplates an explicit feedback button for user to interaction (i.e., bad recommendation), resulting on a perjury of the item, or even a mute on David.

Explicit data can be used as B2B user feedback, in its sparse availability, in ad-hoc contexts. Likes, ignores and dislikes should adapt RS towards its presented suggestions, regulating boldness in recommendations. The expected output is to mitigate J + HD B2B user explicit rating resistance, while retrieving knowledge, and, contextually, educating B2B User that explicit feedback is useful for recommendation purposes.

5 Conclusions

As demonstrated, B2B and industrial e-commerce are a big driver for growth, with expressive sizes and capillary specificities making them an easy target of "information overload". In view of the limited application of RS in industry and B2B, this is a field lacking for innovation in RS. B2B users are also targets of "information overload", thus avoiding typical recommendation while demonstrating vague and fuzzy intents. To mitigate this, users support their decisions on: quality assurance, reputation, service quality, referencing, WOM recommendations, legal status, and location.

RS is regarded as a driver for change in a 2020 e-commerce Report [24], and personalized experiences is highly ranked (3rd) as relevant aspect of purchasing luxury online [25]. J + HD, represents a subset of listed limitations while bringing its own. Production complexity, high running costs (with precious material handling and safety concerns) deters new players, and so, innovation. Product similarity is a complex matter and needs to be addressed with assertion as it may result in an overly complex matrix of similarity, while failing to compare vital terms in the user standpoint.

Staff specialization is also a big concern, as they tend to recognize product similarities, categories, typologies, and customization possibilities with ease. This makes effective staff replacement hard to achieve without performance losses or higher costs (sometimes both). These professionals also play an important role in "teaching" software and discriminating relevant information in a business process [26].

Industrial and B2B successful item classification directly affects business profitability, saving labor costs, number of employees and training hours across multiple product categories [26] and, perceived in this conjecture, a B2B RS is a critical factor for innovation in B2B e-commerce's, between suppliers and customers.

David should be able to improve shopping experience through personalization. CBF (as a David by-product) should provide a baseline for such J + HD through improved similarity for product type comparison. Personnel specialization, needed for categorization, can be less critical, or even, replaced by David in some cases.

Next steps for David include implicit rating matrix compilation and ruleset specification through web-mining and contextual parallel dataset aggregation.

Acknowledgements. This research work was supported by National Funds through FCT (Fundação para a Ciência e a Tecnologia) under the project UI/DB/00760/2020.

References

1. Adomavicius, G., Tuzhilin, A.: Toward the next generation of recommender systems: a survey of the state-of-the-art and possible extensions. IEEE Trans. Knowledge and Data Eng. **17**(6), 734–749 (2005)
2. Chen, Y., Shang, M.-S.: An evaluation of structure based similarity indexes for collaborative filtering. In: 2010 Third International Conference on Knowledge Discovery and Data Mining. Phuket, Thailand (2010)
3. Xiaohui, H., Mai, Z., Zhang, H., Xue, Y., Zhou, W., Chen, X.: A hybrid recommendation model based on weighted bipartite graph and collaborative filtering. In: 2016 IEEE/WIC/ACM International Conference on Web Intelligence Workshops (WIW). Omaha, NE, USA (2016)
4. Chatti, M.A., Dakova, S., Thüs, H., Schroeder, U.: Tag-based collaborative filtering recommendation in personal learning environments. IEEE Transactions on Learning Technologies **6**(5), 337–349 (October-December 2013)
5. Dlab, M.H.: Experiences in using educational recommender system ELARS to support e-learning. In: 2017 40th International Convention on Information and Communication Technology, Electronics and Microelectronics (MIPRO). Opatija, Croatia (2017)
6. Burke, R.: Hybrid recommender systems: survey and experiments. User Modeling and User-Adapted Interaction **12**(4), 331–370 (2002)
7. Wu, C.-J., et al.: Developing a recommendation benchmark for MLPerf training and inference. CoRR vol abs/2003.07336, p. 2003.07336 (2020)
8. Schafer, B.J., Frankowski, D., Herlocker, J., Shilad, S.: Collaborative filtering recommender systems. In: The Adaptive Web: Methods and Strategies of Web Personalization. Springer-Verlag, pp. 291–324 (2007)
9. Adomavicius, G., Huang, Z., Tuzhilin, A.: Personalization and recommender systems. In: INFORMS TutORials in Operations Research, pp. 55–107 (2008)
10. Lucas, J.P., Luz, N., Moreno, M.N., Anacleto, R., Figueiredo, A.A., Martins, C.: A hybrid recommendation approach for a tourism system. Expert Systems with Applications **40**(9), 3532–3550 (2013)
11. Mobasher, B.: Data mining for web personalization. In: The Adaptive Web: Methods and Strategies of Web Personalization, pp. 90–135. Springer-Verlag, Berlin, Heidelberg (2007)
12. Sanchez-Moreno, D., Gil Gonzalez, A.B., Munoz Vicente, M.D., Lopez Batista, V., Moreno-Garcia, M.N.: Recommendation of songs in music streaming services: dealing with sparsity and gray sheep problems. In: Trends in Cyber-Physical Multi-Agent Systems. The PAAMS Collection - 15th International Conference, PAAMS 2017, pp. 206–213. Springer International Publishing (2018)
13. Abdollahpouri, H., Burke, R., Mansoury, M.: Unfair exposure of artists in music recommendation. ArXiv, vol abs/2003.11634, pp. 1–4 (2020)
14. Faria, A.R., Almeida, A., Martins, C., Gonçalves, R., Figueiredo, L.: Personality traits, learning preferences and emotions. In: Eighth International C* Conference on Computer Science & Software Engineering. Yokohama, Japan (2015)
15. Jawaheer, G., Szomszor, M., Kostkova, P.: Comparison of implicit and explicit feedback from an online music recommendation service. In: Proceedings of the 1st International Workshop on Information Heterogeneity and Fusion in Recommender Systems. Barcelona, Spain (2010)
16. Pazzani, M.J.: A framework for collaborative, content-based and demographic filtering. Artificial Intelligence Review **13**(5), 393–408 (1999). Dec
17. Kobsa, A.: Modeling the user's conceptual knowledge in BGP-MS, a user modeling shell system. Computational Intelligence **6**(4), 193–208 (1990)
18. Yoon, Y.L., Yoon, Y., Nam, H., Choi, J.: Buyer-supplier matching in online B2B marketplace: an empirical study of small- and medium-sized enterprises (SMEs). Industrial Marketing Management **93**, 90–100 (2021). Feb

19. Cardoso, J.M.: Integration of Virtual Programming Lab in an Eduscrum-based Programming Teaching Process (2020)
20. ACEPI: IDC Portugal, Economia Digital e o Papel das PME na Região Norte (2018). [Online]. Available: https://www.nortedigital.pt/pt/estudos/
21. Mohamad, A.H., Fathullah, M., Ismail, S., Radzi, A.R.M.: A recommender system for finding products from next door virtual manufacturer or supplier: a conceptual study. In: Proceedings of the 4th International Conference on Green Design and Manufacture 2018 (2018)
22. Wu, D., Zhang, G., Lu, J.: A fuzzy preference tree-based recommender system for personalized business-to-business E-services. IEEE Transactions on Fuzzy Systems **23**(1), 29–43 (2015)
23. Flamingo, S.A.: flamingob2b.pt. Porto (2016)
24. Rotar, A.: eCommerce Report 2020. Statista Digital Market Outlook (2020)
25. Luan, L., et al.: China Luxury Report 2019 - How young Chinese consumers are reshaping global luxury. McKinsey & Company (2019)
26. Nia, A.G., Lu, J., Zhang, Q., Ribeiro, M.: A framework for a large-scale B2B recommender system. In: 14th International Conference on Intelligent Systems and Knowledge Engineering (ISKE) (2019)

Multiple Domain Security Awareness
for Factories of the Future

Sinan Wannous[1,2(✉)] , Tiago Dias[1,2] , Eva Maia[1,2] , Isabel Praça[1,2] ,
and Ana Raquel Faria[1,2]

[1] School of Engineering, Polytechnic of Porto, (ISEP/IPP), Porto, Portugal
{Sinai,tiada,egm,icp,arf}@isep.ipp.pt
[2] Research Group on Intelligent Engineering and Computing for Advanced Innovation and
Development (GECAD), Porto, Portugal

Abstract. In the context of factory digitization, the focus of Industry 4.0 initiative
is to leverage the automation and data exchange in manufacturing processes using
automation, IoT, and advanced technologies. Industry 5.0 has emerged as the next
industrial revolution, to adopt a human-centric approach for digital technologies.
That said, having people, robots, smart machines, and intelligent production systems working together raises challenges in terms of monitoring and securing the
production environment. In other words, the complexity of smart factories makes
it possible for incidents to occur and interrupt the manufacturing process. They
might also cause leaking sensitive information or putting the worker's life in danger as well. Accordingly, designing secure architectures in intelligent factories is
crucial to secure a continuous production lifecycle and safe working conditions.
Nonetheless, due to the decentralized environment of modern factories, creating multi-domain data correlation is crucial to obtain universal monitoring of the
occurring events, as well as to establish cyber situational awareness and adopt
suitable countermeasures in case of attacks. For these purposes, we developed a
holistic multi-domain security and safety mechanism for Factories of the Future.
Our approach consists of individual but integrated modules, each of which is
responsible for capturing alerts from different domains of the factory. Alerts are
then handled by an intelligent correlator to inspect possible attacks or malfunc-
tions on the investigated shop floor. In this paper, we describe the architecture and
design of the developed approach.

Keywords: Factories of the future · Multi-domain security and safety ·
Intelligent correlator

1 Introduction

Industry 4.0 describes a digital revolution of different IT-driven aspects in the manufacturing industry. It combines a variety of fundamental concepts such as smart factories,
cyber-physical systems, and decentralized self-organization [1]. The Fifth Industrial
Revolution (a.k.a. Industry 5.0) was announced by the European Commission to complement Industry 4.0 paradigm. Primarily, it incorporates efforts toward the transition to

A. González-Briones et al. (Eds.): PAAMS Workshops 2022, CCIS 1678, pp. 29–40, 2022.
https://doi.org/10.1007/978-3-031-18697-4_3

a sustainable, human-centric, and resilient European industry [2]. While Industry 4.0 is technology-driven with smart factories as one of its essential initiatives, Industry 5.0 is considered to be value-driven aiming at achieving societal goals beyond jobs and growth [3]. That being said, Industry 5.0 attempts to capture the value of new technologies and place the well-being of the industry workers at the center of the production process [4].

On the other hand, smart factories introduce new digitized facilities that connect machines, systems, and stakeholders in an efficient and flexible manner. The automation of production processes, as well as the introduction of intelligent systems into these processes, pose challenges in terms of monitoring and securing the production environment. That said, the complexity and uncertainty of modern factories make it possible for unexpected incidents to occur, making it likely to interrupt the manufacturing process or to leak important information, as well as to put the worker's life in danger. To this end, designing secure architectures in intelligent establishments is crucial to secure a continuous production lifecycle and safe working conditions.

In many occurrences, sensors are installed in several spots to detect emergency situations and avoid material and human damage. To some extent, these preliminary solutions might help in monitoring and controlling individual assets. Nonetheless, due to the dependency of smart factories on intelligent and decentralized automation mechanisms, a proactive monitoring approach needs to deal with heterogeneous, large, and disparate systems that usually operate in various domains of the manufacturing process. Furthermore, as an essential actor in the manufacturing process, considering human factors such as human behavior and human-machine interactions, is crucial but rather not well covered in building resilience mechanisms [5]. Accordingly, collecting and correlating data streamed from all integrated modules in the factory is the first step toward building a holistic multi-domain protection mechanism.

In this work, we describe an integrated multi-domain security and safety mechanism for the Factories of the Future. Our approach incorporates several modules and employs multiple Machine Learning (ML) techniques to correlate alerts from three distinct analyzers: Energy Analyzer, Human Behavior Analyzer, and Network Analyzer. The proposed domains were selected to provide an integrated security from three crucial aspects that exist in almost any industrial environment: energy, human resources, and networks.

2 State of the Art

Security and safety in smart industrial and residential environments have been widely investigated. With the aim of designing robust architectures to detect emergency situations and avoid both material and human damage.

A multi-agent and multi-sensor based security system for intelligent buildings was developed by Luo, R.C., et al. [6]. The proposed system aims at detecting dangerous situations using sensors and has four agents; fire, intruder, environment, and power detection/diagnosis agents. Furthermore, according to da Silva, M.J., et al. [7], the selection of alerts within an industrial plant is difficult due to the huge amount of involved variables. To address this issue, the authors propose an industrial context-aware recommendation system using Semantic Web and Machine Learning techniques. The solution provides an adaptive interface to make non-intrusive recommendations to assist the operator in the decision-making process. According to Park, S.T., et al. [8], there is insufficient research for analyzing threats to smart factories and systematic management. The authors of this work present a Machine Learning and context-aware intrusion detection system in a smart factory-based environment. The proposed architecture consists of three phases: a) data capturing and parsing from sensors and other resources, b) model building and inferring using unsupervised/supervised learning, and c) threat scoring and visualizing in a real-time graph representation. The verification showed better detection rates for anomaly signs. Additionally, handling heterogeneous sources and maintaining security over large data-driven systems have been addressed by Moustafa, N., et al. [9]. This paper proposes a new threat intelligence scheme that models the dynamic interactions of Industry 4.0 physical and network components. It consists of two modules: smart management and threat intelligence. On the other hand, the safety of workers in a factory shop floor has been investigated by Nwakanma, C.I., et al. [10]. The authors used sensors to gather normal and abnormal data of human activities at the factory, in which a real-life situations dataset was also developed.

Moreover, correlating large amounts of data, gathered from various sources, is crucial to establish cyber situational awareness. It allows to adopt suitable countermeasures in case of attacks [11]. In their work, Settanni, G., et al. [12] proposed a collaborative analysis engine for situational awareness and incident response (CAESAIR). The system aims at supporting security operators in collecting security-relevant data from various sources, investigating on reported incidents, correlating them, and providing possible interpretations. Leszczyna, R. and Wróbel, M. R. [13] present a framework that integrates multiple levels of threat intelligence in energy systems and implements a centralized model of information exchange. As part of the solution, a Situational Awareness Network (SAN) was designed where correlation rules that introduce alert prioritization were also specified. AUSPEX [14] is another framework that uses multi-factor approaches combining big data analytics and security intelligence to support in prioritizing the most likely compromised hosts in large organizations. The system integrates internal and external indicators for early detection and mitigation of Advanced Persistent Threat (APT) activities. The data processed combines security sensors and external information related to the employees.

Creating multi-domain data correlation has been also introduced in many other fields to obtain universal awareness of the occurring events. A Multi-Domain Integration and Correlation Engine (MD-ICE) [15] was introduced to understand the situational context in military missions. The system ingests data from two domains: textual information and sensor network information. The resulted data allows for labelling and inference of inter-domain correlations using Machine Learning tools. Castro, A., et al. [16] presented a novel approach to fault network management for multi-domain environments, based on a shared ontology-based knowledge plane and distributed agent architecture. In this approach, agents receive and analyze alarms, and then use a rule-based mechanism to infer the suitable actions and upgrade the knowledge plane. Another work by Wand, K., et al. [17] investigates a hybrid approach to extract fault information by analyzing multi-domain sequential patterns in time-series signals for fault diagnosis. The proposed approach combines a modified Symbolic Aggregate approXimation (SAX) framework and Kernel Principal Component Analysis (KPCA) and outperforms the methods of SAX-entropy using Support Vector Machine for classification.

The work we present in this research adds to what is being done in this regard, specifically in terms of providing a holistic perspective for the security and safety of the Factories of the Future. This happens by monitoring, integrating, and correlating data gathered from multiple domains within the factory, namely the energy consumption domain, human behavior domain, and network domain.

3   Proposed Multi-domain Architecture

3.1   System Architecture

This solution is divided into five distinctive components, which are: (i) Energy Forecasting Analyzer, (ii) Human Behavior Analyzer, (iii) Network Analyzer, (iv) Intelligent Correlator, and (v) Kafka Server. As shown in Fig. 1, it follows a microservices architecture that contributes to the scalability, maintainability, availability, resilience, and security of the decentralized systems.

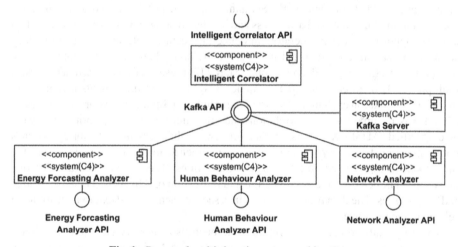

Fig. 1. Proposed multi-domain system architecture

As shown in the diagram, which follows the C4 model for visualizing software architecture [18], this solution uses Apache Kafka as the primary means of communication between systems. Apache Kafka [19] is an open-source distributed event streaming platform used for high-performance data pipelines, streaming analytics, data integration, and mission-critical application. In this work's context, we used Pub/Sub architecture to allow the analyzers to be publishers and to publish to a Kafka topic, and the Intelligent Correlator to be a subscriber and consume the data stored.

This architectural approach allows the components to be small and concise, each with its own responsibility. In this context, each analyzer works as an anomaly detector for each domain: energy, human interactions, and network traffic. Similarly, to anomaly detectors, these analyzers also raise alerts, which are published to a common Kafka topic, making them producers for Kafka Server. The Intelligent Correlator is based on the Hybrid Intrusion Detection System (IDS) presented by Dias, T., et al. [20]. The Hybrid IDS is a highly interpretable and explainable rule-based IDS. In this work, the authors proposed this IDS which stands out for its ML support on the knowledge base, resorting to transparent ML models to generate new rules to be added to the knowledge base, making the IDS much more robust. This Intelligent Correlator maintains much of this work's capabilities regarding the intrusion detection process. This correlator is a Kafka consumer, meaning that it consumes the alerts of the topic, acting on a configured cadency, and correlates them via the rules registered in the knowledge base. Each analyzer module will be further explained in the following subsections.

3.2 Energy Forecasting Analyzer

Obtaining efficient energy predictions is crucial to inspect energy patterns, as it leads to wiser decisions in many aspects. Analyzing energy consumption can be also utilized to monitor buildings and detect deficiencies over time. Studies have been conducted to investigate the impact of energy monitoring in detecting undesirable behaviors [21, 22]. In this regard, we developed the Energy Forecasting Analyzer for buildings and industries. Particularly, this module monitors the actual power consumption for a set of observers/sensors in real-time, predicts future energy records for each observer, compares actual and predicted values, and generates forecasting-based alerts. The workflow of the Energy Forecasting Analyzer consists of two main phases: Training and Scanning.

Training Phase. For each subscribed observer, a training scheduler would be set and triggered as configured in the observer's settings. In every training process, the latest historical energy consumption values for the targeted observer are retrieved, pre-processed, and aggregated into a specific timestamp (minute, hour, day, etc.). Then, it is used to train a predefined supervised ML model. Resulting in an up-to-date trained prediction model for each observer. An input data adapter has been designed to retrieve power data via multiple channels, including APIs, Databases, and static MS Excel files. Furthermore, all involved variables such as training interval, training data source, training data size, aggregation window, and the ML model are configurable for each specific observer.

Scanning Phase. Like the training phase, a separate scanning scheduler with a specific interval is defined for each observer. During the scanning process, the actual energy consumption for the targeted observer is retrieved via the defined data source. Moreover, the previously trained model is loaded and used to predict the observer's expected consumption. Then, the system compares both predicted and actual consumptions and, based on a specific threshold, the difference is being assessed. In case the actual consumption exceeds the normal predicted one, an alert would be generated and triggered to a broadcasting channel (see Fig. 2). An alert triggering mechanism has been developed to allow broadcasting alerts to multiple channels such as: APIs, Databases, and Apache Kafka topics. Likewise, involved variables such as scanning interval, comparison threshold, and distribution channel can be set in the observer's configuration interface.

```
{
  "trigger_time": "2022-01-17T16:24:54.787484+00:00",
  "processing_time": "2022-01-17T16:24:54.997518+00:00",
  "description": "Energy value exceeded the designated threshold during the last HOUR. Energy Value is: 13833 Predicted Value is:
11665.076923076924",
  "analyzer": "Cutting Division",
  "provider":        ,
  "training_details": {
    "start_time": "2022-01-17T16:24:20.562542+00:00",
    "end_time": "2022-01-17T16:24:22.381506+00:00",
    "accuracy_r2": 0.8392024963776039,
    "columns": "[\"year\", \"month\", \"day\", \"hour\", \"target\"]",
    "data_rows_num": 73,
    "data_columns_num": 5,
    "estimator_details": "AdaBoostRegressor()",
    "validation_details": "KFold(n_splits=5, random_state=None, shuffle=True)",
    "aggregation_window": "HOUR"
  },
  "scanning_details": {
    "start_time": "2022-01-17T16:24:53.981535+00:00",
    "end_time": "2022-01-17T16:24:55.184482+00:00",
    "prediction_sample": "[2022, 1, 17, 15]",
    "actual_energy_value": 13833.0,
    "predicted_energy_value": 11665.076923076924,
    "diff_energy_value": 2167.923076923076,
    "threshold_energy_value": 1000.0
  }
}
```

Fig. 2. An example of an alert triggered by the Energy Forecasting Analyzer

3.3 Human Behavior Analyzer

The Human Behavior Analyzer is the system of this multi-domain solution which is responsible for capturing the emotions of the operator of the shop floor. As shown in Fig. 3, this component is composed of two separate modules: Emotion Detector and Camera Application.

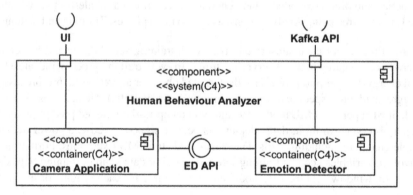

Fig. 3. Human behavior analyzer architecture

Emotion Detector. It is the part of the system that receives images/frames input and classifies the emotion registered regarding the operator caught in that frame. Upon the arrival of a frame, the system preprocesses it by firstly detecting the person in the frame, resorting to a pre-trained detector, and secondly using a pre-trained estimator to focus just on the person's face. With this estimator, the system obtains the coordinates surrounding the person's face. Those are then used to crop the image, for the emotion classification not to be made based on the environment surrounding the captured person. Lastly, the classification is computed using an EfficientNet Convolutional Neural Network. This module considers seven emotions based on the Ekman Model of Basic Emotions [23], including: angry, surprised, disgusted, happy, fearful, sad and neutral. Thus, the system outputs one of those seven emotions, which at last are identified with the computer's IP address that outputted such result, preserving the public integrity and confidentiality of the operator, and is then published to the corresponding Kafka topic.

Camera Application. It is a standalone UI container that can run on one or many devices. This container is responsible for capturing frames in real-time from the computer's webcam and sending them to the Emotion Detector, keeping track of the overall emotions felt by the operator, and suggesting the operator to take a fatigue test when the overall emotions are negative for a long period of time.

3.4 Network Analyzer

Intrusion Detection Systems have been largely used to identify and deal with different threats, by analyzing the network traffic and reporting eventual unnatural occurrences. Suricata [24] is an example of an open-source IDS that supports several protocols and has several rulesets that can be easily extended. Even using several rules to filter the network traffic received, the IDSs deal with large amounts of diverse data. Machine Learning is particularly useful at dealing with large and varied datasets, which are crucial to develop an accurate intrusion detection system. Thus, the huge challenge that intrusion detection represents can be supported by ML techniques. Therefore, we build a Machine Learning engine (ML Engine) that works together with Suricata IDS to identify different threats.

The ruleset of the Suricata IDS instance used was extended with rules designed according to the manufacturing context to match its specific threats and anomalies. This ruleset is completely flexible and allows the administrator to add new detection rules. Each rule consists of an action (what happens when the signature matches), the header (protocol, IP, ports, direction) and options. When a match with a rule occurs, an alert is raised (according to the action defined) and distributed to a Kafka topic.

ML Engine was developed to help in the detection of new attack patterns and new vulnerabilities. It receives the network traffic and uses anomaly detection (unsupervised learning) and misuse-based (supervised learning models) models to detect attacks and anomalies. Then this information is outputted to help in the detection of security incidents. The core of the ML Engine is the ML creator (see Fig. 4). It is responsible for continuously creating new models to improve the performance of the ML Engine. This is very important since due to the fast emergence of new attacks, data needs to be constantly updated. The creation process consists of three main stages: pre-processing, training, and evaluation.

Pre-processing. Most raw traffic network information is not prepared to be fed into ML algorithms. As such most algorithms require some processing of the data to function properly, e.g., removal of 0 variance features, removal of invalid values, etc. Moreover, some parsers also need to be built to ensure the match with ML algorithms input. Feature selection and feature engineering are techniques that aim to reduce the number of variables of the data to remove noise and accelerate the models, and create new features that have better relationships with the target variables.

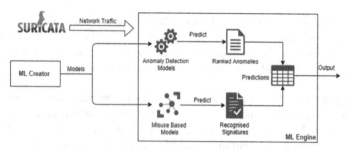

Fig. 4. Network Analyzer – ML Engine

Training. The training process happens after carefully splitting the available data into train and test sets and putting away the testing set for later use. If the data is enough the train set is further split into a validation dataset which is used to evaluate every model trained in the training set until a performance goal is achieved. In a last instance the model is tested on the test set and if the results are satisfactory the model is deployed. In the case of data shortage in the training set, the model can be trained using cross-validation, where the training set is split into k parts or folds and the model is tested independently in each of the parts while being trained on the aggregation of the other k-1 parts. The performance is then calculated as the average of the performance of all folds.

Evaluation. Several experiments were already done using public datasets. Some unsupervised learning techniques, which may hold the key for the detection of Zero-day attacks have been studied. Additionally, feature selection and ensemble methods were applied to recent datasets in order to develop valid models to detect intrusions as soon as they occur. A robust and simplified framework that allows the optimization of any ML model was also built. All these works were developed with the aim of improving the intrusion detection capability.

Note that these experiments correspond to a first phase of the continuous improvement of the ML Engine. In this first phase we used the publicly available datasets that are intended to resemble real data traffic to create the first models to be included in the ML Engine. We used these datasets since they have several different attacks, typically used in real networks, that allow the ML algorithms to learn how to detect them. Then, the ML Engine will be fine-tuned with data from the manufacturing network.

4 Intelligent Correlator

4.1 Correlator Architecture

As previously mentioned, the Intelligent Correlator is based on the Hybrid IDS presented in [20]. However, considering the shift in the domains, some system components were disregarded, as shown in Fig. 5.

In this new architecture, derived from the one presented in the original work, we used only the Drools Backend component since it is the expert system capable of correlating the alerts sent via the analyzers, disregarding the automatic generation of rules

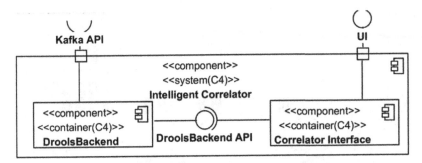

Fig. 5. Intelligent correlator architecture

capability because of the lack of valuable data. Lastly, the presented work also contains the Correlator Interface, a newly developed User Interface.

The Drools Backend maintains its previous responsibilities presented in [20] regarding rules and correlations. Although in previous iterations, this component acted upon arrival of data, in this implementation, a cadence for the consumption of the alerts was defined, making the system act on this value. After consuming the alerts, the system calculates the dynamic evidence, used by Drools engine as evidence to perform the correlation between the gathered data from each domain, resorting to the rules registered in the knowledge base. When the inference results in a warning or a danger state, a justification is created. This confers the system a high transparency, interpretability, and explainability.

The Correlator Interface, presented in the next paragraph, also maintains the same responsibility of providing the means to interact with all Restful APIs of the Intelligent Correlator, by allowing the operator to perform the Create, Read, Update, and Delete (CRUD) operations on the rules, visualizing the correlations, listing all the alerts, and providing means to perform data analysis processes.

4.2 Correlator Interface

As part of the developed methodology, we designed the Correlation Interface to provide an overall overview of the system and its components. The interface is an interactive web-based tool that helps operators obtain details about occurring alerts and their correlations, in addition to controlling and managing the correlation rules. The interface provides the following features:

Alerts List. Displays a list of alerts being received from the three integrated domains: Energy Forecasting Analyzer, Human Behavior Analyzer, and Network Analyzer. Alert details include the alert's origin, triggering time, and other descriptive attributes.

Realtime Dashboard. Provides an instant monitoring interface that displays stats for alerts being triggered from each domain (see Fig. 6).

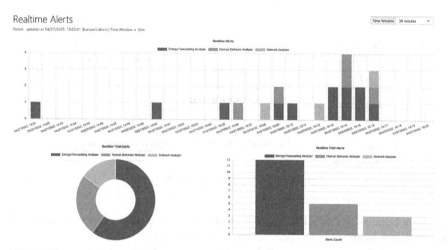

Fig. 6. The realtime dashboard of the Correlation Interface

Network Dashboards. Show multiple visualizations of statistics and details of the alerts that are captured and analyzed by the Network Analyzer. It is possible to visualize the type, severity and time occurrences of network events and alerts, as well as the incident probability according with the ML Engine.

Rules Correlation. Allows the operator to list all the correlations and consult the evidence and rules leading to a warning or danger state correlation. These are presented in a grid ordered by correlation date and time and composed of a color scheme that allows the operator to identify better, which are just warnings, and which represent a danger. Furthermore, the operator can visualize a well-structured justification of that correlation, enhancing the work's explainability and interpretability.

Knowledge Base. The knowledge base interface is where the user can communicate with the Drools backend to perform the CRUD operations on the rules. The rules are displayed as cards in a grid, in which the user can visualize their information, such as the left-hand side and the right-hand side, which are the conditions and the actions of each rule, respectively. Lastly, for more experienced users, the raw Drools format of a rule is also displayed.

5   Conclusion

The combination of traditional manufacturing processes with advanced technologies paved the way for the emergence of smart factories. This came side by side with introducing intelligent systems to automate various aspects of the production process. These kinds of technological advances haven't come with no cost, as the complexity of such intelligent environments opened the doors for attacks and other faults to take place and cause material and human damage. Monitoring smart factories is crucial to keep a continuous and safe production environment. This has been one of the key aspects of Industry

5.0 initiative. The work presented in this paper contributes to what has been done in this field. Specifically, in terms of providing an integrated approach to universally monitor and correlate various domains on a shop floor.

In our approach, we combine inspecting energy consumption profiles, monitoring human behavior interactions, as well as analyzing network traffic, to generate alerts in real-time and correlate them using a rule-based intelligent system. Up to our knowledge, our work is the first to consider such three naturally different but extremely critical aspects to raise awareness and ensure the security and safety in the Factories of the Future. Further efforts would be to evaluate the effect of this approach in a realistic environment. Primarily, by simulating multiple deficiencies occurring at the same time in different domains on a shop floor and trying to capture and correlate the corresponding alerts.

Acknowledgements. The present work has been developed under the EUREKA ITEA3 Project Cyber-Factory#1 (ITEA-17032) and Project CyberFactory#1PT (ANI—P2020 40124) co-funded by Portugal 2020. Furthermore, this work has also received funding from the project UIDB/00760/2020.

References

1. Lasi, H., Fettke, P., Kemper, H.-G., Feld, T., Hoffmann, M.: Industry 4.0. Bus. Inf. Syst. Eng. **6**(4), 239–242 (2014). https://doi.org/10.1007/s12599-014-0334-4
2. Industry 5.0 | European Commission: https://ec.europa.eu/info/research-and-innovation/res earch-area/industrial-research-and-innovation/industry-50_en. Last accessed 26 April 2022
3. Xu, X., Lu, Y., Vogel-Heuser, B., Wang, L.: Industry 4.0 and industry 5.0—inception, conception and perception. J. Manuf. Syst. **61**, 530–535 (2021)
4. Breque, M., De Nul, L., Petridis, A.: Industry 5.0: towards a sustainable, human-centric and resilient European industry. Luxemb. LU Eur. Comm. Dir. Res. Innov. (2021)
5. Becue, A., Maia, E., Feeken, L., Borchers, P., Praca, I.: A new concept of digital twin supporting optimization and resilience of factories of the future. Appl. Sci. **10**, 4482 (2020)
6. Luo, R.C., Lin, S.Y., Su, K.L.: A multiagent multisensor based security system for intelligent building. In: Proceedings of IEEE International Conference on Multisensor Fusion and Integration for Intelligent Systems, MFI2003, pp. 311–316 (2003)
7. de Silva, M.J., Pereira, C.E., Götz, M.: Context-aware recommendation for industrial alarm system. IFAC-PapersOnLine. **51**, 229–234 (2018)
8. Park, S.-T., Li, G., Hong, J.-C.: A study on smart factory-based ambient intelligence context-aware intrusion detection system using machine learning. J. Ambient. Intell. Humaniz. Comput. **11**(4), 1405–1412 (2018). https://doi.org/10.1007/s12652-018-0998-6
9. Moustafa, N., Adi, E., Turnbull, B., Hu, J.: A new threat intelligence scheme for safeguarding industry 4.0 systems. IEEE Access. **6**, 32910–32924 (2018)
10. Nwakanma, C.I., Islam, F.B., Maharani, M.P., Lee, J.-M., Kim, D.-S.: Detection and classification of human activity for emergency response in smart factory shop floor. Appl. Sci. **11**, 3662 (2021)
11. Settanni, G., Shovgenya, Y., Skopik, F., Graf, R., Wurzenberger, M., Fiedler, R.: Acquiring cyber threat intelligence through security information correlation. In: 2017 3rd IEEE International Conference on Cybernetics (CYBCONF), pp. 1–7 (2017)
12. Settanni, G., Skopik, F., Shovgenya, Y., Fiedler, R.: A collaborative analysis system for cross-organization cyber incident handling. In: ICISSP, pp. 105–116 (2016)

13. Leszczyna Rafałand Wróbel, M.: Threat intelligence platform for the energy sector. Softw. Pract. Exp. **49**, 1225–1254 (2019)
14. Marchetti, M., Pierazzi, F., Guido, A., Colajanni, M.: Countering advanced persistent threats through security intelligence and big data analytics. In: 2016 8th International Conference on Cyber Conflict (CyCon), pp. 243–261 (2016)
15. Dron, W., et al.: Multi-domain integration and correlation engine. In: MILCOM 2018-2018 IEEE Military Communications Conference (MILCOM), pp. 1–9 (2018)
16. Castro, A., Fuentes, B., Lozano, J.A., Costales, B., Villagrá, V.: Multi-domain fault management architecture based on a shared ontology-based knowledge plane. In: 2010 International Conference on Network and Service Management, pp. 493–498 (2010)
17. Wang, J., Zhang, Y., Duan, L., Wang, X.: Multi-domain sequential signature analysis for machinery intelligent diagnosis. In: 2016 10th International Conference on Sensing Technology (ICST), pp. 1–6 (2016)
18. The C4 model for visualising software architecture. https://c4model.com/. Last accessed 29 April 2022
19. Apache Kafka: https://kafka.apache.org/. Last accessed 29 April 2022
20. Dias, T., Oliveira, N., Sousa, N., Praça, I., Sousa, O.: A Hybrid Approach for an Interpretable and Explainable Intrusion Detection System. In: Abraham, A., Gandhi, N., Hanne, T., Hong, T.-P., Nogueira Rios, T., Ding, W. (eds.) ISDA 2021. LNNS, vol. 418, pp. 1035–1045. Springer, Cham (2022). https://doi.org/10.1007/978-3-030-96308-8_96
21. Silva, F., Santos, G., Praça, I., Vale, Z.: A context-based building security alarm through power and sensors analysis. Energy Informatics **1**(1), 349–353 (2018). https://doi.org/10.1186/s42162-018-0045-z
22. Wannous, S., Praça, I., Andrade, R.: Intelligence as a Service: A Tool for Energy Forecasting and Security Awareness. In: De La Prieta, F., El Bolock, A., Durães, D., Carneiro, J., Lopes, F., Julian, V. (eds.) PAAMS 2021. CCIS, vol. 1472, pp. 176–186. Springer, Cham (2021). https://doi.org/10.1007/978-3-030-85710-3_15
23. Gu, S., Wang, F., Patel, N.P., Bourgeois, J.A., Huang, J.H.: A model for basic emotions using observations of behavior in Drosophila. Front. Psychol. 781 (2019)
24. Home – Suricata: https://suricata.io/. Last accessed 28 April 2022

Using an Explainable Machine Learning Approach to Minimize Opportunistic Maintenance Interventions

Afonso Lourenço ⓘ, Marta Fernandes(✉) ⓘ, Alda Canito ⓘ, Ana Almeida ⓘ, and Goreti Marreiros ⓘ

GECAD – Research Group on Intelligent Engineering and Computing for Advanced Innovation and Development, Polytechnic of Porto (ISEP/IPP), Porto, Portugal
{fonso,mmdaf,alrfc,amn,mgt}@isep.ipp.pt

Abstract. The industry 4.0 paradigm, with a wide range of sensors, IoT and big data technologies, has facilitated the assessment of faults in complex mechanical systems. In this paper, a fault diagnosis strategy is presented for opportunistic condition-based maintenance decisions of a single failure mode. Focusing on the challenges of the fault identification task, the proposed method was assessed by conducting a case-study using real-world data. To detect symptoms of screen pack degradation in the company's coextrusion process, the devised strategy was based on an anomaly approach and a technique for explainable artificial intelligence (XAI). Experimental results for two consecutive production runs of an extruder show that the proposed method effectively identifies clustered anomalies as symptoms of a clogged screen pack.

Keywords: Machine learning · Industry 4.0 · Explainable AI · Fault diagnosis · Plastic extrusion

1 Introduction

With engineering structures becoming increasingly complex, proactive maintenance plays an important role in keeping the system working under conditions consistent with the required levels of safety, performance, and reliability [1]. However, routine interventions, i.e., replacement of filters or wearing components, require production to be purposefully stopped [2]. As a result, it is a common practice to perform replacement of non-failed components when opportunities arise, e.g., other component failures or change of production materials [3]. By relying on this policy, operators expect to decrease production stoppages and take advantage of the economies of scale of maintenance due to a single set-up cost [4].

Despite being apparently effective, blindly applying this concept of opportunistic maintenance (OM) [5] can turn out to be costly, as some subsystems might still be in good operating condition. In fact, OM only performs economically better than standard preventive maintenance when a system has many components, high set-up costs, high

A. González-Briones et al. (Eds.): PAAMS Workshops 2022, CCIS 1678, pp. 41–54, 2022.
https://doi.org/10.1007/978-3-031-18697-4_4

failure rates and low mean time between interruptions [6]. Aside from that, OM's drawbacks are the challenge of finding whether maintenance activities conducted under the policy are "underdone" or "overdone", as well as sacrificing the possibility of conducting work preparation in advance for routine interventions [7].

To address this, integration of monitoring information in the assessment of system behavior could provide more reliable condition-based opportunistic maintenance decisions [8]. The industry 4.0 paradigm, with a wide range of sensors, increased computational resources, IoT and big data technologies [9], facilitates the analysis of the unavoidable natural phenomenon of degradation. Three analytical modelling approaches are used: physical-based, knowledge-based and data-driven [10]. Developing a physical model is not always possible, as it requires full system design specifications and cumbersome numerical simulations. In such situations, it might be more convenient to derive models from historical records of selected covariates, i.e., variables that are correlated to, but do not define completely or directly the underlying degradation state [11]. To select the proper maintenance action, it is necessary to track the aberrant behavior of each individual component as a symptom of the initiation of the degradation process.

One key issue in doing this is the lack of availability of suitable observations regarding both healthy and degraded subsystems. In such cases, an alternative consists in using temporal unsupervised anomaly detection strategies with proper evaluation [12]. As many statistical-based and machine learning techniques are available, a comparative analysis is required to select the most adequate method according to the different facets and challenges of the specific application [13, 14]. One of the facets that engenders interesting complications is the presence of temporal dependence in the sensor data, i.e., time series data. Characteristics such as autocorrelation, trend, and seasonality, among others, must be considered when working with this type of data [13]. Another facet is dealing with multivariate time series of sensor readings [14], which is commonly done by finding a new set of uncorrelated variables using feature selection methods [15, 16].

Bridging all the knowledge from these fields, the added value of this paper lies in building a fault diagnosis strategy for the interrupting interventions of a manufacturing system. As the literature shows [17, 18], a wide variety of models have been developed for optimizing maintenance, but real case-studies are still not represented very well in this field [18]. This is surprising, since maintenance is something which should be done in practice. Consequently, this paper describes the application of the aforementioned procedure to the domain of blown film extrusion, specifically in the production of flexible packaging. To address this use-case, a fault diagnosis procedure of the screen pack contamination phenomenon is proposed. For fault detection, the Isolation Forest (iForest) was used due to its ability of detecting clustered anomalies and adequacy for real-time deployment [19]. For fault isolation and identification, the Shapley Additive Explanations (SHAP) was applied, since it is the only post hoc explanation model that satisfies local accuracy, missingness and consistency [20]. Additionally, the number of correlated variables was reduced to overcome the weaknesses of these techniques. The adopted feature selection method was the Maximum Relevance Minimum Redundancy (mRmR) algorithm, as it is well suited for real-time deployment [21].

The rest of this document is organized as follows: Sect. 2 presents and justifies the selection of materials and methods used for fault diagnosis. Section 3 presents the implementation of the developed strategy and Sect. 4 describes and discusses the results obtained. Finally, Sect. 5 provides the concluding remarks and directions for future work.

2 Materials and Methods

2.1 Industrial Case Study

The objective of this work is to apply a fault diagnosis procedure for a company that operates with blown film extrusion equipment to produce flexible packaging for the food and medical industries. The fault diagnosis methodology was developed to identify specific faults in extrusion machines, which is one of the most common methods of polymer processing [22]. The purpose of the extruder it to feed plastic granules from a hopper on to the screw and convey them along the barrel where they progressively melt due to the conductive heat of external heaters and the mechanical heat of friction of screw rotation. At the end of the barrel, the mixed polymer melt is filtered with a screen pack to remove contaminants or gels and, finally, enters the die to produce an extrudate of the desired shape [23].

The specific fault that this work focuses on is the screen pack degradation phenomenon. As debris deposit within the filter, defects in the extrudate and risk of damaging the metering pump increase. Therefore, the screen pack must be replaced regularly, which requires shutting down the extruder and disassembling the head. To avoid purposefully stopping production, the company under analysis blindly applies an OM policy for this replacement twice a week. For fault diagnosis, data was obtained from a machine with seven extruders used to produce multiple layers of polymer, which are then combined using an annular coextrusion die. The remaining downstream components related to the blown film application aren't expected to influence the processing conditions. In fact, the present analysis applies to any extrusion process.

For proper troubleshooting and process analysis, five covariates were selected from the sensors installed. The *screw rotational speed* and *throughput* were included to control the shear heating effect and to better interpret the pumping capability, respectively. Also, since variations of shape were constant for each type of material, feeding instabilities should be interpreted by the machine learning model as normal behavior. Three diagnostic covariates have been included, namely the *melt temperature*, which reflects the increased residence time, the *head pressure* (measured just upstream of the screen pack) and the *motor current*. A summary of the available sensor data is shown in Table 1.

Table 1. Sensor data

Environmental covariates	Diagnostic covariates
Screw rotational speed (rpm)	Head pressure (bar)
Throughput (kg/h)	Temperature (°C)
	Motor current (A)

2.2   Anomaly Detection with iForest

Anomaly detection usually involves ranking a set of instances, from the most anomalous to the most normal, solely based on intrinsic properties of the dataset. Several algorithms have been proposed in this area, with distance and density being the most used ranking measure [24]. However, the bias introduced by these measures leads to the problem of masking some of the structure in data distribution [25]. Consequently, to successfully detect both scattered and clustered anomalies, it is more adequate to have a mass-based approach that has no regard for the characteristics of the regions, e.g., shape and size [26].

As anomalies represent our events of interest – symptoms of the component degradation – it is expected that they will affect the subsequent time interval, leading to the existence of clustered anomalies. To address this issue, the score of the iForest is used to identify mass-based anomalies. Additionally, this method has already been shown to perform well on extruder data [19]. Despite reporting more false positives than alternative methods, such as DBSCAN, its stableness under hyperparameter tuning made it more adequate for a real-time deployment in non-stationary extruder data.

As the name suggests, this algorithm builds many isolation trees that compute individual instances' susceptibility to be isolated [27]. In each isolation tree partitions are done randomly by selecting both a feature and split value between the minimum and maximum values until each terminal leaf contains one instance or instances with the same value. The anomaly score is calculated as:

$$s(x, n) = 2^{\frac{-E(h(x))}{c(n)}} \qquad (1)$$

where $E(h(x))$ is the average number of splits given for each data point and $c(n)$ the average path length of an unsuccessful search in a binary search tree [27]. If s is very close to 1 then the observation is an anomaly, a score much smaller than 0.5 indicates the observation is likely normal [28]. The resulting algorithm is a convenient and computationally efficient solution to detect anomalies without assumptions on the data distribution [29]. However, one weakness of the iForest is the bias towards groups of correlated variables, due to the way it computes random splits [30]. One way to address this, is by reducing the number of correlated variables using feature selection techniques [30].

2.3   Explainable Machine Learning with SHAP

The loss of interpretability is a strong limitation of applying the iForest, due to model complexity and ensemble nature. To assess the reason for identifying specific data instances as anomalies, one approach is to build simpler post hoc explanation models [31]. Many techniques are available, but the SHAP [20] is the only one which guarantees the explanations satisfy three properties: local accuracy, missingness and consistency. Detailed information on this can be found elsewhere [32]. In this paper, a model-agnostic approximation, that is Kernel SHAP, was adopted, as it provides more accurate estimates with fewer evaluations of the original model than other sampling-based estimates [33]. This technique is built around linear LIME [33] and coalitional game theory to locally explain the importance of each feature in predicting the data instance's anomaly score. The contribution of a feature is given by the linear function:

$$g(z') = \phi_0 + \sum_{j=1}^{M} \phi_j z_j'$$

(2)

where g is the explanation model, M is the maximum coalition size, $z' \in \{0, 1\}^M$ is the coalition vector to simulate if a feature is present, and $\phi_j \in \mathbb{R}$ is the feature attribution for a feature j. To simulate that a feature value is missing from a coalition, marginalization occurs by sampling values from the variable's marginal distribution. However, when features are dependent, this sampling method can compute unrealistic values from the manufacturing process standpoint [34]. This can be addressed by preprocessing the data with algorithms that reduce the number of correlated variables.

2.4 Feature Selection with mRmR

Feature selection is an essential method in fault diagnosis applications for multiple reasons: (1) dealing with correlated variables; (2) accelerating the training and testing speed; (3) reducing the chance of overfitting; (4) lowering the cost of monitoring and maintaining the model feature pipeline; (5) facilitating the model interpretation [35].

The available methods can be divided into three classes: filter, embedded and wrapper, from the least to most computationally demanding. Filter methods rely only on the data distribution while embedded methods search the optimal feature set within the classifier. Wrapper methods use a learning algorithm to measure the relative importance of a subset of variables. The Maximum Relevance Minimum Redundancy algorithm was chosen for this work, due to its generalizability, computational efficiency, and adequacy for real-time deployment. This filter method ranks the importance of a set of features based on their relevance to the target (computed with the F-statistic), while penalizing features that are redundant among them (given by the average Pearson correlation between the candidate and the features selected at previous iterations) [21]. The score for candidates at each iteration is calculated as follows:

$$score_i(f) = \frac{F(f, target)}{\sum_{s \in features\, selected\, until\, i-1} |corr(f, s)| / (i - 1)}$$

(3)

3 Implementation

3.1 Feature Engineering and Selection for Single Failure Identification

The aforementioned procedure was applied to all the seven extruders in production runs between February and April 2022. Identifying symptoms of the screen pack degradation in the complex extrusion system is a challenging task, due to the high interdependence of process variables and the existence of multiple failure modes. To not mix these hidden data contexts with symptoms of a clogged screen pack, two more features were engineered. As environmental covariate, a measure of motor current variation was created to account for the melting instabilities. The frequently changing value is an indication of solid bed breakup causing inadequate melting rate and surging [36]. Its calculation is given by:

$$MCV_k = \frac{\sum_{i=k-2}^{k+2} MC_i/5}{MC_k} \tag{4}$$

where MCV_k is the motor current variation, MC_k is the motor current and $\sum_{i=k-2}^{k+2} MC_i/5$ is the rolling mean centered to observation k. As diagnostic covariate, a measure of feed rate was engineered to describe the increased effort of pumping the polymer melt, due to a clogged screen:

$$FeedRate = \frac{Throughput}{Speed \times 60} \tag{5}$$

Regarding feature selection, a modified version of the mRmR algorithm was used only with the criterion of minimum redundancy, since no data concerning failures exists. This allowed us to find the n most distinct features. The number of selected variables was decided by checking at each iteration if the feature identified as least redundant had a Pearson correlation coefficient below 0.7 with the already selected features to address the iForest's bias and SHAP's unrealistic permutation problem. In fact, setting this threshold with values between the range 0.6 and 0.9 yielded a stable selection of the same variables.

3.2 Fault Detection with iForest

Historical data relative to each of the seven extruders was collected from the machine's built-in sensors every ten seconds. Prior to building an isolation forest, the data had to be pre-processed to correct some issues. Namely, missing values were filled with linear interpolation. This method was chosen over the alternatives, e.g. spline interpolation, in order to not produce the 'overshoot' situation and falsely impute anomalies in the data. Also, due to the nature of the selected covariates and inexistence of long sequences of missing values, the assumption of linearity was found to be adequate. Additionally, it was necessary to synchronize the time series to deal with discrepancies in the timestamps. This was performed by rounding down the timestamps to a resolution of ten seconds.

In the iForest application, three parameters were considered: the number of trees to build t, the subsampling size ψ and the contamination c, which is the percentage threshold to consider instances as anomalies. An analysis on the effect of parameters t and ψ confirmed the original paper's suggestion that the instances detected as anomalies were insensitive to a wide range of values [27]. As a result, the parameters were set as t = 100 and $\psi = 256$. Regarding the hyperparameter tuning of contamination, models were trained with different values to visually inspect the formation of clustered anomalies in several production runs and extruders. A value of c equal to 1% was found to have the formation of clusters in some production runs and yield a good tradeoff between false positives and false negatives. Therefore, production run data where the identification of clusters required a higher value of contamination should not be representative of screen pack degradation. Also, considering that production runs had between 10,000 and 50,000 observations, values of c lower than 1% resulted in less than 100 anomalies, which were found to not be sufficient to distinguish clusters.

In the dynamically changing environment of any manufacturing process, the data distribution can change over time. In the case study described in this paper, this regime change can manifest in different forms: (1) reduction of the pumping capability of a worn screw, due to a higher volume of melt leaking over the flight tip as clearance increases; (2) variations on the motor current indicative of a change in raw materials; (3) higher melt pressure, because of an unclean or damaged die. To address these non-stationary conditions, this work discarded the general assumption that changes happen unexpectedly by integrating historical data on production and maintenance planning. Upon the occurrence of known environmental events, e.g., shutting down the machine to clean the coextrusion die, the current iForest detector is deleted and another one is built using the data from the following production run.

3.3   Fault Isolation and Identification with SHAP

For model interpretation with the SHAP, a set of conditions were considered to isolate the symptoms of screen pack degradation. These must be carefully defined since it is affected by the business's needs, e.g., tradeoff between false positives and false negatives, and the characteristics of the data. The following set was defined together with the end-users of the system, namely the maintenance managers and operators of the company:

1. if motor current variation increases the anomaly score and the observed value is lower than the mean, then its SHAP value must be less than the sum of all the SHAP values that increase the anomaly score divided by the number of selected features n.
2. if feed rate was selected and,
   a. it increases the anomaly score, then the observed value must be lower than the median,
   b. it decreases the anomaly score, then the observed value must be higher than the first quartile.
3. if temperature, melt pressure or motor current were selected and,
   c. it increases the anomaly score, then the observed value must be higher than the median,
   d. it decreases the anomaly score, then the observed value must be lower than the third quartile.

The rationale behind setting these conditions is based on the extrusion process domain knowledge previously described in Sect. 2.1. Condition 1) allows to isolate instances with low motor current variation with SHAP interpreting the corresponding impact in the anomaly score as positive (but less than the average of other features) or negative. As a result, anomalies related with melting instabilities are expected to be neglected. Conditions 2) and 3) guarantee the diagnostic covariates have the expected behavior, ensuring the alignment between how the observed value is positioned in the data distribution and how SHAP interprets the feature's impact on detection.

To define the thresholds, the measures of spread considered were min-max range, quartiles, and standard deviation. By assessing histograms and Q–Q plots, the data distributions of each diagnostic feature in different production runs and extruders were found to be skewed and have outliers. Therefore, the chosen measure of spread was quartiles since it doesn't consider the extreme values. This loss in the representativeness of data is an advantage for the real time deployment of the fault diagnosis procedure, since it is less affected by the noise introduced by environmental events that can't be tracked, such as: (1) feeding instabilities caused by variations in the shape of raw material; (2) sudden contamination of the material; (3) incomplete maintenance and production planning data failing to update the iForest detector upon a regime change. If a feature increases or decreases the anomaly score, the observation is set to be in 50% or 75% of expected values, respectively.

4 Results

To keep it concise, results are presented from two consecutive production runs of one out of the seven extruders of the machine, tagged as B by the company. The first production run corresponds to the period between the 11th of April 2022 18:06:00 and 13th of April 2022 13:00:30 while the second run starts on 14th of April 2022 14:33:40 and ends on 20th of April 2022 08:10:10. Between these two runs, the machine stopped for a non-related maintenance intervention, namely the cleaning of the coextrusion die. These results should enable us to exemplify the proper execution and interpretation of the proposed fault diagnosis procedure. The experiment was performed on Jupyter Notebook using Anaconda's Python data science libraries, in particular the Scikit-learn and SHAP libraries for the isolation forest and SHAP, respectively.

After the preparation phase, the mRmR algorithm was applied to the multivariate time series. Figure 1 shows the correlation matrix of the four least redundant features in the first production run. The fifth important feature to be considered was speed, but it had a correlation of 0.99 with throughput, which is above the threshold of 0.7 defined in Sect. 3.1.

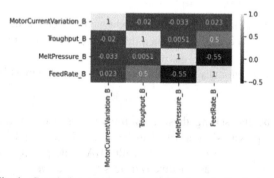

Fig. 1. Correlation matrix of selected features in the first run

As can be seen, the variables have small correlations, which should solve the iForest's bias and SHAP's unrealistic permutation problem described in Sects. 2.2 and 2.3, respectively. Additionally, the physics-based behavior was represented as previously described in Sect. 2.1: (1) throughput is positively correlated with feed rate, as more pumping capability should enable higher throughput rates; (2) melt pressure is negatively correlated with feed rate, indicating that an increase in pressure is related to loss in pumping capability.

The isolation forest was then fit using the four selected variables, returning as a result 0.5 minus the anomaly score described in Sect. 2.2, thus smaller values are attributed to anomalies. Figure 2 shows the time series plots of two of the selected diagnostic features from the first production run data: motor current variation and feed rate. The 0.1% of data instances with higher anomaly scores are marked in red.

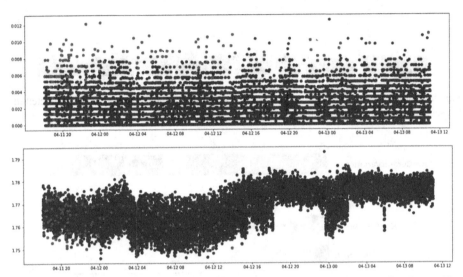

Fig. 2. Motor Current Variation (top) and Feed Rate (bottom) data of the anomalies detected in the first run by the iForest with $t = 100$, $\psi = 256$ and $c = 0.1\%$.

From visual inspection of Fig. 2, anomalies seem to be dispersed over time, being hard to identify any cluster. On the other hand, when observing Fig. 3, which shows the anomalies obtained in the second run data, it can be seen that the iForest identified clustered anomalies. This could be indication of a potential degradation state of the screen pack, but can also be confused for another hidden data context. To properly isolate and identify the detected anomalies, SHAP was applied as an interpretation tool.

Furthermore, to better interpret the results obtained with SHAP, two plots were analyzed: a summary bar chart and a dependence scatter plot. The former shows the mean of the absolute SHAP value for each feature on the final prediction of the anomaly score. This highlights each individual feature's impact, as shown in Fig. 4 for the first run data.

As can be seen, motor current variation was the most important feature for the abnormal behavior of the first run by a considerable difference. Its absolute impact on the anomaly score was 1.16 while the remaining features had an impact between 0.15 and

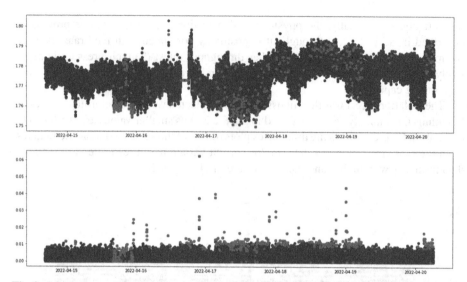

Fig. 3. Motor Current Variation (top) and Feed Rate (bottom) data of the anomalies detected in the second run by the iForest with $t = 100$, $\psi = 256$ and $c = 0.1\%$.

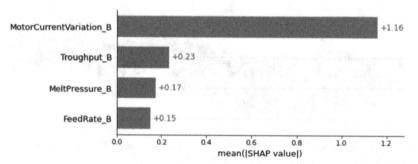

Fig. 4. Global variable importance plot in the first run data

0.23. This is indicative of a predominance of the effect of melting instabilities and a lack of filter contamination. Additionally, Fig. 5 shows two dependence scatter plots, which reveal the relation between observed values and SHAP values for each feature allowing to infer any positive and negative relationships of the variables with the anomaly score.

As can be seen, both motor current variation and feed rate show a relationship pattern with the anomaly score. Higher values of motor current variation are related to lower SHAP values, thus higher anomaly scores. Feed rate has the opposite pattern. Finally, by applying the conditions described in Sect. 3.3, a set of anomalies were identified as events of interest. Figure 6 shows these anomalies for the first run data.

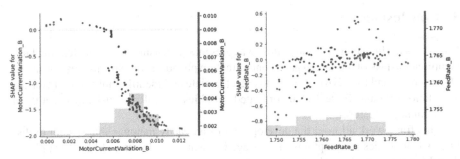

Fig. 5. Individual value plots of motor current variation and feed rate in the first run data

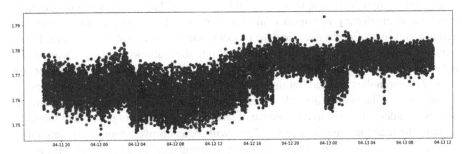

Fig. 6. Anomalies identified in the first run data

Out of the initial 148 detected anomalies, 21 were isolated as potential symptoms of a clogged screen pack. These were dispersed in time, thereby the screen pack was concluded to remain in good conditions. The conclusions differ for the second production run, as shown in Fig. 7.

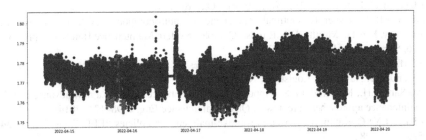

Fig. 7. Anomalies identified in the second run data

In the second production run, 481 instances were detected anomalies with 158 being isolated as potential symptoms of a clogged screen pack. By analyzing the graph, a first cluster was identified between 16:00 and 24:00 on 16th of April 2022, which gives strong evidence of screen pack degradation.

5 Conclusions

In this paper, a fault diagnosis procedure was presented, focusing on the challenging fault identification task of the screen pack contamination phenomenon. Specifically, the usage of the iForest and the SHAP allowed to detect, isolate and identify faults in multivariate non-stationary data. To deal with correlated variables, mRmR was used to select the n least redundant features.

This framework allowed the development of an easily maintainable system to distinguish anomalies as symptoms of a clogged screen pack. Instead of blindly applying the OM policy with the replacement of all extruders twice a week, the condition of each extruder can be assessed whenever opportunity arises to decide if a maintenance action is needed, therefore reducing the number of OM operations. The experimental results have shown the methodology was successful in overcoming the strong correlation between features, the process interactions, and the proper modelling of causal relationships. However, this method still presents limitations. Despite the framework being adequate for real-time deployment, the definition of any automatic alarm, e.g., a threshold for the number of anomalies isolated within a time period, would require frequent updates by the end-users of the system, according to any major changes in the processing conditions of each extruder. Also, due to the absence of labelled data it was not possible to formally evaluate the learning models. Future efforts will focus on overcoming this limitation, through the simulation of an extrusion process with both healthy and degraded behavior.

References

1. Jardine, A.K.S., Lin, D., Banjevic, D.: A review on machinery diagnostics and prognostics implementing condition-based maintenance. Mech. Syst. Signal. Process. **20**, 1483–1510 (2006)
2. Fitch, E.C.: 10 – The proactive approach. In: Fitch, E.C. (ed.) Proactive Maintenance for Mechanical Systems, pp. 287–317. Elsevier, Oxford (1992)
3. Nicolai, R.P., Dekker, R.: Optimal maintenance of multi-component systems: a review. In: Kobbacy, K.A.H., Murthy, D.N.P. (eds.) Complex System Maintenance Handbook, pp. 263–286. Springer London, London (2008)
4. Scarf, P.A., Deara, M.: Block replacement policies for a two-component system with failure dependence. Naval Res. Logist. **50**, 70–87 (2003)
5. Ab-Samat, H., Kamaruddin, S.: Opportunistic maintenance (OM) as a new advancement in maintenance approaches: a review. J. Qual. Maintenance Eng. **2**, 98–121 (2014)
6. Liang, T.Y.: Optimum piggyback preventive maintenance policies. IEEE Trans. Reliab. **34**, 529–538 (1985)
7. Levrat, E., Iung, B., Crespo Marquez, A.: E-maintenance: review and conceptual framework. Prod. Plan. Control **19**, 408–429 (2008)
8. Baur, M., Albertelli, P., Monno, M.: A review of prognostics and health management of machine tools. Int. J. Adv. Manuf. Technol. **107**(5–6), 2843–2863 (2020). https://doi.org/10.1007/s00170-020-05202-3
9. Tao, F., Qi, Q., Liu, A., Kusiak, A.: Data-driven smart manufacturing. J. Manuf. Syst. **48**, 157–169 (2018)
10. Zonta, T., et al.: Predictive maintenance in the Industry 4.0: a systematic literature review. Comput. Ind. Eng. **150**, 106889 (2020)

11. Kalbfleisch, J.D., Prentice, R.L.: The Statistical Analysis of Failure Time Data. John Wiley & Sons (2011)
12. Carrasco, J., et al.: Anomaly detection in predictive maintenance: a new evaluation framework for temporal unsupervised anomaly detection algorithms. Neurocomputing **462**, 440–452 (2021)
13. Gupta, M., Gao, J., Aggarwal, C.C., Han, J.: Outlier detection for temporal data: a survey. IEEE Trans. Knowl. Data Eng. **26**, 2250–2267 (2013)
14. Blázquez-García, A., Conde, A., Mori, U., Lozano, J.A.: A review on outlier/anomaly detection in time series data. ACM Comput. Surveys (CSUR) **54**, 1–33 (2021)
15. Baragona, R., Battaglia, F.: Outliers detection in multivariate time series by independent component analysis. Neural Comput. **19**, 1962–1984 (2007)
16. Papadimitriou, S., Sun, J., Faloutsos, C.: Streaming pattern discovery in multiple time-series (2005)
17. Fernandes, M., et al.: Data analysis and feature selection for predictive maintenance: a case-study in the metallurgic industry. Int. J. Inf. Manage. **46**, 252–262 (2019). https://doi.org/10.1016/j.ijinfomgt.2018.10.006
18. Fernandes, M., Corchado, J.M., Marreiros, G.: Machine learning techniques applied to mechanical fault diagnosis and fault prognosis in the context of real industrial manufacturing use-cases: a systematic literature review. Appl. Intell. (2022). https://doi.org/10.1007/s10489-022-03344-3
19. Fernandes, M., Canito, A., Mota, D., Corchado, J.M., Marreiros, G.: Service-oriented architecture for data-driven fault detection. In: Matsui, K., Omatu, S., Yigitcanlar, T., González, S.R. (eds.) DCAI 2021. LNNS, vol. 327, pp. 179–189. Springer, Cham (2022). https://doi.org/10.1007/978-3-030-86261-9_18
20. Lundberg, S.M., Lee, S.-I.: A unified approach to interpreting model predictions. Advances in Neural Information Processing Systems, vol. 30 (2017)
21. Ding, C., Peng, H.: Minimum redundancy feature selection from microarray gene expression data. J. Bioinform. Comput. Biol. **3**, 185–205 (2005)
22. Gogos, C.G., Tadmor, Z.: Principles of Polymer Processing. John Wiley & Sons (2013)
23. Lafleur, P.G., Vergnes, B.: Polymer Extrusion. John Wiley & Sons (2014)
24. Goldstein, M., Uchida, S.: A comparative evaluation of unsupervised anomaly detection algorithms for multivariate data. PLoS ONE **11**, e0152173 (2016)
25. James, G., Witten, D., Hastie, T., Tibshirani, R.: An Introduction to Statistical Learning. Springer (2013)
26. Ting, K.M., Tan, S.C., Liu, F.T.: Mass: A New Ranking Measure for Anomaly Detection. Monash University, Gippsland School of Information Technology (2009)
27. Liu, F.T., Ting, K.M., Zhou, Z.-H.: Isolation forest. In: 2008 Eighth IEEE International Conference on Data Mining, pp. 413–422. IEEE (2008)
28. Liu, F.T., Ting, K.M., Zhou, Z.-H.: Isolation-based anomaly detection. ACM Trans. Knowl. Discov. Data (TKDD) **6**, 1–39 (2012)
29. Lesouple, J., Baudoin, C., Spigai, M., Tourneret, J.-Y.: Generalized isolation forest for anomaly detection. Pattern Recogn. Lett. **149**, 109–119 (2021)
30. Puggini, L., McLoone, S.: An enhanced variable selection and Isolation Forest based methodology for anomaly detection with OES data. Eng. Appl. Artif. Intell. **67**, 126–135 (2018)
31. Ahmed, I., Jeon, G., Piccialli, F.: From artificial intelligence to eXplainable artificial intelligence in Industry 4.0: a survey on what, how, and where. IEEE Trans. Ind. Inform. **8**, 5031–5042 (2022)
32. Linardatos, P., Papastefanopoulos, V., Kotsiantis, S.: Explainable AI: A Review of Machine Learning Interpretability Methods (2020). https://doi.org/10.3390/e23010018

33. Ribeiro, M.T., Singh, S., Guestrin, C.: "Why should I trust you?" Explaining the predictions of any classifier. In: Proceedings of the 22nd ACM SIGKDD International Conference on Knowledge Discovery and Data Mining, pp. 1135–1144 (2016)
34. Janzing, D., Minorics, L., Blöbaum, P.: Feature relevance quantification in explainable AI: a causal problem. In: International Conference on Artificial Intelligence and Statistics, pp. 2907–2916. PMLR (2020)
35. Guyon, I., Gunn, S., Nikravesh, M., Zadeh, L.A.: Feature Extraction: Foundations and Applications. Springer (2008)
36. Cantor, K.: Blown Film Extrusion. Carl Hanser Verlag GmbH Co. KG (2018)

Workshop on Adaptive Smart areaS and Intelligent Agents (ASSIA)

Workshop on Adaptive Smart areaS
and Intelligent Agents (ASSIA)

This workshop was established to discuss technological solutions for adaptive smart areas, geo-positioned locations with a high need for sensorization, which facilitates their adaptation to significant changes in environmental conditions. Proposed solutions should facilitate decision-making of independent entities fostering collaboration and coordination among them to improve available resources or increase their efficiency in a specific area (cities, buildings, villages, farms, forests, etc...). Adaptive smart areas represent a new way of thinking about any kind of space by shaping a model that integrates aspects like energy efficiency, sustainable mobility, protection of the environment, and economic sustainability. These areas provide potentially unlimited settings for intelligent agents to display their ability to react, act proactively, interact between themselves, or otherwise plan, learn, etc., in an intelligent, or somewhat human, manner.

Therefore, this workshop aims to discuss the use of agent technology for adaptive smart areas to provide intelligence to any of these areas. We welcome any paper about experiences on the use of agents in adaptive smart areas tackling issues related to smart architectures, simulations, intelligent infrastructure, smart transport, robotics, open data, ... We also aim to address specific methodological and technological issues raised by the real deployment of agents in adaptive smart areas.

Organization

Organizing Committee

Vicente Julián	Universitat Politècnica de València, Spain
Adriana Giret	Universitat Politècnica de València, Spain
Carlos Carrascosa	Universitat Politècnica de València, Spain
Juan Manuel Corchado	Universidad de Salamanca, Spain
Sara Rodríguez	Universidad de Salamanca, Spain
Fernando De la Prieta	Universidad de Salamanca, Spain
Alberto Fernández	Universidad Rey Juan Carlos Spain
Holger Billhardt	Universidad Rey Juan Carlos Spain
Marin Lujak	Universidad Rey Juan Carlos Spain

Program Committee

Alfonso González Briones	University of Salamanca, Spain
Ana Belén Gil González	University of Salamanca, Spain
Gonçalo Marques	Polytechnic of Coimbra, Portugal
Jaume Jordán	Universitat Politècnica de València, Spain
Javier Parra	University of Salamanca, Spain
Joao Carneiro	Polytechnic Institute of Porto, Portugal
José Machado	University of Minho, Portugal
Juan M. Alberola	Universitat Politècnica de Valènci, Spain
Jürgen Dunkel	Hochschule Hannover, Germany
Marian Cristian Mihaescu	University of Craiova, Poland
Pasqual Martí	Universitat Politècnica de València, Spain
Radu-Casian Mihailescu	Malmö University, Sweden
Ralf Bruns	Hochschule Hannover, Germany
Ramon Hermoso	University of Zaragoza, Spain
Stella Heras	Universitat Politècnica de València, Spain
Victor Sanchez-Anguix	Universitat Politècnica de València, Spain

Object Recognition-Driven Cultural Travel Guide for the Coffee Cultural Landscape of Colombia

Sebastián López Flórez[1,2(✉)], Luis Hernando Ríos González[1],
Ana María López Echeverry[1], Guillermo Hernández[2,3],
and Fernando de la Prieta[2]

[1] Universidad Tecnológica de Pereira Cra. 27 N 10-02, Pereira, Risaralda, Colombia
{lhgonza,anamayi}@utp.edu.co
[2] BISITE Digital Innovation Hub, University of Salamanca, Edificio Multiusos
I+D+i, Calle Espejo 2, 37007 Salamanca, Spain
{sebastianlopezflorez,guillehg,fer}@usal.es
[3] Air Institute, IoT Digital Innovation Hub, 37188 Salamanca, Spain

Abstract. In recent years, the diffusion of the Colombian Coffee Cultural Landscape as the main tourist axis rich in ancestral traditions, is a country policy that seeks to promote the diffusion of heritage In recent years, the diffusion of the Colombian Coffee Cultural Landscape as the main tourist axis rich in ancestral traditions, is a country policy that seeks to promote the diffusion of heritage tourism and the conservation and promotion of the coffee heritage. Therefore, taking advantage of the growing advances in artificial intelligence (AI) applied to the tourism industry with emphasis on the cultural, artistic, historical and architectural diffusion with the different objects that characterize the culture of the Colombian Coffee Cultural Landscape. This article presents the application of CNN techniques focused on the detection and recognition of objects in the field of Colombian coffee cultural heritage, a line of research little explored. Although AI is just beginning to interact with the built environment through mobile devices, technologies in this field of object detection and classification have been producing and exploring digital models in different industrial sectors for a long time. The interaction between object detection algorithms and state-of-the-art information modeling is approached as an opportunity in heritage tourism as a central axis in a vision of making known the cultural, artistic, architectural and archaeological richness of this area of the country.

Keywords: Artificial intelligence · Heritage tourism · Applications

1 Introduction

Tourism around the coffee culture is in the development stage, which leads to the promotion of projects that allow the use of different technological alternatives that can expand the cultural knowledge of this area. According to Law

A. González-Briones et al. (Eds.): PAAMS Workshops 2022, CCIS 1678, pp. 59–70, 2022.
https://doi.org/10.1007/978-3-031-18697-4_5

2057 of 2020 - Regulatory Manager - Public Function implies proposing and promoting policies that promote tourism in harmony with environmental and social sustainability. Among the different modalities of tourism that currently exist, there is no technological component based on the Colombian Coffee Cultural Heritage (CCLC) that articulates the necessary policies for the social, cultural and historical appropriation of the CCLC. The cultural profile of the coffee grower is characterized by different symbolic objects inherited from the colonization of Antioquia. The settlers were a group of enterprising Antioquians who came to this area in search of land that would allow them to achieve economic independence. This process left impregnated in the culture, values such as hard work, love of work, business acumen and strong family ties, characteristics that continue to be present in the inhabitants of this zone, as well as a series of objects closely related to the development of the coffee activity, among which are the traditional kitchens, clothing and handicrafts. Likewise, the archaeological findings and artistic representations that are still preserved as an ancestral heritage [4,5]. Mobile devices have characteristics that relate the mass dissemination of places and the use of versatile technologies in vision systems. Driven by consumer demand, these systems have a series of elements that can integrate connectivity, computing power and image processing capacity, being a useful tool in the implementation of intelligent models that can interpret the culture and ancestral history of the people of Antioquia, promoting the culture of the CCLC. Machine learning libraries that work in mobile applications [8] such as pytorch [7] and tensorflow [6] allow adopting lightweight encapsulation methodology in mobile systems. Enabling the integration of complex artificial intelligence solutions in portable and easy-to-use devices. Counting with a tool based on artificial intelligence, capable of describing the history of each object as a complement to the coffee tourism guide, strengthening the patrimonial purposes demanded by Unesco since 2011 to Colombia where it establishes the promotion, dynamization and conservation of the CCLC [1,2]. The proposed system consists of a web application [9–11] equipped with an intelligent module based on object recognition Single Shot MultiBox Detector (SSD) [3] capable of interpreting and detecting CCLC objects using convolutional characteristics with a pre-established route according to the coffee zones. In addition, a logic has been implemented to generate an anthropological and cultural description of the object as established by Unesco being necessary to collect the history of coffee objects with the help of a specialized SCCP anthropologist. Statistical techniques are used in the presentation of results to ensure that they are independent of the partition between training and test data. The results show that the system is able to generate a textual description of the object with a detection rate equal to mAP (mean Average Precision) of 0.8.

2   Related Work

Starting from the classic anthropological premise that refers to cultural tourism as a representation of the promotion of living culture (crafts, festivals, rituals, gastronomic practices) which leaves aside some concepts present in ecotourism, ethnographic tourism, rural tourism and in turn stimulate a new form of tourism where its main focus of interest is to promote the set of goods, tangible and intangible, which are identified by a particular society as carriers of cultural values of the community [12]. They are tangible and intangible assets that have a high symbolic content, which makes them worthy of special protection not only related to their conservation but also to the use that can be made of them [13–16] seeking to analyze and deepen the interconnections and dynamic interaction between these two phenomena in the field of UNESCO.

The Declaration of Mexico on Cultural Policies (1982), which redefines cultural heritage to include not only works of authorship, but also material and non-material works that express the creativity of people: language, rituals, beliefs, places and literature are based on traditions, responding to community expectations regarding the expression of their cultural and social identity, which recommends safeguarding popular culture and tradition (1989). The International Conference on the Recommendation on the Safeguarding of Traditional Culture and Folklore held in Washington (1999), which relegates the term folklore and projects the notion of "intangible heritage"; and the program "Masterpieces of Heritage composed of a broad set of aspects that have alternated the classic forms of Oral and Intangible Tourism of Humanity" (1999) that served as the basis for configuring the Representative List of the ICH with three successive proclamations (2001, 2003 and 2005), distinguishing 90 forms of expression and cultural spaces related to 70 countries [17].

2.1 Cultural Heritage Mobile Applications

Artificial intelligence (AI) is now undergoing accelerated development. The deep learning (DL) comprises a series of algorithms that stimulate the solution of challenging problems such as object recognition, scene interpretation, semantic segmentation and others. These models are capable of learning complicated concepts by building them from simpler ones [22]. DL is now emerging and gaining industrial interest thanks to computing power and the development of more compact systems capable of processing complex algorithms in real time. Among the models, convolutional neural networks (CNNs) [18–21] present specialized architectures for computer vision. Currently, CNNs are employed for image recognition in medicine, biology, and many other research fields [23–27]. However, only a few recent studies are employing these technologies for tourism-related research, more specifically heritage tourism.

The DL community [30–32] has shown interest in the recognition of historical cultural representations within the heritage as landmarks in the tourist route. In [33,34] they present research where they seek to highlight applications of image recognition techniques. As of 2012, CNNs started to outperform [18,28,29] algorithms used in object detection and classification from images [38]. The introduction of CNN in heritage studies is proposed by [35], whose targets are ancient inscriptions and a set of 12 monuments in Pisa (Italy), and more recently by [36] with an application on a set of 12 famous Indian monuments. This research is framed in the detection of fixed monuments in an image without exploring the detection of ancient objects representing culture, the progress of this idea corresponds to the inclusion of the YOLO [37] and SDD [3] object detectors, of which no reference has been found to date in the implementation in heritage tourism.

3   Cultural Travel Guide (CTG) Platform

The present research developed an application that allows the user to access data related to a series of objects representative of the culture, art and history of the CCLC by simply capturing an image that can identify the object and describe it. The algorithm exploits the SDD300 single-shot object detector to recognize CCLC objects. The application is based on two main software blocks (Fig. 1). First, a database is generated with the following characteristics: traditional CCLC objects extracted with the indications of the stipulated in anthropological writings suggested by the expert, as well as artistic representations of protected objects within public policies such as the carriel. In order to provide an input to the generalizable robust intelligent system, different representations of images of objects captured from conventional Xiaomi with 32 MP and 13 MP cameras, simulating the images that could be taken by a tourist, following the basic photographic protocol according to criteria of framing, angles and shooting planes [39–44] in the acquisition of the 3600 images that make up the CCLC object database.

For each category according to the normal, counter-chopped and chopped planes, 150 images are taken per class, following the standard in the PASCAL VOC2007 and VOC2012 database [47], the label is subsequently assigned once the taking of historical, social, cultural objects relevant according to the area in which it is located [45]. The label was previously assigned to the process of detection of objects by the SSD, the labelling procedure requires noting and collecting all objects that are relevant to the class, this process is done manually where the human being makes a deep analysis from the relationship-environment concept, on the selection of the different types of objects that are considered relevant within the CCLC. A second component of the software corresponds to the ML module, which encapsulates the intelligent model to optimize the amount of space allowing it to operate in any mobile system.

The labelling process produces annotations necessary to feed the supervised machine learning model. That is, in object detection, an annotation is a process of locating the object within a rectangle, where the boundary of the rectangle will contain it generating a specific label for each patch. This is done through the LabelImg program [46].

Image Pre-processing. Given that the initial training set of the training base is of few images, it is important to have more semantic information of the objects, which allows to have densely sampled objects that help to preserve more local contextual information. It is likely that multiple scales will incorporate more clues and relationships between components, for which it is essential to generate

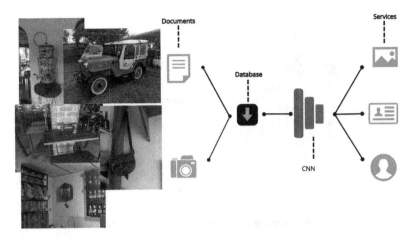

Fig. 1. Schematic of application components: the digital archive, which stores data and documents, and the artificial intelligence engine, which interacts with the site through the application.

an augmented database that includes images with changes in rotation, color and scale. Random transformations will apply the same transformation to all images in a given batch, but will produce different transformations in the calls.

3.1   SSD Network

The SSD network of is one of the most widely used object detection algorithms. For the SSD architecture with an input resolution of 300×300 (SSD300), according to speed/accuracy characteristics presented in the results of Huang et al. [50] and reproducing the experimental methodology described in the paper [3], as well as base frame tracking [48, 49, 51, 52]. The SSD network is based on a feed-forward convolutional network that produces a collection of fixed-size frames, bounding and evaluation denoting the presence of the object class in those frames, followed by a non-maximal suppression step to produce the final detections. The SSD network combines multiple feature maps with different sizes to generate predictions, which make the scale more invariant to the objects. This can be seen in Fig. 2.

Scales and aspect ratios of bounding boxes. The SSD model uses different ratios for its bounding boxes. According to the authors [18], it has a level of sensitivity in its choice, concerning its scale and aspect ratio. The minimum and maximum scales are set for the self-image base at $s_{min} = 0.2$ and $s_{max} = 0.9$ For any feature map among m feature maps, the scale is chosen as [44].

3.2   Loss

The function used is the MultiBox loss [53, 54]. Due to the number of predicted bounding boxes, non-max suppression of IoU is used as a method to ensure detection. The joint function used is defined as $L(x, c, l, g) = L_{conf}(x, c) + L_{loc}(x, l, g)$

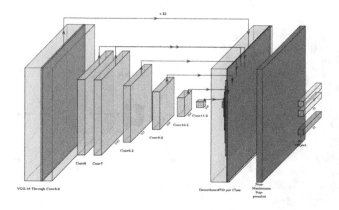

Fig. 2. General scheme of the SCCP object detection system.

Where this function consists of two terms, the $L_{conf}(x, c)$, which is the confidence and regression loss of the bounding box $L_{loc}(x, l, g)$, c is the class confidence (class score), l is the predicted location offset, and g is the true label location.

Location Loss. Location loss In location loss, L_{loc}, is used from huber loss [50]. The predicted frame loss function L_{loc} is defined as.

$$L_{loc}(x, c^p, l_j, g_j) = \frac{1}{N^+} \sum_{i \in Pos}^{N_+} \sum_{m \in cx, cy, w, h} x_{ij}^p L1_s(l_i^m - \hat{g}_j^m) \tag{1}$$

where $N^+ = \sum_{ij} x_{ij}^{p=1}$, which is a scalar for the number of positive matches and li is the location prediction defined as the displacement of the center, height and width.

Loss of Confidence. Loss of confidence. The loss of confidence is essentially the loss of cross-entropy. It is important that the model recognizes the objects that exist in the image and the absence of them. Considering that there are usually only a handful of objects in an image this creates a large imbalance between the background class (negative bounding boxes) and objects (positive bounding boxes), which hinders the optimization process. To counter this problem, negative mining is used. Instead of summing all negative bounding boxes, they are sorted by class confidence and the top negative M bounding boxes that are selected. Where the ratio between M and positive bounding boxes is 3:1. The confidence loss is defined as follows.

$$L_{conf}(x, c) = -\frac{1}{N^+} \sum_{i \in Positivo}^{N_+} x_{ij}^p log(\hat{c}_i^p) - \frac{1}{N^-} \sum_{i \in Negativo}^{N_-} log(\hat{c}_i^0) \tag{2}$$

$$\hat{c}_i^p = \frac{exp(c_i^p)}{\sum_P exp(c_i^p)} \tag{3}$$

where $N^- = M$.

Finally we would have $l = L_{conf} + L_{loc}$ where $alpha = 1$.

Model Encapsulation. Model encapsulation uses Torch libraries that allow saving and loading in a more compact system, using three main functions torch.save that allows saving models, torch.load that allows loading data to query, save and the function torch.nn.Module.load state dict that loads the dictionary.

4   Experiments and Results

After training the SDD-300 network with the PCCC database, the results are compiled in terms of mAP (mean Average Precision), the classification results are shown in Table 1. A database composed of 3600 images was used for this procedure. These images were selected to represent the distinctive features of the SCCP objects to be recognized. For the training and validation protocol, the database was divided into 0.75 for training and 0.25 for validation. This step was repeated 5 times (K-Fold Cross-Validation), reporting an intermediate value of mAP (mean Average Precision) that ruled out possible overtraining or bias in the results.

Table 1. Results of the validation of the SDD-300 on own basis with each object

SSD300			
Adorno	1.0	Maquina de moler	0.909
Bar	1.0	Mueble	1.0
Basenilla	1.0	Pilón	1.0
Baúl	1.0	Pesa	1.0
Bota	1.0	Plancha	1.0
Cafetera	1.0	Plato	1.0
Caperuza	0.984	Radio	1.0
Carriel	1.0	Rocola	1.0
Corazón de jesús	1.0	Silla	0.9083
Elemento de cocina	1.0	Silla de montar	1.0
Fumigador	1.0	Teléfono	1.0
Maleta	1.0	Triciclo	1.0
Maquina de coser	1.0	Silla de montar	1.0
Tv	1.0	Vitrola	1.0
Mean average precision (mAP)			0.990

In the text tests, images were collected with different critical conditions at which the system would have to perform in real aircrafts, changing the perspective of natural illumination. The network was trained from scratch from the proprietary database.

Use Case. For scene recognition of the PCCC regions, a web application capable of running on a mobile device is produced. The application was developed using the Streamlit programming environment, the already encapsulated model is used as the management decision manager by identifying the object and classifying it as shown in Fig. 3.

Fig. 3. Schematic of application components: the digital archive, which stores data and documents, and the artificial intelligence engine, which interacts with the site through the application

5   Conclusión

This article presented the multidisciplinary work that exploit artificial intelligence technologies for the recognition of objects of the CCLC, in order to establish a precedent in the country in the use of new technologies in heritage tourism, and thus promote the ancestral coffee culture inherited by immigrants from Antioquia, along with its transformational from the exploitation of coffee as the main source of input. The technology available in mobile devices offers the opportunity to diversify knowledge through access to information. A tool capable of providing the user with the identification and location of the object in the image, as well as an anthropological description of it, is proposed. The additional developments of the integration of the proposed AI technologies and proprietary databases make the system more scalable and robust, i.e. we tried to cover the spectrum of images simulating the user's behavior, which allowed a successful performance at the time of evaluation. The access to anthropological information in the use of the application is characterized by the implementation of a ML module which provides the decision of textual reproduction according to the object. The SCCP application is only one of the possible applications of the developed technology. With the purpose of continuing to deploy systems like these where the country's public policies encourage researchers to generate new knowledge around issues of interest which relate to heritage with techniques of promotion, awareness and promotion of culture. Therefore a possible future work could integrate possible connections between the virtual environment in natural environments and the PCCC, where ML models could be trained to recognize types of cultural environments, while related information could integrate a personalized narrative description.

References

1. Filocamo, F., et al.: MoGeo, a mobile application to promote geotourism in Molise region (Southern Italy). Resources **9**(3), 31 (2020)
2. Alzate, A.G.: Modelo de diseño para la valoración y apropiación social del Patrimonio en el Paisaje Cultural Cafetero colombiano. Kepes **11**(12), 118–138 (2015)
3. Liu, W., et al.: SSD: single shot multibox detector. In: Leibe, B., Matas, J., Sebe, N., Welling, M. (eds.) ECCV 2016. LNCS, vol. 9905, pp. 21–37. Springer, Cham (2016). https://doi.org/10.1007/978-3-319-46448-0_2
4. Cafetero, P.C.: Excepcional fusión entre naturaleza, cultura y trabajo colectivo. Bogotá: FNC (2014)
5. Castañeda, F.V.Á., Semillero, C.A.T.: Tecnología y cultura en el paisaje cultural cafetero. Cultivando conocimiento: estrategia de acercamiento
6. Abadi, M., et al.: TensorFlow: a system for large-scale machine learning. In: 12th USENIX Symposium on Operating Systems Design and Implementation (OSDI 2016), pp. 265–283 (2016)
7. Paszke, A., et al.: PyTorch: an imperative style, high-performance deep learning library. In: Advances in Neural Information Processing Systems (2019)
8. Ali, I., et al.: The impact of IEEE 802.11 contention window on the performance of transmission control protocol in mobile ad-hoc network. Adv. Distrib. Comput. Artif. Intell. J. **9**(3), 29–48 (2020)
9. Yigitcanlar, T., et al.: Artificial intelligence technologies and related urban planning and development concepts: how are they perceived and utilized in Australia? J. Open Innov. Technol. Mark. Complex. **6**(4), 187 (2020)
10. Casado-Vara, R., et al.: Blockchain framework for IoT data quality via edge computing. In: Proceedings of the 1st Workshop on Blockchain-Enabled Networked Sensor Systems, pp. 19–24 (2018)
11. Abrishambaf, O., et al.: Implementation of a real-time microgrid simulation platform based on centralized and distributed management. Energies **10**(6), 806 (2017)

12. Centella Zea, Y.L.: El patrimonio cultural inmaterial como factor esencial de diversificación de la actividad turística cultural de la ciudad de Puno (2021)
13. Harrison, R. (ed.): Manuel of Heritage Management. Butterworth-Heinemann, Oxford (1994)
14. Prats, L.: El concepto de patrimonio cultural. Política y sociedad **27**(1), 63–76 (1998)
15. Ballart, J., Juan-Tresseras, J.: Gestión del Patrimonio Cultural. Ariel, Barcelona (2001)
16. Hernández hernández, F.H.: El Patrimonio Cultural: La Memoria Recuperada. Trea, Madrid (2002)
17. de Madariaga, C.J., Asencio, F.S.: Patrimonio cultural inmaterial de la humanidad y turismo. Int. J. Sci. Manage. Tour. **4**(2), 349–366 (2018)
18. Alonso, R.S.: Deep symbolic learning and semantics for an explainable and ethical artificial intelligence. In: Novais, P., Vercelli, G., Larriba-Pey, J.L., Herrera, F., Chamoso, P. (eds.) ISAmI 2020. AISC, vol. 1239, pp. 272–278. Springer, Cham (2021). https://doi.org/10.1007/978-3-030-58356-9_30
19. Alonso, R.S.: Low-power distributed AI and IoT for measuring Lamb's milk ingestion and predicting meat yield and malnutrition diseases. In: Novais, P., Vercelli, G., Larriba-Pey, J.L., Herrera, F., Chamoso, P. (eds.) ISAmI 2020. AISC, vol. 1239, pp. 251–257. Springer, Cham (2021). https://doi.org/10.1007/978-3-030-58356-9_26
20. Carneiro, D., Silva, F., Guimarães, M., Sousa, D., Novais, P.: Explainable intelligent environments. In: Novais, P., Vercelli, G., Larriba-Pey, J.L., Herrera, F., Chamoso, P. (eds.) ISAmI 2020. AISC, vol. 1239, pp. 34–43. Springer, Cham (2021). https://doi.org/10.1007/978-3-030-58356-9_4
21. Castanheira, A., Peixoto, H., Machado, J.: Overcoming challenges in healthcare interoperability regulatory compliance. In: Novais, P., Vercelli, G., Larriba-Pey, J.L., Herrera, F., Chamoso, P. (eds.) ISAmI 2020. AISC, vol. 1239, pp. 44–53. Springer, Cham (2021). https://doi.org/10.1007/978-3-030-58356-9_5
22. Goodfellow, I., Bengio, Y., Courville, A.: Deep Learning. The MIT Press, Cambridge (2016)
23. Hosny, A., Parmar, C., Quackenbush, J., Schwartz, L.H., Aerts, H.J.W.L.: Artificial intelligence in radiology. Nat. Rev. Cancer **18**, 500–510 (2018)
24. Webb, S.: Deep learning for biology. Nature **554**, 555–557 (2018)
25. Casado-Vara, R., et al.: IoT network slicing on virtual layers of homogeneous data for improved algorithm operation in smart buildings. Future Gener. Comput. Syst. **102**, 965–977 (2020)
26. Casado-Vara, R., Prieto-Castrillo, F., Corchado, J.M.: A game theory approach for cooperative control to improve data quality and false data detection in WSN. Int. J. Robust Nonlinear Control **28**(16), 5087–5102 (2018)
27. García, Ó., et al.: Energy efficiency in public buildings through context-aware social computing. Sensors **17**(4), 826 (2017)
28. Agostinho, N.B., Wherhli, A.V., Adamatti, D.F.: Development of a multiagent simulator to genetic regulatory networks. In: Novais, P., Vercelli, G., Larriba-Pey, J.L., Herrera, F., Chamoso, P. (eds.) ISAmI 2020. AISC, vol. 1239, pp. 279–283. Springer, Cham (2021). https://doi.org/10.1007/978-3-030-58356-9_31
29. Hernández, G., Rodríguez, S., González, A., Corchado, J.M., Prieto, J.: Video Analysis System Using Deep Learning Algorithms. In: Novais, P., Vercelli, G., Larriba-Pey, J.L., Herrera, F., Chamoso, P. (eds.) ISAmI 2020. AISC, vol. 1239, pp. 186–199. Springer, Cham (2021). https://doi.org/10.1007/978-3-030-58356-9_19

30. Durães, D., Bajo, J., Novais, P.: Supervising attention in an e-learning system. In: Novais, P., et al. (eds.) ISAmI2018 2018. AISC, vol. 806, pp. 389–396. Springer, Cham (2019). https://doi.org/10.1007/978-3-030-01746-0_46

31. Garcia-Alonso, J., Berrocal, J., Murillo, J.M., Mendes, D., Fonseca, C., Lopes, M.: Situational-context for virtually modeling the elderly. In: Novais, P., et al. (eds.) ISAmI2018 2018. AISC, vol. 806, pp. 298–305. Springer, Cham (2019). https://doi.org/10.1007/978-3-030-01746-0_35

32. Freitas, L.O., Henriques, P.R., Novais, P.: Context-awareness and uncertainty: current scenario and challenges for the future. In: Novais, P., et al. (eds.) ISAmI2018 2018. AISC, vol. 806, pp. 174–181. Springer, Cham (2019). https://doi.org/10.1007/978-3-030-01746-0_20

33. Chen, T., Wu, K., Yap, K.-H., Li, Z., Tsai, F.S.: A survey on mobile landmark recognition for information retrieval. In: MDM 2009. IEEE Computer Society, pp. 625–630 (2009)

34. Amato, G., Falchi, F., Gennaro, C.: Fast image classification for monument recognition. J. Comput. Cult. Herit. **8**, 1–25 (2015)

35. Amato, G., Falchi, F., Vadicamo, L.: Visual recognition of ancient inscriptions using convolutional neural network and fisher vector. J. Comput. Cult. Herit. **9**, 1–24 (2016)

36. Gada, S., Mehta, V., Kanchan, K., Jain, C., Raut, P.: Monument recognition using deep neural networks. In: 2017 IEEE International Conference on Computational Intelligence and Computing Research (ICCIC), pp. 1–6 (2017)

37. Redmon, J., Farhadi, A.: Yolo9000: better, faster, stronger. In: Proceedings of the IEEE Conference on Computer Vision and Pattern Recognition (CVPR) (2017)

38. Albawi, S., Mohammed, T.A., Al-Zawi, S.: Understanding of a convolutional neural network. In: International Conference on Engineering and Technology (ICET), vol. 2017, pp. 1–6. IEEE (2017)

39. Gupta, S., et al.: Neural network based epileptic EEG detection and classification (2020)

40. Patil, M.S., et al.: LSTM based lip reading approach for Devanagari script (2019)

41. Pérez-pons, M.E., et al.: Efficiency, profitability and productivity: technological applications in the agricultural sector. Adv. Distrib. Comput. Artif. Intell. J. **94** (2020)

42. Ahmad, P.: A review on blockchain's applications and implementations. Adv. Distrib. Comput. Artif. Intell. J. **10**(2) (2021). https://doi.org/10.14201/ADCAIJ2021102197208

43. Rosenfield, G.H.: The problem of exterior orientation in photogrammetry. Photogramm. Eng. **25**, 536–553 (1959)

44. Milton, E.J., et al.: Measurement of the spectral directional reflectance of forest canopies: a review of methods and a practical application. Remote Sens. Rev. **10**(4), 285–308 (1994)

45. Quattoni, A., Torralba, A.: Recognizing indoor scenes. In: 2009 IEEE Conference on Computer Vision and Pattern Recognition, pp. 413–420. IEEE (2009)

46. Lin, T.: LabelImg (2015). https://github.com/tzutalin/labelImg

47. Everingham, M., Eslami, S.M., Van Gool, L., Williams, C.K., Winn, J., Zisserman, A.: The PASCAL visual object classes challenge (VOC2007) results (2007)

48. Thakkar, Y., Sutreja, A., Kumar, A., Taneja, S., Regunathan, R.K.: Spot a Spot—efficient parking system using single-shot multibox detector. In: Raju, K.S., Senkerik, R., Lanka, S.P., Rajagopal, V. (eds.) Data Engineering and Communication Technology. AISC, vol. 1079, pp. 931–939. Springer, Singapore (2020). https://doi.org/10.1007/978-981-15-1097-7_79

49. Jasim, Y.A., et al.: High-performance deep learning to detection and tracking tomato plant leaf predict disease and expert systems (2021)

50. Huang, J.: Speed/accuracy trade-offs for modern convolutional object detectors. In: Proceedings of the IEEE Conference on Computer Vision and Pattern Recognition, pp. 7310–7311 (2017)

51. Zhang, S., Zhu, X., Lei, Z., Shi, H., Wang, X., Li, S.Z.: S3FD: single shot scale-invariant face detector. In: Proceedings of the IEEE International Conference on Computer Visions, pp. 192–201 (2017)

52. Leng, J., Liu, Y.: An enhanced SSD with feature fusion and visual reasoning for object detection. Neural Comput. Appl. **31**(10), 6549–6558 (2018). https://doi.org/10.1007/s00521-018-3486-1

53. Erhan, D., Szegedy, C., Toshev, A., Anguelov, D.: Scalable object detection using deep neural networks. In: Proceedings of the IEEE Conference on Computer Vision and Pattern Recognition, pp. 2147–2154 (2014)

54. Szegedy, C., Reed, S., Erhan, D., Anguelov, D., Ioffe, S.: Scalable, high-quality object detection. arXiv preprint arXiv:1412.1441 (2015)

Towards Semantic Modelling of the Edge-Cloud Continuum

Iván Bernabé[1]([⊠]) [iD], Alberto Fernández[2] [iD], Holger Billhardt[2] [iD],
and Sascha Ossowski[2] [iD]

[1] Universidad Carlos III de Madrid, Madrid, Spain
ivan.bernabe@uc3m.es
[2] CETINIA, Universidad Rey Juan Carlos, Madrid, Spain
{alberto.fernandez,holger.billhardt,sascha.ossowski}@urjc.es

Abstract. Fog and edge computing paradigms increase the performance of IoT systems compared to those based exclusively on conventional cloud computing. Basically, they propose to move software services that process information to a nearby place where IoT data is collected instead of at the core of the network. The computing continuum concept goes a step further and proposes to run such software services in a transparent manner at any of the different computing paradigms and, if the execution context changes (for example due to unforeseen contingencies), to move the services to other devices if they may increase performance. In this context, advanced mechanisms are required to successfully transfer those software services to devices hosted in different computing platforms located anywhere from the edge to the cloud. This article proposes the Edge Cloud Computing ontology (ECO), an ontology for IoT systems composed of devices and data centers hosted in edge, fog or cloud computing environments. We also expose an example scenario based on a service architecture on which ECO facilitates management actions. These actions include detecting the overload status of system elements, proposals for suitable locations for software deployment or identifying elements potentially affected by problems in the system, such as connection link failures.

Keywords: Ontology · Computing continuum · Internet of Things (IoT)

1 Introduction

Technological infrastructures for smart areas will usually include networks of heterogeneous Internet of Things (IoT) devices (sensors, actuators) that are installed on the field and provide information and services to applications. Data obtained from IoT devices are commonly processed efficiently in large computing data centers, which are usually located in cloud infrastructures that allow resources to be managed flexibly and efficiently ensuring low economic costs and adequate processing capacity at each moment [1]. To reduce the high communication demand for transmitting the vast amount of data generated by IoT devices to remote data centers, the concept of Fog Computing was introduced. Fog Computing [2] provides computing and storage capacity at the edge of the network so data generated by IoT devices can be processed without having to reach

© The Author(s), under exclusive license to Springer Nature Switzerland AG 2022
A. González-Briones et al. (Eds.): PAAMS Workshops 2022, CCIS 1678, pp. 71–82, 2022.
https://doi.org/10.1007/978-3-031-18697-4_6

centralized data centers. However, the integration of IoT devices and fog computing with new application domains increases the complexity and maintenance of the global system, which requires complex self-configuration mechanisms to adapt the system to new conditions.

Therefore, in a typical deployment, IoT devices are connected to other more powerful nodes with varying computing and connectivity capabilities that act as hubs or intermediaries on the edge, and cloud computing services that carry out complex and/or computational demanding processes.

We aim at hard and complex environments where devices are geographically dispersed and external factors (e.g., changing weather conditions, scarcity of energy, connectivity problems, or other contingencies) may negatively influence the reliability of the whole infrastructure. These dynamic changing environments require methods for flexible adaptation to changes and contingencies that may occur more or less frequently in this context. We envision the idea of an edge-cloud continuum, where services or tasks can adapt their behavior or be moved between the edge and the cloud according to the situation in each moment. For example, an agent installed in a particular device may be aware of a reduction of bandwidth or available battery and decide to send data (e.g., monitored field images) to the cloud with lower periodicity or quality. Likewise, the task such agent is carrying out could be moved temporarily to the cloud or to another peer (if it complies with the minimum computing capability).

To this end, methods need to be developed for (i) detecting relevant changes in the edge-cloud context that require actions to ensure the edge-cloud continuum; and (ii) designing decision strategies for adapting task realization between the cloud and edge in case of contingencies. For this, the edge-cloud continuum needs to be formalized.

In this work, we focus on the semantic formalization of the edge-cloud continuum context so as to provide the means for dynamically describing detected contingencies and facilitate decision making regarding the adaptation of the system according to the current situation. In this sense, we propose the use of ontologies and argue that they are appropriate for the IoT domain because they provide a way to represent the information through a common vocabulary which facilitates its exchange with other systems. In addition, ontologies, unlike systems based on traditional databases, provide semantic formal descriptions that can be interpreted by both, people and machines, and new information can be derived through automatic inference.

In this paper, we present an ontology for modelling context in edge-cloud infrastructures. We also give ideas about how this ontology can be used for identifying problems and finding alternative nodes for service execution.

The rest of the paper is organized as follows. Section 2 presents related work on using ontologies to represent knowledge about IoT and cloud infrastructures. In Sect. 3 we describe the ECO ontology as well as how the SPARQL query language can be used to detect problems and assist in solving them. A use case is described in Sect. 4. Finally, we conclude the paper in Sect. 5.

2 Related works

Cloud ontologies have been widely used in recent years. [3] presents some applications of ontologies in cloud environments. In general, it is possible to find works in the literature that propose the use of ontologies to provide security solutions [4], resource management [5] and service discovery [6]. In the case of the use of ontologies to improve the interoperability of cloud-based systems, the most notable work is the mOSAIC cloud ontology [7], which shows a detailed and simple description of cloud computing resources. This ontology is aimed at promoting transparency in access to multiple clouds. The mOSAIC ontology was created more than 10 years ago and has not been updated since then. Thus, new technological elements that have appeared in recent years were not considered and are therefore not supported by mOSAIC. Because of this, new works have emerged and have tried to remove these limitations. For example, Paassage [8] proposes a deployment mechanism for applications in public and private clouds which is controlled by a set of rules described in the CAMEL modeling language [9]. ModaClouds [10] proposes a model-based development for multiple clouds which performs semi-automatic code transformations obtaining compatible implementations on platforms of public and hybrid cloud providers.

These projects provide mechanisms that allow interconnecting services from different providers, improving existing interfaces or providing decision support systems. However, these projects do not support a broad heterogeneous environment, limiting themselves only to resource management, hardware accelerators, or resource abstractions in the same cloud. In addition, these solutions are not oriented to work with IoT devices such as sensors, actuators, gateways, etc. Despite this, there are ontologies that have been specifically developed to model the capabilities, features, and descriptions of devices. One of the efforts made in this regard is the Semantic Sensor Network ontology (SOSA/SSN) [11]. SOSA/SSN describes sensor and actuator networks, their capabilities, their characteristics of interest and their observations. Moreover, it serves as a core or source of inspiration for other ontologies. The ETSI SmartM2M technical committee developed the Smart Applications REFerence Ontology (SAREF) [12] to describe devices and their functions. SAREF is aligned with the oneM2M base ontology [13] which enables syntactic and semantic interoperability between devices and external systems. SAREF and SSN have extensions that allow them to be applied to other more specific domains. For example, in the case of SAREF, CASO extension [14] is oriented to agriculture, EEPSA [12] is oriented to buildings, and the SSN System module models capabilities, systems and things.

Despite the mentioned ontologies, we are not aware of ontologies that provide mechanisms necessary to deal with information of cloud systems, IoT devices at the edge and the fog abstraction in between both. For this reason, we present an ontology for this purpose.

3 Proposed solution

As discussed above, we aim at a computing continuum distributed digital infrastructure over various elements on which software is deployed. This software collaborates with assembling complex applications. In addition, applications are composed of one or more software services that provide functionalities to obtain specific objectives. The solution proposed in this article is oriented to work on software service architectures where applications are based on services that interact with others to provide high-level functionalities. In an IoT system, services can perform a variety of tasks, such as, for example processing measurements received from a network of sensors, or data mining processes in which the received data are analyzed maybe using machine learning techniques.

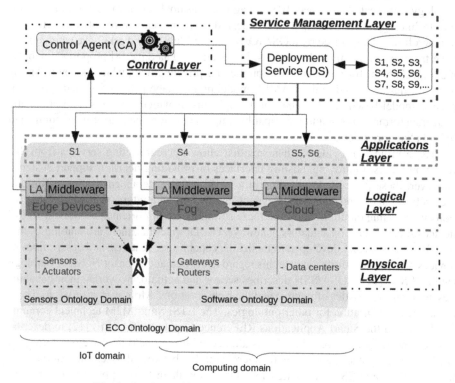

Fig. 1. Service architecture oriented to IoT applications.

Service-oriented architectures are ideal for continuous computing management because they allow to easily install/uninstall/transfer software services to other systems. Fig. 1 presents the reference architecture proposed for this work. The architecture is divided into 5 layers on which the software is distributed. The *Physical Layer* contains the hardware on which the software is deployed. The *Logical Layer* represents the software layer that facilitates the management of services and applications of interest to end-users.

The *Applications Layer* contains the applications of the end-users. The applications are distributed in the form of software services on devices and data centers. The *Control Layer* monitors and manages the operation of the software developed on top of the service architecture. It can dictate the guidelines that orchestrate the configuration of the software. This layer interacts with the *Service Management Layer*, which is responsible for the deployment of the software in an unattended manner. Table 1 describes the elements of Fig. 1 in more detail.

Table 1. Description of the elements that make up the service architecture.

Element	Description
Local Agent (LA)	Local agents are executing on devices and are in charge of 1) obtaining the status of the device on which they are installed by monitoring parameters such as processor load, memory and disk space used at a given time; 2) sending this information to the CA; 3) allowing to make configuration adjustments of the device proposed by the CA; and 4) making decisions about their operations if they lose connection with the CA
Control Agent (CA)	It receives information and notifications from the LAs so it can know the status of all the devices in the system. With this information, the CA can detect problems of operation and the elements involved. In addition, the CA can propose a new distribution of software that solves the detected problems using the Deployment Service to deploy the new software
Middleware	Is the software located between an operating system and the applications that run on it. It enables data communication and management in distributed applications. It avoids having to develop the same software natively for each device
Edge Devices	They are the IoT devices distributed throughout the physical world such as sensors, actuators, etc. These devices are characterized by having low processing capabilities. Normally, they take the measurements and send them to other devices with greater computing power
Fog Devices	They are the devices hosted on the Fog between the IoT part and the cloud. They are responsible for the processing of IoT information and thus avoid sending all IoT information to the cloud, reducing the data traffic in the network
Cloud Data Center	It represents data centers hosted on cloud computing infrastructures. These data centers perform tasks that require high computing capabilities such as data mining, data analysis, predictions, simulations, etc.
Deployment Service	Is a software service in charge of managing how software services are deployed on any device of the architecture. It is responsible for the deployment of any service on devices or data centers of the system, as long as they meet the established requirements
Services	These are software services that provide specific functionalities. Depending on the purpose of the service and the functionality it provides, it can be deployed on IoT devices, in data centers hosted in the cloud or in Fog devices
Applications	They are applications used by end-users. They can be composed of several software services orchestrated with each other providing high-level functionalities to users

3.1 The Edge-Cloud Ontology (ECO)

We propose the use of ontologies to facilitate the management and proper functioning of the architecture presented in Sect. 3. Using ontologies to manage physical devices, software, communications, and processing centers improves the control of the available resources in a system. In addition, it enhances the relationships between the different elements of the system by providing a semantic sense. The fact that the relationships between the elements of the system are enhanced opens up new opportunities for their management beyond those provided by traditional systems, which perform resource management using relational models. Instead of developing an ontology from the scratch and following current ontology development methodologies, we have considered reusing existing ontologies and create only the necessary elements to meet our needs.

There are many ontologies to represent IoT devices and applications through ontologies as mentioned in Sect. 2. However, to address the problem proposed in this work, the authors have started from a perspective based on two fundamental concepts: computing nodes and the connections between nodes. Computing nodes integrate concepts that model elements with computing capabilities such as data centers hosted in cloud infrastructures, devices that are part of the Fog environment or even IoT devices (sensors, actuators, etc.) at the edge.

After analyzing different alternatives, we propose the use of the Smart Energy-Aware Systems (SEAS) ontology [15]. Using SEAS allows to apply a top-down methodology, so it is possible to identify the high-level functions of the IT system and from there go into the details. From this point of view, there is a clearer vision of the topography of the network facilitating the incorporation of parameters on each of the connections and it facilitates the process of semantic modeling. SEAS consists of a set of modules that provide terminology to describe physical systems and their interrelationships by modelling connections between devices. SEAS is aligned with the model perspective based on node and connection concepts.

Figure 2 shows an overview of the main concepts and relationships of the proposed *Edge-Cloud Ontology (ECO)*.

The concepts *seas:System* and *seas:Connection* of the SEAS ontology are used to model complex systems compound of nodes with computing capabilities as well as the connections between them. Computing nodes represent data centers located in the cloud, devices deployed on the Fog, or even sensor devices deployed over an IoT environment at the edge. However, due to the complexity of IoT systems and applications, seas ontology is not sufficient to model other important aspects and factors that need to be considered. To solve this problem, we propose to enhance the ontology with the concepts and properties described below:

- *eco:ComputingNode.* This concept represents any device with computing capabilities, i.e. IoT devices, cloud data centers, or devices hosted on the Fog. Computing nodes are related to *seas:System* through the property *eco:contains*. The resource availability of computing nodes can be specified with the data properties *eco:cpuLoad*, *eco:ramMemoryInstalled*, *eco:ramMemoryFree* and *eco:diskSpaceFree*.
- *eco:Software* represents the software that can be deployed on computing nodes (*eco:ComputingNode*), which is specified through the *eco:deployedIn* property.

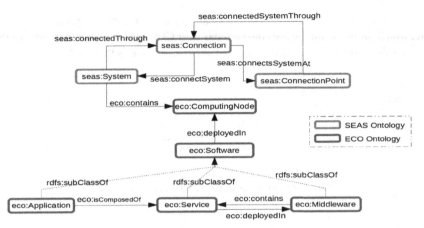

Fig. 2. Main concepts and properties of the ECO ontology. Green concepts are reused from the SEAS[1] ontology, whereas red nodes represent new concepts defined in ECO[2].

- *eco:Application* represents a type of *eco:Software* that is utilized by end-users. An application can be composed of several services (*eco:Services*), which are indicated through the *eco:isComposedOf* property.
- *eco:Service.* Is a type of *eco:Software* that represents the services deployed in a system. The operating requirements of the service are specified with the properties *eco:diskSpaceRequirement* and *eco:ramRequirement*. In the case that services connect to other services on the same or different devices, this information can be indicated with the properties *eco:remoteConnectionTo* and *eco:localConnectionTo*, respectively.
- *eco:Middleware* is a type of *eco:Software* in which software services are deployed. Example of middleware are Java Virtual Machines or Microsoft.NET.

3.2 Using the ECO Ontology: Problem Detection and Adaptation

The main goals of building the ECO ontology consists in the assistance in detecting contingencies (e.g. applications affected by a broken connection) and adapting the infrastructure to ensure continuous computing by selecting the suitable nodes to run software based on their overload and the requirements of the service to be deployed. In the following, we show several scenarios and how SPARQL can be used to obtain information from edge-cloud knowledge represented with the ECO ontology.

Identification of Nodes in an Overload State
The identification of overloaded nodes is important for two reasons: i) it prevents potential service failure due to the nodes overload since it is possible to anticipate and act before failures occur that can cause the collapse of the node and ii) it may reveal that the software executed on the overloaded node may have high response times. Figure 3

---

[1] We use the prefix seas: https://w3id.org/seas/.

[2] We use the prefix eco: https://www.ia.urjc.es/ontologies/eco/.

shows an example of a SPARQL query that can be used to identify nodes in an overload state, which for this example are considered if their CPU load is higher than 90% or that have less than 100 MB of memory or a disk storage space less than 700 MB.

```
SELECT ?computingNode
WHERE {
    ?computingNode eco:cpuLoad ?loadCPU .
    ?computingNode eco:ramMemoryFree ?ramFree .
    ?computingNode eco:diskSpaceFree ?diskFree .
    FILTER (?loadCPU > 90 || ?ramFree <100 || ?diskFree < 700)
}
```

Fig. 3. Query for overloaded nodes identification.

Search for Suitable Computing Nodes for Software Deployment

Continuous computing requires the installation and uninstallation of software automatically at any time. Thus, it is essential to know the functioning topography and available infrastructure resources at any given time. This is especially important when decisions need to be made about where to deploy a specific software in order to have sufficient computing resources and ensure acceptable response times.

The following query (Fig. 4) obtains the list of computing nodes that meet the requirements of service *S4* to be deployed. In particular, those candidate nodes must be connected to a local network managed by router *"routerNetwork01"*, i.e. the node is contained in a system connected through that router. Furthermore, there is a computing node (*?computingNode*) with enough available RAM and disk space, as well as less than 30% of CPU load.

```
SELECT ?computingNode
WHERE {
    ?connectionPoint eco:id "routerNetwork01"     .
    ?connectionPoint seas:connectsSystemThrough ?connection .
    ?connection seas:connectsSystem ?system .
    ?system eco:contains ?computingNode .
    ?computingNode eco:ramMemoryFree ?ramMemoryFree .
    ?service rdf:type eco:Service .
    ?service eco:id "S4" .
    ?service eco:ramRequirement ?ramRequirement .
    FILTER (?ramMemoryFree > ?ramRequirement) .
    ?computingNode eco:diskSpaceFree  ?diskSpaceFree .
    ?service eco:diskSpaceRequirement    ?diskSpaceRequirement .
    FILTER (?diskSpaceFree > ?diskSpaceRequirement) .
    ?computingNode eco:cpuLoad ?cpuLoad .
    FILTER (?cpuLoad < 30 ) .
}
```

Fig. 4. Query for obtaining computing nodes for deploying a specific service.

Detection of Affected Software due to Connection link Drop

Every system is susceptible to errors, breakdowns or attacks that may affect any of the elements that make it up. Connections and network elements are critical in these systems because they allow the communication of some equipment with others. This holds especially in distributed applications where software applications are composed of smaller parts (services) that are not always deployed on the same machine but are rather distributed. In the event of a loss of connection, some software components may not be able to communicate with other software services, thus interrupting their operation.

The query in Fig. 5 obtains the list of applications that may potentially be affected in their operation by a broken connection *C2*. These applications are composed of services that are (i) deployed in a middleware running on a computing node whose connection is broken (i.e. contained in a system whose connection is *C2*) and needs to interact with at least one remote service; or (ii) connected to any remote service deployed in an inaccessible node. The pattern *eco:remoteConnectionTo+* in the query represents the transitive closure of the remote connection property, i.e. an application may be affected by any connection to a remote service in one or more jumps.

```
SELECT   ?application
WHERE {
     ?application eco:isComposedOf ?serviceApp .
     {
         ?serviceApp eco:deployedIn ?middleware   .
         ?serviceApp eco:remoteConnectionTo ?anyRemoteService .
     }
     UNION
     {
         ?serviceApp eco:remoteConnectionTo+  ?remoteService   .
         ?remoteService eco:deployedIn ?middleware   .
     }
     ?middleware eco:deployedIn ?computingNode .
     ?system eco:contains ?computingNode .
     ?connection seas:connectsSystem ?system .
     ?connection eco:id "C2"   .
}
```

Fig. 5. Query identifying applications affected by remote unconnected services.

4 Use case

To evaluate the solutions proposed in this article, a test environment that simulates an Agro-IoT scenario has been designed (see an outline in Fig. 6).

The environment is composed of a network of sensors that monitor a space dedicated to a crop. The sensor network measures temperature and humidity, using devices (*SensorT1*, *SensorT2*, *SensorH1*) with little processing capacities. These devices also check for measurement errors through a simple algorithm and send the data to an information aggregator node, which is a device hosted in the Fog (*NodeFog1*) and obtains the information from all the sensors distributed at the field and calculates the average values. The average values are sent to the data center hosted in the cloud (*NodeCloud*) where data mining and analysis algorithms are applied to generate reports that users can use to evaluate the state of the crop.

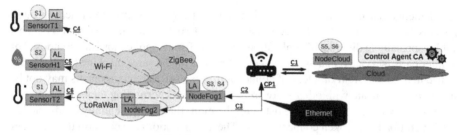

Fig. 6. Example of scenario.

The test environment consists of 3 Arduino devices (sensors), each of them using a different technology (ZigBee, Wi-Fi, LoRaWan) to communicate with a node (*Node-Fog1*) which is connected to the Wi-Fi network provided by a Wi-Fi router (*CP1*). This router also provides an Internet connection to the devices as well as a local Ethernet network in which two Raspberry Pi-based devices (*NodeFog1* and *NodeFog2*) are connected which provides software services to the devices of the Wi-Fi network. These devices provide typical functionalities of Fog computing.

In the proposed scenario, one of the devices (*NodeFog2*) has the backup role. This means that when a problem is detected with the main device (*NodeFog1*), the backup node will take over. Local agents (LA) and control agent (CA) are responsible for detecting possible problems and applying possible corrections through monitoring mechanisms and automatic deployment management. LAs check the processor load, free RAM and disk space of computing nodes on which they are running. If these values are close to a certain threshold, then they are reported to the CA to assess the situation from a global perspective and apply a joint strategy in accordance with other available resources. LAs collect information about the state of the node and send this information periodically to the CA. The CA records the information in a data model according to the specification of the ontology presented in the previous section.

Figure 7 shows part of the scenario modelled using the ECO ontology.

For this example, *NodeFog1* is identified as an overloaded node (query presented in Fig. 3).

Another relevant case in the scenario is the deployment of an additional software service. In this case, it is necessary to obtain the list of appropriate nodes. This can be done with the query shown in Fig. 4 for service *S4*, obtaining as a result the node *NodeFog2*, since it complies with the minimum requirements of *S4*.

Finally, we also show the case of fault detection in some connection link. When the loss of a connection has been detected, it is possible to know which services and applications have been affected by making use of query Fig. 6. Assuming, for example, that connection *C2* is broken, then *Application1* is identified since it is composed of service *S4* (besides *S1*, *S2*, *S3* and *S5*), which is deployed in *MiddlewareFog1*, which in turn is deployed in NodeFog1, which is contained in a system (*System2*) that uses connection *C2*.

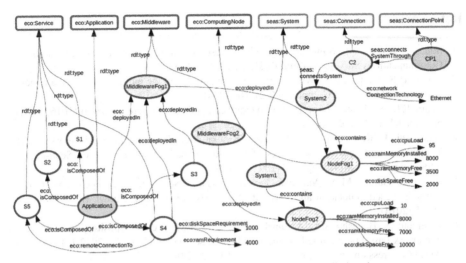

Fig. 7. The figure shows instances of the ECO ontology applied to the use case.

5   Conclusions

In this work, an ontology has been proposed to manage the computing continuum in the field of IoT. The proposed ontology provides concepts and properties to represent the state of each of the devices that make up an IoT system. The design of the ontology is motivated by the need to create an information model that not only records information from each of its components, but also allows to automatically reason with the information asserted and infer information that is relevant to the operation of the applications running on such systems. The Edge Cloud Ontology (ECO) reuses the SEAS ontology and enhances it with classes and properties to model the elements that have been identified in this work.

In the future, we plan to work on improving the use of semantic technologies for monitoring and detection of changes in the edge-cloud context that may require a reconfiguration of the infrastructure or services running on it. In particular, we will explore the use of event stream processing techniques that use semantic representations such as C-SPARQL [16]. Also, we plan to extend the ontology to account for more information requirements and to explore how automatic inferences can be used to infer new knowledge.

Acknowledgements. This work has been partially supported by the Spanish Ministry of Science, Innovation, and Universities, co-funded by EU FEDER Funds, through grant number RTI2018-095390-B-C33 (MCIU/AEI/FEDER, UE) and the AGROBOTS Project funded by the Community of Madrid (Spain). Iván Bernabé has been funded by the Spanish Ministry of Universities through a grant related to the Requalification of the Spanish University System 2021–23 by the University Carlos III of Madrid.

References

1. Sun, X., Ansari, N., Wang, R.: Optimizing resource utilization of a data center. IEEE Communications Surveys & Tutorials **18**(4), 2822–2846 (2016)
2. Atlam, H.F., Walters, R.J., Wills, G.B.: Fog computing and the internet of things: a review. Big Data and Cognitive Computing **2**(2), 10 (2018)
3. Imam, F.T.: Application of ontologies in cloud computing: The state-of-the-art (2016). arXiv preprint arXiv:1610.02333
4. Takahashi, T., Kadobayashi, Y., Fujiwara, H.: Ontological approach toward cyberse-curity in cloud computing. In: Proceedings of the 3rd international conference on Secu-rity of information and networks, pp. 100–109 (2010/09)
5. Rodríguez-García, M.Á., Valencia-García, R., García-Sánchez, F., Samper-Zapater, J.J.: Ontology-based annotation and retrieval of services in the cloud. Knowl.-Based Syst. **56**, 15–25 (2014)
6. Tahamtan, A., Beheshti, S.A., Anjomshoaa, A., Tjoa, A.M.: A cloud repository and discovery framework based on a unified business and cloud service ontology. In: 2012 IEEE Eighth World Congress on Services, pp. 203–210. IEEE (2012/06)
7. Moscato, F., Aversa, R., Di Martino, B., Fortiş, T.F., Munteanu, V.: An analysis of mosaic ontology for cloud resources annotation. In: 2011 federated conference on computer science and information systems (FedCSIS), pp. 973–980. IEEE (2011/09)
8. Sri, K.U., Prakash, M.B., Deepthi, J.: A framework to dropping cost in passage of CDN into hybrid cloud. Int. J. Innov. Technol. Res **5**(2), 5829–5831 (2017)
9. Phase, D.: Cloud application modelling and execution language (CAMEL) and the PaaSage workflow. In: Advances in Service-Oriented and Cloud Computing: Workshops of ESOCC 2015, Taormina, Italy, September 15–17, 2015, Revised Selected Papers, vol. 567, p. 437. Springer (2016/04)
10. Di Nitto, E., Casale, G., Petcu, D.: On modaclouds' toolkit support for devops. In: 4th European Conference on Service Oriented and Cloud Computing Workshops (ESOCC), pp. 430–431 (2016/04)
11. Guha, R.V., Brickley, D., Macbeth, S.: Schema. org: evolution of structured data on the web. Communications of the ACM **59**(2), 44–51 (2016)
12. Daniele, L., Hartog, F.D., Roes, J.: Created in close interaction with the industry: the smart appliances reference (SAREF) ontology. In: International Workshop Formal On-tologies Meet Industries, pp. 100–112. Springer, Cham (2015/08)
13. OneM2M Base Ontology: https://www.onem2m.org/images/pdf/TS-0012-Base_Ontology-V3_7_3.pdf. Accessed 08 May 2022
14. Nguyen, Q.D., Roussey, C., Poveda-Villalón, M., de Vaulx, C., Chanet, J.P.: Development experience of a context-aware system for smart irrigation using CASO and IRRIG ontologies. Appl. Sci. **10**(5), 1803 (2020)
15. Lefrançois, M., Kalaoja, J., Ghariani, T., Zimmermann, A.: The SEAS Knowledge Model (Doctoral dissertation, ITEA2 12004 Smart Energy Aware Systems) (2017)
16. Barbieri, D.F., Braga, D., Ceri, S., Della Valle, E., Grossniklaus, M.: C-SPARQL: SPARQL for continuous querying. In: Proceedings of the 18th international conference on World wide web, pp. 1061–1062 (2009)

A Collaborative Approach to Mobile Crowdsourcing Based on Data Stream Learning

Ralf Bruns[1] , Jeremias Dötterl[1], Jürgen Dunkel[1](✉) ,
and Sascha Ossowski[2]

[1] Hannover University for Applied Sciences and Arts, 30459 Hannover, Germany
{ralf.bruns,juergen.dunkel}@hs-hannover.de
[2] Universidad Rey Juan Carlos, 28933 Mostoles, Spain
sascha.ossowski@urjc.es

Abstract. Mobile crowdsourcing refers to systems where task completion necessarily involves physical movement of crowd workers. Crowdsourced parcel delivery, also called *crowdshipping*, is a particularly relevant example to this respect. Evidence exists that in such systems tasks are frequently abandoned, indicating that crowd workers accept tasks that they misjudge and later prefer to discontinue. In this paper we evaluate as to how far on-the-fly task transfers between crowdworkers can alleviate this problem in a cooperative setting. Its contribution to this respect is twofold. Firstly, it analyses different data stream learning approaches for service quality prediction in mobile crowdshipping. Secondly, it embeds this prediction model into a collaborative agent-based crowdshipping approach where task transfer decisions are taken in a peer-to-peer fashion with limited overhead.

Keywords: Crowdshipping · Agent-based simulation · Data stream learning

1 Introduction

Crowdsourcing has turned out to be a versatile problem-solving paradigm with many useful applications. It usually refers to some entity (the so-called *crowdsourcer*) outsourcing tasks to a huge group of largely independent users (called *crowdworkers*) through an open call, instead of having them performed in a traditional manner by employees or contractors. In some cases crowdworkers come together with the explicit aim of jointly performing the tasks defined by the crowdsourcer, while in others crowdworkers solve a problem as a side-effect of something else they are doing [2].

Mobile crowdsourcing systems – which are also called location-based, spatial, or urban crowdsourcing systems – often belong to the latter class. They refer to crowdsourcing systems with spatial tasks, where task completion necessarily

A. González-Briones et al. (Eds.): PAAMS Workshops 2022, CCIS 1678, pp. 83–94, 2022.
https://doi.org/10.1007/978-3-031-18697-4_7

involves physical movement of crowd workers. Crowdsourced parcel delivery (aka *crowdshipping* [11]) is a particularly relevant example to this respect. It is often applied to solve the *last mile problem*, i.e. to service the delivery leg from the logistics company's parcel hub to the recipients' homes. The aim is doing so in a fast, cost-efficient, and environmentally friendly manner, by making use of spare capacities in private vehicles and piggyback on trips that are made by private citizens anyway. Interested individuals become crowdworkers introducing minor detours to original routes, so as to pick up parcels and to deliver them to their destinations [7].

A major goal of the crowdsourcer (usually a logistics company) with regard to the last mile problem is to establish bilateral agreements with crowdworkers regarding some transportation tasks such that an acceptable quality of service is ensured. Among others, this implies that parcels are delivered as soon as possible, and certainly by some deadline. However, conventional mobile crowdsourcing provides evidence that tasks are frequently abandoned, indicating that crowd workers accept tasks that they misjudge and later prefer to discontinue due to change in opinion or circumstances [8]. Furthermore, during task execution, the crowd worker can face unexpected situations, which can cause delays and task failures. For instance, traffic jams can introduce huge delays to travel plans of crowdworkers moving by car. Weather conditions may put delivery deadlines at risk, especially if the means of transportation is a bicycle. Fatigue can be a reason for a crowdworkers walking or cycling to deliver parcels later than expected [3].

Some recent work on crowdshipping has looked into systems that consider the handover of parcels among crowdworkers [7,11]. In this paper we argue that supporting peer-to-peer task transfers among crowdworkers is a promising approach to prevent task failures in mobile crowdsourcing, and that a key element to this respect is the accuracy of the service quality prediction model that is used to trigger task transfer decisions. Its first contribution is the application and analysis of different data stream learning approaches for service quality prediction. Our second contribution is to embed this prediction model into a collaborative agent-based crowdshipping approach where task transfer decisions are taken locally and with limited overhead.

The paper is organised as follows. Section 2 outlines our collaborative agent-based mobile crowdsourcing model including peer-to-peer task transfers. Section 3 describes the simulation model upon which the approach is evaluated. Section 4 describes in detail the use of different data stream learning models for failure prediction. Section 5 presents experimental results regarding the application of these predictors in the context of collaborative mobile crowdsourcing with peer-to-peer task transfers. After discussing some related work in Sect. 6, we conclude the paper pointing to future lines of work in Sect. 7.

2 Agent-Based Collaborative Crowdshipping with Parcel Transfers

In recent years, mechanisms have been explored that support task transfers among crowdworkers as a means to prevent task failures. This implies (i) detecting that some task t is at risk of failure and (ii) enabling the transfer of t to another crowdworker. Such task transfers are particularly demanding in the crowdshipping domain, as either crowdworkers need to physically meet at some place at a certain time, or the parcel needs to be stored in a secure place and picked up later by the newly responsible crowdshipper. In traditional fleet management systems such task transfers can be arranged in a top-down manner by the logistics company, but the decentralised nature of the crowdshipping approach calls for methods that rely on peer-to-peer interaction [5].

In other work, we have developed a method for peer-to-peer task transfers among *strategic* crowdshippers. Each crowdshipper (aka *courier*) is represented by an autonomous (individually rational) software agent that, once a potential future task failure is predicted, launches second-price auctions to forge task transfer agreements. Once a this is done, the couriers actually meet at a certain location and execute the parcel handover [3].

In this paper, we also take an agent-based approach towards the problem. However, the option of performing a transfer of task t from its bearer i to another agent j is explored only when the couriers i and j "encounter", i.e. when their locations are close to each other. In this case, the expected quality of service provided by i performing t is compared to j's service quality executing t and, if the latter exceeds the former, t is transferred from i to j. Compared to the model from [3], the approach put forward in this paper avoids a major source of complexity: task transfers can be effectively implemented on-the-fly because, as mentioned above, both agents are already near to one another. Of course, such a stance necessarily implies less emphasis on strategic issues.

Algorithm 1 summarises this approach. It can easily be seen that it depends on two key elements:

- the concept of *vicinity* needs to be specified, so as to be able to identify the set CS_c^t of candidate couriers. Notice that the more restrictive the notion of vicinity, more seldomly couriers encounter, and fewer task transfer opportunities exist.
- a function for predicting the *service quality* of an agent with respect to a delivery task is needed. The service quality function $F_{qual}(c, p)$ specifies how good a crowdworker c is able to achieve the delivery of a parcel p, i.e. a high value means better quality.

The following section outlines a cell-based environment model that helps defining the notion of vicinity for the purpose of this paper. Section 4.1 gives an example of a suitable service quality function.

3   Agent-Based Crowdshipping Simulation Model

In order to evaluate the feasibility of our collaborative crowdshipping approach we developed an agent-based simulation environment, which is based on a simple model of the environment, in particular how crowdworkers behave and how the traffic situations change.

Algorithm 1. Collaborative parcel transfer algorithm

1: **procedure** PARCELTRANSFER
2:      Define service quality function $F_{qual}(c, p)$;
3:      **for each** time step t **do**
4:          **for each** courier c with parcel p **do**
5:              Determine the candidate set CS_c^t,   ▷ all couriers c_i in vicinity to c
6:              $cand_{best} = \{c^* \in CS_c^t | F_{qual}(c^*, p) = \min_{\forall c_i \in CS_c^t} (F_{qual}(c_i, p))\}$
7:              **if** $F_{qual}(c, p) > F_{qual}(cand_{best}, p)$ **then**   ▷ *candidate is better suited*
8:                  Transfer parcel p from c to $cand_{best}$
9:              **end if**
10:          **end for**
11:      **end for**
12: **end procedure**

3.1   Environmental Model

Crowdshipping usually operates in highly populated urban areas. In an urban area, the speed at which a crowdworker moves is strongly determined by the current traffic situation.

In order to realize a simple traffic model, we divide our operating area into a grid structure. The area consists of 500 * 500 cells, each 300 m long. We assume that each grid cell can be in one of the following traffic states: *normal traffic, slow traffic and traffic jam*. For crowdworkers moving on the road, the state of the cells affects their velocity. For instance, in a cell with state *traffic jam* the agents using the road do not move at all (travel with 0 km/h). In a cell with state *normal traffic*, all agents in this cell travel with their individual preferred speeds. Figure 1 depicts a typical map with grid cells representing a traffic situation.[1]

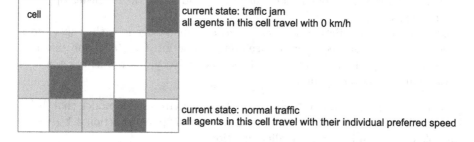

Fig. 1. Grid structure with different traffic states

Of course, the traffic situation in an urban area changes very dynamically and, as a consequence, also the velocity of road users varies over time. We use a

---

[1] For the sake of simplicity, it is assumed that the states of neighboring cells are independent. Of course, this assumption does not hold in reality.

time-discrete Markov chain to model the changing traffic state in a rather simple way. In the simulation the cell states are updated with a frequency of 1 min.

3.2 Crowdworker Agents

The crowd consists of individual worker agents who are registered in the system and interested in delivering parcels. The model distinguishes three types of crowdworker agents with different properties: *walk, bike and motorbike*. The crowd consists of about 1/3 agents of each type. Each agent is defined by an arrival time, start location, end location, and a route with several predefined stopover points. This means, the agents move on different paths of different lengths.

The walk agents and the bike agents do not move on roads, therefore, their speed does not depend on the traffic situation. These two agent types move with a constant speed: walk with 2 m/s and bike with 5 m/s.

The motorbikes travel on the road, and their speed consequently depends on the traffic situation of the grid cell where they are currently located. For the different cell states, a motorbike travels with the following speed:

1. normal traffic: Gaussian mean 9 m/s, with standard deviation 4
2. slow traffic: Gaussian mean 3 m/s, with standard deviation 1.5
3. traffic jam: 0 m/s.

3.3 Parcels and Initial Assignment

Each parcel is specified by randomly drawn pick-up locations, delivery destinations and route lengths (between 1,500 and 5,00 m). The delivery time is calculated by 1 min per 200 m of route length.

The initial assignment of new parcels proceed as follows: New parcels are immediately assigned to the worker agent that is nearest to the pick-up location. Each agent is only allowed to carry one parcel at a time. The delivery destination of the parcel is inserted into the courier agent's pre-defined travel route (by a basic traveling salesman algorithm). The courier agent picks up the parcel at the pick-up location and delivers it to the final destination.

3.4 Agent-Based Crowdshipping Simulator

The model introduced above has been implemented by an agent-based crowdshipping simulator (an extended version of the simulator presented in [4]).

To make the simulation as realistic as possible, we employ real-world GPS data to simulate the physical movements of the agent. We choose open data of a bicycle sharing system because of its conceptual similarity to a crowdshipping system. In both domains, there are users who register in the system, physically move around the urban area, and log out of the system.

Specifically, we employ the GPS data from the Bike Sharing System of Madrid (BiciMAD)[2]. The data set includes the rides logged by users and the GPS events recorded during each ride: start timestamp, start location, end location, and GPS traces. Based on BiciMAD data we simulate parcel delivery in the urban city center of Madrid. The appearance of a worker agent, its start location and destination and its route are derived from the BiciMAD data set.

The simulation runs were conducted with 7986 crowdworker agents and 600 parcels to be delivered. The parcels have randomly selected origin and destination locations within the operating area. Figure 2 shows a screenshot of a simulation run.

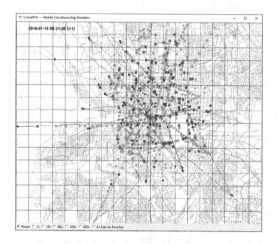

Fig. 2. Agent-based simulator at work

4   Predicting Delivery Success

A key issue of our collaborative crowdshipping approach is the situation-awareness of the crowdworkers: they have to estimate the success of their delivery tasks, i.e. whether they can deliver their package to its destination before the deadline.

4.1   General Prediction Model

The prediction of delivery success can be considered as a binary classification problem. For a crowd agent responsible for a certain parcel, it must be decided whether the parcel can be delivered on time, or in other words, whether the assignment belongs to the class DELAYED or not. More formally, the hypothesis function $h()$ shown in Eq. 1 must be learned.

$$\hat{y} = h(\vec{x}) \tag{1}$$

---

[2] https://opendata.emtmadrid.es/Datos-estaticos/Datos-generales-(1).

with the target $\hat{y} \in \{\text{DELAYED, NOT\_DELAYED}\}$, and the feature vector $\vec{x} = (x_1, x_2, ..., x_n)$, which contains all available data that is used to predict the task delivery outcome.

However, in our crowdshipping scenario, it is not sufficient to only know whether an assignment between courier c and parcel p belongs to class DELAYED; we also need to quantify how certain this prediction is, i.e. the exact value of the delay probability $prob_{delay}(c, p)$. Fortunately, most machine learning algorithms are able to provide probability estimates[3] of their predictions.[4]

Note that the service quality function used in the parcel transfer algorithm from Sect. 2 can be defined as: $F_{qual}(c, p) = 1 - prob_{delay}(c, p)$. A parcel should be transferred to a worker of higher quality, i.e. with a lower delay probability.

The crowdworker can use three types of data to make a realistic prediction about whether or not a packet belongs to the DELAYED class:

(i) worker capabilities: each worker has knowledge about her own speed achieved so far, which is given by the current, mean, maximum and minimum speed.

(ii) parcel delivery state: the current delivery state of a parcel is defined by the remaining distance to the destination and the remaining time until the delivery deadline.

(iii) environmental situation: the traffic situation relevant for parcel delivery can be characterized by the current states of the cells located on the remaining delivery route. We assume that each agent can obtain information about the number of cells on its route in the normal, slow, and traffic jam states via a central service.

For evaluating the quality of a Machine Learning approach, we calculate well-known evaluation metrics for classification problems: precision, recall and F1-score [12].

4.2   Learning from Data Streams

In the crowdshipping scenario, the prediction of the delivery success must be learned on a stream of continuously arriving data: whenever two crowdworkers, one of whom has a parcel, encounter, each of them must estimate the probability with which she could deliver the package on time.

Classification is the task of predicting the correct label (here: DELAYED or NOT_DELAYED) for an unlabeled feature vector $\vec{x_i}$ (as introduced in 1). During training, the classification algorithm observes a data stream D

$$D = \{(\vec{x_i}, y_i) | i = 0, 1, 2, 3, ..., m\} \qquad (2)$$

---

[3] For instance, in a decision tree, if a data item has been traversed to a particular leaf node, then the predicted delay probability is the percentage of delayed items out of all items that have been propagated to that leaf node.

[4] e.g. in scikit-learn provided by the functions decision_function() or predict_proba().

where the i-th training data item $(\vec{x_i}, y_i)$ is the feature vector $\vec{x_i}$ with the corresponding true target label y_i. The machine learning algorithm uses this training data to learn a prediction model. This model can be used to predict, for a newly arriving feature vector $\vec{x}_{new}$, the still unknown and most probable label $\hat{y}_{new}$.

When learning on data streams [6], data cannot be clearly separated between training, evaluation, and testing data (as is the case with batch learning). Instead, when predicting whether a parcel will arrive delayed, the correct result is not available until a later time. For each data item, data stream learning goes through a processing cycle *'predict −> fit model −> evaluate'* with the following steps:

1. get an unlabeled data item $\vec{x_i}$,
2. for $\vec{x}_i$: make a prediction $\hat{y}_i = h(\vec{x}_i)$ using the current model $h()$,
3. determine the true label y_i for $\vec{x}_i$ (here: when at a later time it is known whether a parcel is delayed)
4. use the new correct pair $(\vec{x}_i, y_i)$ to train the current model $h()$,
5. take the pair $(\hat{y}_i, y_i)$ to update statistics for evaluation of the model quality.

Following these steps, we apply an interleaved or *prequential* evaluation approach: Each item is first used to test the model by making a prediction for this previously unseen item. Then, the model is updated (trained) with this item as soon as its label is available.

There are several stream learning algorithms that adapt well-known batch-learning classification algorithms to data streams. Among others we applied K-Nearest Neighbors (KNN), Random Forest and Hoeffding Trees [1,6,9].

4.3   Experiments

Using the data streams generated by the simulator described in Sect. 3.4. we conducted various experiments for predicting the delivery success. Our machine learning experiments are performed with *River*[5] that integrates the data stream learning libraries *scikit-multiflow*[6] and *créme*[7]. Table 1 shows our results using the data stream versions of KNN, Random Forest and Hoeffding.

Table 1. Experiment results for predicting the delivery success

Prediction model	Precision	Recall	F1-score
Random Forest (n = 20)	0.957	0.974	0.966
KNN (K = 10)	0.912	0.904	0.908
Hoeffding	0.879	0.881	0.880

---

[5] https://riverml.xyz/.
[6] https://scikit-multiflow.github.io.
[7] https://pypi.org/project/creme/.

All applied data stream learning methods behave almost the same and provide very good prediction results. In particular, ensemble learning with Random Forest based on $n = 20$ trees yields precision and recall values of better than 95%. Furthermore, appropriate prediction models are learned fast. Figure 3 shows the convergence of the data stream learning process considering the F1-score for the three machine learning methods. After the arrival of about 2000 data items, the F1-score for all methods has reached a value about 90%. After that, the F1-score is almost constant, only for Random Forest it is slightly increasing.

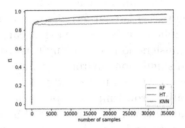

Fig. 3. F1-score convergence for RandomForest (RF), Hoeffing (HT) and KNN

When deriving a prediction model, we are interested not only in its accuracy but also in understanding how the predictions are inferred. A feature importance value can be viewed as a percentage expressing how much a particular feature contributes to the prediction. Table 2 shows how the importance of the features introduced in Subsect. 4.1 is distributed among the different types. To provide a better overview, we have summarized the values of the individual features. The most important features relate to the delivery state of the parcel with an overall importance of about (54%). In particular, the remaining delivery time is by far the most important feature (36%). The features associated with the workers' capabilities, specifically how fast they are, have an overall importance of 19%. The environmental features sum up to about 27% and describe the remaining path with the corresponding traffic states.

Table 2. Aggregated feature importance

Feature	Importance
Worker capability (current, max, min, mean speed)	0.19
Delivery state (remaining time, remaining distance)	0.54
Environmental situation (cell states and distances on remaining path)	0.27

5   Optimizing Delivery Success by Collaborative Parcel Transfers

Whenever a courier agent with an assigned parcel moves, it looks for a more suitable agent in the vicinity. According to Algorithm 1 nearby located crowd-worker agents are potential candidates for a parcel transfer. In our simulation, all agents who are currently in the same cell as the courier agent are considered as candidates. The prediction model learned in previous Sect. 4 is now used to estimate the delivery success probability of each candidate. A parcel transfer takes place if at least one of the candidate agents has a smaller delay probability as the courier agent. The parcel is transferred to that candidate with smallest delay probability. For simplicity, it is assumed that candidates do not yet have an assigned parcel and transfers do not take any time (duration = 0).

Using the agent-based simulation environment introduced in Sect. 3 and the prediction models of Sect. 4, we conducted extensive experimental evaluations of our proposed collaborative crowdshipping approach.

As the baseline of experiments, we implemented a conventional crowdshipping approach where every agent has to deliver its assigned parcel without any possibility of exchange. Taken the simulation parameters introduced in Sect. 3, in this approach without any parcel transfers 39% of the parcels cannot be delivered in time, i.e. 234 of 600 parcels are delayed. The mean completion time over all parcels is 16.28 min.

Table 3. Experimental results of collaborative parcel transfers

Prediction model	Delay	Completion time	Transfers	Reassigned tasks	In time/delayed
Random Forest (n = 20)	20%	12.55 min	249	210	162/48
KNN (K = 10)	22%	12.67 min	256	216	169/47
Hoeffding	21%	11.97 min	227	196	159/37
Convent. crowdshipping	39%	16.28 min	–	–	–

Table 3 shows the simulation results of our collaborative crowdshipping approach with the different prediction models presented in Sect. 4. It can be seen that the percentage of delayed parcels can almost be reduced by half (from 39% to approx. 21%). And the mean completion time drops by 25% from around 16 min to 12 min. The fourth column lists the total number of transfer activities and the fifth column the number of reassigned parcels. It can been seen that some parcels has been exchanged more than once. For instance, 249 transfers from a current courier to a candidate agent took place and 210 parcels were affected. The last column lists the number of parcels in time or delayed after being transferred, respectively. For instance, taken the 210 reassigned parcels, 162 could have been delivered in time after the transfer whereas 48 parcels were still delayed.

The three prediction models applied provide approximately the same results in terms of delay probabilities and completion times. This was to be expected, because the results of the prediction models in Sect. 4 also hardly distinguished from each other.

Overall, the results prove that collaborative crowdshipping has the potential to significantly improve to service quality of last mile delivery processes.

6   Related Work

The focus of crowdshipping research is mainly on three aspects (see [10] for an extensive literature review): (a) *supply*, e.g., the motivational and reward strategies of crowd participants, (b) *demand*, e.g., characteristics of demand and customer trust, (c) *operations and management*, e.g., the initial allocation of parcels to crowd workers.

Only recently, first approaches have been proposed to improve the delivery outcome by exchanging parcels between workers. Sadilek et al. [11] and Giret et al. [7] propose a collaborative delivery of parcels. The delivery path from pick-up to delivery destination is constructed as a chain of collaborative and synchronized deliverers in which the parcel is handed off from deliverer to deliverer that implement different sub-sections of the desired total delivery path.

In [5], we suggest an approach in which the transfer of parcels is seen as an opportunity to react on unforeseen difficulties or problems. Whenever a delay of a courier is predicted (by data stream learning), the system tries to transfer the parcel from the current deliverer to a more promising one nearby. Parcel transfers serve as a means of troubleshooting.

However, to the best of our knowledge, our approach is the first in which collaborative crowdshipping considers parcel transfers repeatedly and in an opportunistic manner, based on situation-aware prediction of the delivery success by data stream learning.

7   Conclusion and Future Lines of Research

In this paper, we presented a novel approach to mobile crowdsourcing. In our collaborative agent-based crowdshipping approach, individual crowdworkers act in cooperation and support each other in completing delivery tasks. A key element is service quality prediction by means of data stream learning, which is used to trigger the transfer of a parcel between worker agents.

In future work, we will focus on some aspects of the practical applicability of our approach. One important aspect to be addressed to this respect are the incentives of *strategic* crowd participants. In such a context, a crowdsourcing platform implementing our present approach can be seen as a "take-it-or-leave-it" offer to potential crowdshippers: they would join the platform when they expect to be better off following its rules than with outside options. However, this may not always be the case. Therefore, we will look into different ways of splitting rewards (penalties) for (un)successful delivery tasks between the involved crowdshippers, such that the transfers required by our mechanism are also individually rational for all stakeholders. This includes investigating the manipulability of information in general, and of the prediction models in particular. Also, our assumption that parcel transfers take no time is a simplification of reality (crowdshippers need to stop, handover the parcel, etc.). We will explore how different notions of transfer costs will affect the task transfer chains.

Acknowledgements. This work was supported by the German *Niedersächsisches Ministerium für Wissenschaft und Kultur* (MWK) in the programme PROFILinternational, by the Spanish *Ministerio de Ciencia e Innovación*, co-funded by EU FEDER Funds, through project grant RTI2018-095390-B-C31/32/33 (InEDGEMobility), and by the Regional Government of Madrid through the AGROBOTS project.

References

1. Aggarwal, C.C.: Data Mining: The Textbook. Springer, Heidelberg (2015). https://doi.org/10.1007/978-3-319-14142-8
2. Arolas, E.E., González-Ladrón-de-Guevara, F.: Towards an integrated crowdsourcing definition. J. Inf. Sci. **38**(2), 189–200 (2012). https://doi.org/10.1177/0165551512437638
3. Dötterl, J.: Mobile crowdsourcing with task transfers: a market-based multi-agent approach. Ph.D. thesis, International Doctoral School, University Rey Juan Carlos, Madrid, Spain (2021). https://en.cetinia.es/activities/cetinia-series
4. Dötterl, J., Bruns, R., Dunkel, J., Ossowski, S.: Evaluating crowdshipping systems with agent-based simulation. In: Bassiliades, N., Chalkiadakis, G., de Jonge, D. (eds.) EUMAS/AT -2020. LNCS (LNAI), vol. 12520, pp. 396–411. Springer, Cham (2020). https://doi.org/10.1007/978-3-030-66412-1_25
5. Dötterl, J., Bruns, R., Dunkel, J., Ossowski, S.: On-time delivery in crowdshipping systems: an agent-based approach using streaming data. In: Giacomo, G.D., et. al. (ed.) 24th European Conference on Artificial Intelligence - ECAI 2020, pp. 51–58. IOS Press (2020). https://doi.org/10.3233/FAIA200075
6. Gama, J.: Knowledge Discovery from Data Streams. Chapman Hall/CRC (2010)
7. Giret, A., Carrascosa, C., Julian, V., Rebollo, M., Botti, V.: A crowdsourcing approach for sustainable last mile delivery. Sustainability **10**(12) (2018). https://doi.org/10.3390/su10124563, https://www.mdpi.com/2071-1050/10/12/4563
8. Han, L., Roitero, K., Gadiraju, U., Sarasua, C., Checco, A., Maddalena, E., Demartini, G.: The impact of task abandonment in crowdsourcing. IEEE Trans. Knowl. Data Eng. **33**(5), 2266–2279 (2021). https://doi.org/10.1109/TKDE.2019.2948168
9. Hulten, G., Spencer, L., Domingos, P.: Mining time-changing data streams. In: Proceedings of the Seventh ACM SIGKDD International Conference on Knowledge Discovery and Data Mining, pp. 97–106. Association for Computing Machinery (2001). https://doi.org/10.1145/502512.502529
10. Le, T.V., Stathopoulos, A., Van Woensel, T., Ukkusuri, S.V.: Supply, demand, operations, and management of crowd-shipping services: a review and empirical evidence. Transp. Res. Part C: Emerg. Technol. **103**, 83–103 (2019). https://doi.org/10.1016/j.trc.2019.03.023, https://www.sciencedirect.com/science/article/pii/S0968090X18314700
11. Sadilek, A., Krumm, J., Horvitz, E.: Crowdphysics: Planned and opportunistic crowdsourcing for physical tasks. In: Proceedings of the Seventh International AAAI Conference on Weblogs and Social Media. AAAI Press (2013)
12. Tharwat, A.: Classification assessment methods. Appl. Comput. Inform., **17**(1), 168–192 (2021). https://doi.org/10.1016/j.aci.2018.08.003

On Balancing Fairness and Efficiency of Task Assignment in Agent Societies

Kendal Cousy[1,2], Marin Lujak[1](✉), Alessio Salvatore[3],
Alberto Fernández[1], and Stefano Giordani[2]

[1] CETINIA, University Rey Juan Carlos, Madrid, Spain
{kendal.cousy,marin.lujak,alberto.fernandez}@urjc.es
[2] Dipartimento di Ingegneria dell'Impresa, University of Rome "Tor Vergata",
Rome, Italy
stefano.giordani@uniroma2.it
[3] Istituto per le Applicazioni del Calcolo "M. Picone", Consiglio Nazionale delle
Ricerche, Rome, Italy
salvatore@iac.cnr.it

Abstract. Agent societies generally aim at collective provision of services (capabilities or resources) in a more efficient way than their agents could individually. In particular, some agents may be more efficient than the others in providing certain tasks. Thus, a task-agent assignment decision determines the overall performance of the society. The conventional linear sum assignment problem handles the assignment of tasks to a society of agents in a one-on-one manner. Such assignments typically only consider efficiency in terms of the overall cost or benefit for the system. However, an assignment strategy may be unfair if it does not explicitly consider fairness. Therefore, the conventional mathematical models for the task assignment problem should be rethought to explicitly consider fairness in the allocation of the tasks to the agents. In this paper, we study the utilitarian, egalitarian, and Nash social welfare in task assignment and propose two new assignment models that balance efficiency and fairness. Since fairness is a relatively abstract term that can be difficult to quantify, we propose three new fairness measures based on equity and equality and use them to compare the newly proposed models. Through functional examples, we show that a reasonable trade off between efficiency and fairness in task assignment can be found through the use of the proposed models.

Keywords: Task assignment · Multi-agent systems · Fairness · Efficiency · Resource allocation · Multi-agent coordination

1 Introduction

In this work, we focus on societies formed by self-concerned individually rational agents that share a common goal but have their own individual, possibly conflicting interests. They may share their capabilities and/or resources to carry out

A. González-Briones et al. (Eds.): PAAMS Workshops 2022, CCIS 1678, pp. 95–107, 2022.
https://doi.org/10.1007/978-3-031-18697-4_8

given tasks in a more efficient way and thus create synergies. Therefore, agents are expected to obtain higher performance by collective action. Examples of such societies are agriculture cooperatives, taxi, ride sharing, and hot meal delivery platforms.

In particular, we study linear sum task assignment problem where a set of tasks needs to be assigned to a set of agents in a one-on-one manner. We assume a centralised decision making process (or algorithm) that is in charge of deciding which agent is assigned to each task. An optimal solution, from a utilitarian point of view, would be the assignment that produces the lowest overall cost (or the highest benefit). However, this globally most efficient solution for the whole system may create large differences among the individual assigned costs of the participating agents (we refer to this as an "unfair" assignment). The perception of an unfair task assignment solution may motivate unsatisfied agents to leave the society, putting the survivability of the society at risk. Thus, assignment decisions in such societies should be made not only based on minimising overall assignment cost but should also consider social welfare and fairness.

The classical linear sum assignment problem is a largely studied, generally computationally easy problem, for which exact solutions can be produced relatively rapidly for even very large instances. However, to the best of our knowledge, related work on balancing fairness and efficiency in task assignment is scarce. Therefore, in this work, we explore the means of balancing the overall cost and fairness in task assignment in agent societies. These two aspects are generally opposed, i.e., solution approaches focusing on cost minimisation are likely to produce unfair assignments for some agents, while fair assignments may be far from the minimum cost solution. In this paper, we study trade-off between these two requirements and focus on finding task assignment solutions that are as fair as possible while not overly penalising the overall system's cost. This implies finding efficient and fair assignments considering the distribution of individual costs among agents.

The main contributions of this paper are twofold. First, we propose three new fairness measures for a multi-agent system composed of self-concerned individually rational agents: Egalitarian Fairness Measure (EFM), Relative All-to-all Fairness (RAF), and Overall Relative Opportunity Cost Fairness (OROCF) measure. Then, we present two new one-on-one task assignment models that maximise social welfare of the system while balancing efficiency and fairness: envy-free utilitarian model that uses the utilitarian social welfare function while constraining the differences of the costs between agents and the Nash model that optimises the Nash product of assigned tasks' benefits or costs of individual agents composing the system. We choose Nash social welfare due to its structure (being product of costs) that explicitly balances efficiency and fairness.

The rest of the paper is organised as follows. In Sect. 2, we give an overview of the state of the art. In Sect. 3, we give motivation for this work and define the general problem of one-on-one task assignment. We propose new equality and equity fairness measures in Sect. 4. The two new mathematical models for efficient and fair task assignment are presented in Sect. 5. Section 6 presents simple functional tests and discusses how the presented models differ based on the proposed fairness measures. In Sect. 7, we conclude the paper by giving an overview of the results and discuss the potential of the new proposed models and fairness measures to make a fairer task assignment. We also give lines of future work to improve the current models and fairness measures.

2 State of the Art

The assignment of resources, capabilities or tasks in a multi-agent society may vary when defining fairness and efficiency depending on mutual inter-dependencies among agents and their relation with the society's objectives (e.g., [4,7,21]).

Collaborative decision making considers a goal that is shared and owned among all agents in a society, while cooperative decision making considers working toward a shared goal even though its ownership is not shared [25]. Thus, cooperative decision making results are generally differentially beneficial to different agents [22], while collaboration is generally about equally sharing efforts, costs and benefits. Collaborative multi-agent task allocation problem is studied in, e.g., [16,19]. This problem has many different real world applications where fairness can be a challenge. For example, in Spatial Crowdsourcing [32], there is a need to minimise the payoff difference among workers while maximising the average worker payoff. Similarly, in Rideshare Platforms, it was shown in [24] that, during high-demand hours, lacking any consideration of fairness and seeking only an optimal number of trips could lead to increased societal biases in the choice of the clients. This problem is relevant for many other applications including manufacturing and scheduling, network routing and the fair and efficient exploitation of Earth Observation Satellites (e.g., [7]).

There exist in the literature many kinds of fairness measures for different contexts, e.g., machine learning (e.g., [10]), neural networks (e.g., [26]) and algorithm development (e.g., [13]). Of our interest are the fairness measures for the allocation of indivisible goods (e.g., [8]), and in more specific, the fairness measures for one-on-one assignment of tasks in collaborative or cooperative multi-agent systems. The most known fairness measures for allocation of indivisible goods are the maxmin of the utility of the agents in the system which maximises the utility of the agent that contributes the least to the global utility of the system; there is also proportionality which states that each agent should receive at least one n^{th} of the utility this agent would have received if it were alone. Max-min fairness is generalised in the case of resource allocation for systems with different resource types in [12] while max-min fairness, proportional fairness and balanced fairness are compared in the setting of a communication network of processor-sharing queues in [3].

The concept of fairness is studied as well in other contexts, like the multi-winner voting problem, machine learning and in recommender systems (e.g., [31]), but also more generally in decision making (e.g., [28]). The importance of the individual perception of fairness within a system in order to keep individual satisfaction high is emphasised in [29]. The potential contradiction between individual fairness and group fairness is studied in [2] in the Machine Learning context. Some works study more generally the concepts of distributive justice, equality and equity (e.g., [9]).

Related to the balance of efficiency and fairness are different social welfare concepts. Their modelling and importance in enhancing the quality of task allocation are studied in [7]. In this work, we study egalitarianism and utilitarianism in this regard. Egalitarianism is a trend of thought in political philosophy that favours equality among the individuals composing the society no matter what their circumstances are (e.g., [11]). Utilitarianism, on the other hand, is a theory of morality that advocates actions that maximise happiness or well-being for all individuals while opposing to the actions that cause their unhappiness or harm. When directed toward making social and economic decisions, a utilitarian philosophy aims at the improvement of the society as a whole (e.g., [23]).

The Nash social welfare combines efficiency and fairness considerations. This function, or variants of it, are studied in literature considering, e.g., fairness in the ambulance location problem [14], and in allocating indivisible goods [6]. The multiagent resource allocation problem considering Nash social welfare (the product of the utilities of the individual agents) is studied in [27].

In resource allocation, there can be agents desiring tasks (resources) more than others, or there can even be agents desiring tasks given to other agents, creating envy in the system (e.g., [7]). Envy-freeness criterion implies that an allocation should leave no agent envious of the other (e.g., [5]). However, it is not always enough to achieve envy-freeness for a fair solution (e.g., [1,15,20]).

3   Motivation and Problem Definition

Most of the State of the art literature on task assignment generally focuses on the efficiency of the assignment and does not consider fairness in the process, thus optimising only the system's overall general assignment cost or profit (e.g., time, distance, monetary value, etc.). This strategy is equivalent to optimising utilitarian social welfare function, a concept from welfare economy that sums the utility of each individual in order to obtain society's overall welfare (see, e.g., [7,30]). All agents are treated the same, regardless of their initial level of utility or cost distribution among the tasks. This strategy is admissible in case of a single decision maker, but might be unacceptable when multiple self-concerned and individually rational agents must decide on the assignment of tasks.

Let us introduce a simple example showing how unfair a task assignment optimising utilitarian social welfare function can be. Let us consider 3 self-concerned, individually rational agents (a_1, a_2, a_3) that need to be assigned to a set of 3 tasks (k_1, k_2, k_3) in a one-on-one manner and vice versa. The cost matrix containing the assignment costs for these agents and tasks is shown in Table 1a.

By applying the conventional (linear sum) task assignment model (i.e., the Utilitarian model) that optimises the overall cost of the system without considering fairness in the assignment (see, e.g., [17,19]), we might get the assignments (called solution s_1) marked in bold in Table 1b. The overall minimum assignment

Table 1. Example of a cost matrix and different one-on-one task assignment solutions with minimum overall cost (in bold)

(a) Cost Matrix

	k_1	k_2	k_3
a_1	50	60	70
a_2	30	40	50
a_3	10	50	30

(b) Solution s_1

	k_1	k_2	k_3
a_1	50	**60**	70
a_2	**30**	40	50
a_3	10	50	**30**

(c) Solution s_2

	k_1	k_2	k_3
a_1	**50**	60	70
a_2	30	**40**	50
a_3	10	50	**30**

(d) Solution s_3

	k_1	k_2	k_3
a_1	50	60	**70**
a_2	30	**40**	50
a_3	**10**	50	30

cost found by this model is 120. However, if we focus on its cost distribution on individual agents, we see large discrepancies. Indeed, the cost of agent a_1 is 60, while the cost of a_2 is only 30. Thus, a_1 is charged twice more than a_2. In Table 1d (i.e., solution s_3), this difference is even larger resulting in 7 times larger cost of the worst-off in respect to the best-off agent. Generally, an upper bound on the difference in the assignment cost is the maximum value in a given cost matrix. In centralised systems, where agents are owned and controlled by a single decision maker, this would not cause any problem. However, in the case of decentralised systems composed of self-concerned and individually rational agents, such an unfair solution might result in the worst-off agents leaving the system due to the lack of fairness in the solution.

Table 1c shows a fairer solution (called s_2) where the costs of the agents are as close as possible, thus minimising the envy of agents. This is an ideal situation in regard to fairness in this case where all agents are assigned tasks of similar costs. Notice that, in this case, we didn't have to sacrifice efficiency to achieve this situation. In case of repetitive task allocations, the assignments can be altered to further facilitate balance in the accumulated assignment costs.

Problem Definition. Given are a set of agents $a \in A$ and a set of tasks $k \in K$ that form a weighted complete bipartite graph $G = (A \bigcup K, E)$ with edge set $E = A \times K$ and with given edge weights c_{ak} on each edge $(a, k) \in E$, where c_{ak} is the cost of assigning task $k \in K$ to agent $a \in A$, $\forall a \in A, k \in K$. W.l.o.g, we assume that the cardinality of the sets is equal, i.e., $|A| = |K|$. In the case of unequal cardinality, we add a sufficient number of dummy vertices and assume that $c_{ak} = 0$ where $a \in A$ or $k \in K$ are dummy vertices. The objective is to assign agents $a \in A$ to tasks $k \in K$ in a one-on-one manner and, therefore, find a perfect matching among vertices in A and vertices in K considering both assignment efficiency and fairness. An edge (a, k) is matched if its (two) extreme vertices $a \in A$ and $k \in K$ are mutually matched, and a matching is perfect if every vertex of A is matched (assigned) exactly to one vertex of K, and vice versa. The following is the mathematical formulation of these constraints.

$$\sum_{k \in K} x_{ak} = 1, \forall a \in A \quad (1) \qquad \sum_{a \in A} x_{ak} = 1, \forall k \in K \quad (2)$$

$$x_{ak} \in \{0, 1\}, \forall a \in A, \forall k \in K \qquad (3)$$

where x_{ak} is a binary decision variable equal to 1 if agent $a \in A$ is assigned to task $k \in K$, and zero otherwise. Constraints (1) and (2) assure that there is one-on-one assignment for each agent $a \in A$ and task $k \in K$, respectively. Constraints (3) fix the ranges of the decision variables.

4   Proposed Fairness Measures

In this section, we introduce different fairness measures for quantifying the balance between fairness and efficiency in task assignment from the egalitarian and equity point of view. All the fairness measures are fractions ranging between 0 and 1. We avoided the division by 0 in some extreme cases by adding a very small number ϵ (e.g., $\epsilon = 1e^{-10}$) to both the numerator and the denominator of these fractions.

Egalitarian Fairness Measure. (EFM) focuses on the assignment cost faced by the worst-off agent (i.e., the agent with the highest assignment cost in a given feasible solution). Given the assignments x_{ak}^{sol}, with $a \in A$ and $k \in K$, of a feasible solution sol, EFM is computed as follows:

$$EFM(sol) = \frac{c_{max} - c_{sol}^{wo} + \epsilon}{c_{max} - c_{min}^{wo} + \epsilon} \qquad (4)$$

where $c_{max} = max_{a \in A, k \in K}\{c_{ak}\}$ is the maximum value in the cost matrix, $c_{sol}^{wo} = max_{a \in A}\{\sum_{k \in K} c_{ak} x_{ak}^{sol}\}$ is the cost paid by the worst-off agent in the given solution, and c_{min}^{wo} is the minimum cost that the worst-off agent could pay. In particular, c_{min}^{wo} is the optimal solution of the given mathematical problem:

$$c_{min}^{wo} = \min \lambda \qquad (5)$$

s.t. (1)–(3) and

$$\sum_{k \in K} c_{ak} x_{ak} \leq \lambda, \forall a \in A \qquad (6)$$

$$\lambda \in \Re \qquad (7)$$

where Constraints (6) impose that the cost (λ) paid by the worst-off agent must be not less than the cost paid by any agent, and Constraints (7) fix the range of the additional variable λ. When the worst-off assigned cost c_{sol}^{wo} is equal to c_{max}, $EFM(sol)$ will equal zero (ignoring ϵ). On the other hand, when c_{sol}^{wo} is equal to c_{min}^{wo}, $EFM(sol)$ will equal one; moreover, this also occurs when there exists an agent $a \in A$ such that $c_{ak} = c_{max}, \forall k \in K$.

For the cost matrix given in Table 1a, where $c_{max} = 70$ and $c_{min}^{wo} = 50$, we calculate the $EFM(sol)$ for each solution reported in Tables 1b–1d. All the solutions reported in Table 1, have minimum overall assignment cost equal to

120, while the values of c_{sol}^{wo} are $c_{s_1}^{wo} = 60$, $c_{s_2}^{wo} = 50$, $c_{s_3}^{wo} = 70$ for the solutions reported in Table 1b, Table 1c, and Table 1d, respectively. $EFM(sol)$ value for these solutions are: $EFM(s_1) = \frac{70-60}{70-50} = 0.5$, $EFM(s_2) = \frac{70-50}{70-50} = 1$, and $EFM(s_3) = \frac{70-70}{70-50} = 0$.

According to EFM measure, solution s_2 is the fairest one. Note that the increase in EFM value in solution s_2 corresponds to a distribution of the costs that leaves the worst-off agent better off than in s_1, and that solution s_3 leaves the worst-off agent with the worst possible cost. Note that, generally, there may be multiple such distributions.

Relative All-to-All Fairness. (RAF) evaluates fairness at a group level by taking into account each agent's perspective in comparison with the others. The measure is based on the sum between the squared differences of the assignment costs of each agent and the costs of the others, as seen in Eq. (8).

$$w_{sol} = \sum_{a \in A} \sum_{a' \in A | a' > a} \left(\sum_{k \in K} c_{ak} x_{ak}^{sol} - c_{a'k} x_{a'k}^{sol} \right)^2, \tag{8}$$

Then, relative all-to-all fairness is computed as follows:

$$RAF(sol) = \frac{w_{max} - w_{sol} + \epsilon}{w_{max} - w_{min} + \epsilon}, \tag{9}$$

where w_{max} and w_{min} represent the maximum and the minimum value of Eq. (8) given Constraints (1)–(3).

For the cost matrix given in Table 1a, the two components of RAF that are independent of the assignment solution are $w_{max} = 5400$ and $w_{min} = 0$, related to solutions s_{max}, with $x_{13}^{s_{max}} = x_{22}^{s_{max}} = x_{31}^{s_{max}} = 1$, and s_{min}, with $x_{11}^{s_{min}} = x_{23}^{s_{min}} = x_{32}^{s_{min}} = 1$, respectively. The values w_{sol} for the solutions reported in Table 1b, Table 1c and 1d are $w_{s_1} = 1800$, $w_{s_2} = 600$, and $w_{s_3} = 5400$, respectively. Related RAF values are: $RAF(s_1) = \frac{5400-1800}{5400-0} = 0.67$, $RAF(s_2) = \frac{5400-600}{5400-0} = 0.89$, and $RAF(s_3) = \frac{5400-5400}{5400-0} = 0$.

Also according to the RAF measure, solution s_2 is the fairest one and the order of the three solutions is the same as for EFM. This is not surprising as both measures evaluate equality in a solution. However, s_2 is not the absolute fairest solution which, with respect to this indicator, is $x_{11} = x_{23} = x_{32} = 1$ where all the agents pay the same cost; in this case the RAF value is equal to 1. This is also not surprising as this particular measure considers not only the worst-off agent, but all of them, therefore making it less likely that one of the solutions with minimum cost also has the highest fairness value.

Overall Relative Opportunity Cost Fairness. (OROCF) focuses on achieving equity among the agents by taking into account the missed opportunities in terms of the assignment cost for each agent. The opportunity cost (e.g., [18]) is the concept in microeconomics of lost benefit that would have been derived by an agent from an option not chosen. As the reference value, we consider a task of the minimum cost and normalise the difference in the cost value between the assigned task and the best-off task (the task with minimum cost) over the amplitude of costs for each agent, as seen in Eq. (10).

$$y_{sol} = \sum_{a \in A} \frac{\sum_{k \in K} c_{ak} x_{ak}^{sol} - min_{k \in K} \{c_{ak}\} + \epsilon}{max_{k \in K} \{c_{ak}\} - min_{k \in K} \{c_{ak}\} + \epsilon} \tag{10}$$

$$OROCF(sol) = \frac{y_{max} - y_{sol} + \epsilon}{y_{max} - y_{min} + \epsilon}, \tag{11}$$

where y_{max}, y_{min} represents the maximum and the minimum value of Eq. (10) given Constraints (1)–(3).

The values y_{sol} for the solutions reported in Tables 1b, 1c and 1d are $y_{s_1} = 1$, $y_{s_2} = 1$, and $y_{s_3} = 1.5$, respectively. For the cost matrix given in Table 1a, the two components of OROCF that are independent of the assignment solution are $y_{max} = 2$ for $x_{13}^{s_{max}} = x_{21}^{s_{max}} = x_{32}^{s_{max}} = 1$ and $y_{min} = 1$ for $x_{11}^{s_{min}} = x_{22}^{s_{min}} = x_{33}^{s_{min}} = 1$. Related $OROCF$ values are: $OROCF(s_1) = \frac{2-1}{2-1} = 1$, $OROCF(s_2) = \frac{2-1}{2-1} = 1$, and $OROCF(s_3) = \frac{2-1.5}{2-1} = 0.5$.

Note that $OROCF$ value is the highest both for s_1 and s_2, meaning that these solutions offer the lowest highest opportunity cost for the sum of all agents. The reader can verify that the solution $x_{11} = x_{23} = x_{32} = 1$ would be the worst choice for agents a_2 and a_3 and would give a value of $OROCF$ equal to 0.

5   Proposed Models Considering Fairness and Efficiency

In this section, we propose new models that mitigate the equity issues posed by the classical linear sum assignment model (e.g., [4]) and achieve a solution that is as fair as possible while sacrificing as little as possible of the overall system's efficiency.

Nash Model. The proposed Nash Model is inspired by the Nash social welfare function, a well studied social welfare function in which the goal is to maximize the product of the utility functions of the agents composing the system. The proposed model is given next:

$$min \prod_{a \in A} \sum_{k \in K} c_{ak} x_{ak} \tag{12}$$

s.t. (1)–(3). Since Eq. (12) is a nonlinear objective function, solving the above problem is computationally expensive. Thus, we propose next its linearised equivalent, which is possible due to the one-on-one assignment constraints (1)–(3).

$$max \sum_{a \in A} \sum_{k \in K} log(M - c_{ak}) x_{ak} \tag{13}$$

s.t. (1)–(3), where $M > max_{k \in K, a \in A} \{c_{ak}\}$.

Envy-Free Utilitarian Model. This model focuses both on efficiency and fairness. We introduce the fairness variable f_u to ensure that all the costs for each agent are inside a certain interval that shrinks as f_u becomes smaller. The model is defined as follows:

$$\min \; \alpha f_u + (1 - \alpha) \frac{\sum_{k \in K} \sum_{a \in A} c_{ak} x_{ak}}{|A|} \tag{14}$$

s.t. (1)–(3), and

$$\sum_{k \in K} c_{ak} x_{ak} - \frac{\sum_{k \in K} \sum_{a \in A} c_{ak} x_{ak}}{|A|} \leq f_u, \forall a \in A \tag{15}$$

$$f_u \in \Re \tag{16}$$

Constraints (15) guarantee that, for each agent, the difference between the cost of its assigned task and the average of the costs of the assigned tasks for all the agents is less than the value f_u. Constraint (16) fixes the range of variable f_u. Parameter α ranges between 0 and 1 and is used to weigh the fairness and the average cost paid by an agent in (14).

6 Functional Tests

To demonstrate the difference between the Nash model and the Envy-free Utilitarian model, we randomly generated three cost matrices (Table 2) with costs ranging from 1 to 1000. The models were solved for each matrix using IBM ILOG CPLEX Optimization Studio 20.0.1.

Table 2. Example cost matrices.

(a) Functional test 1

	k_1	k_2	k_3
a_1	382	816	366
a_2	846	544	175
a_3	578	824	526

(b) Functional test 2

	k_1	k_2	k_3
a_1	450	895	358
a_2	856	233	449
a_3	890	672	976

(c) Functional test 3

	k_1	k_2	k_3
a_1	683	170	699
a_2	943	364	894
a_3	557	741	127

To compare the efficiency of the solutions obtained using the models presented in Sect. 5, we calculate the following normalised efficiency indicator (Eff):

$$Eff(sol) = \frac{z_{max} - z_{sol} + \epsilon}{z_{max} - z_{min} + \epsilon} \tag{17}$$

where $z_{sol} = \sum_{k \in K} \sum_{a \in A} c_{ak} x_{ak}^{sol}$ with x_{ak}^{sol} being the solution returned by the considered model. The values z_{max} and z_{min} are, respectively, the maximum and the minimum values of $\sum_{k \in K} \sum_{a \in A} c_{ak} x_{ak}$ given Constraints (1)–(3).

Table 3. Results and comparison

Functional test 1

Model	Eff	EFM	RAF	$OROCF$
Nash	0.91	1	1	1
Envy-free ($\alpha = 0$)	1	0.07	0	0.68
Envy-free ($\alpha \geq 0.5$)	0.91	1	1	1

Functional test 2

Model	Eff	EFM	RAF	$OROCF$
Nash	0.93	1	0.91	1
Envy-free ($\alpha = 0$)	1	0.28	0.17	0.92
Envy-free ($\alpha = 0.5$)	0.93	1	0.91	1
Envy-free ($\alpha \geq 0.9$)	0	0	1	0

Functional test 3

Model	Eff	EFM	RAF	$OROCF$
Nash	0.93	1	0.73	1
Envy-free ($\alpha = 0$)	1	0	0	0.99
Envy-free ($\alpha = 0.5$)	0.93	1	0.73	1
Envy-free ($\alpha = 0.7$)	0.59	0.94	0.93	0.64
Envy-free ($\alpha \geq 0.9$)	0.05	0.19	1	0.06

Table 3 shows the results of our experiments with all indicators and their values depending on the model used.

The case when $\alpha = 0$ corresponds to the case when we are optimising the global cost only (utilitarian social welfare function). We get very low values of fairness for this case according to our prior assumptions. It is interesting to notice similarities when we set α value to 0.5. Indeed, in that case, the Envy-free Utilitarian model and the Nash model have the same behaviour and give us the same solutions. These solutions for $\alpha = 0.5$ are ideal for the fairness indicators EFM and $OROCF$ in our three tests, while RAF also increases significantly. Moreover, the efficiency (Eff) is greater than 0.9. Equality and equity can be improved without significant decrease in efficiency. We notice in tests 2 and 3 that, generally, the higher the value of α, the lower the overall system's efficiency. This shows that striving for too much equality can be highly detrimental to the system's efficiency and even equity. The results for the cost matrix in Table 1a also support this claim in case $\alpha = 1$. Here, allocation $x_{11} = x_{23} = x_{32} = 1$ is an egalitarian allocation that decreases efficiency and equity simultaneously since agents a_2 and a_3 are allocated to their worst-off tasks and the overall allocation cost is 150 instead of the minimum cost of 120.

7 Conclusions

In this paper, we focused on balancing efficiency and fairness in one-on-one multi-agent task assignment. This problem is of high importance in agent societies composed of individually rational and self-concerned agents where an agent decides to participate only if it brings an individual benefit that is at least as good as when not participating. In this regard, we studied the utilitarian, egalitarian and Nash social welfare, the concepts from economics and philosophy that may be applied in such multi-agent societies to tackle this challenge. Since quantitative fairness measures for task assignment are scarce or missing, we proposed three new fairness measures: egalitarian fairness measure, all-to-all relative fairness measure, and overall relative opportunity cost fairness measure. We proposed the Nash model for task assignment that minimises the product of the costs of each agent, considering one-on-one assignment constraints, and the Envy-Free Utilitarian model which is a model combining the ideas of envy-freeness, equality and the utilitarian social welfare measure. We concluded with 3 functional tests showing that by using our proposed two models, we can achieve a better fairness with little sacrifice in the overall efficiency, and that our Envy-free Utilitarian model can be adjusted depending on the need for fairness.

The fairness measures presented should be computed only for non-dummy vertices to ensure that these measures can still reach either the value of 0 or 1 in practice. In the future, we will further study fairness measures, particularly one encompassing both equality and equity to better support decision-making in collaborative and cooperative open societies where agents can enter and leave as they wish. Moreover, we will focus on three-index assignment problem where each agent needs a tool to perform a task. The assignment here is also performed in a one-on-one manner. Similarly, crafting a multi-objective model which considers equality, equity and fairness for such a problem is a challenge worth facing henceforth.

Acknowledgements. This work has been partially supported by the Spanish Ministry of Science, Innovation, and Universities, co-funded by EU FEDER Funds, through grant number RTI2018-095390-B-C33 (MCIU/AEI/FEDER, UE) and the AGROBOTS Project funded by the Community of Madrid, Spain.

References

1. Alkan, A., Demange, G., Gale, D.: Fair allocation of indivisible goods and criteria of justice. Econometrica: J. Econ. Soc. 1023–1039 (1991)
2. Binns, R.: On the apparent conflict between individual and group fairness. In: Proceedings of the ACM FAccT 2020, pp. 514–524 (2020)
3. Bonald, T., Massoulié, L., Proutiere, A., Virtamo, J.: A queueing analysis of max-min fairness, proportional fairness and balanced fairness. QS **53**(1), 65–84 (2006)
4. Burkard, R., Dell'Amico, M., Martello, S.: Assignment problems: revised reprint. SIAM (2012)
5. Cappelen, A.W., Tungodden, B.: Fairness and the proportionality principle. Soc. Choice Welfare **49**(3), 709–719 (2016). https://doi.org/10.1007/s00355-016-1016-6

6. Caragiannis, I., Kurokawa, D., Moulin, H., Procaccia, A.D., et al.: The unreasonable fairness of maximum Nash welfare. ACM-TEAC **7**(3), 1–32 (2019)

7. Chevaleyre, Y., Dunne, P.E., Endriss, U., et al.: Issues in multiagent resource allocation (2005)

8. Conitzer, V., Freeman, R., Shah, N., Vaughan, J.W.: Group fairness for the allocation of indivisible goods. In: Proceedings of the AAAI Conference on Artificial Intelligence, vol. 33, pp. 1853–1860 (2019)

9. Cook, K.S., Hegtvedt, K.A.: Distributive justice, equity, and equality. Ann. Rev. Sociol. **9**(1), 217–241 (1983)

10. Corbett-Davies, S., Goel, S.: The measure and mismeasure of fairness: a critical review of fair machine learning. arXiv preprint arXiv:1808.00023 (2018)

11. Fleurbaey, M., Maniquet, F.: A Theory of Fairness and Social Welfare, vol. 48. University Press, Cambridge (2011)

12. Ghodsi, A., Zaharia, M., Hindman, B., et al.: Dominant resource fairness: fair allocation of multiple resource types. In: 8th USENIX Symposium NSDI 2011 (2011)

13. Hellman, D.: Measuring algorithmic fairness. VLR **106**(4), 811–866 (2020)

14. Jagtenberg, C., Mason, A.: Fairness in the ambulance location problem: maximizing the Bernoulli-Nash social welfare. SSRN 3536707 (2020)

15. Kranich, L.: Resource-envy-free and efficient allocations: a new solution for production economies with dedicated factors. J. Math. Econ. **89**, 1–7 (2020)

16. Kraus, S., Plotkin, T.: Algorithms of distributed task allocation for cooperative agents. Theoret. Comput. Sci. **242**(1–2), 1–27 (2000)

17. Kuhn, H.W.: The Hungarian method for the assignment problem. Naval Res. Logistics Q. **2**(1–2), 83–97 (1955)

18. Kurzban, R., Duckworth, A., Kable, J.W., Myers, J.: An opportunity cost model of subjective effort and task performance. Behav. Brain sci. **36**(6), 661–679 (2013)

19. Lujak, M., Giordani, S., Omicini, A., Ossowski, S.: Decentralizing coordination in open vehicle fleets for scalable and dynamic task allocation. Complexity **2020**(1047369) (2020)

20. Lujak, M., Giordani, S., Ossowski, S.: Route guidance: bridging system and user optimization in traffic assignment. Neurocomputing **151**, 449–460 (2015)

21. Moulin, H.: Fair Division and Collective Welfare. MIT Press, Cambridge (2004)

22. Moulin, H.: Axioms of Cooperative Decision Making, vol. 15. University Press, Cambridge (1991)

23. Mulgan, T.: Understanding Utilitarianism. Routledge, Milton Park (2014)

24. Nanda, V., Xu, P., et al.: Balancing the tradeoff between profit and fairness in rideshare platforms during high-demand hours. In: Proceedings of the AAAI Conference on Artificial Intelligence, vol. 34, pp. 2210–2217 (2020)

25. Nelson, L.M.: Collaborative problem solving. In: Instructional-Design Theories and Models: A New Paradigm of Instructional Theory, vol. 2, pp. 241–267 (1999)

26. Padala, M., Gujar, S.: FNNC: achieving fairness through neural networks. In: Proceedings of the Twenty-Ninth International Joint Conference on Artificial Intelligence, IJCAI 2020 (2020)

27. Ramezani, S., Endriss, U.: Nash social welfare in multiagent resource allocation. In: David, E., Gerding, E., Sarne, D., Shehory, O. (eds.) AMEC/TADA -2009. LNBIP, vol. 59, pp. 117–131. Springer, Heidelberg (2010). https://doi.org/10.1007/978-3-642-15117-0_9

28. Sampat, A.M., Zavala, V.M.: Fairness measures for decision-making and conflict resolution. Optim. Eng. **20**(4), 1249–1272 (2019). https://doi.org/10.1007/s11081-019-09452-3

29. Schappe, S.P.: Understanding employee job satisfaction: the importance of procedural and distributive justice. J. Bus. Psyc. **12**(4), 493–503 (1998)
30. Sen, A.: Collective Choice and Social Welfare. Harvard University Press, Cambridge (2017)
31. Shrestha, Y.R., Yang, Y.: Fairness in algorithmic decision-making: applications in multi-winner voting, machine learning, and recommender systems. Algorithms **12**(9), 199 (2019)
32. Zhao, Y., Zheng, K., Guo, J., Yang, B., Pedersen, T.B., Jensen, C.S.: Fairness-aware task assignment in spatial crowdsourcing: game-theoretic approaches. In: 2021 IEEE 37th ICDE, pp. 265–276. IEEE (2021)

Plant Disease Detection: An Edge-AI Proposal

C. Marco-Detchart, J. A. Rincon, V. Julian$^{(\boxtimes)}$, and C. Carrascosa

Institut Valencià d'Investigació en Intel·ligència Artificial (VRAIN),
Universitat Politècnica de València, Valencia, Spain
{cedmarde,vjulian}@upv.es, {jrincon,carrasco}@dsic.upv.es

Abstract. Over the last few years, there have been many technological approaches whose application domain is rural areas to provide more advanced services to environments of this kind. In the agricultural environment, several proposals mainly try to develop crop management systems based on the spatial and temporal variability of different factors within a crop field, which is currently known as precision agriculture. One of the most critical tasks in this area is to detect plant diseases. Identifying diseases requires a lot of time and skilled labour. Thus, this paper proposes developing an intelligent device to detect plant diseases using deep learning techniques. Different experiments have been carried out to evaluate the feasibility of the proposed device. The results have shown a high performance with very short execution times.

Keywords: EDGE AI · Deep learning · Precision agriculture

1 Introduction

One of the current problems in Europe and particularly in Spain is the gradual depopulation of rural areas, an effect known in our country as *Empty Spain - España Vaciada*. This phenomenon has repercussions on the abandonment of agriculture and farms, the development of these areas, and the global and sustainable development of the whole country. The well-being of all the citizens of a country lies in the diversity of its territories. Therefore, it is necessary and urgent to engage with rural communities to achieve their economic, social, political and environmental objectives.

To solve this problem, techniques based on Artificial Intelligence (AI) have emerged as a valuable tool to improve this situation by providing mechanisms to facilitate specific tasks in rural areas.

One of the areas in which research has focused is the development of solutions in the agricultural environment. Over the last few years, different approaches have tried to provide AI techniques for sustainable development in the farming sector, especially machine learning techniques. A deeper analysis and further reviews can be consulted in [1,2] and [3].

A. González-Briones et al. (Eds.): PAAMS Workshops 2022, CCIS 1678, pp. 108–117, 2022.
https://doi.org/10.1007/978-3-031-18697-4_9

Early plant disease detection is one of the main problems in agriculture, having consequences on the economy. Early detection of a possible disease can allow early treatment and prevent loss of production. Plant disease detection is traditionally made by manual and ocular inspection completed by an expert/farmer. The manual approach can be a tedious and slow task and generally depends on the knowledge of a restricted group of people. In addition, plants can be affected by multiple diseases, which increments the task difficulty for a person. Moreover, since there are multiple varieties of plants, the number of possible detections increases considerably.

Automatic plant disease detection plays a crucial role in addressing the lack of time and the number of experts to overcome the problems caused by plant diseases. In general, agricultural analysis and plant disease have been addressed using satellite and hyper-spectral imaging. On the one hand, satellite images present advantages as we obtain a broad view of the land and the general performance of the crops. On the other hand, hyperspectral images permit us to see beyond the visible spectrum, allowing the use of specific tools such as the NDVI-index that help measure the level of green on a particular image assisting in locating crop issues. The main disadvantage of this type of image lies in the cost of the material needed to obtain them (specific cameras and satellites) and the processing cost of working with such large pictures. In addition, as we are focusing on an edge context, these types of images are discarded.

Automatic identification of plant disease presents a series of challenges [4] that go from problems in the capture process (*e.g.* noise, fog over the camera, etc.) to unwanted information present in the images (*e.g.* background, soil, other plants, etc.). Beyond image capture material-specific problems, an important issue is the possible presence of multiple diseases in a plant. Automatic plant disease detection is a classification task that can be tackled through two main approaches. First, classic Machine Learning (ML) based approaches, where a collection of features is extracted and selected from images and then classified with techniques such as Support Vector Machines (SVM) [5], K-Means algorithm [6] or Random Forest [7], among others. Second, and nowadays, one of the most popular approaches is the use of Deep Learning (DL) [8] and particularly Convolutional Neural Networks (CNN) [9,10] to train a model to identify the dataset classes.

As seen in the literature, the results obtained by CNN approaches are far from those of ML. Moreover, the training phase does not need considerable preprocessing or feature selection, mainly done inside the network. Additionally, our objective is to build a robust model capable of working on an edge platform.

Consequently, this paper presents an EDGE device that incorporates the necessary hardware and software components for the automatic detection of plant diseases from an image of the plant leaf. The device can be easily incorporated into an agricultural robot, a drone, or a tractor to facilitate automatic image acquisition in a crop field.

The rest of the paper is structured as follows. Section 2 presents the description of the proposed device, Sect. 3 describes the experiments carried out, and finally, some conclusions are presented in Sect. 4.

2   System Description

This Section describes the system's operation for plant disease classification using an EDGE device, detailing the different software and hardware tools used. The proposed approach is shown in Fig. 1.

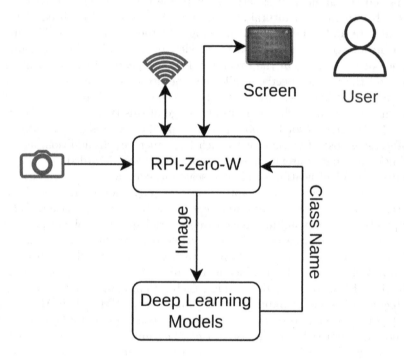

Fig. 1. Description of the system.

The main components are the machine vision and data processing module, the decision-making module incorporating the classification models, the WiFi communication system to send the classified data to the cloud, and a visualisation system through an LCD. The following sections describe the hardware components and the classification models developed in more detail. At a general level, the EDGE system uses the camera to capture the images and uses classification models to determine whether the plant has any of the 38 diseases present in the training database.

2.1   Hardware Description

This Section describes the hardware used for plant disease recognition using a *Raspberry Pi Zero W* (Fig. 2). The Raspberry Pi Zero W development system has a 1 GHz BCM2835 single-core processor with 512 MB of RAM. Within this hardware, trained models can be run. To capture the images, the Raspberry has a camera, which captures the images with a size of 224 × 224. The models will then use these images to obtain the name of the plant's disease. One of the advantages of this hardware is its small size, making it easy to transport in the field where it is to be used. At the same time, it can be coupled to robots or drones, thus extending the range of action when classifying.

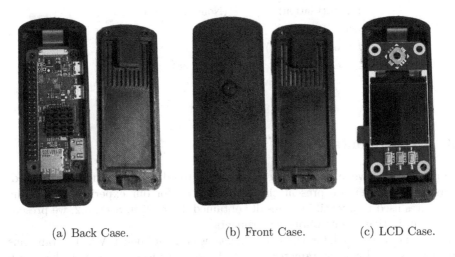

(a) Back Case.   (b) Front Case.   (c) LCD Case.

Fig. 2. The system proposed based on Raspberry Pi Zero

2.2   Software Description

This Section will describe the software used for the classification of plant diseases. Our system uses deep learning techniques to classify plant diseases using EDGE devices. A MobileNet v2 network architecture was used to train the model.

The MobileNet v2 [11] architecture is based on an inverted residual structure where the input and output of the residual block are thin bottleneck layers, unlike traditional residual models that use expanded representations at the input. MobileNet v2 uses lightweight convolutions in-depth to filter features in the intermediate expansion layer. In addition, non-linearities in the narrow layers have been removed to maintain representational power. Research presented by Kristiani et al. [12] showed from the experiments that Mobilenet outperforms Inception in terms of speed, accuracy and file size. The speed in Inception V3 is 9 frames per second, while that value in Mobilenet is 24 frames per second.

Table 1 shows the structure of the model obtained after compilation. The compiled structure is common to the different configurations (Table 2) used in this work. At the end of the training process, this model will be stored as a *.tflite file to be embedded in the Raspberry Pi Zero. This model can be easily replaced if the model undergoes a modification that improves classification or if a new class (disease) has been added.

Table 1. Summary of the model.

Layer (type)	Output shape	Param #
keras_layer (KerasLayer)	(None, 1280)	2257984
flatten (Flatten)	(None, 1280)	0
dense (Dense)	(None, 512)	655872
dropout (Dropout)	(None, 512)	0
dense_1 (Dense)	(None, 38)	19494

3   Experimental Setup

In this Section, we analyse the performance of the different configurations used. First, in Sect. 3.1, we present the data set used for our experiments and the measures used to quantify the results obtained. Second, in Sect. 3.2, we present the quantitative results of our experiments.

The network used for the experiments was a Mobilenet V2. To train this network, several hyperparameters were defined; some were fixed in all the experiments, while others were varied to determine with which of them the best results were obtained. It was decided to use a maximum of 7 epochs, as a higher number of epochs would lead to overfitting. The learning rate for all models is the same; data augmentation and fine training were turned on or off, depending on the experiment. The hyperparameter settings can be seen in the Table 2.

Table 2. Hyperparameters used to configure the neural net used in the experiments.

#	Net type	N-Epochs	Learning rate	Transfer learning	Data augmentation	Data set
S_1	Mobilenet V2	7	0.001	✗	✗	Raw Image
S_2	Mobilenet V2	7	0.001	✓	✗	Raw Image
S_3	Mobilenet V2	7	0.001	✗	✓	Raw Image
S_4	Mobilenet V2	7	0.001	✓	✓	Raw Image

(a) Tomato - Blight   (b) Grape - Esca   (c) Strawberry - Scorch   (d) Apple - Rust

Fig. 3. Example of images included in the PlantVillage dataset [13] from different plants diseases.

3.1 Dataset and Quantification of the Results

The data set used to train and validate our model was PlantVillage [13] which consists of approximately 87.000 RGB images of healthy and diseased crop leaves that are classified into 38 different classes. The images are taken from individual leaves of each plant and disease over a homogeneous background. This dataset was divided into three subsets with an 80/20 ratio, 80% for training, 10% for testing and the remaining 10% for validation. We used raw images (Fig. 3) to train and validate the models without image pre-processing.

To interpret the results obtained in the confusion matrix, we use the following Precision/Recall measures:

$$Prec = \frac{TP}{TP + FP}, \; Rec = \frac{TP}{TP + FN}, \; F_\beta = (1 + \beta^2)\frac{Prec \cdot Rec}{\beta^2 \cdot Prec + Rec}.$$

We select the values of $\beta = 0.5$ and $\beta = 1$ as the most commonly used in the literature.

3.2 Experimental Results

This Section presents the results obtained with the different configurations from Table 2. We show its quantitative results in Table 3. Moreover, we tested our models in a real environment in the exposed proposal with a Raspberry Pi Zero.

Figure 4 shows how each of the different configurations used behaves similarly during the different epochs. In terms of validation, S_2 and S_4 have more erratic behaviour and begin with low accuracy, then increment suddenly and go up and down until training ends. In contrast, the learning curve of S_1 and S_3 is more constant and stabilises at the end of the epochs. The behaviour of each of the configurations is further reflected in the quantitative results obtained in the test phase.

As we can see in Table 3 the best results (validated on the training machine) are obtained with configuration S_1, without applying neither transfer learning nor data augmentation. The second-best result is obtained with S_2, which uses only data augmentation. This behaviour indicates that, for the particular task of

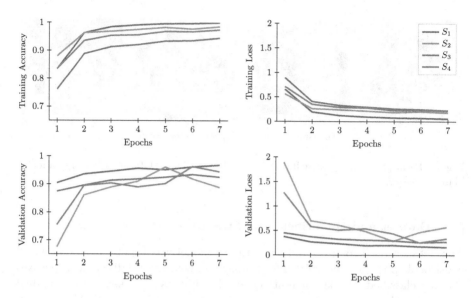

Fig. 4. Training and validation accuracy and loss obtained with the different configurations from Table 2

identification of plant diseases with MobileNet v2 using transfer learning, it does not produce any improvement, on the contrary, it makes all the measures decay. This behaviour occurs because the weights used for transfer learning come from the Imagenet dataset, which has a large number of classes. We can see how it affects the results in S_3 where no transfer learning is used, and the result is quite similar to S_1, so neither transfer learning nor data augmentation is beneficial.

The training and validation of the models were conducted on a machine with an Intel i5-9500 processor at 4.4 GHz and 16 GB of RAM running Ubuntu 20.04.4 LTS. The actual validation of the model was carried out on a Broadcomm BCM2835 ARM11 1 GHz, dideoCore IV GPU and RAM memory 512 MB.

Table 3. Resulting test performance of the model trained with the parameters in Table 2

#	Precision	Recall	$F_{0.5}$	F_1
S_1	**.881**	**.904**	**.882**	**.886**
S_2	.829	.852	.813	.807
S_3	**.881**	.897	.881	.883
S_4	.852	.862	.836	.831

Figures 5 and 6 below show the $\Delta(t)$ of the validation process between the computer and the Raspberry Pi for each experiment.

As expected, the validation times on the computer are more stable due to its processor and memory characteristics. However, the validation times on the Raspberry are less regular. It can be seen that experiment S_1 has the highest peak time, with a maximum run time of about 90 ms. This may be because this experiment has no data augmentation or fine-tuning, as this experiment was trained from scratch. This means that this model does not use pre-trained weights compared to the other models. Another possible explanation is that its weight in bytes is higher than that of the others, so memory storage and resource consumption are higher. Nevertheless, these values make the models suitable for our application.

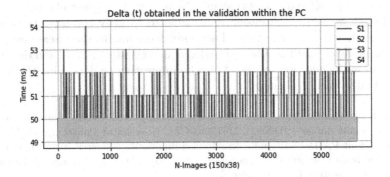

Fig. 5. Delta (t) obtained in the validation within PC.

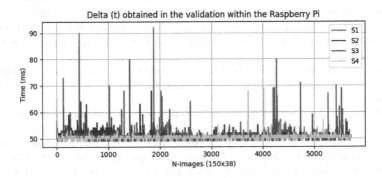

Fig. 6. Delta (t) obtained in the validation within the Raspberry Pi.

4   Conclusions and Future Work

This work presents a low-cost smart device for the identification of plant diseases. A Raspberry Pi Zero with its respective camera has been used for its development. The device integrates a deep learning model responsible for classifying and presenting information through an LCD screen. At the same time, the device is easy to install on a drone, a robot, or any agricultural equipment.

The device presents a more effective way to visualise disease spots in plants. It will save costs by avoiding the unnecessary application of fungicides, pesticides, and herbicides.

The results obtained show how the proposed device demonstrates that with current EDGE technology, it is possible to carry out plant disease classification and detection systems. These do not require an Internet connection to perform the classification, which is reflected in the costs associated with the transmission and analysis of the images. At the same time, it allows the farmer to perform a preanalysis of possible diseases that may be present in his/her plants.

In future work, it is proposed to be able to identify the severity of plant diseases as they change over time. Therefore, according to the disease evolution cycle, the models should be adapted to detect and classify diseases and the degree of affectation. In addition, it would also be interesting to determine the impact of mixed infections in plants.

Acknowledgements. This work was partially supported by the Spanish Government with grant numer PID2021-123673OB-C31, Universitat Politecnica de Valencia Research Grant PAID-10-19 and Consellería d'Innovació, Universitats, Ciencia i Societat Digital from Comunitat Valenciana (APOSTD/2021/227) through the European Social Fund (Investing In Your Future).

References

1. Jha, K., Doshi, A., Patel, P., Shah, M.: A comprehensive review on automation in agriculture using artificial intelligence. Artif. Intell. Agric. **2**, 1–12 (2019)
2. Vadlamudi, S.: How artificial intelligence improves agricultural productivity and sustainability: a global thematic analysis. Asia Pac. J. Energy Environ. **6**(2), 91–100 (2019)
3. Benos, L., Tagarakis, A.C., Dolias, G., Berruto, R., Kateris, D., Bochtis, D.: Machine learning in agriculture: a comprehensive updated review. Sensors **21**(11), 3758 (2021)
4. Barbedo, J.G.A.: A review on the main challenges in automatic plant disease identification based on visible range images. Biosyst. Eng. **144**, 52–60 (2016)
5. Camargo, A., Smith, J.S.: Image pattern classification for the identification of disease causing agents in plants. Comput. Electron. Agric. **66**(2), 121–125 (2009)
6. Gueye, Y., Mbaye, M.: KMeans kernel-learning based AI-IoT framework for plant leaf disease detection. In: Hacid, H., et al. (eds.) ICSOC 2020. LNCS, vol. 12632, pp. 549–563. Springer, Cham (2021). https://doi.org/10.1007/978-3-030-76352-7_49
7. Khan, S., Narvekar, M.: Novel fusion of color balancing and superpixel based approach for detection of tomato plant diseases in natural complex environment. J. King Saud Univ. - Comput. Inf. Sci. (2020)
8. Schuler, J.P.S., Romani, S., Abdel-Nasser, M., Rashwan, H., Puig, D.: Reliable deep learning plant leaf disease classification based on light-chroma separated branches. In: Villaret, M., Alsinet, T., Fernández, C., Valls, A. (eds.) Frontiers in Artificial Intelligence and Applications. IOS Press (2021)

9. Gui, P., Dang, W., Zhu, F., Zhao, Q.: Towards automatic field plant disease recognition. Comput. Electron. Agric. **191**, 106523 (2021)
10. Atila, Ü., Uçar, M., Akyol, K., Uçar, E.: Plant leaf disease classification using EfficientNet deep learning model. Eco. Inform. **61**, 101182 (2021)
11. Sandler, M., Howard, A., Zhu, M., Zhmoginov, A., Chen, L.-C.: MobileNetV2: inverted residuals and linear bottlenecks. In: Proceedings of the IEEE Conference on Computer Vision and Pattern Recognition, pp. 4510–4520 (2018)
12. Kristiani, E., Yang, C.-T., Nguyen, K.L.P.: Optimization of deep learning inference on edge devices. In: 2020 International Conference on Pervasive Artificial Intelligence (ICPAI), pp. 264–267. IEEE (2020)
13. Xu, H.: PlantVillage Disease Classification Challenge - Color Images (2018). https://gitlab.com/huix/leaf-disease-plant-village

Machine Lerning for the Analysis of Vegetation in the Heritage City of Salamanca

Raúl López-Blanco[1]([✉]) [ID], Ricardo S. Alonso[1,2] [ID], Javier Parra-Domínguez[1] [ID],
Angélica González-Arrieta[1] [ID], Jose A. Flores-Villarejo[1] [ID],
Miguel Á. Fuertes-Prieto[1] [ID], Beatriz Diosdado-Calvo[3],
Román Andrés-Bondía[1] [ID], and Javier Prieto[1] [ID]

[1] BISITE Research Group, University of Salamanca, Edificio Multiusos I+D+i,
Calle Espejo 2, 37007 Salamanca, Spain
{raullb,ralorin,javierparra,angelica,flores,fuertes,
roman.andres,javierp}@usal.es
[2] AIR Institute - Deep Tech Lab, IoT Digital Innovation Hub, Salamanca, Spain
ralonso@air-institute.com
[3] Ayuntamiento de Salamanca, Plaza Mayor, 1, 37001 Salamnca, Spain
bdiosdado@aytosalamanca.es
https://bisite.usal.es, https://air-institute.com

Abstract. Pollution in cities has emerged as one of the main concerns of the citizens who live there. Cities, increasingly overcrowded, are suffering the effects of Climate Change. However, they can also play a key role in mitigating these consequences thanks to the new Smart Cities, based on IoT technologies, Big Data tools and Artificial Intelligence techniques such as Machine Learning. This article presents a successful case study carried out in the world heritage city of Salamanca in which a platform has been used for the management, analysis and visualisation of the data produced and on which unsupervised machine learning techniques have been applied through clustering (K-means) and supervised through K-Nearest Neighbors (K-NN). The results have proved vital in directing and explaining present and future environmental actions in the city of Salamanca.

Keywords: Vegetation index · Smart Cities · Climate change · Clustering · K-Nearest Neighbours

1 Introduction

Citizens in today's cities suffer from a strong concern about Climate Change. A survey carried out in [16] shows that more than 90% of those questioned during the study were concerned about the climate situation. In fact, mental affectations related to this fact are beginning to appear among the youngest people [20],

A. González-Briones et al. (Eds.): PAAMS Workshops 2022, CCIS 1678, pp. 118–128, 2022.
https://doi.org/10.1007/978-3-031-18697-4_10

which is inexorably advancing and whose effects are increasingly noticeable [15], especially in cities due to their overcrowding, but which must also be established for the same reason as the centre of Climate Change mitigation, by means of sustainable development strategies.

The participation of cities in this mitigation process is vital [22], as local strategies specific to each urban area [5] are those that citizens really perceive in their day-to-day lives and which can reduce their levels of climate anxiety and mitigate the effects of climate in urban centres [38]. These actions involve the use of new technologies to manage the data produced in cities today thanks to the new Smart Cities concepts [11].

The technologies that Smart Cities make use of range from the use of IoT devices in different areas such as livestock feed [24], Industry 4.0 [29] or even seeking citizen involvement in matters such as recycling [3]. Also, around Smart Cities, Big Data [19] and Artificial Intelligence [6] technologies are increasingly used.

For the management of all the data produced in the data by IoT devices, which is expected to reach 80 zettabytes in 2025 [27]. This is why it is necessary to use some framework or intermediate platform that provides mechanisms for the ingestion, analysis and visualisation of the data [11]. In addition to this it is desirable and increasingly important to have mechanisms that allow us to apply Artificial Intelligence techniques on the data [36].

The use of new technologies is one of the bases of the European Union's LIFE projects, always bearing in mind the objectives of preserving nature and biodiversity. With these aims, that of mitigating the effects of Climate Change and improving the quality of life of citizens through environmental actions, the LIFE Vía de la Plata [25] project was born. This project is aligned with the specific objectives of Adaptation to Climate Change [5] of the European LIFE projects [30].

The remainder of the article is divided into Sect. 2, which contains a series of papers related to the one presented in this paper. Section 3 then sets out some of the functionality contained within the platform that manages the data for the case study. In Sect. 4, the data and the platform are used to draw a series of conclusions set out in Sect. 5, together with lines of future work.

2   Related Works

Climate change and its long-term effects on citizens [26] and on the climate are increasingly noticeable [4] and Smart Cities aim to be one of the solutions to these effects [35] by generating more sustainable lifestyles through precise knowledge of the consequences of each of our actions thanks to the power of data.

The technologies applied for this sustainable future will be the key to the success of this strategy [13]. In these Smart Cities [8] of the future, which are becoming more and more a reality, it will be necessary to count on permanent technological allies to combat the consequences of Climate Change [2]. Some of the most widely used technologies for this purpose are the Internet of Things (IoT) [28], the blockchain [14], platforms for managing the data produced by the IoT and the Blockchain [10] and Artificial Intelligence [23].

Through the data collected and with all these technologies, the aim is to achieve an intelligent urban management [36] that helps to control from the efficiency of the buildings [12] to the control of all the complex processes, sectors and activities that happen every day in a city [37]. Ultimately, this sustainability model is intended to improve the lives of citizens by improving the quality of the spaces they live in [1].

As alternative options to mitigate the problem of Climate Change, there are already some solutions that work through Artificial Intelligence and Machine Learning such as the studie of [6] that use clustering to make Climate Change predictions. To feed into these, geospatial data is often used to create [33] groupings within cities thanks to clustering algorithms. In addition, other works are using Green Infrastructure and urban actions to improve the quality of life [18]. The case presented brings together these two strategies in search of the best results.

Previous work, such as [34], has already used clustering methods (K-means) and the NDVI index to characterise cities into zones based on vegetation. However, the novelty of this study lies in the application of this technique in a world heritage city and the subsequent use of the classification (K-NN) to check the optimal choice of the points where the environmental measurement stations will be installed.

3   Requirements to Meet the Needs of Smart Cities

The management of the data produced by Smart Cities is the first step to be able to work with them with an efficient strategy since the heterogeneity of the data makes it necessary to bring them together in some way in order to work with them as a whole. For this reason it is necessary to use a platform for data management [7]. In this section, the functionalities implemented by the platform used in the case of Sect. 4 will be presented.

The platform used composes a working ecosystem based on layers [9] to allow users to work in a modular way that can be extended to all possible models of smart cities [17] to facilitate the transition model towards them.

The first layer consists of a *source* system (see Fig. 1) whose functions are to handle the data received from the devices. This source concept is the base component where the data is stored. The origin of the source data can have very different origins such as databases (relational and non-relational), direct sources (local files), derived sources (from sources already created) and other cloud-based services. The platform also has different levels of security, ingesting data securely thanks to elements such as certificates, passwords or encryption of the data itself on arrival at the platform.

In the second layer resides the data management, where processes such as type conversion take place, knowing during the ingestion process the types of

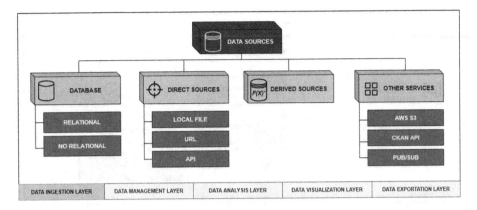

Fig. 1. Data ingestion process options [9].

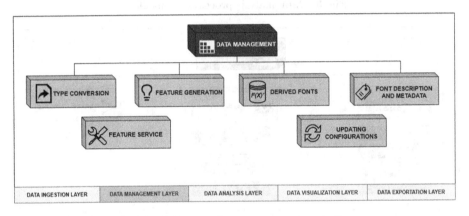

Fig. 2. Data management process options [9].

data that are being added during the loading. Derived sources are also another element that provides versatility to the data management process, it consists of using existing sources to perform filtering or merging with other sources. Other interesting points are the generation of features, the updating of configurations or the description and metadata of the source (see Fig. 2).

The differential point of this platform lies in its analysis section (see Fig. 3). Through this layer, data can be used to feed different supervised and unsupervised learning algorithms to create models to solve clustering, classification, regression, classification and some other types of problems.

The fourth layer of the platform includes the functionality to create graphs and explanatory panels for the user. This functionality helps to understand the information obtained from the sources in a graphical way thanks to the versatility of modifying titles, colors, filters within each graph, among all the types offered by bar charts, line charts, maps and many others that can be seen in Fig. 4.

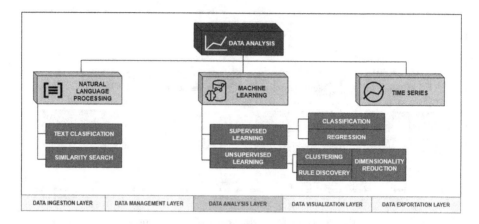

Fig. 3. Data analysis process options [9].

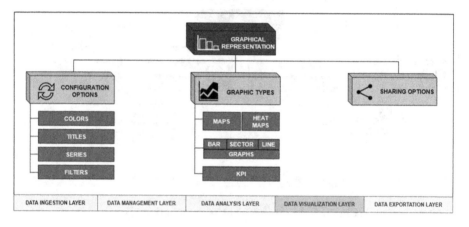

Fig. 4. Data visualization process options [9].

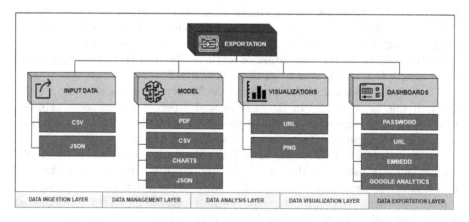

Fig. 5. Data exportation process options [9].

The last layer is the one that integrates the export and sharing of data, since the visualizations can be grouped in panels that are shared as dashboards or simply as images resulting from what is being visualized. There is also the functionality to share all the information through public links and even through downloadable files in standardized formats Fig. 5.

4   K-Means and K-NN for Vegetation Classification

In this section we will explain the application of the unsupervised algorithm, clustering with K-means and the subsequent use of K-Nearest Neighbour (K-NN) classification to obtain useful information for the actions of the LIFE Vía de la Plata project.

4.1   Clustering Process

In this work we have started with a series of data from Copernicus [31] containing normalized difference vegetation index (NDVI) [32] data on the city of Salamanca. Attached to these data are the positions of the air quality stations of the Government of Castile and León. As previously described, an unsupervised algorithm has been used to make the predictions, which works by dividing a data set into groups (clusters) with *similar* internal properties, K-means. The number of clusters k is defined in advance according to mathematical criteria of *closeness* using the elbow method, so that each observation is assigned to the cluster whose distance is smaller. The assignment procedure is repeated until the centroids of each group stop moving or are under a threshold distance. The equation in charge of this is Eq. 1.

$$\min_{\mathbf{S}} E\left(\boldsymbol{\mu}_i\right) = \min_{\mathbf{S}} \sum_{i=1}^{k} \sum_{\mathbf{x}_j \in S_i} \|\mathbf{x}_j - \boldsymbol{\mu}_i\|^2 \quad (1) \tag{1}$$

The objects are represented by real number vectors with $\mathbf{b}$ dimensions like $(\mathbf{x}_1, \mathbf{x}_2, \ldots, \mathbf{x}_n)$. The operation of the mathematical construction K-means distributes into $\mathbf{x}$ groups. The objective of this consists in minimizing the sum of the distances with respect to the objects, within each of the groups $\mathbf{S} = \{S_1, S_2, \ldots, S_k\}$, with respect to the centroid. As far as the definition of $\mathbf{S}$ is concerned, it is explained as the data set whose elements are the objects $\mathbf{x}_j$ (vectors). For the resolution we have $\mathbf{k}$ groups, whose centroids are updated by means of the condition fulfilled by the function $E\left(\boldsymbol{\mu}_i\right)$ which, in its quadratic form is Eq. 2.

$$\frac{\partial E}{\partial \boldsymbol{\mu}_i} = 0 \implies \boldsymbol{\mu}_i^{(t+1)} = \frac{1}{\left|S_i^{(t)}\right|} \sum_{\mathbf{x}_j \in S_i^{(t)}} \mathbf{x}_j \tag{2}$$

The clusters obtained from the NDVI index are those shown in Fig. 6 which has allowed to characterize the city in several vegetation groups, allowing to give a first approximation of where the actions on the Green Infrastructure can

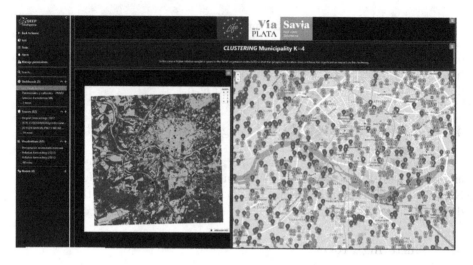

Fig. 6. Clustering based on NDVI data.

be carried out. After this process, a supervised learning algorithm K-Nearest Neighbors (K-NN) will applied in the Sect. 4.2.

To check that the chosen k is optimal, the elbow method has been used as shown in Fig. 7, which consists of finding the best number of clusters by comparing the sum of the mean squared error (SSE). The point chosen must be the one with the angle of the bend, in this case four, which is why $K = 4$ has been chosen.

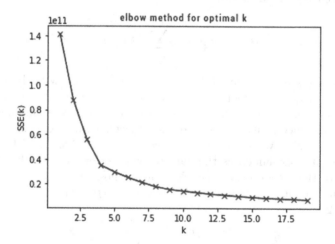

Fig. 7. Elbow method for testing the performance of the number of clusters.

This algorithm works correctly for continuous variables, in this case we are using geographical data and the NDVI vegetation index to find the groups that divide the city of Salamanca into similar zones. The implementation of the K-means algorithm also allows to parameterise the weight of the variables involved and thus obtain different groupings based on this configuration of relative weights. Figure 6 shows the areas grouped according to the different weights of the geographical variables (latitude and longitude) and the NDVI variable. The graph on the left shows the geographical points, the cluster to which each of them belongs and the location of the stations (marked with an X). The graph on the right shows some of these points on the map of Salamanca and the location of the stations (in grey).

4.2 Classification Process

After obtaining this characterisation by groups with the vegetation of the city of Salamanca, we wanted to carry out a supervised learning process by classification to associate the air quality stations to each zone discovered by the clustering algorithm. For this process, the K-Nearest Neighbour (K-NN) algorithm has been used, where K means the number of "neighbouring points" that we have in the vicinity of the previously discovered clusters, in this case 4.

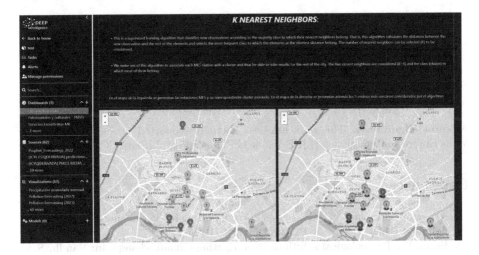

Fig. 8. Classification with K-Nearest Neighbors.

In order to perform the classification, K has been chosen in order to associate each environment monitoring station to a cluster. For this purpose, the result shown in Fig. 8 has been obtained, where the map on the left shows the stations and their corresponding associated cluster and the map on the right also shows the 5 nearest neighbours considered by the algorithm.

5   Conclusions and Future Work Lines

The results of this research confirm that a form of data management is necessary when working with massive sources that undergo frequent updating processes and come from different origins with different forms of integration. This Section includes the conclusions drawn from the use of the platform described in Sect. 4 and the lines of future work.

- The data collected from IoT sensors and open data sources do not guarantee results if they are not intervened through a versatile data manager as is the platform used in the case study of the city of Salamanca.
- The result of the analysis processes has managed to characterize the city of Salamanca through its vegetation levels, this provides a baseline to know where local actions may become more necessary.
- The results of supervised and unsupervised learning application processes have been successfully graphed. These visualisations provide value to citizens in understanding the actions of their governments, to data scientists in seeing the results, and to local authorities themselves in informing their decisions.

The mass of data that is produced within the new Smart Cities conception is something that is in the process of learning to be managed by local authorities using data scientists as allies [21]. Future work streams are as follows:

- Collection of new data from other sources to complement the analyses performed and presented in this study, taking advantage of the data ingestion versatility of the platform.
- Application of new machine learning techniques, both supervised and unsupervised, to check how the data behave with new models that can improve the learning process performed so far.

Acknowledgements. This work has been partially supported by the LIFE program of the European Commission (LIFE Vía de la Plata project: LIFE19 CCA/ES/001188).

References

1. Arroyo, Á., Corchado, E., Tricio, V.: Soft computing models to analyze atmospheric pollution issues. Log. J. IGPL **20**(4), 699–711 (2012)
2. Betts, R.: Technological solutions to mitigating climate change. In: Bandh, S.A. (ed.) Climate Change, pp. 329–368. Springer, Cham (2022). https://doi.org/10.1007/978-3-030-86290-9_19
3. Briones, A.G., et al.: Use of gamification techniques to encourage garbage recycling. A smart city approach. In: Uden, L., Hadzima, B., Ting, I.-H. (eds.) KMO 2018. CCIS, vol. 877, pp. 674–685. Springer, Cham (2018). https://doi.org/10.1007/978-3-319-95204-8_56
4. to Bühne, H.S., Tobias, J.A., Durant, S.M., Pettorelli, N.: Improving predictions of climate change-land use change interactions. Trends Ecol. Evol. **36**(1), 29–38 (2021)

5. Bushnell, J., Peterman, C., Wolfram, C.: Local solutions to global problems: climate change policies and regulatory jurisdiction. Rev. Environ. Econ. Policy (2020)
6. Carvalho, M., Melo-Gonçalves, P., Teixeira, J., Rocha, A.: Regionalization of Europe based on a k-means cluster analysis of the climate change of temperatures and precipitation. Phys. Chem. Earth Parts A/B/C **94**, 22–28 (2016)
7. Chamoso, P., González-Briones, A., De La Prieta, F., Venyagamoorthy, G.K., Corchado, J.M.: Smart city as a distributed platform: toward a system for citizen-oriented management. Comput. Commun. **152**, 323–332 (2020)
8. Corchado, J.M.: Blockchain and its applications on edge computing, Industry 4.0, IoT and smart cities. Dieleman, S (2014)
9. Corchado, J.M., et al.: Deepint.net: a rapid deployment platform for smart territories. Sensors **21**(1), 236 (2021)
10. Corchado, J.M., Pinto-Santos, F., Aghmou, O., Trabelsi, S.: Intelligent development of smart cities: deepint.net case studies. In: Corchado, J.M., Trabelsi, S. (eds.) SSCTIC 2021. LNNS, vol. 253, pp. 211–225. Springer, Cham (2022). https://doi.org/10.1007/978-3-030-78901-5_19
11. Corchado, J.M., Trabelsi, S.: Advances in sustainable smart cities and territories (2022)
12. Corchado, J.M., et al.: Smart buildings (2021)
13. Corchado, J.M.: Technologies for sustainable consumption - researchgate.net (2021). www.researchgate.net/profile/Juan_Rodriguez331/publication/353755163_Technologies_for_sustainable_consumption/links/610ea9491e95fe241abaae5e/Technologies-for-sustainable-consumption.pdf
14. Corchado Rodríguez, J.M., et al.: DeepTech-AI-IoT in Smart Cities (2021)
15. Deilami, K., Kamruzzaman, M., Liu, Y.: Urban heat island effect: a systematic review of spatio-temporal factors, data, methods, and mitigation measures. Int. J. Appl. Earth Obs. Geoinf. **67**, 30–42 (2018)
16. Dettori, M., et al.: Environmental risks perception among citizens living near industrial plants: a cross-sectional study. Int. J. Environ. Res. Public Health **17**(13), 4870 (2020)
17. Garcia-Retuerta, D., Chamoso, P., Hernández, G., Guzmán, A.S.R., Yigitcanlar, T., Corchado, J.M.: An efficient management platform for developing smart cities: solution for real-time and future crowd detection. Electronics **10**(7), 765 (2021)
18. Giannico, V., Spano, G., Elia, M., D'Este, M., Sanesi, G., Lafortezza, R.: Green spaces, quality of life, and citizen perception in European cities. Environ. Res. **196**, 110922 (2021)
19. Hassani, H., Huang, X., Silva, E.: Big data and climate change. Big Data Cogn. Comput. **3**(1), 12 (2019)
20. Ingle, H.E., Mikulewicz, M.: Mental health and climate change: tackling invisible injustice. Lancet Planetary Health **4**(4), e128–e130 (2020)
21. Matheus, R., Janssen, M., Maheshwari, D.: Data science empowering the public: data-driven dashboards for transparent and accountable decision-making in smart cities. Gov. Inf. Q. **37**(3), 101284 (2020)
22. Mi, Z., et al.: Cities: the core of climate change mitigation. J. Clean. Prod. **207**, 582–589 (2019)
23. Milojevic-Dupont, N., Creutzig, F.: Machine learning for geographically differentiated climate change mitigation in urban areas. Sustain. Urban Areas **64**, 102526 (2021)
24. Pérez-Pons, M.E., Parra-Domínguez, J., Chamoso, P., Plaza, M., Alonso, R.: Efficiency, profitability and productivity: technological applications in the agricultural sector. ADCAIJ: Adv. Distrib. Comput. Artif. Intell. J. **9**(4) (2020)

25. Vía de la Plata, L.: Proyecto life vía de la plata (2022). www.lifeviadelaplata.com/
26. Querejeta, M.U., Alonso, R.S.: Modeling air quality and cancer incidences in proximity to hazardous waste and incineration treatment areas. In: Second International Workshop on Data Engineering and Analytics (WDEA 2019), pp. 108–122 (2019)
27. O'Dea, S.: Global IoT connections data volume 2019 and 2025 (2020). www.statista.com/statistics/1017863/worldwide-iot-connected-devices-data-size/
28. Sittón-Candanedo, I., Alonso, R.S., Corchado, J.M., Rodríguez-González, S., Casado-Vara, R.: A review of edge computing reference architectures and a new global edge proposal. Futur. Gener. Comput. Syst. **99**, 278–294 (2019)
29. Sittón-Candanedo, I., Alonso, R.S., Múñoz, L., Rodríguez-González, S.: Arquitecturas de referencia edge computing para la industria 4.0: una revisión. In: Memorias de Congresos UTP, pp. 16–23 (2019)
30. European Union: Regulation (EU) no 1293/2013 of the European parliament and of the council (2013). https://eur-lex.europa.eu/legal-content/ES/TXT/?uri=CELEX3A32013R1293
31. European Union: Copernicus (2022). https://www.copernicus.eu
32. European Union: Normalized difference vegetation index (2022). https://land.copernicus.eu/global/products/ndvi
33. Wang, X., Wang, J.: Using clustering methods in geospatial information systems. Geomatica **64**(3), 347–361 (2010)
34. Yang, Z., Shen, Y., Li, J., Jiang, H., Zhao, L.: A clustering method for inter-annual NDVI time series. Remote Sens. Lett. **12**(8), 819–826 (2021)
35. Yigitcanlar, T., Butler, L., Windle, E., Desouza, K.C., Mehmood, R., Corchado, J.M.: Can building "artificially intelligent cities" safeguard humanity from natural disasters, pandemics, and other catastrophes? An urban scholar's perspective. Sensors **20**(10), 2988 (2020)
36. Yigitcanlar, T., Corchado, J.M., Mehmood, R., Li, R.Y.M., Mossberger, K., Desouza, K.: Responsible urban innovation with local government artificial intelligence (AI): a conceptual framework and research agenda. J. Open Innov.: Technol. Market Complex. **7**(1), 71 (2021)
37. Yigitcanlar, T., Mehmood, R., Corchado, J.M.: Green artificial intelligence: towards an efficient, sustainable and equitable technology for smart cities and futures. Sustainability **13**(16), 8952 (2021)
38. Zhongming, Z., Wei, L., et al.: Urban adaptation to climate change in Europe 2016—transforming cities in a changing climate (2016)

Demand-Responsive Mobility for Rural Areas: A Review

Pasqual Martí$^{(\boxtimes)}$ ⓘ, Jaume Jordán ⓘ, and Vicente Julian ⓘ

Valencian Research Institute for Artificial Intelligence (VRAIN),
Universitat Politécnica de Valéncia, Camino de Vera s/n, 46022 Valencia, Spain
pasmargi@vrain.upv.es, {jjordan,vinglada}@dsic.upv.es

Abstract. Demand-responsive mobility is currently considered an environmentally conscious transportation option that can improve user experience and cut operating costs. Many works propose and analyse demand-responsive transportation systems for urban areas with a high displacement demand. However, the number of works that propose these systems for rural settlements, where scattered populations and low demand are present, is reduced. This work discusses the challenges and open issues found in rural demand-responsive transportation extracted from the review of various recent publications. The commented solutions are approached through artificial intelligence and computer science techniques. Finally, conclusions on the topic are presented, including recommendations for better quality future research.

Keywords: Demand-responsive · Rural mobility · Artificial intelligence

1 Introduction

Demand-responsive transportation (DRT) initially appeared in the UK around the 1960s, conceived as a rural mobility mode [23] with a flexible route and dial-a-ride scheme. Historically, it has been used to assist physically impaired people with on-demand transportation services. These early projects were reliant on government financing, and if that funding was withdrawn, they eventually vanished. In fact, financing has always been a crucial issue in DRT, as usually, the flexibility in a transportation mode incurs higher operational costs [8,10]. Nowadays, in a world dominated by dial-a-ride private transportation [11] (taxi, Uber, Cabify) supported by smartphones and applications, public transport providers have recovered an interest in DRT systems. The reason is twofold: On the one hand, the technological advancements in computation and electronics make it possible to solve complex problems such as online vehicle scheduling, routing and detouring in brief computational times. Moreover, the popularisation of smartphones has made on-demand mobility more accessible than ever for the newer generations. Finally, the advances in autonomous mobility made demand-responsive transportation more promising. On the other hand, the flexibility and

A. González-Briones et al. (Eds.): PAAMS Workshops 2022, CCIS 1678, pp. 129–140, 2022.
https://doi.org/10.1007/978-3-031-18697-4_11

responsiveness of DRT are intuitively good attributes for an environmentally conscious, more sustainable transportation mode that may be able to reduce empty-vehicle displacement, thus reducing energy consumption and greenhouse-gas emissions.

The number of DRT research papers published in the last few years has been rising, although most of the studied and proposed systems are developed for high-density urban areas. In contrast, the application of DRT solutions to rural settlements or areas is less explored. Rural areas count with scattered residents, a low level of transportation demand and, on average, an older population with respect to urban areas. Its usual transportation methods vary depending on the concrete application case but generally feature a single line with a mid-to-high capacity vehicle and a low frequency. The lack of quality public transportation is reflected in the usage of individual motorised transport, which is the most popular form of transportation in some rural areas [25].

Besides what the literature reflects, rural mobility demand seems a good match for a demand-responsive system which, if implemented correctly, could save costs to the operator and be more sustainable for the environment thanks to its on-demand activation. In addition, passenger experience could be improved by lower waiting and riding times. To design such a system it is necessary to gather data from the application area, model the system and develop algorithmic solutions to its different planning and scheduling tasks. Moreover, such a system should be simulated to observe its dynamics and fine-tune its parameters to optimise the fleet's operation.

The present work aims to review the state of the art research in rural demand-responsive transportation. To do so, we first describe how demand-responsive mobility works, presenting diverse configuration options for concrete DRT services and techniques to model and solve their challenges (Sect. 2). Following, classification for the reviewed works is presented and discussed (Sect. 3). Then, we comment on the observed research gaps and discuss approaches for them (Sect. 4). Finally, the work is concluded, emphasising good practices for the future development of rural-DRT research (Sect. 5).

2   Demand-Responsive Transportation Description

A demand-responsive transportation (DRT) system is composed of a series of subsystems, each in charge of solving one of the many challenges that a transportation system involves. These subsystems are highly configurable and can be adapted to the concrete mobility needs of a concrete area. Because of that, the variety among DRT services is wide. Nevertheless, all of them deal with a concrete set of issues presented below:

– *Demand prediction and estimation* is the main attribute of DRT systems, as it is used to optimise its operation. All systems need a demand prediction based on historical data or techniques to control future and current demand. Many solutions require the passengers to explicitly state their desire to use the service by issuing a request.

– *Planning of services and scheduling of requests.* Whether it is performed in advance or in real-time after receiving transportation requests, a DRT operator must plan the operation of its fleet according to its resources. Depending on the type of system, such planning may include routing and stop assignment. In addition, in a request-based system, passengers must be assigned to a vehicle (or a concrete line) that will serve them. This assignment implies the rescheduling of the vehicle planning to include new customers while worsening as little worse as possible other passengers' experiences.
– *Optimising fleet resources*; the goal is to select the appropriated vehicles with a concrete capacity such that the operation of the DRT system yields an acceptable quality of service while being economically viable and sustainable.
– *Validation* through the definition of appropriated metrics to evaluate and compare different configurations.

Solutions to the above issues are dependent on the concrete type of DRT system that will be implemented in addition to the modelling and optimisation techniques used for that. Following, we describe the different characteristics that a DRT system can have (Sect. 2.1) and the techniques that have been observed in the literature for their implementation (Sect. 2.2). Finally, we enumerate the optimisation perspectives of the reviewed material (Sect. 2.3).

2.1   System Types

DRT systems have a series of standard elements present in all of them. Different authors apply different labels to those elements. For the current work, we have followed the terminology described in this survey [29].

In a DRT system, a *service* is the departure of a vehicle to serve the transportation requests it has assigned. One service is generally tied to a concrete area or line the transport will follow. In contrast, a *route* is the concrete path the vehicle follows connecting all the pickups and drop-offs. A route does not necessarily include all existing stops in a line or area. Customers are picked up and dropped off in a predefined set of *stops* within the serviced area or line. Alternatively, a *door-to-door* service can be offered, in which any user-specified location within a particular area may act as a stop. This type of mobility is thought to be *shared*; i. e: multiple customers are served by the same vehicle. Typical vehicle choices for demand-responsive services include a taxi-like car with a capacity of 4 passengers, mini-vans with 9 to 12 seats, and mini-buses or buses with 20 to 30 seats, respectively.

Many use cases exist for demand-responsive transportation. Specifically, for rural-DRT, we find the following: transportation within rural settlements, transportation between rural settlements and transportation between rural and urban settlements. In practice, these cases can be reduced to two systems: *many-to-many*, with a set of multiple origins and destination locations, and *many-to-one*, where origin and destination locations share a unique pick up or drop off point. The last type is usually the so-called feeder line, where flexible transportation service is used to move passengers to another, less accessible service (for instance, communications from rural settlements to an airport). Figure 1 shows a schematic representation of the commented used cases.

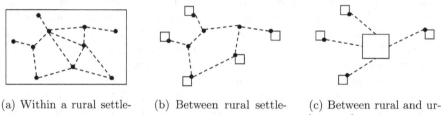

(a) Within a rural settlement   (b) Between rural settlements   (c) Between rural and urban settlements

Fig. 1. Observed uses cases for rural demand-responsive transportation systems. Boxes indicate rural/urban settlements. Black dots represent stops. Dashed lines represent demand-responsive lines. Pictures (a) and (b) are cases of many-to-many transportation, while (c) represents a many-to-one model.

If the customer is required to send a *request* to access transport, then the service is provided *on-demand*. The time between sending a request and the customer's pick up is the *lead time*, and it is used to adapt the fleet operation or *planning* to include such a request. In a stop-based operation, the customer will be assigned a stop from which they will be picked up. On-demand systems can operate in real-time, accepting last minute bookings, or with a hybrid approach, accepting bookings in advance too. DRT systems which are not on-demand are also possible. These systems consider current demand or demand predictions for the service planning but do not require requests to run.

The period of time for which the DRT service is planned and optimised is referred to as *planning horizon*. The duration of planning horizons is usually a whole day. In addition, the operator may plan for a few hours to adapt to high/low demand periods. According to the influence of the demand data on the service planning, the system will be *fully-flexible* if routes are planned from scratch according to current demand or *semi-flexible* if a predetermined plan exists but vehicles are allowed to modify it influenced by demand.

2.2   Modelling and Optimisation Techniques

Once the concrete type of DRT system has been chosen, it must be modelled and tested to check its performance and adjust its attributes. We will discuss below the different steps this involves, citing relevant research and the methods their authors employ. Please be aware that not every paper cited in this section explores rural-DRT.

Most rural-DRT works are set in a concrete rural settlement or area. In general, the main transportation network (roads, highways) of the area is mirrored thanks to services like OpenStreetMap (www.openstreetmap.org) or OpenSourcingRoutingMachine (OSRM, www.project-osrm.org) [9]. Ideally, the actual organisation of the area, its types of districts, population or socio-economic reality, among others, should also be considered. Authors in [16] describe a seven-step analysis method for the optimisation of any transportation system, based on reproducing the features of the currently implemented transport service (that would potentially be replaced) Alternatively, some works employ grid-like modellings of the area where the system will run [6]. More insight on area modelling is given in Sect. 4.4.

Demand modelling is also crucial. Passenger demand has two main aspects: (1) frequency and intensity and (2) shape (location of origin-destination pairs). Demand attributes can be extracted from datasets of different transportation modes and extrapolated, as in [13], where taxi data is used. Moreover, real data of pilot DRT services [7, 27] can be reproduced when available. However, the most observed technique is the use of synthetic demand data that can be generated statistically [6], based on socio-demographic information [30], via surveys [9, 16, 25] or generated in a (semi-)random [28] way according to the properties of the reproduced area (population, age, occupation, vehicle ownership). Demand data sourcing is an open issue within DRT research and discussed in detail in Sect. 4.3. Finally, if traffic intensity data is available, it is useful to include it in the model, although not as relevant for rural areas with respect to city-centred studies, since the former tend to have lower intensity.

The operation of the DRT system requires automated planning and scheduling of vehicle services. At the same time, these tasks need information on the time and travelled kilometres that a concrete detour would imply, which makes routing algorithms also necessary. In addition, since it is common to find online systems that accept real-time requests, the computation time for detours and new request insertions must be kept low. The use of multi-modal planning [9] is common to solve the scheduling of vehicle services. Moreover, some simulation platforms, such as MATSim [2] include their own implementations of the algorithms mentioned above. These implementations usually employ (meta)heuristic techniques [30] that optimise vehicle-passenger assignments (insertion heuristics [5], for instance) or vehicle routing in a short computational time. Besides that, other less exploited techniques such as automated negotiation could be used to decide assignments from a decentralised perspective [3]. The topic of decentralised operation is amplified in Sect. 4.5

Finally, to observe the system's dynamics and its operation and adjust its attributes, it is necessary to simulate it. This can be performed through mathematically modelling [16] provided detailed data is available. However, a more popular way of achieving this is through multi-agent simulation (MAS). Among the observed choices we find NetLogo [26], used in [14], the already mentioned MATSim and even custom simulators [9, 22].

2.3 Optimisation Goals

The main goal of people transportation services is to supply the displacement needs of its users. Ideally, the operation of the service shall be performed optimising three factors: (1) the economic viability of the service; (2) the customer's experience (or quality of service); and (3) the sustainability of the service. These three factors are translated into scopes when it comes to transportation research, and thus we can find works that asses one (only operator perspective [19]), or many of them from a multi-objective perspective (passenger and operator perspectives [18]), The optimisation of customer experience implies the reduction of passenger travel times, whereas the economic viability is ensured by reducing operational costs. Finally, optimising sustainability requires reducing vehicle travelled kilometres (VTK).

The greatest challenge of demand-responsive transportation systems is finding the equilibrium among the factors above to offer a competitively-priced, economically viable and flexible mobility alternative to private cars and traditional public transportation. For the case of rural-DRT, economic viability is especially difficult, taking into account the relatively low demand.

3   Previous Work Classification

Table 1. Classification of rural demand-responsive transportation papers. Asterisks (*) indicate analysis papers which do not propose a system configuration. Ref. = Reference, net. = network, MAS = Multi-agent simulation, Math. = Mathematical modelling.

Ref.	Service type		Use case		On-demand	Flexibility	
	Stop-based	Door-to-door	Many-to-many	Many-to-one		Fully-flexible	Semi-flexible
[30]	X	X	X		X	X	
[16]	X		X	X	X		X
[25]		X	X		X	X	
[9]	X		X		X	X	
[6]	X			X	X	X	

Ref.	Area model		Demand model		Planning/Scheduling		Operation	
	Real net.	Grid net.	Survey/statistics	Pilot data	Heuristic	No heuristic	MAS	Math.
[30]	X		X		X		X	
[16]	X		X			X		X
[25]	X		X		X		X	
[9]	X		X		X		X	
[6]		X	X		X		X	
[7]*				X				
[1]*			X					

Table 1 shows a classification of the rural-DRT system research items cited in Sect. 2. The upper half is centred around the type of DRT service, while the lower half indicates modelling, optimisation and visualisation techniques. As it can be seen, there is an apparent lack of variability among proposals. All of them model on-demand service, which is to be expected in rural areas, as the trips between settlements are, on average, longer than in an urban area, and therefore it is not economically viable to deploy a vehicle if there is no demand. In addition, since most of the research analyses current public transport options, the already established stops are preserved, giving rise to stop-based proposals. There is clear popularity among the use of survey data to model demand among those works that perform experimentation over their proposals. Also, whenever MAS is employed, its integrated heuristic algorithms are employed too. Those works which make no use of such techniques generally perform numerical analysis with average values for waiting times and trip kilometres. Finally, since most of the studies are done over real rural areas, road networks are the most common way to model the scenario.

4 Open Issues

This section assesses the issues that rural-DRT research presents as observed after analysing existing works. Some are central in most DRT research, while others have not been addressed. Each issue includes a brief description and discuss potential techniques that could be applied in future works.

4.1 Issuance of Bookings

On-demand DRT services require their users to issue bookings (or travel requests) for them to be serviced. This action may pose a barrier to the use of the service, although it could be argued that it is solved entirely with today's smartphone technology. Mobile and web applications are an excellent gateway for communicating users and operators. They can be used for bookings and give general information about waiting times, assigned stops and vehicles, and any other relevant data to the user. All this contrasts with the demographic reality of rural areas, where the ageing population may have difficulty with the technology discussed above. Because of this, there will always be a need for a telephone hotline for travel bookings and information provision, which, in turn, implies higher service maintenance costs. An AI-based solution to this issue could be intelligent assistants [17]. With a little learning effort, a person of any age can learn to use voice commands to operate an assistant that, integrated into the application of the demand-responsive transport system, can be used to consult information or confirm reservations.

4.2 Adoption Rate of DRT

A significant number of papers that explore rural-DRT propose to replace part (or the whole) of the current transportation system with them. Among them, those with demand data available assume the new system would absorb all of such demand without considering its adoption rate. Many DRT pilot projects show poor adoption percentages among the population of the areas where it was implemented. Considering how dependent on demand DRT systems are to be economically viable, this may be a cause for their failure.

An interesting technique to promote the adoption of a new transportation service could be *persuasion strategies*, specifically those based in natural language *argumentation* [12]. Such a technique aims to influence user behaviour through interaction with the computer. In this case, the computer could be an intelligent agent embedded in the DRT system application.

Other ways to promote the service and even encourage better use (from the operator's point of view) are the so-called *pricing strategies*. Dynamic variations in the price of services have been explored to regulate electricity demand [31] and, more recently, on-street parking [21]. Through these policies, the operator can influence the booking times of users, offering more competitive prices to those users whose location is nearby the planned route of an already departed vehicle, for instance. Similarly, the price could increase in periods where deploying a new vehicle would be too costly or when the operator predicts the system to be overflown with demand. Nevertheless, the introduction of these strategies is delicate, as the public acceptance can be generally low [24].

4.3   Data Sourcing

The lack of input data is a common problem of demand-responsive research. In the context of rural-DRT, this issue is aggravated by the lack of rural-specific or low-demand datasets. There are a small number of DRT pilot projects, and among them, an even smaller number share the collected data. Still, the data that can be found about pilot projects is very dependent on the specific area and the socio-demographic context where the pilot took place.

Two main trends have been observed in dealing with data shortage. On the one hand, some authors recur to using datasets for other modes of transportation (such as taxi or public bus systems) to ground their use cases and experimentation. However, results from real implementations of DRT services show how the user usage decays when substituting a transportation mode with another [7]. In addition, according to the type of the studied system, it may require other datasets for tasks such as stop allocation (in stop-based models). On the other hand, several works claim to use real-life data. The specific meaning of "real-life" has different implications. For the analysed rural-centred works it implied the following: (1) Synthetic demand data generated (1.1) statistically, based on socio-demographic information [6] or (1.2) via survey [1,9,16,25,30]; and (2) demand data from actual field tests [7].

Synthetic survey-based data appears to be the more popular option. This is partly explained because the reviewed works are more centred in the field of transportation research than computer science. Nevertheless, computing methods and, in particular, artificial intelligence can aid in this issue. Artificial mobility data generation techniques seem like a potential solution. This generation would consider the attributes of the concrete area where the experimentation will take place, increasing the quality and reliability of future research. Ideally, the generators should be configurable to create fictitious yet realistic scenarios for various problems and diverse circumstances, including concrete transport demand patterns, traffic arrangements, settlement layouts, and population, among others.

4.4   Stop Location and Mobility Hubs

As commented throughout the work, it is usual that rural-DRT systems are proposed as a substitution for the public transportation mode currently serving the area. The authors consider the same set of stops (in stop-based proposals) that the traditional mobility option had when doing this. We believe it is worth exploring the deactivation or relocation of existing stations and the creation of new ones.

A wide variety of heuristic techniques can be applied to the optimal allocation of resources. In addition, evolutionary computation can be directly employed. The evaluation function needs to define the improvement of a particular arrangement over another. For our concrete problem, the first step would be to evaluate the current stop location. For this, we propose the use of multi-agent simulation. The authors of the present work have experience in this topic, having proposed an electric station allocation method supported by genetic algorithms whose solutions are evaluated through multi-agent simulation [15].

A concrete case within stop allocation is the creation of a mobility hub (see Fig. 2). A hub is a shared destination point for all transportation lines in a specific area. The hub has the function of accumulating passengers to make a journey to a more distant destination or in a more direct way (e.g. without stops). Similarly to the case of stops, the proposal of a mobility hub has to be accompanied by a careful study of how its location influences the transportation system to decide the optimal one.

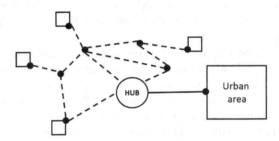

Fig. 2. Schematic representation of a mobility hub within a demand-responsive transportation system. Dashed connections represent medium-capacity demand-responsive lines; meanwhile, continuous connections represent high-capacity fixed lines. A circle represents the hub. Small boxes represent rural settlements; meanwhile, the big box indicates an urban area. Black dots are stops.

4.5   Decentralised Fleet Operation

The DRT operator should consider the willingness of vehicle drivers to work on dynamic services. In general, DRT services are thought of as centralised systems in which new requests are assigned to a vehicle so that the travel time and vehicle kilometres are minimised while preserving the time windows of the customer booking. A centralised entity performs the assignment without consideration for the driver's desires or preferences (understanding a driver as an intelligent agent or human). This system poses no problem if vehicles are *autonomous* and work without human drivers. However, the technology for autonomous vehicles is still premature, making it unfeasible to implement for current systems. For human-driven vehicles, a sudden change in the route, a detour or servicing a remote customer may require an extra effort from the driver. Decentralised systems often give the option to vehicle drivers to accept or reject some requests according to their interests, as long as more than one vehicle can serve such a request. The acceptance or rejection comes with bonuses or penalties for the driver, respectively, which gives the driver the chance to make an informed decision [4].

Automated negotiation techniques can also be applied, most directly with autonomous vehicles, although it is also suitable for human drivers. With these, drivers can negotiate among themselves to which vehicle should new requests be assigned. In general, consensus can be reached in a relatively low time. Finally, *game theory* can also be applied when more than one driver is interested in serving a concrete request [20]. Game-theoretic processes can be computationally costly, and should be carefully researched and refined before their applications.

5   Conclusions

The present work has described in-depth demand-responsive transportation systems, enumerating the different types, the strategies followed for modelling and optimisation, and their objectives. Then, open and less researched issues have been discussed, focusing on those relevant to rural-DRT. We hope the insights given to each issue and the comments throughout the paper help guide future research in the field.

The field of demand-responsive transportation is young as a whole. The lack of standards has caused authors to arrange their own systems, each with its particular name, resulting in a significant number of proposals. Nevertheless, when analysed closely, most systems are very similar, differing merely in a few details. In addition, the number of works that provide insight into the attributes of their model is low. Although exploring algorithms and techniques is expected in a field with many open issues such as DRT, authors need to centre their discussions on the particular contributions these algorithms and system modellings bring to passengers, operators, and drivers. Given a system, it is crucial to fine-tune its configurable parts (stops, assignments, vehicle capacity, among others) to the concrete, real-life application case.

Following the current research, we want to arrange a series of works that assess the commented issues by modelling, implementing, and testing AI solutions for them. Ideally, this path will lead to a unified proposal containing various optimisation methods for the different parts of a DRT system.

Acknowledgements. This work is partially supported by grant RTI2018-095390-B-C31 funded by MCIN/AEI/10.13039/501100011033 and by "ERDF A way of making Europe. Pasqual Martí is supported by grant ACIF/2021/259 funded by the "Conselleria de Innovación, Universidades, Ciencia y Sociedad Digital de la Generalitat Valenciana". Jaume Jordán is supported by grant IJC2020-045683-I funded by MCIN/AEI/ 10.13039/501100011033 and by "European Union NextGenerationEU/PRTR".

References

1. Anburuvel, A., Perera, W., Randeniya, R.: A demand responsive public transport for a spatially scattered population in a developing country. Case Stud. Transp. Policy **10**(1), 187–197 (2022)
2. Balmer, M., Rieser, M., Meister, K., Charypar, D., Lefebvre, N., Nagel, K.: MATSim-T: architecture and simulation times. In: Multi-agent Systems for Traffic and Transportation Engineering, pp. 57–78. IGI Global (2009)
3. Bertelle, C., Nabaa, M., Olivier, D., Tranouez, P.: A decentralised approach for the transportation on demand problem. In: Aziz-Alaoui, M.A., Bertelle, C. (eds.) From System Complexity to Emergent Properties, pp. 281–289. Springer, Heidelberg (2009). https://doi.org/10.1007/978-3-642-02199-2_13
4. Billhardt, H., Fernández, A., Ossowski, S., Palanca, J., Bajo, J.: Taxi dispatching strategies with compensations. Expert Syst. Appl. **122**, 173–182 (2019)
5. Bischoff, J., Maciejewski, M.: Proactive empty vehicle rebalancing for demand responsive transport services. Procedia Comput. Sci. **170**, 739–744 (2020)
6. Calabrò, G., Le Pira, M., Giuffrida, N., Inturri, G., Ignaccolo, M., Correia, G.: Fixed-route vs demand-responsive transport feeder services: an exploratory study using an agent-based model. J. Adv. Transp. **2022** (2022)
7. Coutinho, F.M., van Oort, N., Christoforou, Z., Alonso-González, M.J., Cats, O., Hoogendoorn, S.: Impacts of replacing a fixed public transport line by a demand responsive transport system: case study of a rural area in Amsterdam. Res. Transp. Econ. **83**, 100910 (2020)
8. Currie, G., Fournier, N.: Why most DRT/micro-transits fail-what the survivors tell us about progress. Res. Transp. Econ. **83**, 100895 (2020)
9. Dytckov, S., Persson, J.A., Lorig, F., Davidsson, P.: Potential benefits of demand responsive transport in rural areas: a simulation study in Lolland, Denmark. Sustainability **14**(6) (2022)
10. Enoch, M., Potter, S., Parkhurst, G., Smith, M.: Why do demand responsive transport systems fail? In: Transportation Research Board 85th Annual Meeting, Washington DC, USA (2006)
11. Ho, S.C., Szeto, W., Kuo, Y.H., Leung, J.M., Petering, M., Tou, T.W.: A survey of dial-a-ride problems: literature review and recent developments. Transp. Res. Part B: Methodol. **111**, 395–421 (2018)
12. Hunter, A., Chalaguine, L., Czernuszenko, T., Hadoux, E., Polberg, S.: Towards computational persuasion via natural language argumentation dialogues. In: Benzmüller, C., Stuckenschmidt, H. (eds.) KI 2019. LNCS (LNAI), vol. 11793, pp. 18–33. Springer, Cham (2019). https://doi.org/10.1007/978-3-030-30179-8_2
13. Hyland, M., Mahmassani, H.S.: Operational benefits and challenges of shared-ride automated mobility-on-demand services. Transp. Res. Part A: Policy Pract. **134**, 251–270 (2020)
14. Inturri, G., Giuffrida, N., Ignaccolo, M., Le Pira, M., Pluchino, A., Rapisarda, A.: Testing demand responsive shared transport services via agent-based simulations. In: Daniele, P., Scrimali, L. (eds.) New Trends in Emerging Complex Real Life Problems. ASS, vol. 1, pp. 313–320. Springer, Cham (2018). https://doi.org/10.1007/978-3-030-00473-6_34

15. Jordan, J., Palanca, J., Marti, P., Julian, V.: Electric vehicle charging stations emplacement using genetic algorithms and agent-based simulation. Expert Syst. Appl. **197**, 116739 (2022)
16. Lakatos, A., Tóth, J., Mándoki, P.: Demand responsive transport service of 'dead-end villages' in interurban traffic. Sustainability **12**(9) (2020)
17. Liu, J., Zhu, B.: An intelligent personal assistant robot: BoBi secretary. In: 2nd International Conference on Advanced Robotics and Mechatronics (ICARM), pp. 402–407 (2017)
18. Liyanage, S., Dia, H.: An agent-based simulation approach for evaluating the performance of on-demand bus services. Sustainability **12**(10) (2020)
19. Marković, N., Kim, M.E., Kim, E., Milinković, S.: A threshold policy for dispatching vehicles in demand-responsive transit systems. Promet - Traffic & Transp. **31**(4), 387–395 (2019)
20. Martí, P., Jordán, J., De la Prieta, F., Billhardt, H., Julian, V.: Demand-responsive shared transportation: a self-interested proposal. Electronics **11**(1) (2022)
21. Mo, B., Kong, H., Wang, H., Wang, X.C., Li, R.: Impact of pricing policy change on on-street parking demand and user satisfaction: a case study in Nanning, China. Transp. Res. Part A: Policy Pract. **148**, 445–469 (2021)
22. Palanca, J., Terrasa, A., Carrascosa, C., Julián, V.: SimFleet: a new transport fleet simulator based on MAS. In: De La Prieta, F., et al. (eds.) PAAMS 2019. CCIS, vol. 1047, pp. 257–264. Springer, Cham (2019). https://doi.org/10.1007/978-3-030-24299-2_22
23. Ryley, T.J., Stanley, P.A., Enoch, M.P., Zanni, A.M., Quddus, M.A.: Investigating the contribution of demand responsive transport to a sustainable local public transport system. Res. Transp. Econ. **48**, 364–372 (2014)
24. Schade, J., Schlag, B.: Acceptability of urban transport pricing strategies. Transport. Res. F: Traffic Psychol. Behav. **6**(1), 45–61 (2003)
25. Schlüter, J., Bossert, A., Rössy, P., Kersting, M.: Impact assessment of autonomous demand responsive transport as a link between urban and rural areas. Res. Transp. Bus. Manag. **39**, 100613 (2021)
26. Tisue, S., Wilensky, U.: NetLogo: a simple environment for modeling complexity. In: International Conference on Complex Systems, Boston, MA, vol. 21, pp. 16–21 (2004)
27. Vallée, S., Oulamara, A., Cherif-Khettaf, W.R.: Maximizing the number of served requests in an online shared transport system by solving a dynamic DARP. In: Bektaş, T., Coniglio, S., Martinez-Sykora, A., Voß, S. (eds.) ICCL 2017. LNCS, vol. 10572, pp. 64–78. Springer, Cham (2017). https://doi.org/10.1007/978-3-319-68496-3_5
28. van Engelen, M., Cats, O., Post, H., Aardal, K.: Enhancing flexible transport services with demand-anticipatory insertion heuristics. Transp. Res. Part E: Logist. Transp. Rev. **110**, 110–121 (2018)
29. Vansteenwegen, P., Melis, L., Aktaş, D., Montenegro, B.D.G., Vieira, F.S., Sörensen, K.: A survey on demand-responsive public bus systems. Transp. Res. Part C: Emerg. Technol. **137**, 103573 (2022)
30. Viergutz, K., Schmidt, C.: Demand responsive - vs. conventional public transportation: a MATSim study about the rural town of Colditz, Germany. Procedia Comput. Sci. **151**, 69–76 (2019)
31. Ye, B., Ge, F., Rong, X., Li, L.: The influence of nonlinear pricing policy on residential electricity demand—a case study of Anhui residents. Energ. Strat. Rev. **13**, 115–124 (2016)

Workshop on Character
Computing (C2)

Workshop on Character Computing (C2)

The fourth consecutive Workshop on Character Computing addressed the emerging field and the opportunities and challenges it poses. Character computing is any computing that incorporates the human character within its context (for more details see https://www.springer.com/gp/book/9783030159535 and https://en.wikipedia.org/wiki/Character_computing). The character includes stable traits (e.g., personality) and variable affective, cognitive, and motivational states as well as history, morals, beliefs, skills, an appearance, and socio-cultural embeddings, to name a few. As the next step towards further putting humans at the center of technology, novel interdisciplinary approaches such as character computing are developing. The extension and fusion between the different computing approaches, e.g., affective and personality computing, within character computing is based on well-controlled empirical and theoretical knowledge from psychology. This is done by including the whole human character as a central part of any artificial interaction.

Character computing has three main modules that can be investigated and leveraged separately or together: 1) character sensing and profiling, 2) character-aware adaptive systems, and 3) artificial characters.

The aim of the workshop is to inspire research into the foundations and applications of character computing by investigating novel approaches by both computer scientists and psychologists. C2 addresses applications, opportunities, and challenges of sensing, predicting, adapting to, affecting, or simulating human behavior and character.

This workshop seeks to promote character computing as a design material for the creation of novel user experiences and applications by leveraging the evolving character of the user.

The main goals of this workshop are to

- Provide a forum for computer science, technology, and psychology professionals to come together and network for possible future collaboration.
- Share experience obtained and lessons learned from past projects to understand the current state of the art of research conducted related to character computing.
- Identify challenges and opportunities that researchers face to set up a current R&D agenda and community in this field.

C2 brings together researchers and industry practitioners from both computational and psychology communities to share knowledge and resources, discuss new ideas, and build foundations of possible future collaborations. The primary aim is to further the research into character computing by discussing potential ideas, challenges, and sharing expertise among the participants. This year, the workshop was held in a hybrid format like the main PAAMS conference, allowing registrants to participate virtually or in-person in L'Aquila (Italy).

Organization

Organizing Committee

Alia El Bolock   German International University, Egypt
Cornelia Herbert   Ulm University, Germany
Slim Abdennadher   German International University, Egypt

Program Committee

Friedhelm Schwenker   Ulm University, Germany
Yomna Abdelrahman   Bundeswehr Universität München, Germany
Caroline Sabty   German International University, Egypt
Dirk Reichardt   DHBW Stuttgart, Germany
Amr ElMougy   German University in Cairo, Egypt
Walid El Hefny   German University in Cairo, Egypt
Jailan Salah   German University in Cairo, Egypt

FAN-VE: A Tool for Facial Animation Generation in Virtual Reality Education

Mostafa Alaa[1,2]([✉]) and Slim Abdennadher[2]

[1] German University in Cairo, Cairo, Egypt
mostafa.talaat@guc.edu.eg
[2] German International University, Cairo, Egypt
slim.abdennadher@guc.edu.eg

Abstract. Teachers play a critical role in the education process. The importance of this role is not diminished when transitioning into Education inside Virtual Reality. With the rise of popularity in VR and remote education, the optimization of virtual teachers becomes needed. In this paper, we present a tool that provides facial animations to virtual teachers. The tool is designed to be user friendly, generic, and work across different models and facial expressions in order to serve a wide range of use cases. The tool was tested for usability and feedback was collected regarding its functionality. Our results indicate that our tool is user friendly and needed and has potential for further development and adoption.

Keywords: Virtual Reality · Education · Pedagogical agents

1 Introduction

Virtual Reality (VR) technology is considered one of the highly disruptive technologies that can provide new capabilities to our daily life. VR offers a simulated environment allowing the users to experience a world that does not really exist.

On the other hand, in the field of education, the same traditional approaches have been applied for decades. The students go to schools or universities, where they usually have to sit in classrooms all day to listen to their tutors explaining their lessons. This might have some negative side effects and can become monotonous and boring. This approach also has the disadvantage of not being available to everyone; some students can not afford going to schools and universities and some other students live in cities where there are no schools or universities available. This was specially evident in light of the recent Covid-19 pandemic where school physical attendance was not possible.

However, the major leap in technology and innovation that is being experienced nowadays brings many new and innovative opportunities to the education field. VR is one of the technology trends that promises a great improvement and evolution to education as it introduces a whole new concept in the education system.

A. González-Briones et al. (Eds.): PAAMS Workshops 2022, CCIS 1678, pp. 145–156, 2022.
https://doi.org/10.1007/978-3-031-18697-4_12

At the center of the VR integration in education is the characteristics and behavior of the virtual teacher avatar. Many aspects should be considered when designing the virtual teacher; the looks, the movements, the speech to lips synchronization, as well as the facial expressions all play a vital role in the education process in VR. All these aspects can affect the student, both directly and indirectly, and cause certain consequences to the learning outcome. That is why, in this paper, our aim is to create a tool that can help users in creating better virtual teachers, keeping these aspects in mind.

2   Background and Related Work

2.1   Facial Expressions

A facial expression is one or more motions of the small muscles of the face. It is a type of non verbal communication, where emotions can be expressed without uttering any single world. Facial expressions are common between human beings, most of the mammals and some different species of animals [6].

There are 7 universal facial expressions, each is related to a main human's emotion. These main emotions are Happiness, Sadness, Fear, Disgust, Anger, Contempt and Surprise. In the late 20th century, Dr. Paul Ekman and his team conducted a study and concluded that the emotional facial expressions are innate and not related to a specific culture or race [9]. However, there exists what is known as a compound facial expression of emotions. They are the result of combining different basic expressions, for example a person shows an expression when he is happily surprised in a different way than when he is angrily surprised. When observing all the combined options of the basic expressions, we find that human beings can perform twenty one different facial expressions. Moreover, all of them are distinguishable from the other [8].

2.2   Facial Expressions in Education

Teachers' facial expressions are extremely crucial when it comes to the relationship between the teacher and the students and the academical performance of the students. It is proven that non verbal communication in a classroom plays a vital role in the classroom's management, which is the techniques that a teacher follows to ensure that the students remain attentive to what he is saying and to improve academically. The teacher's facial expressions during explanation increases the students' engagement and motivation as well as improves the students' academical level [12]. Furthermore, it is the perfect way of managing the emotions of all the students in the classroom, no matter how many they are, in a controlled and fast way. They can also force the bored students to be enthusiastic about what the teacher is saying by frequently drawing their attention to the teacher and his explanation. Another important aspect is that the facial expressions of the students are found to be of prime importance in the classroom as they help the teacher to get a better insight about the students' apprehension to the explanation and their satisfaction level.

2.3 VR in Education

VR is very useful in the education field as it has a lot of benefits. First of all, VR includes elements of social presence, cognitive presence and teaching presence so it offers a rich educational experience. Moreover, it has the advantage of visualization of difficult models and the experiential learning of abstract concepts. In addition to that, it provides a space to explore different things and test their solutions without proposing any risk. It was demonstrated that it enhances the learning due to immersion, as the more the students are involved, the less distracted they will be and the more they will achieve [2]. It was also shown that it eliminates the boundaries because students will be exposed to a lot of people and worlds that are normally inaccessible [13].

It also has significant effects on enhancing the students' competencies such as communication, challenging practice and major foundation. It was found that these competencies are better enhanced in VR classrooms than in traditional classrooms [16]. It also removes the language barriers as subtitles can be added as an option in the software.

Many studies have been conducted to explore the benefits of VR in the educational field. The aim of some studies was to determine the outcomes of using VR in the educational field generally; whether for schools or universities [17,19,22]. While other studies focused on the effect of using VR while teaching certain topics such as Engineering or Chemistry [2,10,14,18,21]. Others aimed to explore the upshot of VR learning environments on students with special needs such as students with Autism Spectrum Disorder (ASD) [4,15,20]. Moreover, some studies' aim was to see the effects that a virtual teacher has and how does the presence of a virtual teacher affect the students [1,11,23].

2.4 Virtual Teacher

Teachers have an important role in teaching the students. The teacher has a great impact on the students' academical performance and their test scores, as the qualities of a teacher are as important as the methods that a teacher uses to convey information to the students. The relationship between the teacher and the student is found to be very effective, as this relationship has a direct effect on the students' emotional well-being and the students' social and academical skills [26].

The revolutionizing of education has been proven to play a critical role in strengthening the relationship between the students and the teachers. For example, using internet in the classroom has led to more group work and more communication between the teacher and the student which affected the relationship between the teacher and the students positively. Additionally, it helps to diminish the conflicts between the teacher and the students [24].

A study by Doswell [7] provided a Pedagogical Embodied Conversational Agent (PECA) which is a virtual instructor system that provides a multi-modal interface for human computer interaction. It combines input processors, a multilingual dialogue generator, facial recognition systems, gesture recognition systems and voice recognition systems among other components to ensure that the virtual teacher will have human-like characteristics and will be able to interact with the students in real-time. It was shown that the presence of a virtual teacher allows the students to better interact in the VR environment and facilitates the tailored instruction. Likewise, it creates an efficacious and pleasurable environment for education which makes the students more interested and motivated.

In [5] a study was conducted aiming to observe the positive outcomes of Asynchronous Learning Networks where the internet is used to support class activities and the perks of having a virtual professor in the virtual classroom and how it imposes a big change in the virtual education. The focus was on the effect this technology has on the teachers themselves and not just the students. The changes in cognitive roles, affective roles and managerial roles have been captured. The study was conducted across different research projects that took almost twenty years to be conducted. It was found that a virtual university had an effect on the instructors' cognitive role. The cognitive role contains numerous aspects of intellectual functions such as thinking, information storage, problem solving and reasoning. It was proven that it changed to one of deeper cognitive complexity. However, they noticed that to make a bigger change in the affective role, which influences the classroom's spirit and the relationships between the students and the teacher, they still need to find ways to express emotions in the virtual world. Nevertheless, it was clear that the relationship between the professors and students became more intimate.

Another study [25] was conducted to investigate the effect of the facial expressions of the virtual teachers on the virtual students and the relation between these expressions and the student's interactions to these expressions. The relation between these expressions and the students' performance was also observed. The study focused on differentiating between the expressions that really had an effect on the students and the expressions that the students neglected. In this study, two experiments were conducted. In the first, it was observed that the lecturer's facial expressions made the students concentrate more and to be more responsive. They were also more interested and motivated during the lecture. It was reported that the main facial expression that had quite an impact on the students was the Smiling. The students most probably would smile back to the lecturer when he smiles. It also showed that students' interest and motivation increased when the virtual lecturer used facial expressions and gestures and that they even scored higher grades. They felt that they were engaged in the virtual environment more when the lecturer was capable of doing facial expressions and otherwise they would lose focus and they felt bored. They said that only virtual lecturers with facial expressions and gestures should be used.

In the second experiment, it was reported that by increasing the facial expressions used by the virtual teacher, the student's interest and motivation gets higher. Moreover, the students have also obtained higher scores when the teacher did some form of facial expression compared to when they did not.

3 Approach

The aim of this project is to create a tool that can provide the users with the ability to augment virtual teachers with lip syncing, facial expressions, as well as body movements. Special attention was given to the design in order to make sure that the tool will be scalable and not limited to a specific provision. The simplicity of the project was also taken into consideration as to ensure that users can quickly work with this tool without facing any difficulties.

The tool was designed for the Unity3D platform. Unity is a very popular game engine that is used for content creation across different industries. It supports cross platform development as well as integration with VR. It also provides a huge community of developers and support personnel. This makes Unity a very suitable choice for our tool. Additionally, in order to achieve our goals, the tool was designed according to the following criteria.

3.1 Characters

It was very important to make this project very generic, scalable and modular as much as possible by allowing the users to have any character they want without restraining them to choose between only some characters. This was fulfilled by granting the users the possibility to import any character into Unity with the condition that the character must have the same avatar animation rig as the one used in the project.

The avatar animation rig that is used in the project is the same as the default rig used by the Character Creator software. Character Creator is a software used to design characters for games, cartoons, AR and VR. It allows the users to customize any 3D character they want. The characters can either be a male or female. They can have different heights, different body shapes as well as different body poses. Furthermore, it's possible to customize the skin textures to get any skin tone that is wanted, the makeup of the character, the style of the hair and its color. Moreover, the character can be dressed in many different clothing items by either choosing clothes from the available assets or by creating new clothes. With all these options available for customization, the user faces no boundaries while creating the characters. Additionally, four different characters were provided by default in the project and the user can choose any character from them.

3.2 Audio

The user can add any audio clip they want to the audio clip field. This allows the user to choose any topic for the virtual teacher to explain, without being restricted to some specific topics. Also, there are no limitations regarding the duration of the audio clip. The lip sync animation is done automatically and is automatically saved to an animation clip inside the project. The user can choose to save the lip sync animation in the default animations directory or any other directory they want.

3.3   Facial Expressions

Another feature that was added to ensure that the project will be generic, scalable and modular was to allow the users to import the facial animation of any facial expression. However, the imported animation's avatar animation rig must have the same avatar rig used in the project. Additionally, 13 different facial expressions were already added to the project for the user to choose from. The inclusion of facial expressions in the animation is optional; users can choose to play the audio without any facial expression, just the lip sync animation.

The different facial expressions are shown in Fig. 1. If the user wants to add a facial expression, they simply add it before pressing the play button. Otherwise, no facial expression will be added to the character.

Fig. 1. Drop down list of all the different facial expressions built into the tool.

3.4   Body Animations

The feature of having different body animations was also added. A folder named "Sample animations" is added with different body animations to allow the user to choose from them the animation that they want. These animations are shown in Fig. 2. Additionally, the user has the option of importing any body animation that they want inside the project. The user also has the possibility to play the audio without adding any body animation to the character. The user has to choose the body animation before they press the play button, otherwise no body animation will be added to the character.

3.5   Recording

If the user adds a new audio clip, they must choose to record its lip sync animation at least once. However, if it is already recorded, then they have the option

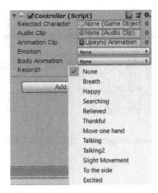

Fig. 2. Drop down list of all the different body animation built into the tool

to choose whether to record it again or just play the already recorded animation file.

The user can see whether it is now recording or just playing a saved animation clip from the game view. If it is recording then the message "Preparing animation" will be found beside the character. In addition to that, the user will not be hearing the audio clip's sound while seeing that the character's lips are moving as an indication that recording is in progress.

When the message disappears that means that it finished recording and that the just recorded animation will be played directly and the audio's sound will be heard. If the user chose from the start not to record the lip sync, then the saved animation will be directly played and the user will not see any message in advance.

3.6 User Interface

A user interface was also created by creating a Unity Custom Inspector, as shown in Fig. 3. The aim of creating the user interface was to ensure that this project will be user friendly and that the workflow will be facilitated. The user just adds the character they want by choosing the character prefab, the audio clip that would serve as the speech of the teacher, the facial expression of the teacher during that speech from the drop-down menu, the body animation of the teacher while speaking, and then whether they want to record the lip sync animation or just play the saved one.

It's worth noting that the facial expressions and body animations are not recorded in the lip sync animation. This was done in order to ensure that the user can use the same lip sync animation as many times as they want with any of the expressions and body animations without being restricted to the specific facial expression or an animation used at the time of recording. So by doing that, they always have the chance of trying different expressions and body animations with the same lip sync animation that was recorded before.

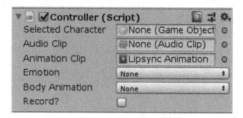

Fig. 3. Custom inspector built into Unity Engine

4   Experiment

4.1   Participants

There were 12 participants. They were all teaching assistants, who were working at the German University in Cairo. The participants were chosen in such a way to ensure that they all have at least basic knowledge of how to use Unity in order to be able to use our tool and give the feedback about the usability of it.

4.2   Procedure and Setup

Testing was done by exporting the tool as a package from Unity and sending it to the participants to test it themselves. A Read Me file was sent to help the participants in using the tool and to explain how to use the system features. Two videos were also recorded as a sample of the output of the project and sent also to the participants.

4.3   Test and Questionnaires

To collect subjective information and feedback from the participants, they were asked to answer a questionnaire. The first part of the questionnaire was to test the System Usability and it was done using the System Usability Scale (SUS) [3]. The SUS is a standardized method to measure the usability of the system. It consists of 10 different questions with five response options; from strongly agree to strongly disagree.

The second part of the questionnaire was to know the participants' opinion of the output of the project and whether the presence of facial expressions and body animations is really a plus to the system or not. The participants were asked the following questions:

1. Please rate your level of satisfaction with the overall quality of the system.
2. Do you think that the character's lip sync matches the audio?
3. Does the presence of facial expressions and body animation help you to concentrate more with what the character was saying?
4. In your opinion, what are the features that should be added/modified to the system?

5   Results and Discussion

5.1   SUS Questionnaire

In order to calculate the score the sum of the even numbered questions is calculated and then this value is subtracted from 25. The sum of the odd numbered questions is also created and then 5 is subtracted from this value. These 2 values are then added to each other and the result is multiplied by 2.5. To get the SUS Test result, the average of all the scores has to be calculated. When the average of the participants' scores was calculated, our tool scored an average of 81.1. This result is in the 90–95 percentile range and is interpreted as excellent [13].

5.2   Participants Feedback

The first question in this part was to know whether the participants were satisfied with the overall quality of the system. This question had five response options ranged from Very Satisfied to Very Unsatisfied. The results of this question where that 8.3% of the participants chose Neutral, 50% chose Satisfied and 41.7% chose Very Satisfied.

The second question was to know whether the participants think that the lip sync animation generated matches the audio and is in sync or not. It was a question with three response options; Yes, No, Sometimes. 8.3% of the participants chose No, 25% chose Yes and 66.7% chose Sometimes.

The third question was to know their impression on the presence of the facial expressions and body animations. The aim of the question was to know whether they would prefer to see a character with facial and body animations or they would prefer if the character spoke only without any other animations. This question had two response options; Yes and No. Choosing a Yes meant that they prefer the presence of the facial and body animations. The results show that 33.3% of the participants chose No while 66.7% chose Yes.

In the final question, the participants were asked about the features that they would like to add or modify in the system. It was suggested that the facial expressions and body animations should be customized instead of choosing from a drop down menu. The idea of allowing the users to change the audio and to update the animation during run time was also recommended. Furthermore, it was suggested to make the facial expressions more visible and to add more facial expressions to the system. It was also suggested that the character needs to have more eye contact with the users. Moreover, some of the participants said that the synchronisation of the lip sync animation needs to be further improved. In addition to that, it was recommended that the timing of the body animations should be specified to help the user while choosing the animation with the audio and to work on improving the body animation. Another comment was to put the audio, facial emotion and body animation in a scriptable object and to assign it in the controller component so that it would be easier to create combinations of animations.

6 Conclusion and Future Work

A scalable, modular and flexible tool has been implemented and its design is presented in this paper. This tool allows the users to automatically add audio clip lip syncing to virtual teachers in any Unity project. Different 3D characters were created to perform the role of the virtual teacher within the tool. Additionally, the user can also opt to use their own characters as the virtual teachers.

Various facial expressions and gestures have been built into the tool and they can all be applied to any of the characters within the project. Moreover, different body animations were also provided by default within the tool. The user is free to choose any of the created characters, add any audio clip to the tool, choose the facial expression that matches the audio as well as the body animation that will be applied to the character.

The system was tested by showing sample videos of the system's output to the participants and giving them the tool to try it themselves. The aim of the testing was to measure the usability of the tool by using the SUS Test and to measure the overall satisfaction of the users with the quality of the output. The results obtained from the testing indicate that 66.7% of the participants have found that adding the facial expressions and body animations helped them to concentrate better with what the character was saying. In addition to that, the score of the SUS Test was 81.1 which is equivalent to excellent. That means that the tool can be used by the user in an effective and an efficient way.

As part of extending our tool, we plan to add different facial expressions and different body animations to the same audio as to match exactly what the teacher is saying at a specific moment. This will make the matching of the facial expressions and the body animations to the character's speech more accurate.

Furthermore, adding eye contact to the characters can be added. Allowing the users to change the audio, facial emotions and body animations during run time can also be added to the system. This will give the users the possibility of trying different combinations together quickly without having to start from the beginning each time.

Various background scenes can also be provided by the tool and the user can have the option to choose one of these scenes. A background scene can help in making the whole experience more realistic as the students can be more immersed and help provide the feeling of being inside a classroom.

References

1. Afifi, B.M., El Bolock, A., Alaa, M., Herbert, C., Abdennadher, S.: VRacter: investigating character-based avatar preference in education. In: De La Prieta, F., et al. (eds.) PAAMS 2020. CCIS, vol. 1233, pp. 71–82. Springer, Cham (2020). https://doi.org/10.1007/978-3-030-51999-5_6
2. Alhalabi, W.: Virtual reality systems enhance students' achievements in engineering education. Behav. Inf. Technol. **35**, 1–7 (2016). https://doi.org/10.1080/0144929X.2016.1212931
3. Brooke, J.: SUS: a retrospective. J. Usabil. Stud. **8**, 29–40 (2013)

4. Cai, Y., Chiew, R., Nay, Z., Indhumathi, C., Huang, L.: Design and development of VR learning environments for children with ASD. Interact. Learn. Environ. **25**, 1–12 (2017). https://doi.org/10.1080/10494820.2017.1282877

5. Coppola, N., Hiltz, S., Rotter, N.: Becoming a virtual professor: pedagogical roles and ALN, p. 10 p. (2001). https://doi.org/10.1109/HICSS.2001.926183

6. Darwin, C.: The expression of the emotions in man and animals (1872). https://doi.org/10.1037/10001-000

7. Doswell, J.: Building the virtual reality instructor (2004). https://doi.org/10.1145/1186107.1186128

8. Du, S., Tao, Y., Martinez, A.: Compound facial expressions of emotion. Proc. Natl. Acad. Sci. U.S.A. **111**, E1454–E1462 (2014). https://doi.org/10.1073/pnas.1322355111

9. Ekman, P.: Darwin, deception, and facial expression. Ann. New York Acad. Sci. **1000**, 205–221 (2004). https://doi.org/10.1196/annals.1280.010

10. Elgewely, M., Nadim, W., ElKassed, A., Yehiah, M., Talaat, M., Abdennadher, S.: Immersive construction detailing education: building information modeling (bim)-based virtual reality (VR). Open House Int. **ahead-of-print** (2021). https://doi.org/10.1108/OHI-02-2021-0032

11. Faltaous, S., el Bolock, A., Talaat, M., Abdennadher, S., Schneegaß, S.: Virtual reality for cultural competences, pp. 457–461 (2018). https://doi.org/10.1145/3282894.3289739

12. Haneef, M., Faisal, M.A., Alvi, A.K., Zulfiqar, M.: The role of non verbal communication in teaching practice. Sci. Int. (Lahore) **26**, 513–517 (2014)

13. Hu-Au, E., Lee, J.: Virtual reality in education: a tool for learning in the experience age. Int. J. Innov. Educ. **4**, 215–226 (2018). https://doi.org/10.1504/IJIIE.2017.10012691

14. Isabwe, G.M.N., Moxnes, M., Ristesund, M., Woodgate, D.: Children's interactions within a virtual reality environment for learning chemistry. In: Andre, T. (ed.) AHFE 2017. AISC, vol. 596, pp. 221–233. Springer, Cham (2018). https://doi.org/10.1007/978-3-319-60018-5_22

15. Ke, F., Im, T.: Virtual-reality-based social interaction training for children with high-functioning autism. J. Educ. Res. **106**, 441–461 (2013). https://doi.org/10.1080/00220671.2013.832999

16. Lee, H., Shvetsova, O.: The impact of VR application on student's competency development: a comparative study of regular and VR engineering classes with similar competency scopes. Sustainability **11**, 2221 (2019). https://doi.org/10.3390/su11082221

17. Lee, M., Spryszynski, A., Nersesian, E.: Personalizing VR educational tools for English language learners (2019)

18. Limniou, M., Roberts, D., Papadopoulos, N.: Full immersive virtual environment CAVETM in chemistry education. Comput. Educ. **51**, 584 (2008). https://doi.org/10.1016/j.compedu.2007.06.014

19. Lin, M.: A study on the effect of virtual reality 3D exploratory education on students' creativity and leadership. EURASIA J. Math. Sci. Technol. Educ. **13**, 3151–3161 (2017). https://doi.org/10.12973/eurasia.2017.00709a

20. Parsons, S., Cobb, S.: State-of-the-art of virtual reality technologies for children on the autism spectrum. Eur. J. Spec. Needs Educ. **26**, 355–366 (2011). https://doi.org/10.1080/08856257.2011.593831

21. Raikwar, A., et al.: CubeVR: digital affordances for architecture undergraduate education using virtual reality, pp. 1623–1626 (2019). https://doi.org/10.1109/VR.2019.8798115

22. Rodríguez, C.: Virtual teaching in postgraduate programmes: the importance of social collaboration in virtual communities. Proc. - Soc. Behav. Sci. **237**, 1430–1438 (2017). https://doi.org/10.1016/j.sbspro.2017.02.223
23. Safwat, S., El Bolock, A., Alaa, M., Faltaous, S., Schneegass, S., Abdennadher, S.: The effect of student-lecturer cultural differences on engagement in learning environments - a pilot study. In: De La Prieta, F., et al. (eds.) PAAMS 2020. CCIS, vol. 1233, pp. 118–128. Springer, Cham (2020). https://doi.org/10.1007/978-3-030-51999-5_10
24. Schofield, J., Davidson, A.: The impact of internet use on relationships between teachers and students. Mind Cult. Act. **10**, 62–79 (2003). https://doi.org/10.1207/S15327884MCA1001_06
25. Theonas, G., Hobbs, D., Rigas, D.: Employing virtual lecturers' facial expressions in virtual educational environments. IJVR **7**, 31–44 (2008)
26. Wentzel, K.: Students' relationships with teachers as motivational contexts. In: Handbook of Motivation at School, pp. 301–322 (2009)

Vaxera: An Empathetic Chatbot
for COVID-19 Vaccination

Walid El Hefny[1(✉)], Mohamad Elshimy[1], Alia El Bolock[2],
and Slim Abdennadher[2]

[1] German University in Cairo, Cairo, Egypt
`walid.elhifny@guc.edu.eg`, `mohamad.elshimy@student.guc.edu.eg`
[2] German International University, Cairo, Egypt
`{alia.elbolock,slim.abdennadher}@giu-uni.de`

Abstract. Rumors about the COVID-19 vaccines are spreading rapidly
on social media platforms, questioning their intentions and efficiency.
Currently, chatbots are used to combat the risk of misinformation amplification during the pandemic. They provide users with information from
trusted and reliable sources. However, most of the current COVID-19
chatbots are non-personalized and do not focus on the vaccination process, rather they focus on answering general questions and performing
symptom checking. In this paper, an empathetic chatbot named "Vaxera" was developed to provide users with accurate and up-to-date information about COVID-19 and its vaccines specifically. Vaxera provides
users with information regarding COVID-19 frequently asked questions,
advice and precautions, available vaccines, rumors and myths, and travel
regulations. Additionally, it clears the circulating misconceptions about
the vaccines and motivates the users on social media platforms to get
vaccinated in a friendly manner. It tries to build a bond with the users
through empathy and humor, so users will not feel forced. The results
showed positive feedback from the participants who found the chatbot
friendly and informative, as it corrected multiple rumors they believed.
Moreover, a significant increase in the participants' intentions to get vaccinated was observed after interacting with the chatbot.

Keywords: Conversational agents · Chatbots · Healthcare ·
COVID-19 · Coronavirus · Character computing

1 Introduction

Nowadays, COVID-19 has become one of the most searched topics globally [16].
People are searching for information regarding the virus and its vaccines on the
web. However, some people refuse to take the vaccines due to the spread of
rumors and false information on social media platforms. The results of a study
showed that the percentage of people planning to vaccinate decreased, while
the percentage of people refusing to vaccinate increased [26]. It was found that
the decline in vaccination was due to the exposure to misinformation regarding

A. González-Briones et al. (Eds.): PAAMS Workshops 2022, CCIS 1678, pp. 157–168, 2022.
https://doi.org/10.1007/978-3-031-18697-4_13

the vaccines, and concerns over the vaccines' safety [26]. The rapid spread of false information could harm people, especially during a pandemic. Therefore, chatbots were used to combat the risk of misinformation amplification during the COVID-19 pandemic by providing accurate medical information, promoting health behaviors, and decreasing the psychological damage caused by fear and isolation [21].

Chatbots are software applications that simulate conversations with humans in an intelligent way [23]. They use modern technologies such as natural language processing and machine learning to understand the users' input and respond accordingly [18]. Moreover, they are used in multiple domains such as education and healthcare where they answer inquiries without letting the users navigate through numerous pages to find the required information. Users can easily retrieve information about any product, helping them in their decision-making process [13]. Additionally, chatbots are used to support or replace the human factor, especially in responding to repetitive questions due to their constant availability. For several years, healthcare institutions have been developing a variety of chatbots to provide medical information or screen patients and redirect them to in-person appointments or phone call support [16].

Currently, most healthcare chatbots provide an artificial conversation and lack human empathy [4]. They do not take into consideration the users' preferences and needs [12]. Therefore, it was proposed to build personalized and adaptive chatbots to satisfy their needs and prevent any biases towards particular user groups [12]. The quality of interaction is influenced by multiple factors such as affect and personality [15], as advocated by Affective [24] and Personality Computing [27]. However, they are not the only factors that affect the user's behavior. All variable state (affect, cognition, well-being, etc.) and stable trait (personality, sociocultural embeddings, beliefs, etc.) markers of an individual, as well as the situation should be considered. A person's character is constituted by these factors [7,15], and any type of computation that includes the human character within its context falls under the inter-disciplinary field of Character Computing [3].

A framework was proposed in [8] for building character-based chatbots. It provides a flexible way for creating and customizing chatbot characters for any domain. Moreover, it was used to build personalized chatbots for different domains such as academic courses management [9], university admission [11], and COVID-19 [9,10]. Current personalized COVID-19 chatbots do not offer a vaccination feature, as they only support displaying the number of cases per country, answering frequently asked questions, providing advice and precautions, and performing symptoms checking [9,10,16]. Therefore, we propose building a character-based chatbot that provides users with accurate information regarding the COVID-19 vaccines. The chatbot will answer questions regarding the vaccines in an empathetic manner to clear the misconceptions circulating them. The main goal is to motivate the users to get vaccinated and boosted on a regular basis. Additionally, we investigate how our chatbot overcomes some of the limitations and weaknesses of healthcare and COVID-19 chatbots [4,16].

The structure of this paper is as follows: Sect. 2 presents the related work. Section 3 describes the chatbot design, features, and implementation. Moreover, Sect. 4 discusses our evaluation, results, and discussion. Finally, Sect. 5 concludes the paper and presents future work.

2 Related Work

A study was conducted to evaluate the use of chatbots during the COVID-19 pandemic [21]. It was mentioned that the main challenge posed by the pandemic is the fast spread of false information. People are drifted away from the correct precautions to be performed during the pandemic, so to avoid boosting false information, we need to retrieve the information from trusted and reliable sources [2]. Chatbots can provide users with information from verified healthcare sources in short sentences, which is easier to follow compared to long paragraphs displayed by search engines. This is important as rumors and disinformation spread online faster than correct information [28]. Moreover, since chatbots are constantly available, they can respond to users at any time with up-to-date information sourced from verified websites, unlike human agents who can not handle simultaneous queries nor be updated with the latest information immediately [21]. Therefore, COVID-19 chatbots answering questions from verified sources are needed to combat the risk of misinformation amplification.

The authors in [16] evaluated 24 COVID-19 chatbots against 12 heuristics. Some of the heuristics were about visibility, dealing with input errors, flexibility, and whether the chatbot accomplished its goal or not. Some chatbots failed to respond when the users typed the queries manually instead of using the quick replies provided by the chatbot, which frustrated them [16]. Moreover, almost all chatbots did not give the user the control or freedom to change the flow of the conversation. Additionally, 50% of the evaluated chatbots had either a persistent menu or help options. Therefore, our proposed chatbot will support external user input by typing the desired question, a persistent menu to give the users a quick overview of the main features provided by the chatbot, and quick replies to guide the users when the chatbot asks them a question.

A COVID-19 chatbot was introduced in [1] to answer questions regarding the different vaccines. The study aimed to determine whether interacting with a COVID-19 vaccination chatbot will affect their decision in taking the vaccine or not. One of the chatbot's drawbacks was not allowing the users to type questions, rather they had to select from a pool of 51 questions. Moreover, the chatbot responses contained the resources it got the information from. The results showed that the participants who had a positive impact on the vaccines significantly increased by 37%, while those who had negative impact decreased by 20% [1]. As a result, our chatbot will provide extra reading material for the users from verified sources, and it will motivate the users to get vaccinated and boosted.

The weaknesses of healthcare chatbots were identified by the authors in [4] including the artificial conversation, lack of human empathy, and the failure to understand complex conversations. Multiple efforts were made to overcome them by building personalized chatbots. A character-based COVID-19 chatbot was designed to display the number of cases per country, provide advice and precautions, answer frequently asked questions, and perform symptoms checking [9,10]. The chatbot had two characters "Formal and Informal" which have opposing characteristics and traits. According to the selected chatbot character, the information provided by the chatbot was personalized. However, the chatbot did not answer questions regarding the vaccines. Therefore, we included vaccines questions and answers in our chatbot.

3 Chatbot Design

We designed a personalized COVID-19 chatbot named "Vaxera" to answer questions related to the vaccines and vaccination process per country. Vaxera was equipped with a sufficient pool of data to be able to provide people with the required information. Upon using the chatbot for the first time, the user will be prompted to choose their country as regulations and processes differ from one country to another. Afterward, the user will be able to retrieve the requested vaccination information based on the selected country.

3.1 Features and Functionalities

Vaxera's large knowledge base enables it to answer most of the users' inquiries. The COVID-19 information provided by the system includes available vaccines and their details, frequently asked questions, advice and precautions, common rumors and myths, vaccine registration process, and travel regulations. Moreover, our chatbot aims to correct the rumors by providing facts from reliable sources such as the World Health Organization (WHO), Centers for Disease Control and Prevention (CDC), and official government websites.

Vaxera can personalize the responses depending on the user's country. It is useful for users who travel from one country to another, so they can know the regulations of their destination country. Additionally, it keeps track of the conversation context which overcomes the failure to maintain the conversation context weakness stated in the literature. For example, if the user asked "What is the Pfizer-BioNTech vaccine type?", they do not need to mention its name again if they want to ask follow-up questions. They can type "How many doses does it require?" without mentioning the vaccine's name. Furthermore, it will try to motivate the users to take the vaccine by redirecting them to the vaccination registration website, and it will ask them whether they registered or not. If they did not register, the chatbot will state the drawbacks of getting infected without being vaccinated as an attempt to influence their decision. It will also ask them about the reasons behind their decision, and it will try to provide clarifications regarding their concerns as shown in Fig. 1. Finally, the chatbot supports small talk to provide a human-like feeling to the users by answering social queries such as "Hello", "Goodbye", and "Thank you".

Fig. 1. A sample dialogue between a user and Vaxera.

3.2 Social Cues

Researchers have demonstrated that people unwittingly apply social expectations while dealing with technology that employs natural language [22]. These
expectations contribute significantly to determining the users' contentment and
chatbot adoption [14]. As a result, it is critical to develop chatbots with human-
like conversational skills. It can be accomplished by including social cues into the
chatbot design [5]. Moreover, chatbot humanness is determined by verbal and
visual social cues. We designed an empathetic chatbot character that uses verbal
and visual social cues to provide a human-like feeling to the users. Verbal social
cues are conversational standards represented by chatbots. The small talk functionality is an example as it enables the chatbot to respond to social and personal
messages, resulting in human-like conversations that meet the emotional requirements of users. It replies to user inputs like "You're great" and "I'm upset". Users
regularly leave these comments, and replying to them encourages the users to
communicate more with the chatbot and grow their interest in the technology
[6]. Consequently, small talk functionality was added to Vaxera to answer social
messages that are not related to the vaccination process, thus eliminating the
artificial conversation and lack of human empathy weaknesses. The small talk
responses were extracted from the "EmpatheticDialogues" dataset to answer
the users' social messages in an empathetic manner [25]. It was proven in [19]
that extracting sentences from personality-tagged datasets delivers the intended
chatbot personality to the users. Meanwhile, visual social cues are graphical char-

acteristics that indicate human behavior. Examples of these features are names, avatars, and emojis. Accordingly, our chatbot was given a name and uses emojis and images (static and animated) in its responses as shown in Fig. 2.

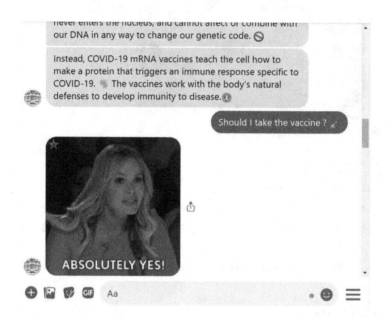

Fig. 2. Vaxera responding using emojis and animated images.

Moreover, it is critical to recognize that while social cues might increase the user's satisfaction level, they can also elicit negative feedback. Users are much more satisfied when a chatbot's social cues are appropriate and relevant to the chatbot's intended use. Additionally, quick replies were implemented which are suggestions that appear to the users as replies instead of typing. They assist the users when they feel lost or do not know what to say when the chatbot sends a message. A persistent menu was added to provide shortcuts to the most frequently used chatbot features. We decided to create one character as a start to perform early/initial testing before implementing additional characters, as we follow an agile model for the system development life cycle. This will help us determine the chatbot limitations and weaknesses before adding new characters and features.

3.3 Chatbot Implementation

Vaxera was built using the framework proposed in [8] for building character-based chatbots. Our chatbot consists of four main components which are the messaging application, chatbot engine, web server, and database. The messaging application acts as the conversational user interface where it takes inputs from the users and displays outputs to them. Moreover, the chatbot engine analyzes the users' input. It consists of entity extraction and intent matching. Entities are keywords extracted from user messages such as numbers, dates, and cities. Meanwhile, the intention of a user for one conversational turn is called intent. If the user wants to greet the chatbot, they can say "Hello", "Hi", or "Good evening", which will be matched to the greetings intent that contains training phrases similar to these messages. The chatbot engine extracts the entities present in a user message and matches it to an intent, so the chatbot will know the context of the message. The extracted entities are then passed to the web server to retrieve a personalized response from the database based on the matched intent.

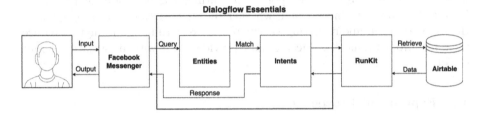

Fig. 3. An overview of the chatbot architecture.

An overview of the technologies used to implement the chatbot is shown in Fig. 3. Facebook Messenger was chosen as the messaging application because it was one of the early platforms to adopt chatbot technology. Moreover, it provides developers with a variety of application programming interfaces (APIs) and libraries to ease the process of chatbot deployment. Also, since we are combating the spread of false information on social media, Facebook is one of the leading social media platforms with a huge user base. Therefore, our chatbot can correct the misconceptions related to the vaccines which are spreading on Facebook by non-expert users and fake pages. After receiving a message from the user, Facebook Messenger will send the message to the chatbot engine. We used Dialogflow Essentials by Google to build the chatbot engine. It is a non-programming chatbot development tool that provides a graphical user interface for developers to create entities and intents without any programming skills. It provides flexibility and easy scaling to add new features instantly. We identified the possible user questions to create intents and determined the required entities that will be extracted from the user messages. Afterward, the identified questions and all of their possible formats were mapped into intents. Additionally, follow-up intents were used to maintain the conversation context by predicting the user's upcoming questions. Flow charts were used to predict the possible direction of a conversation. Dialogflow Essentials will extract the entities in a user query and send their values along with the matched intent to the web server to retrieve the personalized response. Our back-end code is deployed on RunKit which provides a sandboxed JavaScript environment for hosting our code. Moreover, it processes the received entities and matched intent from the chatbot engine, and retrieves a customized response from the database accordingly. The user information and personalized responses are stored in Airtable which is a relational cloud-based database.

4 Experimental Design

An initial study was conducted to allow users to evaluate the different aspects of Vaxera before implementing additional characters and other features such as motivating the users to get boosted. It is beneficial as they will provide feedback regarding their experience to identify points of strengths and weaknesses. Afterward, we will use the identified points to continue the development process of Vaxera. Moreover, we investigated whether the chatbot can affect or emphasize the users' decision about getting vaccinated, correct rumors and myths, reduce their fear from taking the vaccine, and provide them with information about COVID-19 in general.

4.1 Experiment Procedure

We invited 40 university students (57.5% males and 42.5% females) aged from 18 to 24 years (M = 21.43, SD = 1.36). We had 3 participants (7.5%) who got vaccinated, while 37 participants (92.5%) did not take the vaccine at the time of the experiment. The participants were asked to fill the pre-use questionnaire regarding their opinion on the vaccination, and then they were told to interact with the chatbot and ask questions regarding COVID-19 and its vaccines. After interacting with the chatbot, they were asked to fill out the post-use questionnaire. The post-use questionnaire evaluated the overall chatbot usability using the System Usability Scale (SUS) and the Chatbot Usability Questionnaire (CUQ), and their attitude towards the vaccination after using the chatbot.

The pre-use questionnaire contained two questions on a scale from 1 to 10 regarding their intention on getting vaccinated, and whether they are afraid to get vaccinated or not. Moreover, they were asked if they will get vaccinated if they knew that the vaccines are 100% safe or not. On the other hand, the post-use questionnaire contained the SUS survey which is a widely used 10-item scale that tests a system's usability and learnability [20]. It consists of 10 questions with five response options from strongly agree to strongly disagree. Moreover, the SUS score is calculated out of 100. Additionally, the post-use questionnaire contained the CUQ survey as the SUS is not enough to evaluate all aspects of a chatbot interface [17]. It evaluates seven different aspects, which are personality, onboarding, navigation, understanding, responses, error handling, and intelligence of a chatbot. It consists of 16 questions with five response options from strongly agree to strongly disagree, and the score is calculated out of 100. Finally, the two pre-use questionnaire questions were asked again, as well as, questions on a scale from 1 to 10 regarding the trustworthiness and information delivery of the chatbot, and whether it affected their vaccination decision or not.

4.2   Results and Discussion

The results of the pre-use and post-use questionnaires are shown in Table 1. Originally, the participants had neutral feelings about the vaccination. However, after using the chatbot, the participants were encouraged to get vaccinated, and most of them were no longer afraid. Accordingly, using Vaxera decreased the participants' fears about taking the vaccine. Moreover, the chatbot performed well in the SUS (M = 93.3, SD = 5.7) as shown in Fig. 4 and the CUQ (M = 93.8, SD = 6.51) as shown in Fig. 5. According to the literature, the acceptance value is 71.1, and a score of 80.3 or higher puts the system in the "A" category. After analyzing the scores of the individual SUS and CUQ questions, it was found that the participants praised the chatbot's ease of use. At the beginning of the conversation, Vaxera presented itself adequately, and briefly mentioned its purpose in a friendly and welcoming manner. Additionally, the participants did not find the interaction complex, and they did not believe they needed technical assistance or orientation on using it. The participants believed that other users will adjust to using it quickly. Moreover, the chatbot understood most of their questions, but not all, and the participants did not feel that the chatbot responses were robotic or monotonic due to the responses personalization and the use of emojis and GIFs. The trustworthiness and information delivery of the chatbot results were high, meaning that the participants trusted the chatbot responses (M = 9.68, SD = 0.69) and its rumors correction feature (M = 9.63, SD = 0.66), and found the answers sufficient to their questions (M = 9.93, SD = 0.27). Finally, the participants were convinced that the chatbot affected their decision in getting vaccinated (M = 8.68, SD = 1.27). Although this study provided positive results, some participants rejected the idea of getting vaccinated. In the pre-use survey, we asked the participants if they knew that the vaccines are 100% safe, will they take it?. Some participants stated that they will not take it even if it is 100% safe. Accordingly, our chatbot was not able to change all participants' minds, but it increased the users' intentions on getting vaccinated significantly.

Table 1. The pre-use and post-use questionnaires results.

Question	Pre-use		Post-use	
	Mean	SD	Mean	SD
I want to take the COVID-19 vaccine	6.2	3.21	8.78	1.4
I am afraid of getting vaccinated	5.6	3.98	2.53	1.81
I trusted the information provided by the chatbot	–		9.68	0.69
The chatbot was informative about COVID-19 and its vaccines	–		9.93	0.27
The chatbot cleared the rumors I heard regarding the vaccines	–		9.63	0.66
The chatbot affected my decision in getting vaccinated	–		8.68	1.27
System Usability Scale (SUS)/100	–		93.3	5.7
Chatbot Usability Questionnaire (CUQ)/100	–		93.8	6.51
	Yes		No	
If you know that the vaccine is 100% safe, will you take it?	94.6%		3.4%	

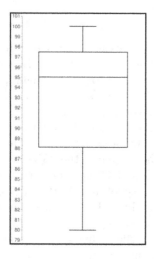

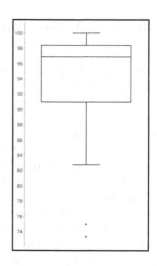

Fig. 4. The SUS scores boxplot.   **Fig. 5.** The CUQ scores boxplot.

5   Conclusion and Future Work

Current COVID-19 chatbots answer frequently asked questions and perform symptom checking. However, there are only a few non-personalized COVID-19 chatbots that focus on the vaccination process. Therefore, we proposed a character-based chatbot named "Vaxera" to answer inquiries related to COVID-19 generally and the vaccine specifically in an empathetic manner. We added social cues to provide a human-like interaction with the users to motivate them to take the vaccine. Moreover, we invited 40 participants to evaluate the chatbot. A pre-use and post-use questionnaires were given to the participants. We used the SUS and CUQ surveys to evaluate the overall usability of the chatbot. Vaxera performed well in the SUS (M = 93.3, SD = 5.7) and the CUQ (M = 93.8, SD = 6.51). The participants were satisfied with the chatbot responses and found it informative, and perceived it as a useful tool. In the beginning, the participants had neutral feelings about getting vaccinated. However, the chatbot had an impact on their decision and they were motivated to take the vaccine after Vaxera corrected the rumors they knew about the vaccines. However, some limitations were faced during the study. The participants did not test all of the chatbot features as they had specific questions in mind. A graphical user interface provides a finite amount of options that are visible to the users, compared to a conversational user interface with an infinite amount of combinations that can be tested. Moreover, we had a small and non-diverse sample size as most of them are university students from the same major and age group.

We implemented an empathetic chatbot character as a start to evaluate our chatbot purpose and goals. However, future work should focus on adding more characters and allowing the users to modify the inner traits of each character.

It is feasible since Vaxera is built using the proposed framework in [8] which allows for full chatbot character customization. Users can create or select the chatbot character they want to interact with. Moreover, we can allow the chatbot character to adapt to the users based on their current affective state or mood. It will be useful to deliver the information in a way that suits the user without forcing them towards a particular direction using a specific tone. Additionally, multiple languages can be added to reach more people on social media platforms who do not understand English. Finally, speech support can be added instead of the basic text interface. The challenge will be in customizing the chatbot's tone of voice, as it should not be monotonic.

References

1. Altay, S., Hacquin, A.S., Chevallier, C., Mercier, H.: Information delivered by a chatbot has a positive impact on COVID-19 vaccines attitudes and intentions. J. Exp. Psychol.: Appl. (2021)
2. Blog, B.: COVID-19: how do we encourage the right behaviours during an epidemic (2020)
3. Bolock, A.E., Abdelrahman, Y., Abdennadher, S. (eds.): Character Computing. Human Computer Interaction Series, Springer, Cham (2020). https://doi.org/10.1007/978-3-030-15954-2
4. Cameron, G., et al.: Best practices for designing chatbots in mental healthcare- a case study on iHelpr. In: Proceedings of the 32nd International BCS Human Computer Interaction Conference, vol. 32, pp. 1–5 (2018)
5. Candello, H., Pinhanez, C., Figueiredo, F.: Typefaces and the perception of humanness in natural language chatbots. In: Proceedings of the 2017 CHI Conference on Human Factors in Computing Systems, pp. 3476–3487 (2017)
6. Dutta, D.: Developing an intelligent chat-bot tool to assist high school students for learning general knowledge subjects. Technical report, Georgia Institute of Technology (2017)
7. El Bolock, A.: What is character computing? In: El Bolock, A., Abdelrahman, Y., Abdennadher, S. (eds.) Character Computing. HIS, pp. 1–16. Springer, Cham (2020). https://doi.org/10.1007/978-3-030-15954-2_1
8. El Hefny, W., El Bolock, A., Herbert, C., Abdennadher, S.: Towards a generic framework for character-based chatbots. In: De La Prieta, F., et al. (eds.) PAAMS 2020. CCIS, vol. 1233, pp. 95–107. Springer, Cham (2020). https://doi.org/10.1007/978-3-030-51999-5_8
9. El Hefny, W., El Bolock, A., Herbert, C., Abdennadher, S.: Applying the character-based chatbots generation framework in education and healthcare. In: Proceedings of the 9th International Conference on Human-Agent Interaction, pp. 121–129 (2021)
10. El Hefny, W., El Bolock, A., Herbert, C., Abdennadher, S.: Chase away the virus: a character-based chatbot for COVID-19. In: 2021 IEEE 9th International Conference on Serious Games and Applications for Health (SeGAH), pp. 1–8. IEEE (2021)
11. El Hefny, W., Mansy, Y., Abdallah, M., Abdennadher, S.: Jooka: a bilingual chatbot for university admission. In: Rocha, Á., Adeli, H., Dzemyda, G., Moreira, F., Ramalho Correia, A.M. (eds.) WorldCIST 2021. AISC, vol. 1367, pp. 671–681. Springer, Cham (2021). https://doi.org/10.1007/978-3-030-72660-7_64

12. Følstad, A., Brandtzæg, P.B.: Chatbots and the new world of HCI. Interactions **24**(4), 38–42 (2017)
13. Ghose, S., Barua, J.J.: Toward the implementation of a topic specific dialogue based natural language chatbot as an undergraduate advisor. In: 2013 International Conference on Informatics, Electronics and Vision (ICIEV), pp. 1–5. IEEE (2013)
14. Gnewuch, U., Morana, S., Adam, M.T., Maedche, A.: Faster is not always better: understanding the effect of dynamic response delays in human-chatbot interaction. In: Frank, U. (ed.) 26th European Conference on Information Systems: Beyond Digitization-Facets of Socio-Technical Change, ECIS 2018, Portsmouth, UK, 23–28 June 2018, p. 143975 (2018)
15. Herbert, C.: An experimental-psychological approach for the development of character computing. In: El Bolock, A., Abdelrahman, Y., Abdennadher, S. (eds.) Character Computing. HIS, pp. 17–38. Springer, Cham (2020). https://doi.org/10.1007/978-3-030-15954-2_2
16. Höhn, S., Bongard-Blanchy, K.: Heuristic evaluation of COVID-19 chatbots. In: Følstad, A. (ed.) CONVERSATIONS 2020. LNCS, vol. 12604, pp. 131–144. Springer, Cham (2021). https://doi.org/10.1007/978-3-030-68288-0_9
17. Holmes, S., Moorhead, A., Bond, R., Zheng, H., Coates, V., McTear, M.: Usability testing of a healthcare chatbot: can we use conventional methods to assess conversational user interfaces? In: Proceedings of the 31st European Conference on Cognitive Ergonomics, pp. 207–214 (2019)
18. Khan, R., Das, A.: Introduction to chatbots. In: Khan, R., Das, A. (eds.) Build Better Chatbots, pp. 1–11. Springer, Berkeley (2018). https://doi.org/10.1007/978-1-4842-3111-1_1
19. Kowatsch, T., Nißen, M., Rüegger, D., Stieger, M., Flückiger, C., Allemand, M., von Wangenheim, F.: The impact of interpersonal closeness cues in text-based healthcare chatbots on attachment bond and the desire to continue interacting: an experimental design (2018)
20. Lewis, J.R., Sauro, J.: The factor structure of the system usability scale. In: Kurosu, M. (ed.) HCD 2009. LNCS, vol. 5619, pp. 94–103. Springer, Heidelberg (2009). https://doi.org/10.1007/978-3-642-02806-9_12
21. Miner, A.S., Laranjo, L., Kocaballi, A.B.: Chatbots in the fight against the COVID-19 pandemic. NPJ Digit. Med. **3**(1), 1–4 (2020)
22. Nass, C., Moon, Y.: Machines and mindlessness: social responses to computers. J. Soc. Issues **56**(1), 81–103 (2000)
23. Nimavat, K., Champaneria, T.: Chatbots: an overview types, architecture, tools and future possibilities. IJSRD-Int. J. Sci. Res. Dev **5**(7), 1019–1024 (2017)
24. Picard, R.W., Picard, R.: Affective computing, vol. 252. MIT Press, Cambridge (1997). EEG-detected olfactory imagery to reveal covert consciousness in minimally conscious state. Brain Injury **29**(13–14), 1729–1735
25. Rashkin, H., Smith, E.M., Li, M., Boureau, Y.L.: Towards empathetic open-domain conversation models: A new benchmark and dataset. arXiv preprint arXiv:1811.00207 (2018)
26. Robinson, E., Jones, A., Daly, M.: International estimates of intended uptake and refusal of COVID-19 vaccines: a rapid systematic review and meta-analysis of large nationally representative samples. Vaccine **39**(15), 2024–2034 (2021)
27. Vinciarelli, A., Mohammadi, G.: A survey of personality computing. IEEE Trans. Affect. Comput. **5**(3), 273–291 (2014)
28. Vosoughi, S., Roy, D., Aral, S.: The spread of true and false news online. Science **359**(6380), 1146–1151 (2018)

Personalized Avatars Without Agentic Interaction: Do They Promote Learning Performance and Sense of Self in a Teaching Context? A Pilot Study

Cornelia Herbert[(⊠)] [iD] and Joanna Daria Dołżycka[iD]

Department of Applied Emotion and Motivation Psychology, Institute of Psychology and
Education, Ulm University, 89081 Ulm, Germany
`cornelia.herbert@uni-ulm.de`

Abstract. Virtual agents are becoming promising opportunities for augmenting
human-human interaction in the analog world in a diversity of domains such as
health care or education. This experimental study explores the impact of virtual
self- and virtual other presence on e-learning performance in a virtual classroom
setting. In addition, the relevance of virtual teachers is explored. The classroom
setting is designed to simulate to study either alone with one's self-representative
avatar or together with virtual classmates. Participants could take part in an online
course thought by a virtual teacher. First results show that the mere representation
of the virtual Self or of virtual Others by static avatars without any functionality of
the avatars to serve as interactive agents has no differential impact on the learner's
immediate learning performance, even when the avatars representing the Self are
self-chosen by the participants. However, the online course taught by a humanoid
avatar as virtual teacher was positively related with the learning performance. This
suggests that embodying teachers as virtual educators in online learning could help
improve the learner's cognitive performance with or without virtual presence of
one's Self or peers.

Keywords: Agent-based human interaction · Sense of self · Social presence ·
Virtual self · Psychology · Education · Embodiment · Experimental
manipulation · Character computing

1   Introduction

Virtual agents have conquered the internet and are supporting human service and human-
human interaction in the analog world, be it at public service places or in more private
or academic contexts such as counseling, health care or education including teaching at schools or at universities. Theoretically, there is no single definition of virtual
agents or of the characteristics determining them. Psychologically, however, it makes
sense to describe and categorize virtual agents along some key dimensions such as
the *abstractness* and *(computational) functionality* of the agent. These two dimensions

© The Author(s), under exclusive license to Springer Nature Switzerland AG 2022
A. González-Briones et al. (Eds.): PAAMS Workshops 2022, CCIS 1678, pp. 169–180, 2022.
https://doi.org/10.1007/978-3-031-18697-4_14

might influence the user's experience, behavior, and the user's interaction with the agent significantly [1]. *Abstractness* of the agent can vary along the degree of *humanness* [2], whereas *(computational) functionality* describes the degree of interaction, i.e., the degree or extent to which for the user, the interaction with the agent mimics real human-human interaction or just follows e.g., scripted rules to provide automated service or guidance (for an overview [1]). Both dimensions (*abstractness* and *functionality*) might not be independent from each other. Moreover, each of these two dimensions (*abstractness* and *functionality*) might comprise further subcategories and taxonomies such as *humanness* as proposed by [3]. This may include the distinction between agent and avatars [4] that describes the degree of *computational functionality* (an avatar being a mere representation of a virtual human vs. an agent having flexibility and control of the interaction with the user as a computer program), for an overview [5].

1.1 Aim of the Present Study

The present study focuses particularly on the first of the two dimensions *(abstractness)*. Specifically, the study explores the mere impact of the virtual self- and virtual social presence realized by avatars with *low functionality* on the learner's e-learning performance in a virtual classroom setting. In addition, the virtual presence of humanoid teachers is explored. The virtual classroom was designed to study either alone with one's self-representative avatar or together with virtual others, or with both, virtual self- and virtual others or without the presence of any visual avatar (control condition). All participants took part in an e-learning course whose content was explained by a humanoid avatar as teacher. This study design allows to investigate the following major research questions. First, will the mere visual presence of avatars considered to represent the Self or Others positively improve the learner's performance compared to compared to the experimental conditions including no avatar presence? Second, will the effects differ depending on whether the avatar representing the Self is preselected and predefined by the experimental design or self-chosen by the participants? In virtual reality, people often do not chose a visual character that resembles their actual Self, but instead choose a character that resembles the ideal Self (for an overview [1]). Allowing the participants to study in the online course with avatars of own choice or with avatars preselected by the experimental design aims to shed further light on this question and especially its impact on the learner's performance. Third, will the mere visual presence of avatars representing other classmates significantly affect the individual learner's learning performance? Previous studies suggest, that this seems to hold true especially when the avatars show certain emotional traits relevant for the learning context such as taking over the role of a caring co-learner or the role-model (mastery model for novice learners), see [1]. Therefore, the present study additionally explores whether the mere presence of avatars representing the peer learners will facilitate the participants' learning performance even without assigning specific peer-roles to the avatars, and without any interaction between own and other avatars taking place. Exploring this question in the absence of any virtual interaction between self-avatar and other-avatar characters will add to a better understanding of the role the user's perception of virtual others plays in virtual scenarios without confounding the user's perception by factors evoked by the social interaction with the avatar (i.e., low vs. high *(computational) functionality*). To this end, akin to the own avatar condition, the visual presence of other avatars is varied in terms of the degree of *abstractness* (presence of visual avatar vs. presence of verbal labels for others avatars only vs. no presence of other avatars, see Fig. 1). Fourth, the online course was thought by a virtual teacher to explore the relevance of the teacher's role in online education. By choosing this study design (for an overview see Fig. 1), potential interactions between virtual self-presence and virtual other-presence (including peers and teacher) on learning performance and learner's experience can be explored.

2 Methods

2.1 Participants, Procedure, Study Design and Methods

The study was conducted as an online survey study by the Department of Applied Emotion and Motivation Psychology, Ulm University. Participants were recruited via local email lists, SurveyCircle (SurveyCircle, 2022), and Prolific (https://www.prolific.co/; [7]). SurveyCircle and Prolific are international platforms for participants interested in taking part in online scientific studies. Participants could take part in the study at the age of 18 years and older. Given that the study was provided in English language, further inclusion criteria of study participation were high proficiency of the English language or being a native speaker of English. The participants should not have any history of a disorder affecting the participant's understanding of the course material provided within the study. In addition, participants should hold a student status. The participants were debriefed about the purpose of the study and gave written informed consent. They were told that this study is aimed at improving online teaching of neuroimaging methods for students during the COVID-19 pandemic and that, to this end, they will take part in a neuroimaging course in which a short introduction on neuroimaging methods will be provided in a webinar format with a virtual teacher presenting the content. Depending on the experimental group to which the participants were randomly assigned, they were told to be a student of an online course studying the course material in a virtual classroom session in self-presence or with presence of virtual others or alone. The participants in the groups with self-presence through avatars received further instructions how they could choose an avatar (groups: self-chosen avatar) or were instructed that a preselected avatar is representing themselves in the class (groups: preselected self-avatar). They were told that their avatar is visible to the other students during the class. In addition, the groups assigned to the experimental conditions in which virtual peers were visually present were told that they would study the course material in virtual presence of other peers who will be represented by avatars and whose avatars and nicknames will be displayed on screen together with their own avatar in the virtual classroom. The participants who were assigned to the control conditions (no self-avatars or no peer avatars) were given no information about self- or other-presence during the course. Taken together, there were six possible experimental conditions to which the participants could be assigned (see Table 1):

Table 1. Experimental conditions to which the participants could be randomly assigned

Experimental Condition A Group 1 in the figures	preselected self-avatar with nickname and visual representation of other peers in the class with nicknames
Experimental Condition B Group 2 in the figures	self-chosen visual avatar with nickname and visual representation of other peers in the class with nicknames
Experimental Condition C (control condition 1) Group 3 in the figures	no visual self-avatar with nickname but symbolic representation of other peers in class by nickname
Experimental Condition D Group 4 in the figures	preselected self-avatar with nickname but no visual representation of other peers in the class
Experimental Condition E Group 5 in the figures	self-chosen visual avatar with nickname but no visual representation of other peers in the class
Experimental Condition F (control condition 2) Group 6 in the figures	no visual self-avatar with nickname and no visual representation of other peers in the class

As shown in Table 1, all participants could choose a nickname as a virtual identity (besides the participants of Group 6 /experimental condition F in Table 1). Moreover, as shown in Table 1, in the experimental condition C, virtual others were represented by nicknames only to control for the potential impact of symbolic representation of others. Participation in the study was voluntary and anonymous. Participants could withdraw from the study without giving reasons for quitting. The online study was provided to the participants via Lime Survey software [8], an open, an open source survey tool with the possibility to save data on local servers (https://www.limesurvey.org). After giving written informed consent, the participants were asked sociodemographic questions including age, gender, country of residence, their English proficiency that could affect study participation as checks of inclusion criteria. Next, the participants were asked to give a brief description of their previous teaching experiences and preferences. The questions focused on teaching and learning as suggested in the questionnaire used in [9] asking about teaching preferences of preferring to study and learn alone or with peers, in presence or online. Next, the participants could choose a nickname to take part in the random assignment to one of the experimental groups. Random assignment to the groups was realized by using the randomizer function implemented in the LimeSurvey software package. Hereafter, participants who were randomly assigned to the experimental group B and E (see Table 1 or Fig. 1) could choose their avatar from a variety of avatar options that were presented as static images and created via the virtual characters provided by the Python package for multicultural avatar generation Multiavatar [10]. The virtual avatars representing classmates in the experimental conditions A and B (see Table 1 or Fig. 1) were also taken from the same source. The Multicultural Avatar Maker is a freely available open source toolbox that contains virtual characters whose display (torso from front view) can vary according to several visual human identity features including genetic and social features such as sex or gender, culture, age, facial expressions including discrete emotions, hair or eye color and clothing style. For the purpose of the present study, only those virtual characters were chosen as avatars for self- and other-presence whose visual features could not be compromised by computer settings such as brightness, contrast or other physical properties such as color (red and green due to vision blindness). An overview of the virtual characters from the list of avatars chosen in the present study to represent virtual classmates or the participant's self-avatar is provided in Fig. 1. As illustrated in Fig. 1, the visual presentation of classmates was arranged in a way to simulate a real classroom setting (characters sitting at a desk in tandems of two with the number of classmates chosen according to the average size of seminar classes which is approximately 20 students).

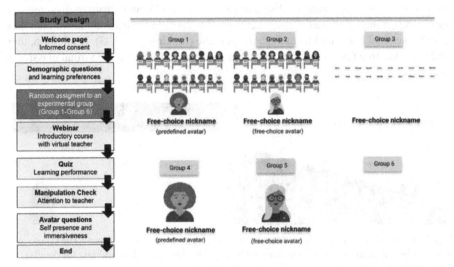

Fig. 1. Illustration of the study design and of the virtual avatars representing either the Self or the virtual classmates taken from the software Multiavatar [10].

After group assignment and answering the questions described above, all participants took part in an online course about neuroimaging methods. The course was digitally created by using Figma and Synthesia.io in-browser software [11] as well as Wondershare Filmora [12] and Clideo [13] for editing video and text animations. The content of the course was an introduction to neuroimaging methods. It was conceptualized according to an in house teaching protocol of the author and digitally designed by the Department of Applied Emotion and Motivation Psychology, Ulm University (see for an illustration Fig. 2a/b). The webinar course lasted 9 min, it was embedded within the survey and could be streamed by the participants. As illustrated in Fig. 2, the content of the webinar was offered by a humanoid avatar chosen to represent the online teacher. The humanoid avatar was chosen from Synthesia software [11] that offers several virtual characters (AI generated humanoids). The virtual characters are engineered and designed to read out text provided by a software user. The voice of the humanoid avatars can be chosen according to the purpose of the generated content. For this study, the natural American English voice was chosen as a familiar prosody of speech. After watching the webinar, the participants were asked to take part in a quiz testing their learning performance.

The quiz was a mix of open questions asking for particular course content. The quiz included attention questions (asking about appearance features of the virtual teacher) as manipulation check to control the degree to which the participants paid attention to the digital teacher being visible on the slides. After having completed the quiz, the participants were asked to answer questions about their experience with the course setting. The participants of the experimental groups A, B, D and E were presented questions taken from the embodiment avatar questionnaire [14] including the subscales 'body ownership' and 'external appearance' that assess the degree to which participants feel a sense of Self for the avatars representing their own person. Participants were asked for providing their answers on a 5-point Likert scale ranging from strongly agree (5), agree (4), neither agree or disagree (3), disagree (2), and strongly disagree (1), respectively. Finally, all participants were asked to provide feedback on how much they thought they had benefitted from the online course (ranking from 1–5). In addition, they could provide free text to describe the experience they made with the virtual classroom context.

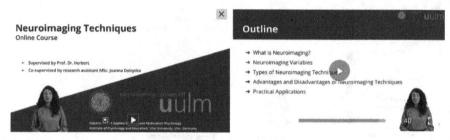

Fig. 2. Illustration of the webinar "Introduction to Neuroimaging Techniques" The course was provided by a human avatar as a teacher shown on each slide (see below and text for details).

3   Data Analysis and Results

3.1   Data Analysis

Data analysis of the survey items included descriptive analysis as well as statistical non-parametric and parametric testing of group differences. Specifically, learning performance, the degree of embodiment and self-presence through avatar presence and online course experience were chosen as variables. Data analysis was performed with XLSTAT software (https://www.xlstat.com/de/). Differences between the experimental conditions are reported at a significance level of $p < .05$ uncorrected .

3.2   Results

In total, N = 70 participants, mean age = 24.44 (SD = 7.36) took part in the study. Analysis of country of residence revealed a broad distribution of the participants across European countries including countries outside Europe (United States or South America). N = 35 participants reported to be male, N = 31 reported to be women, N = 1 preferred diverse, and N = 3 preferred not to mention the gender. All participants reported to speak English with good proficiency. According to outlier analysis, N = 5 participants did not provide answers to all of the survey items, resulting in a final sample of N = 65 participants. Of these, N = 23 participants N = 23 participants (35.38%) reported to have a bachelor's degree, N = 5 participants reported to have a master's degree. The majority of the participants (N = 34, 52.31%) reported to have a high school diploma. N = 3 participants reported "other" as a category (e.g., degree higher than a master degree). 63.08% of the participants (N = 41) reported to have little knowledge of neuroimaging methods (learners), N = 6 participants (9.23%) reported to have advanced knowledge. N = 20 (30.77%) reported to be a little familiar with the topic.

Learner's Performance

Table 2. Test Items (multiple choice questions) including the questions asking for paying attention to the virtual teacher while watching the webinar and test items (quiz) asking for the learner's learning performance, statistical analysis, see text.

Test Items (Multiple Choice Questions)	
The following is a control question to verify you watched the course video. What was the teacher's hairstyle?	
The following is a control question to verify you watched the course video. Did the teacher wear glasses?	
Which of the following are target groups for neuroimaging studies?	
Which of the following is the least invasive method?	
Which research fields can neuroimaging studies contribute to? Multiple choices can be correct	
Which research fields can neuroimaging studies contribute to? Multiple choices can be correct	
Which research fields can neuroimaging studies contribute to? Multiple choices can be correct	
Pick the only true statement about EEG	

Individual comparisons between the six experimental groups by means of non-parametric tests and post-hoc comparisons between groups showed no consistent significant patterns that would suggest a clear advantage of one of the six experimental groups in quiz performance, $H(5) = 6.33$, $p = .275$, nor in paying more or less attention to the virtual teacher, $H(5) = 4.194$, $p = .522$ (Fig. 3). The groups with the pre-selected or self-chosen visual avatars and the visual presence of the avatars of the virtual classmates (group 1 and group 2 in Fig. 3) and the groups with the pre-selected or self-chosen visual avatars but no visual presence of the avatars of the virtual classmates (group 4 and group 5 in Fig. 3) did, on average (sum of all items), not outperform the groups of participants who attended the class without visual self-representation or without visual representation of other peer learners. The control group that conducted the webinar (online course) without virtual presence of Self and Others obtained on average and descriptively the best learning performance, see group 6 in Fig. 3b.

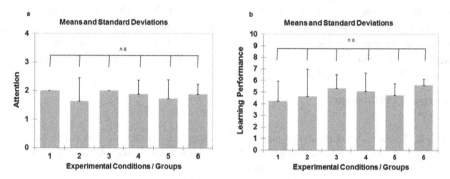

Fig. 3. a/b. Answers (means and standard deviations) of the items of the manipulation check (paying attention to the virtual teacher, 3a) as a function of experimental group assignment. Figure 3b displays the mean quiz performance as a function of the experimental groups. Group 1: predefined self-avatar plus visual avatars of classmates; Group 2: self-chosen self-avatar plus visual avatars of classmates; Group 3: no self-avatar but nicknames of classmates; Group 4: predefined self-avatar no visual avatars of classmates; Group 5: self-chosen self-avatar and no visual avatars of classmates, Group 6: no avatars. *n.s.*: not significant.

Relevance of the Virtual Teacher

As shown in Fig. 3a/b the experimental groups did not differ significantly in the degree of attention to the teacher during the online course (see Fig. 3a). However, the quiz items (learning performance) and the items of the manipulation check (attention to the virtual teacher) were related. The sum scores of the attention items and the sum scores of the total quiz performance were positively correlated (Spearman Rho $= 0.344$, $p < .05$; Kendalls Tau-c $= 0.158$, $p < .05$). This suggests that paying attention to the virtual teacher and learning performance are related. The correlation holds true irrespective of group assignment, i.e., whether the Self or Others are being virtually present in the class or not. Given that the teacher was a highly realistic humanoid avatar shown on any slide, this suggests that substituting the real teacher by a realistic visual avatar in online learning is more important than substituting the learner or the peers by visual avatars to simulate virtual presence.

Self-reported Learning Preferences

The results about learning performance and teacher relevance should not be discussed independently from the self-reported learning preferences of the participants. The majority of the participants reported to generally prefer learning in presence over learning online. Moreover, 50% of the participants did not feel to have previously benefitted

Table 3. Correlation analysis between paying attention to the humanoid teacher avatar and the participants' learning performance (for details, see text).

Items (Sum Scores)	Attention	Learning Performance
Attention	1	**0.344***
Learning Performance	**0.344***	1

$^*p < .05$

better from online teaching than from classes being attended in presence. The present online course however received a mean ranking of 4 points ($SD = 0.92$) on a Likert scale ranging from 1 (not good) to 5 (very good). This is supporting the hypothesis that teacher-guided online courses were perceived as effective. And this, although the teacher was a realistic humanoid avatar and the majority of the participants seemed not to be convinced about online courses for their study from their experience in the past.

Table 4. Identification with the self-avatar as assessed by questions taken from standardized avatar embodiment questionnaires [14] (for details see Methods).

Questions	Experimental Groups		
	Self-chosen avatar $M(SD)$	Preselected avatar $M(SD)$	P
1. I would say the avatar is a mirror of myself	3.1 (1.1)	2.2 (1.1)	0.01*
2. I recreated someone else through my avatar	2.1 (0.9)		
3. The virtual avatar resembled my own real physical appearance	3 (1.2)	2 (1)	0.002*
4. I had fun choosing my avatar	3.9 (0.9)		
5. I would use such avatar again, in other online teaching environments	3.5 (1)	2.8 (1.1)	0.007*
6. The avatar was a great means of self-expression	3.3 (1.1)	2.4 (1)	< 0.001*
7. The avatar had realistic features	3 (1)	2.6 (1)	0.074
8. Do you think you had enough avatar options to choose from? You may leave a comment in the text box on the right, to further detail on your answer	1.5 (0.8)		

Self-presence and Immersiveness, and Gender
Comparison between the experimental groups with a self-chosen vs. preselected avatar showed significant results between the groups. The groups significantly differed in their answers on the items asking for the degree of embodiment or self-identification with the avatar (see Table 4). In addition, the group that could choose the avatar on its own was more motivated to use the avatar again, and evaluated the possibility to represent the Self by an avatar as funny and as a good means of self-expression (see Table 4). In addition, most of the participants with self-chosen avatars preferred to choose an avatar that matched to the own character including physical appearance. Given that the experimental groups with self-avatars did not differ in learning performance, it seems that self-determined choice of one's character seems not to have a significant impact on the learning efficiency as such, but might affect other factors such as the motivation to learn online in a more self-determined and pleasurable way. Finally, comparisons across gender did not show any significant gender effects in any of these variables (all $p > .05$).

4   Discussion, Conclusion and Future Outlook

The COVID-19 pandemic has significantly increased the need for teaching and learning concepts that support university students worldwide in their effort to learn in a self-determined and self-regulated context, off campus, asynchronously and detached from face-to-face or any kind of analog interaction with peers in presence. Recent surveys have shown that this change in teaching from face-to-face to full digital learning formats was perceived as a big burden for many students and associated with a drop in well-being and academic performance [6]. According to the literature, several suggestions have been made how to design the content of online teaching in a way beneficial to the students and the teachers [15]. In parallel, the influence of virtual agents on human users' experience and behavior has been investigated in several virtual reality studies: the results of these studies are underscoring the relevance and impact of virtual self-presence and other-presence in the gaming context [16]. The present study explored whether virtual learning contexts also benefit from virtual presence. Specifically, it was explored whether substituting the Self of the learner or peers by virtual avatar characters can improve learning performance and feelings of presence in an online teaching context, even without interaction between the learners. Regarding self-presence, previous studies suggest that customized characters can increase self-presence and the learner's engagement [21]. Also, the influence of peers has been studied and it is theoretically assumed to have a huge impact on the cognition, motivation and the mood of the learner, in particular when there is agentic interaction or communication between the virtual agents, for an overview, [1]. Still little is known about the benefits of the mere presence of virtual peers and virtual self-representation in an online teaching format. Also, little is known about the relevance of virtual teachers. In summary, the results of the present study, although preliminary, do not support that the mere representation of the Self or of virtual Others has a significant impact on the learner's learning performance in an online course taught by a human-like teacher avatar. As outlined in detail in the Results, one tentative explanation of this is the previous experience of the participants regarding online teaching. In addition, the lack of interaction with the avatar might reduce the effects of embodiment that often has been suggested to have beneficial effects on the extent to which users immerse into a plot or accept the virtual character as a representation of the Self and of their identity. Embodiment has been defined as the sense of ownership that occurs when integrating the avatar as a tool within one's self or body image [17]. In the present study, embodied interaction was missing and only static avatars without a body but torso (face and shoulders) were used. Nevertheless, the group of participants who could choose their avatar on their own reported self-presence (see Table 4). Moreover, most of the participants decided to choose realistic avatars that closely resembled the own identity and physical appearance. This suggests that in contrast to other context such as in gaming in which users often prefer to choose avatars that might more closely fit to the ideal self [1], in a teaching context, a realistic representation of the virtual Self as one's own Self seems to be more important than representing oneself in an "ideal" format regarding character traits and physical appearance. This assumption should be followed up in future studies investigating larger study samples that additionally analyze whether specific avatar features such as facial expression may be related to differences in the user's preferences (see for a discussion e.g., [18]. Importantly, future studies should determine further the benefit of using human-like avatars as teachers in the teaching context. In the present study this seemed to have had an impact on the learning performance of all of the participants. In addition, the participants evaluated the online course as good (4 of 5 stars). Future studies could include additional measures to assess changes in mood, learning motivation and changes in the capacity of self-regulated learning such as the learner's self-efficacy to further exploit the conditions in which learners benefit from avatars as virtual agents in the learning context. In summary, this pilot study furthered the understanding of the role virtual characters can play in online contexts other than gaming. In addition, it adds to the discussion of how to theoretically frame the analysis of human behavior in digital contexts. Models such as the Character Computing Model introduced in [19] and [20] that aim to compute and predict the user's behavior by taking psychological approaches, human factors and situational factors into consideration could serve as theoretical heuristic approach in future studies.

References

1. Baylor, A.L.: Promoting motivation with virtual agents and avatars: role of visual presence and appearance. Philosophical Transactions of the Royal Society B: Biological Sciences **364**(1535), 3559–3565 (2009)
2. Blascovich, J., Loomis, J., Beall, A.C., Swinth, K.R., Hoyt, C.L., Bailenson, J.N.: Immersive virtual environment technology as a methodological tool for social psychology. Psychol. Inq. **13**(2), 103–124 (2002)
3. Hassan, M.: Online teaching challenges during COVID-19 pandemic. Int. J. Info. Edu. Technol. **11**(1), 41–46 (2021). https://doi.org/10.18178/ijiet.2021.11.1.1487
4. Bailenson, J., Blascovich, J.: Avatars. In: In: Bainbridge, W.S. (ed.) Encyclopedia of Human-Computer Interaction, pp. 62–64 (2004)
5. Michael-Grigoriou, D., Kyrlitsias, C.: Social interaction with agents and avatars in immersive virtual environments: a survey. Frontiers in Virtual Reality (2022)
6. Noor, S., Isa, F.M., Mazhar, F.F.: Online teaching practices during the COVID-19 pandemic. Educational Process: International Journal **9**(3), 169–184 (2020). https://doi.org/10.22521/edupij.2020.93.4

7. Bradley, P.: Prolific | Online participant recruitment for surveys and market research (2014). Retrieved 14 March 2022. from https://www.prolific.co

8. Limesurvey GmbH: LimeSurvey: An Open Source survey tool. LimeSurvey GmbH, Hamburg, Germany. https://www.limesurvey.org

9. Muthuprasad, T., Aiswarya, S., Aditya, K.S., Jha, G.K.: Students' perception and preference for online education in India during COVID -19 pandemic. Social Sciences & Humanities Open 3(1), 100101 (2021). https://doi.org/10.1016/j.ssaho.2020.100101

10. Katon, G.: Multiavatar - Multicultural Avatar Maker. Multiavatar (2020). Retrieved 3 September 2021. From https://multiavatar.com

11. Riparbelli, V., Niessner, M., Agapito, L., Tjerrild, S.: Synthesia (2017). Retrieved 9 March 2022. From https://app.synthesia.io

12. Wu, T.: Wondershare Filmora - Easy, Trendy and Quality Video Editing Software (2003). Retrieved 10 March 2022. From https://filmora.wondershare.com

13. Softo Ltd.: Clideo — Online Video Tools (2014). https://clideo.com/tools

14. Gonzalez-Franco, M., Peck, T.C.: Avatar embodiment. Towards a standardized questionnaire. Frontiers in Robotics and AI 5(74), (2018). https://doi.org/10.3389/frobt.2018.00074

15. Andrew, L., Wallace, R., Sambell, R.: A peer-observation initiative to enhance student engagement in the synchronous virtual classroom: a case study of a COVID-19 mandated move to online learning. J. Univ. Teach. Learn. Prac. 18(4), 184–205 (2021). https://doi.org/10.53761/1.18.4.14

16. Domínguez, A., Saenz-de-Navarrete, J., De-Marcos, L., Fernández-Sanz, L., Pagés, C., Martínez-Herráiz, J.: Gamifying learning experiences: practical implications and outcomes. Comput. Educ. 63, 380–392 (2013). https://doi.org/10.1016/j.compedu.2012.12.020

17. Ratan, R., Sah, Y.J.: Leveling up on stereotype threat: the role of avatar customization and avatar embodiment. Comput. Hum. Behav. 50, 367–374 (2015). https://doi.org/10.1016/j.chb.2015.04.010

18. Ducheneaut, N., Wen, M.-H., Yee, N., Wadley, G.: Body and mind: a study of avatar personalization in three virtual worlds. In: Proceedings of the SIGCHI Conference on Human Factors in Computing Systems. Boston, MA, pp. 1151–1160 (2009). https://doi.org/10.1145/1518701.1518877

19. Herbert, C.: An experimental-psychological approach for the development of character computing. In: Character computing, pp. 17–38. Springer, Cham (2020)

20. El Bolock, A., Salah, J., Abdelrahman, Y., Herbert, C., Abdennadher, S.: Character computing: computer science meets psychology. In: Proceedings of the 17th International Conference on Mobile and Ubiquitous Multimedia, pp. 557–562 (November 2018)

21. Chen, Z.H., Lu, H.D., Lu, C.H.: The effects of human factors on the use of avatars in game-based learning: customization vs. non-customization. Int. J. Human–Computer Interaction 35(4–5), 384–394 (2019)

The Effects of Personality Traits on Rumors

Nada Ibrahim$^{(\boxtimes)}$, Mariam Elzayany, and Amr Elmougy

German University in Cairo, Cairo, Egypt
{nada.abdelfattah,amr.elmougy}@guc.edu.eg,
mariam.elzayany@student.guc.edu.eg

Abstract. The spread of rumors has often been linked to major social and political impacts with consequences that oftentimes may prove to be severe. While there are multiple factors that could make a rumor more believable, this paper focuses on investigating the effects of personality traits on believing or disbelieving rumors. Participants were given a survey which included rumors relating to a single topic, COVID-19, to avoid topic-bias. Participants were also given a personality test which assessed the participants' traits based on the Big 5 Model and categorized them as high or low. The effect of valence (pleasure) and arousal (excitement) on believing or disbelieving rumors was also explored, along with how this effect differs from one trait to another. The results showed that people with high agreeableness tend to believe rumors more than people with low agreeableness and that there was a correlation between valence and believing rumors for people with high neuroticism and people with low agreeableness. No correlation was found between arousal and believing rumors for any of the personality traits.

Keywords: Rumors · Big 5 · Personality traits · Character Computing · Self-assessment manikin · COVID-19

1 Introduction

A rumor is defined as a statement that is an unproven narration or explanation of an event that concerns the public [3], which means that it is not verified as either true or false. Despite this, rumors have been proven to have a rather significant effect on people as well as enough power to influence them and their actions just as much as true and verified information can [1]. Inspiring feelings of hope, fear and hate, rumors can also weaken people's trust in their governments, shape public opinion, as well as cause political tensions [2]. Consequently, it is evident that rumors play a very important role in people's lives and that is why social psychologists and other scientists are motivated to understand what rumors are, how they spread, who believes them, how they can be identified and what their effects are.

Most studies [3–6] are concerned with two aspects when studying rumors; rumor detection and rumor analysis. Rumor analysis is studied in multiple fields,

A. González-Briones et al. (Eds.): PAAMS Workshops 2022, CCIS 1678, pp. 181–192, 2022.
https://doi.org/10.1007/978-3-031-18697-4_15

including economics, psychology and social science, where rumors are classified based on different criteria, characteristics and dimensions. The criteria are: how rumors differ, where they originate, what topics they address, the emotions they evoke, how they spread and how users interact with them [3]. Other classifications consider whether the rumor is deemed newsworthy or not. Rumors are classified as newsworthy if they concern the public and are of interest to social media users, whereas non-newsworthy rumors only concern a small community or group of people and are more personal [4]. Rumors are also classified based on the emotions they evoke, varying from positive to negative and the need to take action [4]. The emotions evoked are evaluated based on 3 dimensions that measure human reactions to different stimuli: valence (pleasure), arousal (excitement) and dominance (sense of control) [29].

Since the majority of the studies focused on the different facets of the rumor itself, this study was carried out in an attempt to examine a factor not often focused on: the personality traits of people who accept or reject rumors. This is Phase II of a previously conducted study which analyzed the effect of buzz users on rumors' lifetime [7] and generated author profiles on Arabic-speaking social media users in Egypt. The study found that buzz users were capable of sparking a rumor as well as significantly affect its lifetime due to their believable and trustful features, leading more people to believe them.

Identifying personality traits can help predict behavioral patterns a person tends to display [14], since personality captures a person's stable individual characteristics, and this allows us to understand which types of people would be more likely to accept or reject rumors. This can be done using trait models, which can represent an individual's personality in terms of numerical values. One of these trait models is the five-factor model of personality (FFM). Often referred to as the "Big- Five", FFM is currently the "dominant paradigm in personality research, and one of the most influential models in all of psychology" [15] and consists of five traits: extraversion, agreeableness, conscientiousness, neuroticism and openness. Ergo, the aim of this study is to examine three major problem statements:

– Do personality traits have an effect on believing rumors in general?
– Does valence have an effect on believing rumors for each personality trait?
– Does arousal have an effect on believing rumors for each personality trait?

By addressing these problem statements, we are attempting to understand if personality and emotions play a role in affecting people actually believing the rumors that circulate online, which are aspects of Character Computing and can contribute to our understanding of how humans process rumors.

In order to understand the effects of personality traits, valence and arousal on believing rumors, this study explored and evaluated personality traits of several participants, as well as the emotions evoked by the participants upon reading a set of rumors.

The entire study is documented in this paper and the remaining sections of this paper are organized as Related Work, Implementation and Methods, Results and Analysis, Discussion and Conclusion.

2   Related Work

2.1   Believing a Rumor

While examining the factors that lead people to believe and spread rumors, researchers have looked into the characteristics and contents of a rumor and have found that the length, sentiment and presence of pictures in a rumor affect people's intention to believe and spread the rumor [5]. One study by Schwarz et al. [6] found that the metacognitive experience of people - which is how easy it is to recall and understand new information based on how it is presented - leads them to believe or disbelieve a rumor; meaning that when statements are made easier to read by writing them in color, people will be more likely to accept these statements as true. Another study [5] found that people tend to support a rumor that is spread on Twitter before it has even been verified rather than deny it.

People also tend to believe rumors based on the trustability of the person who tweeted the rumor, where trust in Twitter's retweet network includes two factors: trustworthiness and trustingness. Trustworthiness is when user A finds user B trustworthy and chooses to trust user B and believe and retweet a rumor that user B has shared. Trustingness is when user A trusts the rest of the people in the network which leads user A to believe the rumors that people share easily. People with high trustworthiness tend to be more careful with what they share and their reputation, leading them to be less likely to spread and believe unverified or false information compared to people with low trustworthiness. The trustworthiness of a user can be measured using several factors including the number of retweets of a user's tweet; the higher the number of retweets, the more trustworthy the user is [8]. Trustability can also be extended to the language used to express the rumor, where linguistic relativity, i.e. the way a particular language spoken influences thoughts [9], can be a source of bias for social media users when reading rumors in certain languages.

To further understand people's inclination to believe rumors, researchers started looking into people's characteristics such as demographics, cognition, and behaviors and how they contribute to them believing rumors [10]. Chua and Banerjee [11] showed that people's personal involvement with the content of the rumor would make them more likely to believe it. Psychological factors such as uncertainty, belief, lack of control, and anxiety, were also proven to have an effect on the tendency to believe rumors. Grinberg et al. [12] found that more conservative and older people are more likely to believe and spread rumors. Young users are more immune to misinformation and the stress caused by rumors since they spend more time on social media, while older users are more prone to the anxiety caused by rumors, which makes them more likely to believe and share rumors [10]. Therefore, after surveying 171 university students on 16 motivations regarding believing and spreading rumors, Chen and Sin [13] found the top motivations to spread rumors were to acquire other people's' opinions on the information being spread, to convey their own opinion on the information, and to interact with other people. They also found that while gender showed no significant effect in the spread of rumors, personality did; consequently, they found that extroverts shared more rumors in order to socialize more. Accordingly, studying the personalities of people who spread rumors is of high importance to understand the characteristics of people and how they affect the belief of rumors.

2.2   Social Media, Misinformation and Personality

Due to the flexibility and incredible ease of sharing up-to-date news on social media, as well as it being highly unregulated, it is incredibly easy for rumors to spread amongst social media users [17] and multiple studies [18–23] have shown that Facebook, YouTube and Twitter all play major roles in the spread and circulation of rumors and misinformation on multiple topics including medical ones.

According to Heinstrom [24], out of the five personality traits, extraversion and neuroticism personalities are more associated with online activities, where social media users with high extraversion or high neuroticism are more engaged with online activities. In a study by Amnieh and Kaedi [25], it was found that those with high extraversion eagerly await new messages and are more likely to forward them on Twitter, which leads us to expect those with high extraversion to be more likely to believe and spread rumors. Conscientious people were found to be more likely to use social media for academic or work purposes, and hence, when gathering information, they tend to make more effort in verifying facts and searching for resources [24]. As a result, it is expected that conscientious people be less inclined to believe rumors without further investigating them. Meanwhile, neurotic people tend to spend more time online, but usually do not use information- related features [26], and due to their fear of producing a negative outcome when communicating, they avoid exchanging a lot of information on social media and are less likely to share rumors [27], but that does not necessarily mean that neurotic people are less likely to believe rumors.

Open people were found to be more likely to use news and information features as well as personal information features on Facebook [28]. They are also more open to new and unexpected ideas and are more likely to question authority; therefore, it is expected that open people tend to believe rumors for their "unconventional ideas" [24].

Moreover, Hamburger and Ben- Artzi [26] suggest that gender may change the effect of personality on social media usage. For example, women's internet use of social services was negatively related to extraversion and positively related to neuroticism, while for men, it is positively related to both.

3   Implementation and Methods

3.1   Collecting Rumors

Being one of the most sought after and controversial topics for the past 2 years, COVID-19 has had - and continues to have - a profound effect on people's lives. Thus, people follow it closely on news outlets and on social media platforms,

Table 1. Rumors collected from websites

Rumor number	Rumor details	Language rumor was shown in	Were further details provided for the rumor?	Type of emotion evoked by the rumor
R1	The UK Medicines and Healthcare Products Regulatory Agency (MHRA) will use artificial intelligence to monitor the safety of COVID-19 vaccines because the agency knows that vaccines are extremely dangerous	English	Yes	Positive
R2	Chinese doctors confirmed that African people are "genetically resistant" to new coronavirus	English	No	Positive
R3	COVID tests and PCRs contain the carcinogenic chemical compound Ethylene Oxide and the packaging belonging to the tests provided by the UK Medicines and Healthcare Products Regulatory Agency (MHRA) are marked as using Ethylene Oxide	Arabic	Yes	Negative
R4	The COVID-19 vaccines will cause "pathogenic priming" or "disease enhancement", meaning that vaccinated individuals will be more likely to develop severe cases of COVID-19 if they are infected with the COVID-19 virus	English	Yes	Negative
R5	A person who has already previously caught COVID-19 does not need to be vaccinated against it	Arabic	No	Positive

eagerly waiting for any and all updates, some of which may simply be rumors. Accordingly, five rumors related to COVID-19 - shown in Table 1 - that were already circulating on the internet were collected from four different websites; *nashra.com*, *arabic.cnn.com*, *snopes.com*, and *britannica.com*.

The general topic of the rumors collected was kept constant to avoid having the topic become a factor in determining whether people will believe the rumor or not, and the rumors were collected based on specific criteria that could trigger some personality traits, thus possibly causing people exhibiting these traits to believe the rumor more. The criteria were:

– How much detail was given in the rumor (how specific was the rumor).
– If the person found the rumor positive or negative (emotion evoked on the person by the rumor).
– Whether or not the rumor would have been more believable if more details were added.
– Whether the rumor was in Arabic or English.

3.2   Study Survey Conducted

The survey was filled by participants residing in Egypt (where Arabic is the main language used). All participants spoke both English and Arabic, and consequently, both languages were used to convey different types of phrasing in an attempt to prevent bias based on linguistic relativity. As shown in the sample screenshots in Figs. 1 and 2, the survey consisted of demographic questions on the age, gender, and education level of the participants, the Big Five Inventory BFI-10 personality test [16] to assess the personality traits of the participants, and four questions on each of the five the rumors collected. The survey also included using the Self-Assessment Manikin (SAM) [29] in order to evaluate the emotional response and reaction of a person after a certain stimulus [30], which in this case was reading the rumor. A summary of the questions asked on each rumor is shown in Table 2, along with the measurement or scale used. The null hypotheses of the experiment are:

1. None of the five personality traits have any effect on believing rumors in general.
2. Valence does not have an effect on believing rumors for each personality trait.
3. Arousal does not have an effect on believing rumors for each personality trait.

Table 2. The questions asked about the rumors in the questionnaire and the measurements used for the response for each question

Question	Measurement of response
Please rate how strongly you believe or disbelieve the rumor	Likert scale
How did the rumor make you feel?	SAM
How intense was this feeling?	SAM
Do you believe the rumor would have been more believable if it had more details?	Yes/No

Since highly conscientious people pay more attention to detail than lowly conscientious people, it is expected that highly conscientious people will believe rumors more if the rumors include more detail; however, people with low conscientiousness will not be affected by the extra detail.

Fig. 1. Survey screenshots of the general questions and some of the BFI-10 questions

Fig. 2. Survey screenshots of the rest of the BFI-10 questions and the questions asked on one of the rumors

It is also expected that a positive rumor - or a rumor that evokes positive emotions - may lead people who are high in neuroticism to believe the rumor more, while people who are low in neuroticism are not affected by the positive or negative emotions evoked by the rumor. The reasoning behind this is that those who are high in neuroticism may experience a lot of stress, feel anxious and get upset really quickly, while those low in neuroticism are more emotionally stable and can deal well with stress. Furthermore, because people high in agreeableness have more empathy for others, it is expected that this may lead them to refuse to accept negative rumors - or rumors evoking negative emotions - more than those low in agreeableness.

4   Results and Analysis

There were 69 participants in the study, more of which were female (n = 36, 52.1%) than male (n = 33, 47.8%), all aged 16 and above. The largest age group was 16–24 (n = 53,76.8%), the second age group was 25–40 (n = 13, 18.8%), and the last age group was 40 years and above (n = 3, 4.3%).

As shown in Table 3, the most prevalent personality trait among all the participants was low agreeableness (n= 41, 59.4%) and the least prevalent was high agreeableness (n= 28, 40.5%).

Table 3. Percentage of prevalence of the different personality traits

Personality trait	n value	Percentage
High openness	39	56.5%
Low openness	30	43.4%
High conscientiousness	39	56.5%
Low conscientiousness	30	43.4%
High extraversion	34	49.2%
Low extraversion	35	50.7%
High agreeableness	28	40.5%
Low agreeableness	41	59.4%
High neuroticism	34	49.2%
Low neuroticism	35	50.7%

4.1   Personality Trait vs. Believing Rumors

As the data sample collected was categorical, non-linear and small in size, Chi-square analysis was used. As shown in Table 4, only two traits showed a relationship with believing some of the rumors: openness showed a correlation with believing R3 ($P = .009$), while agreeableness showed a correlation with R2 ($P = .019$) and R3 ($P = .016$).

Table 4. Correlation between personality traits and believing each of the rumors

Personality Trait	R1 p-value	R2 p-value	R3 p-value	R4 p-value	R5 p-value
Openness	0.52935	0.54617	0.00887	0.229857	0.67395
Conscientiousness	0.91047	0.89950	0.49952686	0.3252282	0.252512453
Extraversion	0.4017834	0.5486375	0.7657644	0.42952997	0.8556222
Agreeableness	0.1191626	0.018854	0.01565293	0.1324283	0.4810904
Neuroticism	0.759667	0.1476201	0.55592045	0.7217332	0.8271240

4.2 Valence per Personality Trait Versus Accepting or Rejecting Rumors

As shown in Table 5, all personality traits, except for low openness and high conscientiousness, were affected by valence when choosing to accept or reject at least one of the given rumors. However, there were traits that showed a higher contribution to the influence of valence on accepting or rejecting rumors and the two traits that showed the most contribution were low agreeableness ($P = .05$ for R2 and $P < .001$ for R3, R4, R5) and high neuroticism ($P = .05$ for R1, $P = .006$ for R2, $P = .003$ for R3 and $P < .001$ for R4).

Table 5. Correlation between the valence of each personality trait and the possibility of accepting each rumor

Personality Trait	R1 p-value	R2 p-value	R3 p-value	R4 p-value	R5 p-value
High openness valence	0.1331651	0.000017037	0.171593	0.0962218	0.001121672
Low openness valence	0.0517629824	0.307635	0.5944507	0.35916584	0.413165513
High conscientiousness valence	0.52155245	0.119177652	0.117761106	0.62624263	0.272043603
Low conscientiousness valence	0.230635052	0.01206255894	0.547834171	0.284658810	0.0231353339
High extraversion valence	0.07132987	0.0003366619	0.67799819376	0.45599853002	0.18153383001
Low extraversion valence	0.14962214	0.091825102	0.330169598	0.024595058	0.00744932
High agreeableness valence	0.038449660	0.00207923231	0.1606250326	0.50888909258	0.6651729006
Low agreeableness valence	0.4911898	0.0556049563	0.000735770977	0.00028821553	0.0001292718
High neuroticism valence	0.0512704	0.006350	0.002894440	0.00000283652	0.06529042
Low neuroticism valence	0.12100129	0.000774485	0.16212025	0.57744021	0.0939897

4.3 Arousal per Personality Trait Versus Accepting or Rejecting Rumors

The results in Table 6 showed that arousal in general did not affect the participants' decision in rejecting or accepting the rumors. The traits that showed some relation between arousal and accepting and rejecting just one of the rumors were low openness ($P = .03$ for R3), high extraversion ($P = .01$ for R4), low extraversion ($P = .002$ for R4), high agreeableness ($P = .004$ for R4), low agreeableness ($P = .001$ for R3), and low neuroticism ($P = .002$ for R4).

Table 6. Correlation between arousal of each personality trait and the possibility of accepting each rumor

Personality Trait	R1 p-value	R2 p-value	R3 p-value	R4 p-value	R5 p-value
High openness arousal	0.246276879	0.565881055	0.46933748	0.087082806	0.1431241204
Low openness arousal	0.127228911	0.24701788	0.01982169	0.123556055	0.487592128
High conscientiousness arousal	0.349923249	0.3499374	0.14761635	0.56912347	0.64115717
Low conscientiousness arousal	0.823926938	0.491547057	0.142330876	0.20571553	0.16639188
High extraversion arousal	0.78239310810	0.9304412413	0.5350930017	0.012362447	0.7718887
Low extraversion arousal	0.42865151	0.2246352385	0.09755469	0.002110787	0.22180383
High agreeableness arousal	0.828949169	0.52472195	0.19314369	0.0427318310	0.451340170
Low agreeableness arousal	0.481146830	0.35475609	0.01305601	0.06855075	0.31706365
High neuroticism arousal	0.3152544	0.44227017	0.32759874	0.15231373	0.055832
Low neuroticism arousal	0.529083	0.393220317	0.50007492	0.022406515	0.749199563

5 Discussion

The null hypothesis for all of the rumors for conscientiousness, extraversion, and neuroticism were accepted as there was no correlation between these personality traits and believing each of the rumors. For openness, the null hypothesis was only rejected for R3; consequently, it was not rejected for all the other rumors; therefore, it was accepted that openness has no effect on believing rumors.

For agreeableness, the null hypothesis was rejected for two rumors: R2 and R3; however, this was also not enough for the null hypothesis for agreeableness to be rejected for all the other rumors as well. As a result, the results concluded that there is no great effect of personality traits on rumors and the null hypothesis was accepted. On the other hand, people with high extraversion were expected to believe rumors more since they spend more time on social media, are more exposed to rumors and tend to share rumors more; however, the results showed no correlation. This could be due to the increase of social media use during COVID-19 quarantine and as a result, introverted people may have been spending just as much time on social media as extroverted people did.

Highly conscientious people were expected to reject the rumors since all the rumors had no citations and conscientious people tend to check the source and make sure the information is correct before accepting it. However, the results showed no correlation between conscientiousness and believing rumors. It was also expected that highly agreeable people believe rumors more because they tend to be more trusting than lowly agreeable people. The results support this hypothesis; open people were expected to believe rumors that contained unconventional ideas. R3 may contain a different idea that is not often heard of, which may be the reason it showed a correlation between believing it and high agreeableness.

In regards to valence, agreeableness and neuroticism showed the most correlation; hence, the null hypothesis was rejected, which shows that highly neurotic people tend to believe rumors more if they are negative since they have a tendency to be drawn to negative feelings, which was expected, and this means they may rely on emotions more than lowly neurotic people. Meanwhile, arousal showed a correlation for only some traits when believing at most 1 rumor, the null hypothesis was accepted for all of the personality traits Table 7.

Table 7. Summary of the acceptance and rejection of the three null hypotheses

Personality trait	Null hypothesis 1	Null hypothesis 2	Null hypothesis 3
Agreeableness	Accepted	Rejected	Accepted
Openness	Accepted	Accepted	Accepted
Conscientiousness	Accepted	Accepted	Accepted
Extraversion	Accepted	Accepted	Accepted
Neuroticism	Accepted	Rejected	Accepted

6   Conclusion and Future Work

The only trait that showed any significant effect on believing or disbelieving rumors was agreeableness, showing that highly agreeable people are more likely to believe rumors than lowly agreeable people. The rest of the traits may have shown some relation to believing rumors; however, they were not significant enough to reject the null hypothesis for each of the remaining traits. Furthermore, valence has been found to affect accepting or rejecting rumors for highly neurotic and lowly agreeable people, whereas arousal does not show any significant correlation with accepting or rejecting rumors for any of the personality traits.

Since the scope of this experiment only included rumors that were related to COVID-19, it would be interesting to explore other rumor topics such as but not limited to political rumors and celebrity gossip. This would produce a larger data set to study the personality traits of Internet users and shed more light on the personality traits most likely to accept rumors on social media as true without further investigation. Moreover, future experiments can also investigate the effect of age, gender and social standing on believing rumors, which can then lead us to further understand the character traits of social media users and what causes them to believe rumors online.

References

1. Shi Liao, L.: She gets a sports car from our donation: rumor transmission. In: A Chinese Microblogging Community. 2013 Conference on Computer Supported Cooperative Work, ACM (2013)
2. Hosni, A.I.E., Li, K.: Minimizing the influence of rumors during breaking news events in online social networks. Knowl. Based Syst. **193**, 105452 (2020)
3. Nourbakhsh, A., Liu, X., Shah, S., Fang, R., Ghassemi, M., Li, Q.: Newsworthy rumor events: a case study of Twitter 11 (2015)
4. Chua, A., Aricat, R., Goh, D.: Message content in the life of rumors: comparing three rumor types. In: 2017 Twelfth International Conference on Digital Information Management (ICDIM), pp. 263–268 (2017)
5. Berinsky, A.J.: Rumors, truths, and reality: a study of political misinformation. Massachusetts Institute of Technology Department of Political Science (2012)
6. Schwarz, N., Sanna, L.J., Skurnik, I., Yoon, C.: Metacognitive experiences and the intricacies of setting people straight: implications for debiasing and public information campaigns. Adv. Exp. Soc. Psychol. **39**, 127–161 (2007)
7. Michel, M., Soueidan, A. Elmougy, A.: Analyzing the effect of buzz users on rumors' lifetimes (2020)
8. Rath, B., Gao, W., Ma, J., Srivastava, J.: From retweet to believability: utilizing trust to identify rumor spreaders on Twitter. In Proceedings of the 2017 IEEE/ACM International Conference on Advances in Social Networks Analysis and Mining 2017, ASONAM 2017, pp. 179–186. NY, USA (2017)
9. Lucy, J.A.: Linguistic relativity. Ann. Rev. Anthropol. **26**, 291–312 (1997)
10. He, L., Yang, H., Xiling, X., Lai, K.: Online rumor transmission among younger and older adults. SAGE Open **9**, 7 (2019)

11. Chua, A.Y., Banerjee, S.: Intentions to trust and share online health rumors: an experiment with medical professionals. Comput. Hum. Behav. **87**, 1–9 (2018)
12. Grinberg, N., Joseph, K., Friedland, L., Swire-Thompson, B., Lazer, D.: Fake news on twitter during the 2016 US Presidential election. Science **363**, 374–378 (2019)
13. Chen, X., Sin, S.J.: Misinformation? What of it? Motivations and individual differences in misinformation sharing on social media. In: Proceedings of the American Society for Information Science and Technology, vol. 50, no. 1, pp. 1–4 (2013)
14. Matthews G., Deary I.J., Whiteman M.C.: Personality traits, third edition. personality traits, Third Edition, pp. 1–568 (2009)
15. McCrae, R.R.: The five-factor model of personality traits: consensus and controversy. In: Corr, P.J., Matthews, G. (eds.) The Cambridge handbook of personality psychology, pp. 148–161. Cambridge University Press, Cambridge (2009)
16. Rammstedt, B., John, O.P.: Measuring personality in one minute or less: a 10-item short version of the big five inventory in English and German. J. Res. Pers. **41**(1), 203–212 (2007)
17. Alkhodair, S.A., Ding, S.H.H., Fung, B.C.M., Liu, J.: Detecting breaking news rumors of emerging topics in social media. Inf. Process. Manage. **57**(2), 102018 (2020)
18. Bora, K., Das, D., Barman, B., Borah, P.: Are internet videos useful sources of information during global public health emergencies? A case study of Youtube videos during the 2015–16 zika virus pandemic. Pathog. Glob. Health **112**(6), 320–328 (2018)
19. Oi-Yee Li, H., Bailey, A., Huynh, D., Chan, J.: YouTube as a source of information on COVID-19: a pandemic of misinformation? BMJ Glob. Health **5**, e002604 (2020)
20. Sharma, M., Yadav, K., Yadav, N., Ferdinand, K.C.: Zika virus pandemic - analysis of Facebook as a social media health information platform. Am. J. Infect. Control **45**(3), 301–302 (2017)
21. Broniatowski, D.A., et al.: Weaponized health communication: Twitter bots and Russian trolls amplify the vaccine debate. Am. J. Pub. Health **108**(10), 1378–1384 (2018)
22. Ortiz-Martínez, Y., Jiménez-Arcia, L.: Yellow fever outbreaks and Twitter: rumours and misinformation. Am. J. Infect. Control **45**, 815–816 (2017)
23. Kouzy, R., et al.: Coronavirus goes viral: quantifying the COVID-19 misinformation epidemic on Twitter. Cureus **12**(3), e7255 (2020)
24. Heinstrom, J.: Five personality dimensions and their influence on information behaviour. Inf. Res. **9**, 9-1 (2003)
25. Amnieh, I.G., Kaedi, M.: Using estimated personality of social network members for finding influential nodes in viral marketing. Cybern. Syst. **46**, 355–378 (2015)
26. Hamburger, Y.A., Ben-Artzi, E.: The relationship between extraversion and neuroticism and the different uses of the internet. Comput. Hum. Behav. **16**, 441–449 (2000)
27. Amiel, T., Sargent, S.L.: Individual differences in internet usage motives. Comput. Hum. Behav. **20**(6), 711–726 (2004)
28. Ryan, T., Xenos, S.: Who uses Facebook? An investigation into the relationship between the big five, shyness, narcissism, loneliness, and Facebook usage. Comput. Hum. Behav. **27**, 1658–1664 (2011)
29. Lang, P.J., Bradley, M.M.: Measuring emotion: the self-assessment manikin and the semantic differential. Behav. Ther. Exp. Psychiatry **25**, 49–59 (1994)
30. Suci, G., Tannenbaum, C.: The Measurement of Meaning. University of Illinois, Urbana (1957)

Workshop on Deep Learning Applications (DeLA)

Workshop on Deep Learning Applications (DeLA)

Deep learning is an artificial intelligence (AI) function that imitates the workings of the human brain in processing data and creating patterns for use in decision making. Deep learning is a subset of machine learning in artificial intelligence that has networks capable of learning unsupervised from data that is unstructured or unlabeled. Also known as deep neural learning or deep neural networks.

The objective of the workshop on Deep Learning Applications is to give an opportunity for researchers to provide further insight into the problems solved at this stage, advantages and disadvantages of the various approaches used, lessons learned, and meaningful contributions to enhance applications based on deep learning. In this sense, the first workshop on Deep Learning Applications (DeLA) provided a forum for the presentation and discussion of novel research ideas or actual deployments focused on the development of advanced applications based on Deep Learning.

Organization

Organizing Committee

Dalila Durães	University of Minho, Portugal
Cleber Zanchetin	Northwestern University, USA
Leonardo Matos	Federal University of Sergipe, Brazil
Flávio Santos	University of Minho, Braga, Portugal

Program Committee

Ricardo Matsumura Araujo	Federal University of Pelotas, Brazil
Adriano Lorena Inacio de Oliveira	Federal University of Pernambuco, Brazil
Francisco Marcondes	University of Minho, Portugal
Bruno Fernandes	University of Minho, Portugal
Tiago Oliveira	Tokyo Medical and Dental Univerity, Japan
Ângelo Costa	Technical University of Valencia, Spain
Hector Moretón	University of Leon, Spain
Javier Bajo	Technical University of Madrid, Spain
Paulo Novais	University of Minho, Portugal
Hugo Peixoto	University of Minho, Portugal
Pedro Oliveira	University of Minho, Portugal

A Computer Vision Model for Detecting Suspicious Behaviour from Multiple Cameras in Crime Hotspots Using Convolutional Neural Networks

Omobayo A. Esan[1]([⊠]) [iD] and Isaac O. Osunmakinde[2] [iD]

[1] School of Computing, College of Science, Engineering and Technology, University of South Africa, Pretoria, South Africa
58525483@mylife.unisa.ac.za
[2] Computer Science Department, College of Science, Engineering and Technology, Norfolk State University, Norfolk, VA, USA
ioosunmakinde@nsu.edu

Abstract. Conventional security surveillance systems detect suspicious behaviours by the active participation of human operators constantly watching monitors showing video streams of activities captured from different cameras. The datasets are manually retrieved and analyzed after the occurrence of the incidents. This often leads to misinterpretation and late detection in a real-life environment. Recent studies have investigated the current surveillance systems for the challenges of the detection of suspicious incidents. The research question here is: How can suspicious breaking into run be detected being a common red flag leading to most crimes? This research develops a computer vision framework based on feature engineering, convolutional neural network (CNN), and median filtering to address the lacuna faced by the surveillance systems. Experiments were conducted on real-life image frames captured from multiple camera datasets. The proposed model outperforms the conventional approaches in terms of the detection of suspicious behavioural patterns with an average F1-score of 0.9661, a false positive rate of 0.0734, and an accuracy of 94.81%. The deployment of this proposed model in a crowded environment can help to augment the work of security personnel in raising awareness regarding possible crime at hot spots.

Keywords: Computer vision · Convolutional neural networks · Deep learning · Security · Surveillance

1 Introduction

Surveillance cameras are the predominant security mechanisms used in many organizations to monitor and protect people's lives and properties against crime [1]. The conventional surveillance camera often requires the active participation of human operators. Such vigilant personnel constantly watch the monitors showing all the video streams

A. González-Briones et al. (Eds.): PAAMS Workshops 2022, CCIS 1678, pp. 197–209, 2022.
https://doi.org/10.1007/978-3-031-18697-4_16

captured from various cameras. The technological capability of the system is therefore determined by the human operators who monitor the system [2].

The deployment of surveillance cameras in many public places involves the passive recording of all activities that take place at every moment, resulting in huge video datasets [2]. In the detection of any suspicious behaviours, these archived video datasets are manually retrieved and analyzed by the security operators after the occurrence of the incident. Consequently, analyzing a huge dataset of video sequences manually can overwhelm the security operators who needed the information to make an accurate decision [3]. Furthermore, most conventional surveillance cameras exhibit static localization properties. The exposed image frames captured are susceptible to environmental noises such as illuminations, occlusions, shadows, low camera resolution, etc., resulting in low-quality image scene resolution of incidents occurring in the environment [3].

Crime is one of the major issues confronted by many nations on the continent, leading to death and loss of valuable properties [4]. Recent studies have investigated the significant effects of crime on the economy of many nations in the world [4]. Figure 1 shows the estimated statistics of the death rates by crime index in some African countries between 2012 and 2021 [5].

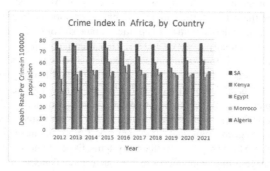

Fig. 1. Death rates by crime in some African countries 2012–2021 adapted from [5]

Figure 1 shows the statistics of the estimated death rate by crime incidents in some African countries from 2012 to 2021. These crime incidences include riots, protests, and gun-related offenses, inter alia. From Fig. 1, one can see the negative effect of crime incidents in terms of death per 100,000 people in each nation in African countries [5]. This prevalence of a high crime rate in many African countries has led to great financial loss, together with the loss of investors in the economy. To address this issue of crime, it is imperative to develop a preventive security system that can detect suspicious patterns before they manifest in crime.

Conventional surveillance security systems have proven deficient in certain aspects of detecting suspicious behaviour that could lead to crime. Intelligent components have been absent, therefore full reliance on human assessment [3]. Thus, there is a need to develop an intelligent surveillance security system that can give security personnel advance notice of the locations where crime is likely to occur. Deep learning technology with the convolutional neural network (CNN) has shown promising results in video surveillance suspicious detection due to its strong capability of feature extraction from high dimensional image data with complex structures and ability to handle imbalance data which might result in a bias towards the majority group (i.e., true cases) during detection [3]. This study, therefore, develops a computer vision framework based on feature engineering, median filtering, and a deep learning convolutional neural networks model that can intelligently detect suspicious behavioural patterns, creating early warning about a crime. In doing so, the main research question is raised below.

1.1 Research Question and Contributions

Based on the above background, this research poses the question: *How can a crowded environment be monitored to detect suspicious breaking into a run from a set of camera frames possibly affected by environmental noise?* The computer vision model, which addresses the research question first utilizes a deep learning model to obtain suspicious behavioural patterns in image frames before security personnel makes a conclusive decision. The contributions of this paper are as follows:

- Development of a computer vision framework that encompasses multi-cameras, feature engineering, median filtering, and image processing components to address the issue of environmental noise in the image, feature extraction, and deep learning convolutional neural network to train relevant features from the image frames.
- Feature engineering for statistical extraction of numerical features from image frames compared with direct pixels extraction from the image frames.
- Early knowledge generation can give security personnel advance notice of suspicious behaviors and the locations where crime is likely to occur even when image frames are affected by environmental noise such as occlusions, shadows, smoke, illuminations, etc.
- Benchmarking the performance evaluations of the proposed model with other related detection models and publicly available University Minnesota (UMN) datasets rather than scientific/simulated datasets.

The deployment of this approach with application to a crowded environment is an emerging area. The remainder of this paper is arranged in the following order: Sect. 2 provides a review of the existing related techniques and the theoretical background of the proposed model. Section 3 presents a detailed explanation of the computer vision model on median filtering and CNN; Sect. 4 discusses various experiments and evaluations of the model. The concluding remarks are shared in Sect. 5.

2 Backgrounds

2.1 Related Techniques

Different research has been conducted on the prediction of crime to assist security personnel in forecasting the criminal behavioural patterns in a crowded environment. The summary of existing crime prediction methods in terms of the problem addressed, the method used, the result obtained, and their limitations are presented in Table 1.

Table 1. Summary of related works on crime prediction methods

Citations	Problem addressed	Method used	Result obtained	Limitations
[6]	Crime prediction due to randomness and possibility of re-occurrence anywhere at anytime	The use of classification techniques such as Naïve Bayes, Random Forest, and Gradient Boosting decision tree were used on the San Francisco crime dataset	The system gives accuracy as follows: Gradient Boost Decision Tree produces 98.5% Naïve Bayes produces 65.82% Random Forest gives 63.43%	The was only conducted on violent and non-violent crime activities, which does not justify how the performance of the approach will be when used with other criminal activities
[7]	Crime location classification and predictions	Deep learning architecture (Convolutional Neural Network and Long Short-Term Memory) is used	Experimental conducted using 5 different publicly available datasets with 10 state-of-the-art methods demonstrate that deep learning-based methods consistently outperform the existing best methods	The approach is computationally intensive
[8]	Effective understanding of criminal behavioural patterns	Four learning techniques; the K-NN, SVM, Random Forest, and XGBoost were used	Experimental results show that the proposed approach achieves up to 89% of precision for crime tendency, and 70% of precision for crime occurrences	The approach did not consider the extraction of features. Furthermore, using all proposed algorithms might require close ire assistance of domain experts

(continued)

Table 1. (*continued*)

Citations	Problem addressed	Method used	Result obtained	Limitations
[9]	Uncovering hidden patterns and correlation data analysis on large data to prevent crime	The multinomial logistic regression method was used for prediction purposes	Experimental results show that the model was able to successfully predict crime based on weekdays, districts, and hours of the incidents	It gives high false-positive errors

Although conventional techniques for the detection of suspicious behavioural patterns have been investigated in the literature. However, no enough work has considered noise disturbances, and the shortfall of revealing suspicious behavioural patterns that could lead to crime, as an early warning in crowded scenes for the security personnel. This research develops a convolutional neural network inclined on a deep learning model to address the misinterpretation and late detection behavioral patterns in surveillance security systems. The theoretical background used in this research is explained in Sect. 2.2.

2.2 Selected Theoretical Techniques

Median Filtering.
Median filtering is a nonlinear filter-processing technology that removes noise value in an image by replacing the median value of the neighbours (mask) [12]. This is as in Eq. (1), where (x, y), $g(x, y)$ is the original image and the output image, W is the two-dimensional mask which can be linear, square, circular, etc. One of the advantages of median filtering is that it is an efficient filter to remove unwanted noise from an image.

$$g(x, y) = med\{f(x - i, y - j), i, j \in W \tag{1}$$

Convolutional Neural Network.
A CNN is a type of artificial neural network that uses a convolutional layer to filter inputs for obtaining useful information for the network [13]. The layers of CNN are further discussed in detail in the subsequent sections.

Convolutional Layer.
This layer uses convolutional filters called kernels, with a defined size, which cover the entire input data to perform a convolution operation. The filter slides over the input matrix with a stride, and this process teaches how to detect patterns from the previous

layers as in Eq. (2), where $(f_k)_{i,j}$ is the convolved image, $X_{i,j}$ represents the input image, W_k is the weight, and b_k is the bias.

$$(f_k)_{i,j} = (W_k * X)_{i,j} + b_k \tag{2}$$

Rectified Linear Unit.
ReLU (rectified linear unit) applies a non-saturating activation function to remove negative values from an activation map by setting them to zero as in Eqs. (3)–(4). The ReLU increases the non-linear properties of the decision function and the overall network without affecting the receptive field of the convolutional layer.

$$f(x) = \max(0, x) \tag{3}$$

$$\frac{d}{dx}\text{ReLU}(x) = \begin{cases} 1 \; if \; x = 0 \\ 0 \; otherwise \end{cases} \tag{4}$$

Pooling Layer.
The purpose of the pooling layer in CNN is to summarize the nearby neighborhood pixels, replacing them in the output at a location with summarized features as in Eq. (5), where $x[i]$ is the 2D input image, $w[k]$ is the filter of length k, r is the stride with which the image input is sampled, and $y[i]$ is the output of the convolution image. The subsequent section gives a detailed explanation of the methodology used for the implementation of the proposed model for the detection of break into run suspicious.

$$y[i] = \sum_{k=1}^{k} x[i + r.k]w[k] \tag{5}$$

3 Development of Deep Learning Computer Vision Framework

The system architecture is designed to detect the likely suspicious behaviour patterns as break into run in a crowded environment is divided into three stages, including the data acquisition stage, image pre-processing stage, and detection stage, see Fig. 2.

3.1 Stage 1: Data Acquisition

The image frames used in this research were acquired from the multiple surveillance cameras mounted at various hotspot locations in the campus environment. The frames were directed to image pre-processing for further processing.

IMAGE ACQUISITION STAGE

IMAGE PRE-PROCESSING

DETECTION STAGE

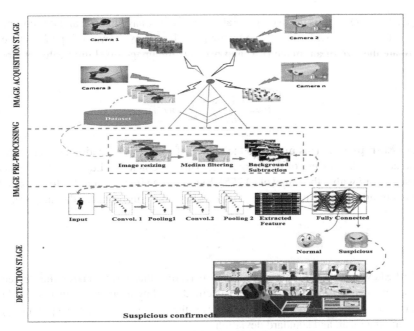

Fig. 2. Detection of suspicious patterns in image frames

3.2 Stage 2: Image Pre-processing

Image pre-processing has become a regular operation in image processing for computational efficiency. This is illustrated in the upper layer see Fig. 2.

Image Resizing and Noise Removal.
In this research, the original image captured from the camera is 576×576. To reduce the computational complexity of the image data, this image is resized by 256×256 using a bilinear interpolation algorithm [12]. This is then passed to median filtering for further processing as shown on the middle layer of Fig. 2.

Background Subtraction.
The background subtraction is performed on the filtered image by separating the current image background $I(x, y, t)$ at the time (t) from the previous image frame $I(x, y, t - 1)$ at a time (t–1) using the frame differencing technique [12], as in Eq. (6), where $I(x, y, t)$ is the current image background at the time (t), and $I(x, y, t - 1)$ is the previous image frame at a time (t–1). This operation keeps the foreground image which is then passed to the next stage for further processing.

$$Foreground = |I(x, y, t) - I(x, y, t - 1)| \tag{6}$$

Feature Engineering Stage
The foreground image is fed into the feature engineering stage where the features in the image are statistically extracted using the image mean, entropy, skewness, and kurtosis.

[i] Mean (μ): This is the average of all pixels in the image matrix, and it is computed to reflect the grey distribution of the image [12]. This is as shown in Eq. (7), where M and N are the size of an image (i, j) and $p(i, j)$ is the image pixel grey value at a point (i, j).

$$\mu = \frac{1}{MN} \sum_{i=1}^{N} \sum_{j=1}^{M} p(i, j) \tag{7}$$

[ii] **Entropy** (E): This measures the degree of image pixel randomness and is used to characterize the texture of the image [12]. This is depicted in Eq. (8), where p_i is the probability of i within the range of [0,255]. Entropy is an important index to measure the richness of information in an image; it reflects how much information the image carries.

$$E = - \sum_{i=0}^{255} p_i log_2 p_i \tag{8}$$

[iii] **Skewness** (S_{sk}): This is a statistical feature that characterizes the degree of asymmetry of pixel distribution in the specified window around its mean value [12]. This is computed using Eq. (9), where, $p(i, j)$ is the image pixel value at a point (i, j), μ and σ are the mean and standard deviation.

$$S_{sk} = \frac{1}{MN} \sum_{i=1}^{M} \sum_{j=1}^{N} [p(i, j) - \mu)/\sigma]^3 \tag{9}$$

[iv] **Kurtosis** (k): This measures the peak or flatness of a distribution related to a normal distribution in the image [12], and this is computed as in Eq. (10), where $p(i, j)$ is the image pixel value at a point and (i, j), μ is the mean value of the pixel.

$$k = \frac{1}{MN} \sum_{i=1}^{M} \sum_{j=1}^{N} [p(i, j) - \mu]^4 - 3 \tag{10}$$

3.3 Stage 3: Detection

The output of the extracted image is used as the input of the CNN model for training and detection purposes. The CNN takes the original image of size 256×256 with 1×1 kernel size and 1 filter produced $256 \times 256 \times 1$ output. The output is passed as input to the convolution layer 1, where a convolution operation is performed on the image with the 3×3 kernel size and filters of 24 to obtain $128 \times 128 \times 24$ as the output. The pooling layer 1 takes the output of the convolutional layer 1 as input and uses a 2×2 kernel size with a filter of 32 to obtain $64 \times 64 \times 32$ as a feature map. The output of convolutional layer 2 is fed as input to the pooling layer 2 as shown in Table 2.

The ReLU activation function is applied to increase the non-linear properties of the decision function in the neural network, as in (4). Thereafter the Softmax function is implemented to classify the behavioural patterns in the image as either normal or suspicious.

Table 2. Parameters for the CNN architecture for detection of suspicious behavioural patterns

Layers	Kernel size	Filters	Input	Output
Original image	1×1	1	$256 \times 256 \times 1$	$256 \times 256 \times 1$
Convolutional layer 1	3×3	24	$256 \times 256 \times 1$	$128 \times 128 \times 24$
Pooling layer 1	2×2	32	$128 \times 128 \times 24$	$64 \times 64 \times 32$
Convolutional layer 2	3×3	48	$64 \times 64 \times 32$	$32 \times 32 \times 48$
Pooling layer 2	4×4	32	$32 \times 32 \times 48$	$16 \times 16 \times 32$

3.4 Evaluation Metrics

To evaluate the performance of the proposed model, the confusion matrix and hold-out cross-validation technique are adopted, the detailed metrics can be found in [13].

4 Experimental Evaluation and Results

4.1 Data Description and Experimental Settings

The experimental set-up utilizes three analogous high definitions (AHD) surveillance cameras with a 576×576 resolution at 30 frames per sec to obtain real-life image frames at various crowded hotspot locations in the campus environment with different scenarios as explained in Sect. 3.1. The publicly available suspicious dataset used for the experiments was obtained from the University of Minnesota (UMN) [14] repository. The implementation software used in this research is MATLAB R2017. The suspicious behaviour was deliberately mixed with normal behavioural patterns image frames, making 12700 images, and trained with the proposed model for detection purposes as previously explained in Sect. 3.3.

4.2 Experiment 1: Detection of Suspicious Suddenly Breaking into a Run on Real-Life Datasets

This section shows the visualized performance of the proposed model on suspicious suddenly breaking into a run using real-life image frames see Fig. 3

Figure 3(a)–(c) is the original noisy frame; Fig. 3(d)–(f) presents the output of noise removal on the image using median filtering. Figure 3(g)–(i) has extracted foreground region result using background subtractions; while finally, Figs. 3(j)–(l) presents the image detection region with the red part showing the suspicious suddenly breaking into a run compared with the labelled ground truth. To further ascertain the performance of the proposed model, the proposed approach is compared with other detection models (such as optical flow, and GoogleLeNet CNNs) to detect suspicious behavioural patterns. This is done by conducting a quantitative experiment using a cross-validation technique of 90% for training and 10% for testing. The confusion matrix for suspicious suddenly breaking into a run see Fig. 4(a)–(d).

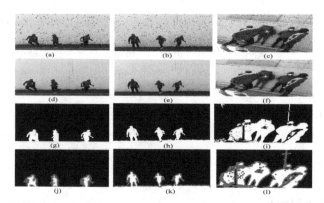

Fig. 3. Visual inspection of suspicious suddenly breaking into a run from cameras

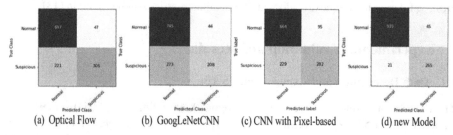

(a) Optical Flow   (b) GoogLeNetCNN   (c) CNN with Pixel-based   (d) new Model

Fig. 4. Confusion matrix for suspicious suddenly breaking into a run using Optical flow, GoogleLeNet CNNs, CNN with Pixel-based extraction, and the proposed model

Figure 4(a)–(d) depict the confusion matrix for detection of suspicious suddenly breaking into a run using three different models with the proposed model. Furthermore, the summary of model performance used compared with the proposed model in terms of recall, precision, F1-score, and accuracy is shown in Table 3.

Table 3. Summary of performance metrics on conventional techniques

Models	Recall	Precision	FPR	F1-score	Accuracy (%)
Optical flow	0.9368	0.7593	0.4202	0.83887	78.89
GoogleLeNet CNNs	0.9442	0.7318	0.5676	0.8245	75.04
CNN with pixel	0.8748	0.7436	0.4481	0.8039	74.49
Proposed model	0.9543	0.9781	0.0734	0.9661	94.81

Table 3 produces optical Flow with a recall of 0.9368; for GoogleLeNet CNNs it is 0.9442, and the proposed model is 0.9543. The precision of optical Flow, GoogleLeNet CNNs, and the proposed model are found to be 0.7593, 0.7318, and 0.9781, respectively. The accuracy of optical Flow is 0.7889, the GoogleLeNet CNNs is 0.7504, and the proposed model is 94.81%. It is worth noting that the high detection accuracy in the proposed technique on the real-life dataset compared with other detection models was due to the feature engineering and quality noise removal characteristics of median filtering and CNN, which are used during the detection process.

4.3 Experiment 2: Benchmarking Popular Publicly Available UMN Video Dataset for Detection of Suddenly Breaking into a Run

The intention here is to determine whether the proposed model can detect suspicious suddenly breaking into a run. For the visual result of the proposed model, see Fig. 5

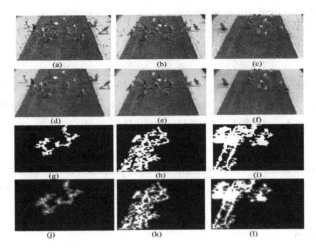

Fig. 5. Visual inspection of a sudden breaking into a run

Figure 5(a)–(c) consists of the original noisy suspicious behavioural frame; Fig. 5(d)–(f) presents the output of noise removal median filtering which removes the environmental noise on the image frames. Figure 5(g)–(i) presents the extracted foreground output obtained using background subtraction. Figure 5(j)–(l) presents the result of detection regions. The red highlight indicates the suspicious suddenly breaking into a run detected in the image frame. To further ascertain the performance of the proposed model, the proposed approach is compared with other detection models by using a similar cross-validation technique as in experiment 1. The confusion matrix for suspicious suddenly breaking into a run see Fig. 6(a)–(d).

Figures 6(a)–(d) depict the confusion matrix for detection of suspicious suddenly breaking into a run using four different models. The summary of model performance used compared with the proposed model in terms of recall, precision, F1-score, and accuracy is shown in Table 4.

Considering all the metrics used for comparison in Table 4, one can observe that the proposed model consistently outperforms other models. These results show that using feature engineering with CNN can improve overall suspicious detection in a crowded environment. For example, one can observe an increase in accuracy by 0.2–0.31% across

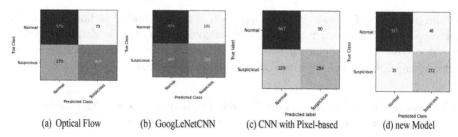

| (a) Optical Flow | (b) GoogLeNetCNN | (c) CNN with Pixel-based | (d) new Model |

Fig. 6. Confusion matrix using Optical flow, GoogleLeNet CNNs, CNN with Pixel-based extraction, and the proposed model on the UMN dataset

Table 4. Summary of performance metrics on conventional techniques

Models	Recall	Precision	FPR	F1-score	Accuracy (%)
Optical flow	0.8865	0.6786	0.4306	0.8389	72.99
GoogleLeNet CNNs	0.7835	0.5802	0.5158	0.8245	62.68
CNN with pixel	0.8811	0.6604	0.4464	0.8069	74.88
Proposed model	0.9502	0.9632	0.1140	0.9661	93.47

different detection models. This result attests to the proposed model of feature engineering and quality noise removal being suited to use for the detection of suspicious activities in crowded scenes.

5   Conclusion

Early detection of suspicious behavioural pattern systems is an effective tool that can be used to curb potential security threats. Nonetheless, detecting suspicious patterns in a crowded environment has proven to be a difficult problem due to the shortfall of revealing adequate suspicious behavioural patterns most especially in a noisy image frame. The classical techniques and most current practices on campuses rely heavily on surveillance cameras monitored by humans, often leading to misinterpretation of events. This research develops a computer vision framework based on feature engineering and a convolutional neural network model based on deep learning, to address the delays of revealing suspicious behavioural patterns to security operatives. Experimental evaluations of the proposed model were conducted on both real-life and publicly available datasets; benchmarked with other related detection methods (see Tables 3–4), indicating that the proposed model was able to accurately detect suspicious behavioural patterns and outperform other popular detection models. Future work can find possible interactions between the crime types/trends at various locations.

References

1. Karmakar, K., Kundu, S., Paul, S.: Design and implementation of information security using neural network architecture. Int. J. Appl. Eng. **13**(11), 9916–9923 (2018). ISSN: 0973–4562

2. Malathi, A., Baboo, S.S.: An enhanced algorithm to predict a future crime using data mining. Int. J. Comput. Appl. **21**(1), 1–6 (2011). ISBN:0975-8887
3. Shilpa, H., Prathap, L., Sunitha, M.R.: A survey on moving object detection and tracking techniques. Int. J. Eng. Comput. Sci. **5**(5), 16376–16382 (2016)
4. Shojaee, S., Mustapha, A., Sidi, F., Jabar, M.A.: A study on classification learning algorithms to predict crime status. Int. J. Digital Content Technol. Appl. **7**(9), 361–369 (2013). https://doi.org/10.4156/jdcta
5. Numbeo: Crime index by Country [Online] Available: https://numbeo.com/crime/rankings_by_country.jsp?title=2020
6. Rajenderan, S.V., Thang, K.F.: Real-time detection of suspicious human movement. In: Proceedings of the International Conference on Electrical, Electronics, Computer Engineering and their Applications, pp. 56–69 (2014)
7. Zhang, X.: Image denoising using local Weiner filter and its method noise. Optik Journal **127**(17), 6821–6828 (2016)
8. Dheepa, V., Dhanapal, R.: Behaviour-based credit card fraud detection using support vector machines. ICTACT J. Soft Comput. **2**(4), 391–397 (2012). ISSN: 2229-6956(Online)
9. Ha, R., Liu, P., Jia, K.: An improved adaptive median filter algorithm and its application. In: Advances in Intelligent Information Hiding and Multimedia Signal Processing, vol. 64, pp. 179–186, ISBN: 978-3-319-50212-0 (2017)
10. Chauhan, R., Ghanshala, K.K., Joshi, R.C.: Convolutional Neural Network (CNN) for image detection and recognition. In: 2018 First International Conference on Secure Cyber Computing and Communication (ICSCCC), vol. 2, pp. 1–7, ISBN:978-1-5386-6374-5 (2018)
11. Titus, J., Geroge, S.: A comparison study on different interpolation methods based on satellite images. Int. J. Eng. Res. Technol. **2**(6) (2013). ISSN (Online): 2278-0181
12. Zhao, J., Zhou, C., Huang, L., Yang, X., Xu, B., Liang, D.: Fusion of unmanned aerial vehicle panchromatic and hyperspectral images combining joint skewness-kurtosis figures and a non-subsampled contourlet. Sensors **18**(3467), 1–23 (2018)
13. Yu, T., Yan, J., Lu, w.: Combining background subtraction and convolutional neural network for anomaly detection in pumping-unit surveillance. Algorithm **12**(115), 1–13 (2019). https://doi.org/10.3390/a12060115
14. Nayau, N., Sahu, S.S., Kumar, S.: Detecting anomalous crowd behavior using correlation analysis of optical flow. SIViP **13**, 1233–1241 (2019)

Analysis of Machine Learning Algorithms for Violence Detection in Audio

Bruno Veloso📧, Dalila Durães(✉)📧, and Paulo Novais📧

ALGORITMI Centre, University of Minho, Braga, Portugal
a78352@alunos.uminho.pt, dalila.duraes@algoritmi.uminho.pt,
pjon@di.uminho.pt

Abstract. Violence has always been part of humanity, however, there are different types of violence, with physical violence being the most recurrent in our daily lives. This type of violence increasingly affects many people's lives, so it is essential to try to combat violence. In recent years, human action recognition has been extensively studied, but mainly in video, an important computer vision area. Audio appears as a factor capable of circumventing these problems. Audio sensors can be omni-directional, requiring less processing power and hardware and software performance when compared to the video. The audio can represent emotions. It is not affected by lighting or temperature problems, nor does it need to be at a favourable angle to capture the intended information. That said, audio is seen as the best way to recognize violence, applied with *Machine Learning/Deep Learning/Transfer Learning techniques.* In this paper we test a Convolutional Neural Network (CNN), a ResNet50, VGG16 and VGG19, in order to classify audios. Later we see that CNN obtains the best results, with a 92.44% accuracy in the test set. ResNet50 was the worst model used, obtaining an 86.34% accuracy. For the VGG models, both show a good potential but did not get better results than CNN.

Keywords: Audio violence detection · Deep learning · Transfer learning · Audio action recognition

1 Introduction

In 2020, 66408 cases were reported to the Portuguese Association for Victim Support (APAV- Associação Portuguesa de Apoio à Vítima), of which 31% correspond to 'crimes and other forms of violence' (it is a category in the study). Of these 31%, 94% represent acts of violence against people [1]. The detection and recognition of violence have been areas of research interest, mainly in surveillance. The main objective of detecting and recognizing violence is to carry it out automatically and in real time, in order to be able to provide assistance to victims in a timely manner [2].

Supported by organization ALGORITMI Centre.

A. González-Briones et al. (Eds.): PAAMS Workshops 2022, CCIS 1678, pp. 210–221, 2022.
https://doi.org/10.1007/978-3-031-18697-4_17

Violence has always been part of humanity, and it can be expressed in different ways. The fact that there are different ways of practicing violence, means that it has to be reduced in society. One of the types that is more present in society is domestic violence. Domestic violence is then recognized as a serious public health problem, which can not only cause physical harm to the victim, as well as mental harm to the victim [3, 4].

When talking about violence detection, it is mainly associated with detecting violence through the video. However, capturing video requires great capacity and performance of hardware and software. Another method that can be used to violence detection is with the use of audio, as it can be identified and/or classified through *machine learning (ML)* [5]. Audio can be easily captured by microphones. These sensors are very powerful and can capture human behavior and emotions. Thus, a good representation of audio is critical to complement and prove the video classification [6, 7].

Audio plays a critical role in understanding the environment around us, containing information that visual data cannot represent. Hence, its analysis is important, since, when analyzing the content of audio, it is possible to interpret the medium in which it was captured or its present situation. After analysing the importance of audio for understanding and environment, it is interesting that this can be used to build systems capable of automatically detecting and recognizing violence [3, 8].

In this way, we find that automatic audio classification is a growing research area, with results that allow its application in real cases. The study and classification of audio can be very important for the resolution of several issues, namely in the detection of violence, where one can recognize whether the environment, in which a particular person is inserted, is in any way prone to violence or not. For that, we propose the use of *deep learning (DL)/transfer learning (TL)* to classify the audios in terms of violence or not.

The paper is organized as follows: next section presents the Literature Review with explanations of recognition og Human Actions, audio vs video, audio representation, and dataset. Section 3 described the dataset where it was explained the preprocessing, while Sect. 4, Experiments, describe the models of deep learning used and training details of the experiments. Section 5, present the results and the discussion. Finally, Sect. 6 concludes this work with some future directions.

2 Literature Review

This literature review begins with the explanations of recognition of Human Actions and the difference between action predictions and action recognition. Then some difference between audio and video is described. Following it analyses the audio representation as well as the different methods. Finally, it presents some existing public datasets.

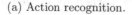

(a) Action recognition.   (b) Action prediction.

Fig. 1. Classification of human actions, where a) represents an action recognition, and b) represents a prediction of an action. All rights belong to *DarrenLevyOfficial* [19]

2.1 Recognition of Human Actions

In the last decade, the analysis of human movement and recognition of actions have been extensively studied by researchers [2,3,3,6,9].

All human actions are done with some purpose. For example, to complete a physical exercise, the person interacts and responds with the environment using legs, arms, hands, etc. One of the biggest goals of artificial intelligence is to build a machine capable of understanding actions and human interactions.

As technological advances increase, it is becoming possible to develop machines capable of understanding human actions. There are two cores topic, which are: action prediction, trying to predict the human action using data that do not correspond to the totality of the action; and action recognition, which tries to recognize/classify the action using data regarding the total execution of the action [9].

Action prediction focuses on the future state. Often, machines cannot wait for the execution of total action before acting, so it's important that they are able to predic whether we will be facing a risky action [9], using the data collected so far, that could put people'se lives at risk. For example, trying to predict that a robbery will occur, in order to prevent or contain it as soon as possible, as can be seen in Fig. 1b, the passenger, dressed in black, extends his hand around the driver, and not having the complete action, you can only try to predict what will happen next, in this case it was an assault on the driver.

Action recognition attemps to identify human action based on data that represent the action in its entirety. One of the biggest problems with recognizing human actions is the detection of violence. As the Fig. 1a illustrates, the previously mentioned scene of the robbery is already complete, so we can try to recognize what the action is, which in this case this recognition would say that it was a robbery.

2.2 Audio vs Video

The signal produced by the sound of an audio contains information that visual data cannot represent [3].

Audio sensors (microphones) have very interesting particularities, to which video sensors (cameras) cannot compete. When detecting violence through audio, the need for bandwidth, storage, and computational resources are much lower then when compared to video [14]. This is due to the fact that audio is one-dimensional (time), unlike video which is three-dimensional (width × height × time), and this allows for a greater number of audio sensors (since its cheaper per unit) and also having a more complex signal processing due to requiring less computing resources. Cameras have a limited angular field of view, while the microphones are omnidirectional, this allowing a spherical field of view. Audio sensors do not have problems with lighting and temperatures, so the audio to be processed is not affected. A video, by itself alone, cannot represent information such as screams, explosions, words of abuse, or emotions [6]. Audio event acquisition is better because the audio wave length is longer and many surfaces allow reflections of acoustic waves, so obstacle in the way can be bypassed [14].

However, audio also has its problems, and sometimes these are difficult to avoid. Some of these problems are: there may be an overlap of several audios, for example a song that is in the background, which can affect the classification of the audio, when there is multipath propagation that results in an echo, and if the microphone is far from the audio we want to capture, it makes it harder to understand what kind of environment this one was captured [6].

The main problem, regarding any type of data capture, is due to privacy. The capture of images or audio raises very important ethical issues, which can lead to some debates about whether it is correct or not, but, as there is no other form of surveillance, this was put aside for the continuation of the study and it will be used audio.

2.3 Audio Representation

The audio can be represented, so that it can be interpreted by the human being. The main idea is in taking the audio signal and converting it into a visual image. These images, generated from the audio, can then be used to extract features from them, either by hand, or fed directly to a DL/TL classifier, as there are classifiers that can learn and extract features [15].

There are some methods that can be used to create this images (spectrograms), that represent the audio, and some are: *Short-Time Fourier Transform, Chromagram, Mel-Spectrogram* [14]. As we will only be using mel-spectrograms, this will be the only to be explained.

A Mel-spectrogram is a spectrogram whose y-axis has been applied a mel scale. For this to be obtained, some steps have to be fulfilled. These are [16]:

1. Divide the audio into fixed-size windows, with a smaller hop size between windows than division size.
2. For each window, apply *Fast Fourier Transform* to move from the time domain to the frequency domain.
3. Take the frequency spectrum, originated in the previous step, and apply *mel scale*.
4. For each window, decompose the magnitude of the signal and its components, corresponding to the frequencies from the mel scale.

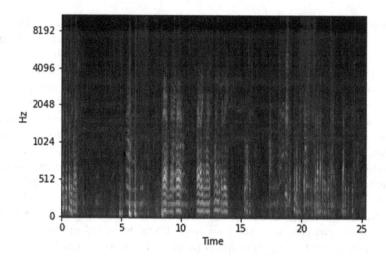

Fig. 2. Representation of a *mel-spectrogram*.

The Mel-spectrogram, over time (x-axis), shows successive frequencies (y-axis), as well as the different amplitudes (colors, measured in dB) for each instant, as can be seen in the Fig. 2.

2.4   Public Datasets

To find a dataset with audios involving violence or not, is really hard. But there are some datasets that are worth mentioned.

The Real Life Violence Situations dataset (RLVS) has 2000 videos. 1000 videos are classified as violence videos and the other 1000 are classified as non-violence videos. These videos were extracted from *YouTube*. The violent videos are extracted from many environments like prisons, streets, schools, etc., and the non violent videos represent different human actions like sports, eating, walking, etc. This dataset includes a wide variety of race, gender and age. Some of the videos, that the dataset contains, have no sound, and resolution can go from 480p to 720p (indoor or outdoor environments) [11].

NTU CCTV-Fights dataset has 1000 videos, some without sound, taken from *YouTube*. The actions in this dataset, goes from pushing, to kicking, fighting, pulling, among others. The dataset is divided into CCTV, which are videos captured by surveillance cameras, and NON-CCTV, which are videos capture by dash-cams, cell phone cameras, drones and helicopters. The CCTV group consists of 280 files, which include different types of fights, ranging from 5 s to 12 min, 8.54 h in total. The NON-CCTV group has 720 videos, ranging from 3 s to 7 min, giving a total of 9.13 h of videos [12].

XD-Violence dataset, contains 4754 videos, not all of them contain audio, these videos are divided into two categories, violence with 2405 videos and 2349 without violence, giving a total of 217 h in videos. Videos marked with violence can be further distinguished between six different types of violence, which are: abuse, car accident, explosion, fight, riot and shooting. Each video of violence can also contain between 1 and 3 labels inclusive, and the order of the labels corresponds to the importance they have for the different events during the video. The videos in this dataset are clips from movies, cartoons, video games, news, sports, music, fitness, live scenes (captured by surveillance cameras, people recording with cell phone, etc.), etc. [13].

3   Dataset

The dataset is required in order to evaluate the models implemented, but no dataset was found that contained the specific restrictions. So, a group of researchers created their own dataset, making all the recording of all the scences of violence, and non violence, inside a car with people who are not actors and during the pandemic. The dataset consist in videos, all of them have sound, and they represent 20 different scenarios. From that 20 different scenarios, 12 of them have violence included and the other 8 only contain non violence. Violence scenarios are: push and punch, three fight scenarios (one is only push, and the other two are real fighting), discussion and one person strangles another, discussion and slap, two scenarios involving sexual harassment, three scenarios involving robbery (using knife or gun), and lastly, one person forcing to see the phone of another. Non violence scenarios are: people hug each other, two scenarios involving taking photos, one person fix the hair and the other sleeps, one person sneezes and the other reads a book, one person yawns and the other listens to music, one person answers a call and the other coughs and uses a notebook, and lastly, one person writes something and the other uses alcohol gel. Each scenario was recorded with 16 different pairs of actors. Some scenes contain the use of objects as well.

3.1   Preprocessing the Dataset

The dataset had 795 violence videos and 494 non-violence videos. The next step was to go through each of these files and convert them to mp3 files, once that it is only necessary the audio of them. For this, a python script was created that traverses the folders and, with the use of a python library called *moviepy*[1] converts mp4 and MOV files to mp3. Due to the existence of very large non-violent audio files, it was decided that, for all those that had more than 40 s, they would be divided in half, using a python library called *pydub*[2] thus creating a new entry in the dataset. As for the audios of violence, these were generally longer than non-violence, and had the problem that, for the most part, the first 10 to 25 s did not contain violence. So, the solution was to analyze audio by audio and see when violence started, and using the *pydub* library it was possible

---

[1] Biblioteca *moviepy* https://github.com/Zulko/moviepy.

[2] Biblioteca *pydub* https://github.com/jiaaro/pydub.

to split the audio into two audios, in which the first corresponds to non-violence and the second to violence. There were also some audios that did not contain any content, this could be because they accidentally recorded it or because they didn't know it was recording, and these were all removed, thus giving a total of 1175 non-violence and 755 violence audios. After all this process, the non-violence audios were analyzed again to see which ones could be removed in order to balance the dataset. The result was a dataset with 860 non-violence audios and 755 violence audios. The next step was to go to the RLVS dataset and see the violence audios that could be inserted to balance the dataset. We got 105 violent videos from the RLVS dataset, and these were converted to audio and added to the final dataset, giving us a total of 860 non-violence audios and 860 violence audios. The last thing to do was to loop through all the audios and create a mel spectrogram of each audio, using the python library called *librosa*[3] to be fed into the deep learning models. Finally, the dataset was then divided into 80% for training and 20% for testing. The training folder contains 1376 mel spectrograms, of which, 688 correspond to non violence mel spectrograms and 688 violence mel spectrograms. In the test folder there are a total of 344 mel spectrograms, and of these, 172 are non violence and 172 are violence.

4   Experiment

In this section we are going to present the experiments that we did. Starting with the presentation of the models that were tested, in Subsect. 4.1. Later in this section, we present all the training details regarding our networks implemented, and refering the conditions where the models were trained, in the Subsect. 4.2.

4.1   Deep Learning Models

In this subsection we present the four models that have been used, the reason is that they are some of the most used in the literature [14]. The models that we have applied are: Convolutional Neural Network (CNN), ResNet50, VGG16 e VGG19.

Convolutional Neural Network is a deep learning model that is focused on image classification. This neural network, with sufficient training, can learn features that are present in the images, and is able to capture spatial and temporal dependencies, in an image, by applying relevant filters. The architecture, of a CNN, was inspired by the connection of neurons in the human brain [17].

Residual Network (ResNet) was developed to resolve the vanishing gradient problem by skipping layers with identity functions. ResNet can have multiple network depths and the depth is followed by their name, for example the one we use is ResNet50 which means that it has depth 50 [10].

---

[3] Biblioteca *librosa* https://librosa.org/doc/latest/index.html.

VGG, meaning Visual Geometry Group, is a deep CNN architecture with multiple layers. The deep refers to the number of layers they have. This is a transfer learning model, used for the classification of images, and it was trained using the *ImageNet* dataset [18]. We used two implementations of VGG, which are VGG16 and VGG19, the first has 16 convolutional layers and the last one has 19 convolutional layers, and these convolutional layers are used to extract features from the images [18].

To prepare for the algorithms, the train part of the dataset was divided, randomly, into train and validation. So 20% of the train folder will be for validation, which means that we have 1102 for the training part and 274 images for the validation part. Each class has the same quantity of images.

4.2 Training Details

All the networks were fed with only the images, using the dataset presented in the Sect. 3.1. The images are mel spectrograms of the audio in itself, and we never fed the networks with audio.

During the experiments, the CNN network was trained for 600 epochs, and ResNet50, VGG16 and VGG19 were trained for 35 epochs. As for CNN, the learning rate used was 0.01 and for ResNet50, VGG16 and VGG19, the learning rated applied was 0.001. All the models were trained on desktop with a NVIDIA GeForce GTX 1070 Ti GPU, 16 Gb of RAM, and has an AMD Ryzen 5 2600 processor.

Each model has the same callbacks. *EarlyStopping* callback that is checking validation loss and has a patience of 10, *ModelCheckpoint* to save the weights and is checking validation loss aswell, and last *ReduceLROnPlateau* to reduce learning rate when a metric has stopped improving, checking validation loss with a patience of 20 and a factor of 0.1.

Table 1 shows all the training parameters applied.

Table 1. Training details for every trained model.

Model	Optimizer	Learning rate	Epochs
CNN	Adam	0.01	600
ResNet50	Adamax	0.001	35
VGG16	Adamax	0.001	35
VGG19	Adamax	0.001	35

5 Results and Discussion

Before talking about results, we need to say that this study is limited to the 20 different scenarios used (recorded inside a car) and we didn't try this approach with another type of scenarios like violence in the street.

In Fig. 3, for each model we present two graphs, the first one is for the accuracy curve, and the second one is to analyze the loss curve. In all the graphs, the orange line represents the train set, and blue line is the validation set. Analyzing the loss curve, can give us an idea of how the model is learning, and if the model is underfitting or overfitting.

As shown in Fig. 3, the accuracy, for the train set and validation set, are close to each other in all models, except in the ResNet50 model. In ResNet50, validation set takes a much higher accuracy than the training set. As for the loss, it follows the same principle, where ResNet50 is the only model that have a much higher difference in training loss and validation loss. *EarlyStopping* callback, CNN only trained for 36 epochs.

The Fig. 3 also shows that validation accuracy, in the CNN, almost did not improve during every epoch, and it also had a similar behaviour compared to VGG16. With that said, the validation loss, in CNN, did not decrease during every epoch.

Table 2 shows the best accuracy obtained for every model, in the train set, validation set and test set. The model that obtained best accuracy in the train set was VGG16, in validation set the best model was VGG9 and for the test set was the CNN.

This results show that CNN had the best results so far, and ResNet50 may be to much complex for the problem to solve. As for the VGG, both VGG16 and VGG19 show good potential.

Table 2. Best accuracy results in every model.

Model	Train	Validation	Test
CNN	92.83	94.16	92.44
ResNet50	87.02	91.97	86.34
VGG16	95.01	93.43	90.41
VGG19	93.74	94.89	90.41

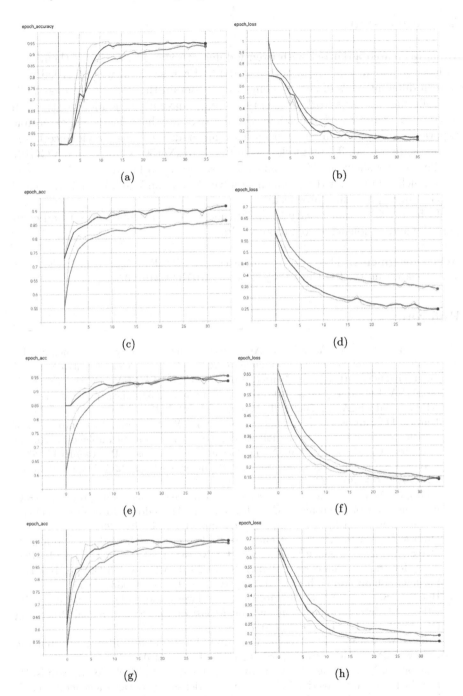

Fig. 3. Accuracy curve, on the left, and loss curve, on the right. Orange line is train set and blue line is validation set. a) and b) represent the use of CNN, c) and d) the use of ResNet, e) and f) model VGG16, and, g) and h) the VGG19. (Color figure online)

6   Conclusion

We have created a dataset with twenty different scenarios, twelve of them have violence included, and the other eight don't. Each scenario was recorded with sixteen different pairs of actors. Some scenes contain the use of objects as well.

Following previous work in the literature, we have used the Mel-spectrogram method for represented the audio signal. Next, we have made an extensible experience using four different deep learning models to classify violence based on the audio signal. These models were CNN, ResNet50, VGG16, and VGG19.

The results show that CNN had the best results so far, and ResNet50 may be to much complex for the problem to solve. As for the VGG, both VGG16 and VGG19 show promising prospects.

In future work is necessary to apply this models to public dataset and compare the audio violence recognition results.

Acknowledgments. This work is supported by: FCT Fundação para a Ciência e Tecnologia within the RD Units Project Scope: UIDB/00319/2020.

References

1. Souto, H., Mello, R., Furtado, A.: An acoustic scene classification approach involving domestic violence using machine learning. In: Anais do XVI Encontro Nacional de Inteligência Artificial e Computacional. SBC, 2019. APAV (2021). Estatisticas_APAV_Relatorio_Anual_2020.Pdf., apav.pt/apav_v3/images/pdf/Estatisticas_APAV_Relatorio_Anual_2020.pdf. Accessed 22 Oct 2021
2. Durães, D., Santos, F., Marcondes, F.S., Lange, S., Machado, J.: Comparison of transfer learning behaviour in violence detection with different public datasets. In: Marreiros, G., Melo, F.S., Lau, N., Lopes Cardoso, H., Reis, L.P. (eds.) EPIA 2021. LNCS (LNAI), vol. 12981, pp. 290–298. Springer, Cham (2021). https://doi.org/10.1007/978-3-030-86230-5_23
3. Souto, H., Mello, R., Furtado, A.: An acoustic scene classification approach involving domestic violence using machine learning. In: Anais do XVI Encontro Nacional de Inteligência Artificial e Computacional, pp. 705–716. SBC (2019)
4. Durães, D., Marcondes, F.S., Gonçalves, F., Fonseca, J., Machado, J., Novais, P.: Detection violent behaviors: a survey. In: Novais, P., Vercelli, G., Larriba-Pey, J.L., Herrera, F., Chamoso, P. (eds.) ISAmI 2020. AISC, vol. 1239, pp. 106–116. Springer, Cham (2021). https://doi.org/10.1007/978-3-030-58356-9_11
5. Hershey, S., et al.: CNN architectures for large-scale audio classification. In: 2017 IEEE International Conference on Acoustics, Speech and Signal Processing (ICASSP), pp. 131–135. IEEE (2017)
6. Crocco, M., Cristani, M., Trucco, A., Murino, V.: Audio surveillance: a systematic review. ACM Comput. Surv. (CSUR) **48**(4), 1–46 (2016)
7. Marcondes, F.S., Durães, D., Gonçalves, F., Fonseca, J., Machado, J., Novais, P.: In-vehicle violence detection in carpooling: a brief survey towards a general surveillance system. In: Dong, Y., Herrera-Viedma, E., Matsui, K., Omatsu, S., González Briones, A., Rodríguez González, S. (eds.) DCAI 2020. AISC, vol. 1237, pp. 211–220. Springer, Cham (2021). https://doi.org/10.1007/978-3-030-53036-5_23

8. Jesus, T., et al.: Review of trends in automatic human activity recognition using synthetic audio-visual data. In: Analide, C., Novais, P., Camacho, D., Yin, H. (eds.) IDEAL 2020. LNCS, vol. 12490, pp. 549–560. Springer, Cham (2020). https://doi.org/10.1007/978-3-030-62365-4_53

9. Kong, Y., Fu, Y.: Human action recognition and prediction: a survey. Int. J. Comput. Vision **130**(5), 1366–1401 (2022)

10. Wu, Z., Shen, C., Van Den Hengel, A.: Wider or deeper: revisiting the resnet model for visual recognition. Pattern Recogn. **90**, 119–133 (2019)

11. Soliman, M.M., Kamal, M.H., Nashed, M.A.E.M., Mostafa, Y.M., Chawky, B.S., Khattab, D.: Violence recognition from videos using deep learning techniques. In 2019 Ninth International Conference on Intelligent Computing and Information Systems (ICICIS), pp. 80–85. IEEE (2019)

12. Rapid-Rich Object Search Lab, NTU CCTV-Fights Dataset. https://rose1.ntu.edu.sg/dataset/cctvFights/. Accessed on 08 Jan 2022

13. Wu, P., et al.: Not only look, but also listen: learning multimodal violence detection under weak supervision. In: Vedaldi, A., Bischof, H., Brox, T., Frahm, J.-M. (eds.) ECCV 2020. LNCS, vol. 12375, pp. 322–339. Springer, Cham (2020). https://doi.org/10.1007/978-3-030-58577-8_20

14. Santos, F., et al.: In-car violence detection based on the audio signal. In: Yin, H., et al. (eds.) IDEAL 2021. LNCS, vol. 13113, pp. 437–445. Springer, Cham (2021). https://doi.org/10.1007/978-3-030-91608-4_43

15. Nanni, L., Costa, Y.M., Aguiar, R.L., Mangolin, R.B., Brahnam, S., Silla, C.N.: Ensemble of convolutional neural networks to improve animal audio classification. EURASIP J. Audio Speech Music Process. **2020**(1), 1–14 (2020)

16. Gartzman, Dalya, Getting to Know the Mel Spectrogram (2019). https://towardsdatascience.com/getting-to-know-the-mel-spectrogram-31bca3e2d9d0. Accessed on 29 Jan 2022

17. O'Shea, K., Nash, R.: An introduction to convolutional neural networks. arXiv preprint arXiv:1511.08458 (2015)

18. Gujjar, J.P., Kumar, H.P., Chiplunkar, N.N.: Image classification and prediction using transfer learning in colab notebook. Global Transit. Proc. **2**(2), 382–385 (2021)

19. DarrenLevyOfficial (2021). https://www.youtube.com/watch?v=BB5Y0j8RLE4. Accessed 30 Jan 2022

Improving the Effectiveness of Heart Disease Diagnosis with Machine Learning

Catarina Oliveira⬤, Regina Sousa⬤, Hugo Peixoto$^{(\boxtimes)}$⬤, and José Machado⬤

ALGORITMI Research Center/LASI, University of Minho, Braga, Portugal
a88327@alunos.uminho.pt, regina.sousa@algoritmi.uminho.pt,
{hpeixoto,jmac}@di.uminho.pt

Abstract. Despite technological and clinical improvements, heart disease remains one of the leading causes of death worldwide. A significant shift in the paradigm would be for medical teams to be able to accurately identify, at an early stage, whether a patient is at risk of developing or having heart disease, using data from their health records paired with Data Mining tools. As a result, the goal of this research is to determine whether a patient has a cardiac condition by using Data Mining methods and patient information to aid in the construction of a Clinical Decision Support System. With this purpose, we use the CRISP-DM technique to try to forecast the occurrence of cardiac disorders. The greatest results were obtained utilizing the Random Forest technique and the Percentage Split sampling method with a 66% training rate. Other approaches, such as Naïve Bayes, J48, and Sequential Minimal Optimization, also produced excellent results.

Keywords: Heart disease · Classification · Data mining · Machine learning · Decision support systems

1 Introduction

A "heart disease" is a catch-all term for a wide range of conditions that affect the structure and function of the heart. It is important to remember that all heart diseases are Cardiovascular Diseases, but not all CVDs are heart diseases. Coronary heart disease is the most common type of heart disease, killing 360.900 people in 2019. Heart disease is the leading cause of death in the United States for men, women, and people of most racial and ethnic groups [1,2].

Every year, approximately 659.000 people in the United States die from heart disease, accounting for one out of every four deaths. In the United States, someone dies from cardiovascular disease every 36 s, and someone has a heart attack every 40 s. In terms of costs, heart disease cost the United States approximately $363 billion per year between 2016 and 2017 [2].

Focusing now on CVDs, which involve not only the heart but also the blood vessels, these were responsible for an estimated 17.9 million deaths in 2019, accounting for 32% of all global deaths, and remain the leading cause of death

A. González-Briones et al. (Eds.): PAAMS Workshops 2022, CCIS 1678, pp. 222–231, 2022.
https://doi.org/10.1007/978-3-031-18697-4_18

globally. Eighty-five percent of these deaths were caused by heart attacks and strokes (cerebrovascular diseases). Tobacco use, unhealthy diet and obesity, physical inactivity, harmful use of alcohol, diabetes, high blood pressure, and others are all risk factors for CVDs that should be considered when performing patients' exams [3,4].

Because heart diseases claim so many lives each year and cost so much money to countries, it is critical to keep track of people's health in order to make an accurate diagnosis or choose the best treatment available.

This is where Machine Learning (ML) and Data Mining (DM), two features that have revolutionized the Decision Support Systems paradigm in Healthcare, come into play. There are Knowledge-Based Clinical Decision Support Systems (CDSS), which are typically divided into three components: the knowledge base, the inference or reasoning engine, and Non-knowledge-Based CDSS, which use ML to allow the computer to learn from previous experiences or recognize patterns in clinical data [5].

The primary goal of this paper is to determine the presence or absence of a heart disease in patients using data collected from their clinical records and any hidden knowledge they may have. To be successful, the current work required some prior research on this theme as well as existing work on it, as well as familiarity with the CRISP-DM methodology.

2   State of the Art

Since heart diseases have such a big impact in today's society, many are the studies around this theme and around DM techniques allied to Clinical Decision Support Systems. Therefore, in this section, a few studies will be mentioned in order to give the reader a better understanding of what already as been done and studied and the background which inspired this paper.

Pattekari et al. developed a prototype Heart Disease Prediction System using Naïve Bayesian Classification technique and defended that this was the most effective model to predict patients with heart disease. The data source was linked to questionnaires that contemplated many attributes that will be taken into consideration in this paper, such as age, sex, blood pressure, blood sugar, and others. In fact, these medical profiles could predict the likelihood of patients getting a heart disease because they enabled significant relationships between medical factors related to heart disease to be established [6].

Esfahani et al. used a new DM technique for cardiovascular disease detection which consisted in a fusion strategy of the three best classifiers in terms of the result achieved on the F-Measure value. Therefore, Neural Network, Rough Set and Naïve Bayes were combined by a weighted majority vote and achieved an F-Measure of 86.8%, a better result than when comparing with the F-Measure values of each classifier independently (Neural Network alone achieved an F-Measure of 86.1%, Rough Set achieved 85.7% and Naïve Bayes with 84.6%) [7].

Abdullah and Rajalaxmi developed a DM model using Random Forest Classifier in order to improve not only the prediction accuracy, but also, in order to investigate some events related to (Coronary) Heart Disease. The results showed that this classification was successful in terms of predicting the events and the risk factors related to it and even had better results when compared to Decision Trees, used in other similar studies [8].

Almustafa performed a comparative analysis of different classifiers for the classification of a heart disease dataset for positive and negative diagnosed participants and the results ended up being very promising in terms of accuracy for the K-NN (K=1), Decision Tree J48 and JRip classifiers when compared to others, mentioned earlier, such as Naïve Bayes and SVM [9].

Martins et al. also mentioned in their study that not all metrics had the same importance and that realizing if a patient was correctly diagnosed with CVD (precision) and the amount of diseased patients who were correctly predicted (sensitivity) were more relevant than knowing the amount, of all the patients, who were correctly labeled (accuracy) and the amount of healthy people who were predicted as being healthy (specificity). A threshold was also defined as the combination of the four metrics mentioned, in order to filter the most suitable models [10].

3   Data Mining Approach

The main aim of this study was to develop a solution that would be able to predict the presence of a heart disease in patients through knowledge hidden in their medical records. Indeed this is extremely important due to the problematic in question and because of the impact it has in people's lives and in Healthcare systems globally. In order to conduct this study, WEKA software was used.

In order to achieve such results, the starting point of this work was the CRISP-DM methodology. This methodology counts with a flexible sequence of six phases, such as Business Understanding, Data Understanding, Data Preparation, Modeling, Evaluation and Deployment. All this phases allowed the construction of a DM model to be later used and to deal with the real world problems, in this case, related to the prediction of heart diseases. An overview representation of the steps in this work is presented in Fig. 1.

3.1   Heart Disease Dataset

The dataset used to develop this work was the result of the combination of 5 different datasets over the common features already available independently [11]. The total number of observations was 1190, however, since there were 272 duplicated observations, the final dataset only counted with 918 observations. Table 1 presents a brief description of the dataset's attributes and the Table 2 counts with an analysis of the same attributes. There were no missing values. Adding to this, the distribution of the class if of 44,7% with no presence of heart desiease, i.e. normal individuals, and 55,3% with presence of heart disease, i.e. not normal. This indicates that the dataset is well balanced.

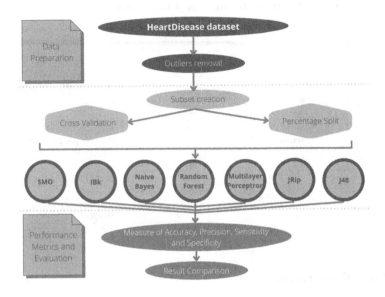

Fig. 1. Overview of the steps in this study.

Table 1. Attribute Description of Heart Disease Dataset

No.	Attribute	Type	Description
1	Age	Numeric	Age of patient [years]
2	Sex	Nominal	Sex of patient [M: male; F: female]
3	ChestPainType	Nominal	[TA: Typical Angina; ATA: Atypical Angina; NAP: Non-Anginal Pain; ASY: Asymptomatic]
4	RestingBP	Numeric	Resting blood pressure [mm Hg]
5	Cholesterol	Numeric	Serum cholesterol [mm/dl]
6	FastingBS	Nominal	Fasting blood sugar [1: if FastingBS >120 mg/dl; 0: otherwise]
7	RestingECG	Nominal	Results [Normal; ST: ST-T wave abnormality, LHV: probable/definite left ventricular hypertrophy]
8	MaxHR	Numeric	Maximum heart rate achieved [Numeric value between 60 and 202]
9	ExerciseAngina	Nominal	Exercise-induced angina [Y: Yes; N: No]
10	Oldpeak	Numeric	ST [Numeric value measured in depression]
11	ST_Slope	Nominal	The slope of the peak exercise ST segment [Up: upsloping; Flat; Down: downsloping]
12	HeartDisease	Nominal	Output class [1: heart disease; 0: normal]

Table 2. Attribute Analysis of Heart Disease Dataset

No.	Unique	Distinct	Max/Most	Min/Least	Average	Deviation	Distribution
1	3	50	77	28	53.511	9.433	–
2	0	2	–	–	–	–	M (79%); F (21%)
3	0	4	ASY	TA	–	–	ASY (54%); NAP (22.1%); ATA (18.8%); TA (5%)
4	14	67	200	0	132.397	18.514	–
5	66	222	603	0	198.8	109.384	–
6	0	2	–	–	–	–	0 (76.7%); 1 (23.3%)
7	0	3	Normal	ST	–	–	Normal (60.1%); LVH (20.5%); ST (19.4%)
8	19	119	202	60	136.809	25.460	–
9	0	2	–	–	–	–	N (59.6%); P (40.4%)
10	15	53	−2.6	6.2	0.887	1.067	–
11	0	3	Flat	Down	–	–	Flat (50.1%); Up (43%); Down (6.9%)
12	0	2	–	–	–	–	1 (55.3%); 0 (44.7%)

3.2 Data Preparation

In this step, there was a need to prepare and clean the data by eliminating duplicated data, removing outliers, dealing with missing values and other inconsistencies. As mentioned previously in the Data Understanding stage, this dataset had no missing values and the duplicated data had already been removed. Adding to that, no inconsistencies were found, therefore, the main focus was detecting outliers using WEKA's *InterquartileRange* filter and then eliminating these instances.

3.3 Modeling

With the data already prepared, it was possible, in this stage, to define the Data Mining Model (DMM). DMM can be described through a few aspects such as the type of approach (A), the set of scenarios considered (S), the chosen DM techniques (DMT), the sampling methods used (SM), the data approaches followed (DA) and finally the target variable (T). The number of generated simulations can be calculated using Eq. 1 [12].

$$DMM_n = A_f \times S_i \times DMT_y \times SM_c \times DA_b \times T_t \qquad (1)$$

For this work it was defined that:

- A = {Classification}
- T = {HeartDisease}
- S = {S1, S2}
- DMT = {Naïve Bayes (NB), Sequential Minimal Optimization (SMO), RandomForest (RF), JRip, J48, IBk, MultilayerPerceptron (MP)}
- SM = {Cross-validation 10 Folds, Percentage Split 66%}
- DA = {Without Oversampling and Undersampling}

Where:

- S1 = {all attributes}
- S2 = {Age, Sex, ChestPainType, Cholesterol, MaxHR, ExerciseAngina, Old-peak, St_Slope, HeartDisease}

Therefore, and having Eq. 1 in mind, 28 simulations were generated (1 [A] × 1 [T] × 2 [S] × 7 [DMT] × 2 [SM] × 1 [DA]).

In order to generate S2, WEKA's supervised filter *AttributeSelection* (Cfs-SubsetEval) was used. This filter is responsible for selecting only the most relevant attributes and, therefore, reducing the number of attributes that have to be analyzed.

The DMT chosen were NB, SMO, RF, JRip, J48, IBk and MP. This way it would be possible to evaluate which of the DTMs mentioned in the different papers previously worked best for this situation.

The SM used were cross validation with 10 folds and percentage split with 66%. Percentage Split is helpful for getting a fast impression of a model's performance. According to the literature, a common split value for train and test sets is 66% to 34%. All other configurations were used as WEKA's default.

In terms of DA and since the class was balanced, there was no need to follow approaches such as *Oversampling* or *Undersampling*.

3.4   Evaluation

Performance metrics play a very important role at this stage, since they are responsible for the validation of the result's reliability obtained with the different algorithms. The performance metrics considered in this study were:

- *Accuracy:* Correctly true positive (TP) classified instances. [10] In a more practical way it is translated to the amount of patients who were correctly labeled out of the total patients in study. This value can be obtained through Eq. 2.

$$Accuracy = \frac{TP + TN}{TP + TN + FP + FN} \tag{2}$$

- *Precision:* It measures the classifier's exactness. [10] It is the amount of patients who really had heart disease out of all the labeled as having it. Precision can be obtained with the help of Eq. 3.

$$Precision = \frac{TP}{TP + FP} \tag{3}$$

- *Sensitivity:* It measures the classifier's completeness. [10] It is the amount of patients who were correctly predicted as having heart disease out of all the patients who had heart disease. This value can be calculated by using Eq. 4.

$$Sensitivity = \frac{TP}{TP + FN} \tag{4}$$

– *Specificity:* Correctly true negative (TN) classified instances. The amount of healthy patients who were predicted as so, out of all healthy patients. This value can be obtained by using Eq. 5.

$$Specificity = \frac{TN}{TN + FP} \tag{5}$$

Similar to what was mentioned in the related works section of this piece, even though all these four performance metrics have a great impact and importance for the result's credibility, for this study and because of its Healthcare related theme, precision and sensitivity, are the key most relevant ones. Indeed, it is much more crucial to detect correctly a patient that has a heart disease when compared to a healthy patient who was wrongly labeled as a carrier of a heart disease, simply because the wrong diagnosis in one might be fatal and in the other, at least most of the time, isn't.

The best values for accuracy, sensitivity, specificity and precision, according to each technique used, are presented in terms of percentage in Table 3.

Despite these individual best values, it was of interest to find the best overall results and, therefore, a threshold was defined. The best results to be considered would be those that had all the performance metrics above the average, that contemplated the 28 simulations, of each performance metric. In a more practical way, the only situations to achieve the title of overall best results would be those that had an accuracy >85,7%, a sensitivity >87,7%, a specificity >83,1% and lastly a precision >85,6%. However, because JRip and IBk did not achieve very good results when compared to others, the average for each metric decreased and 11 out of the 28 situations had its metrics above the conditions previously mentioned.

In order to reduce this number and do a better filtering, out of these 11 best situations, an average was calculated for the 4 performance metrics of each situation. The top 5 best results of these averages determined the top 5 overall best results which are represented in Table 4.

Since it was mentioned before that the key most relevant performance metrics were precision and sensitivity, another variation of this filtering was done. While calculating the average, the weight of these parameters was duplicated, in other words, they were considered twice, in order to represent its' importance. Despite this new filtering, the top 5 best results did not change, only the positions in this ranking did, with No.2 switching positions with No. 3 and No.4 switching with No.5, as it is possible to observe when comparing the results between Table 4 and Table 5.

Table 3. Best values for each performance metric according to each technique

DM Technique	Scenario	Sampling method	Accuracy	Sensitivity	Specificity	Precision
Naïve Bayes	S2	Percentage split	88,1	–	87,3	–
	S1		–	90,4	–	88,7
Random Forest	S1	Percentage split	90,4	93,8	85,8	90,4
	S2		–	–	–	–
SMO	S1	Percentage split	89,1	90,4	87,3	89,1
JRip	S2	Percentage split	85,5	91,0	–	85,6
		Cross validation	–	–	80,4	–
J48	S1	Percentage split	90,0	93,2	85,8	90,1
IBk	S1	Percentage split	85,5	85,9	85,1	85,6
MultilayerPerceptron	S2	Percentage split	87,5	89,8	84,3	87,4

Table 4. Top 5 overall and above threshold results unconsidering the importance of each metric

No.	DM technique	Scenario	Sampling method	Metrics' average	Accuracy	Sensitivity	Specificity	Precision
1	Random Forest	S1	Percentage split	0,913	0,904	0,938	0,858	0,904
2	J48	S1	Percentage split	0,902	0,887	0,904	0,866	0,887
3	Naïve Baye	S1	Percentage split	0,897	0,900	0,932	0,858	0,901
4	SMO	S1	Percentage split	0,892	0.881	0.887	0.873	0,881
5	Naïve Baye	S2	Percentage split	0,890	0,891	0,904	0,873	0,891

Table 5. Top 5 overall and above threshold results considering the importance of each metric

No.	DM technique	Scenario	Sampling method	Metrics' average
1	Random Forest	S1	Percentage split	0,911
2	Naïve Bayes	S1	Percentage split	0,897
3	J48	S1	Percentage split	0,896
4	Naïve Bayes	S2	Percentage split	0,893
5	SMO	S1	Percentage split	0,890

4   Discussion and Contributions

In this study, we evaluated the possibility of determining the presence of cardiac disease by employing data mining. For this purpose, the CRISP-DM methodology was followed, and WEKA software was used. Two scenarios were evaluated, one where all attributes were taken into account (S1) and the other where attribute selection was performed using WEKA software (S2).

The CfsSubsetEval evaluator assessed feature selection in S2 provided nine attributes. The method calculates each attribute's correlation with the degree of redundancy between the attributes, choosing the ones with the best correlation. Based on the results obtained, scenario (S1), which includes all attributes, gave the best results, unlike scenario (S2), where RestingBP, FastingBS, and RestingECG were excluded. Despite their low correlation, the excluded attributes provided necessary information that would have improved the prediction accuracy of the algorithm. Based on this result, it would be recommended to repeat the task using other methods of attribute selection by WEKA, and compare their respective impacts on the accuracy prediction.

The data set was evaluated by 10-fold cross-validation and standard split-percentage with 66% training and 34% for testing. Split-percentage showed the best results compared to cross-validation. By Cross-validation, the dataset was divided into ten equally sized segments. Then ten iterations took the place of training, followed by testing, ensuring that a different segment of data was used for testing in each iteration. Not all models were able to be evaluated by cross-validation, and it is recommended in future work to evaluate the rest of the methods with it. Using cross-validation, we could better understand and evaluate the prediction accuracy and variance of the dataset in the models.

The evaluation results obtained by split percentage were positive, especially in the S1 scenario. Random-Forest was the technique that showed better results than the rest of the presented methods. It achieved the best overall results with an accuracy of 90,4%, a sensitivity of 93,8%, a specificity of 85,6%, and a precision of 90,4%. NB, J48, and SMO algorithms also achieved excellent results. The advantage of these techniques is that they are not as slow in training as the random forest technique. In the case of larger datasets could be more beneficial [13]. The two techniques that consistently and independently from the situation showed the worst results when compared to others were JRip and IBk. Indeed, JRip implements propositional rules; these are rules that follow an IF - Then structure, and the lower results of the metrics might be an outcome of a not-so-strong rule [14]. On the other hand, the poor results related to IBk might be a consequence of either a lack of representation or even a not meaningful and efficient distance measure.

5   Conclusions and Future Work

To increase the effectiveness of a heart disease diagnosis and, consequently, to improve the patient's quality life and also to reduce costs in the Healthcare systems through the implementation of a Clinical Decision Support System, different data mining techniques, sampling methods and scenarios were tested.

In this study, RF technique, through a 66% Percentage Split and using S1 achieved the best results and, therefore, should be used in the future. However, NB, J48 and SMO also achieved great results and must be on the table for future works and implementations. In terms of sampling methods, Percentage Split and Cross Validation were studied, and the best results were mainly and curiously associated with Percentage Split.

Future work can be done with a dataset closer to what would be found in reality, in other words, with a larger dataset and also with more instances, in order to assess the previous conclusions in terms of the best techniques and sampling methods. Assessing other ways to differentiate the weights of importance of the 4 performance metrics considered in this study can also be a field for study. The same goes for other performance metrics that weren't studied in this paper.

Acknowledgments. This work has been supported by FCT-Fundação para a Ciência e Tecnologia within the R&D Units Project Scope: UIDB/00319/2020.

References

1. Know the Differences: Cardiovascular Disease, Heart Disease, Coronary Heart Disease. https://www.nhlbi.nih.gov/sites/default/files/media/docs/Fact_Sheet_Know_Diff_Design.508_pdf.pdf. Accessed 27 Dec 2021
2. Heart Disease Facts, Centers for Disease Control and Prevention. https://www.cdc.gov/heartdisease/facts.htm. Accessed 26 Apr 2022
3. Cardiovascular diseases (CVDs). World Health Organization. https://www.who.int/news-room/fact-sheets/detail/cardiovascular-diseases-(cvds). Accessed 27 Dec 2021
4. Ahmad, T., Munir, A., Bhatti, S.H., Aftab, M., Raza, M.A.: Survival analysis of heart failure patients: a case study. PLoS One **12**(7), e0181001 (2017)
5. Berner, E.S.: Overview of Clinical Decision Support Systems, vol. 233, 2nd edn., pp. 4–8. Springer, Heidelberg (2007)
6. Pattekari, S.A., Parveen, A.: Prediction system for heart disease using Naïve Bayes. Int. J. Adv. Comput. Math. Sci. **3**, 290–294 (2012)
7. Esfahani, H.A., Ghazanfari, M.: Cardiovascular disease detection using a new ensemble classifier. In: 2017 IEEE 4th International Conference on Knowledge-Based Engineering and Innovation (KBEI), pp. 1011–1014. IEEE (2007). https://doi.org/10.1109/KBEI.2017.8324946
8. Abdullah, S.A., Rajalaxmi, R.R.: A data mining model for predicting the coronary heart disease using random forest classifier. In: IJCA Proceedings on International Conference in Recent trends in Computational Methods, Communication and Controls (ICON3C 2012), vol. 3, pp. 22–25 (2012)
9. Almustafa, K.M.: Prediction of heart disease and classifiers' sensitivity analysis. BMC Bioinform. **21**, 278 (2020). https://doi.org/10.1186/s12859-020-03626-y
10. Martins, B., Ferreira, D., Neto, C., Abelha, A., Machado, J.: Data mining for cardiovascular disease prediction. J. Med. Syst. **45**, 1–8 (2021)
11. fedesoriano, Heart Failure Prediction Dataset. kaggle 2021. https://www.kaggle.com/fedesoriano/heart-failure-prediction?select=heart.csv. Accessed 20 Dec 2021
12. Fonseca, F., Peixoto, H., Miranda, F., Machado, J., Abelha, A.: Step towards prediction of perineal tear. Proc. Comput. Sci. **113**, 565–570 (2017)
13. Peixoto, H., et al.: Predicting postoperative complications for gastric cancer patients using data mining. In: Cortez, P., Magalhães, L., Branco, P., Portela, C.F., Adão, T. (eds.) INTETAIN 2018. LNICST, vol. 273, pp. 37–46. Springer, Cham (2019). https://doi.org/10.1007/978-3-030-16447-8_4
14. Melo, I., Medeiros, N., Silva, I., Lira, L., Moraes, R.: Evaluation of the performance of the JRIP algorithm in the classification of heart disease diagnosis. In: 2019 IV National Congress of Research and Teaching in Sciences (2019)

Workshop on Decision Support, Recommendation, and Persuasion in Artificial Intelligence (DeRePAI)

Workshop on Decision Support, Recommendation, and Persuasion in Artificial Intelligence (DeRePAI)

Decision support systems are applied in different fields to support individuals and groups, as well as to influence human behavior and decision-making. Decision support systems are expected to facilitate decision-making while enhancing the quality of that decision, as well as recommender systems which are expected to facilitate the choice process to maximize the user satisfaction. In decision support and recommendation for groups, it is important to consider the heterogeneity and conflicting preferences of its participants. In addition, decision support and recommendation systems must have strategies for configuring preferences and acquiring user profiles in a nonintrusive (implicit) and time-consuming manner.

On the other hand, the acceptance and effectiveness of the hints and recommendations provided by the system depends on several factors. First, they must be appropriate for the objectives and profile of the user, but also, they must be understandable and supported by evidence (the user must understand why the recommendation is provided and why it is good for him/her). Thus, it is necessary to provide these systems with a mechanism that supports suggestions by means of artificial intelligence. In this way, computational argumentation is a technique that builds upon the natural way humans provide reasons (i.e., arguments) for which a recommendation is suggested and should be accepted. Therefore, a system that uses these technologies must be persuasive to obtain the desired results by influencing human behavior.

In this workshop, we aim to explore the links between decision-support, recommendation, and persuasion to discuss strategies to facilitate the decision/choice process by individuals and groups. This workshop also aims to be a discussion forum on the latest trends and ongoing challenges in the application of artificial intelligence technologies in this area.

Organization

Organizing Committee

Jaume Jordán	Universitat Politècnica de València, Spain
João Carneiro	Polytechnic Institute of Porto, Portugal
Goreti Marreiros	Polytechnic Institute of Porto, Portugal
Stella Heras	Universitat Politècnica de València, Spain

Program Committee

Patrícia Alves	Polytechnic Institute of Porto, Portugal
Andreas Brännström	Umeå University, Sweden
Carlos Carrascosa	Universitat Politècnica de València, Spain
Vicente Julián	Universitat Politècnica de València, Spain
Diogo Martinho	Polytechnic Institute of Porto, Portugal
Jorge Meira	Polytechnic Institute of Porto, Portugal
Juan Carlos Nieves	Umeå University, Sweden
Paulo Novais	Universidade do Minho, Portugal
Víctor Sánchez-Anguix	Universitat Politècnica de València, Spain
Ichiro Satoh	National Institute of Informatics Tokyo, Japan

Planning Model for Visiting Tourist Attractions with Minimum Costs

Costel Bălcău, Ion Alexandru Popescu, and Nicolae Bold[(✉)]

Department of Mathematics and Computer Science, University of Pitesti, Pitesti, Romania
bold_nicolae@yahoo.com

Abstract. In the current context, when the tourist offers are many and with various facilities, hotels and travel agencies must bring something new in their offer to attract customers and propose them opportunities to spend their free time. In this paper we propose a model for planning the visit of tourist objectives, which can be used to optimize the expenses of the organizers and to satisfy as much as possible the wishes of the clients. The model is based on the centralization of tourists' options at the time of hotel accommodation and then, depending on this information and budget, it will be decided which tourist attractions can be included in the tour circuits. Weighted graphs and algorithms for generating spanning trees in ascending order of costs were used to model these activities. This approach can also be used for city-break or circuit tourism – to visit the main tourist attractions in a country. For the implementation of the model, web or mobile technologies can be used to obtain a useful and friendly computer product.

Keywords: Tourist attractions · Graph · Spanning tree · Cost of tree

1 Introduction

We live in a time where people travel a lot and are eager to visit sights. In the category of tourist objectives there are not only museums, cathedrals, mosques, temples but also botanical gardens, zoos, parks, stadiums and many other objectives in various fields of activity. All these objectives can be used by tour operators, hotel managers, travel agencies to make tourist tours.

Strategies and categories for creating tourist circuits in various geographical areas are presented in detail in [2, 4] and [11]. In order to achieve the best possible advertising of the tourist objectives and to ensure pleasant activities for the tourists, the circuits must be well analyzed before the organization, in this sense important studies have appeared, such as those in [8, 9] and [12]. The economic impact of the tourist circuits can be particularly high because it involves transportation, trade, entertainment, public institutions activities as it is also specified in [11].

In this paper we will present a way to plan tourist circuits using modeling by weighted non-oriented graphs. The tourist objectives are nodes, and their edges are the connections between the objectives, depending on the road access in most cases. The weights of the edges are dependent on the time, the distance traveled and the difficulty of the route

© The Author(s), under exclusive license to Springer Nature Switzerland AG 2022
A. González-Briones et al. (Eds.): PAAMS Workshops 2022, CCIS 1678, pp. 237–245, 2022.
https://doi.org/10.1007/978-3-031-18697-4_19

between the tourist objectives. Having this weighted graph we can generate all spanning trees in ascending order of costs using specific algorithms such as those in [1, 13] and [14]. From the generated spanning trees we select only those that fulfill the property that they have the degree of each node at most NrD. This is equivalent to the fact that the tourist circuit associated with the spanning tree does not contain the passing past the same tourist objective more than NrD times. In the example in Sect. 4, NrD = 3 was used.

In Sect. 2 we will describe the planning model, and in Sect. 3 we present the results used to generate tourist routes. In Sect. 4 we describe an example of using the model on some concrete situations, and in Sect. 5 we present the main aspects regarding the implementation of the model presented in Sect. 2.

2   Planning Model

In order to plan the tourist circuits, some information is needed. This information can be grouped into two categories:

- The tourist objectives chosen by tourists for visiting
- Costs related to visiting tourist attractions, visiting schedule, transportation costs

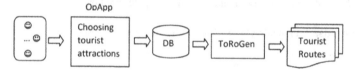

Fig. 1. Model for planning some tourist visits

Figure 1 shows the main components of the circuit planning model. On the left side appear the tourists, who at the moment of arrival (for example at the accommodation) through a mobile application or web applications noted by us with OpApp choose the tourist objectives they want to visit. The OpApp application enters the information taken from tourists in the DB database. After completing the tourist information process, the data from the DB database are taken over by a generator, in Fig. 1 marked with ToRoGen and used to build a weighted graph and generate routes with tourist objectives that constitute the tourist circuits, they are saved in the files noted by us in the planning model with Tourist Routes.

For the tourist circuits, the organizer can impose restrictions related to its total cost, which can be in a range of values [Min, Max] and the number of tourist objectives marked with No. Thus, the ToRoGen generator uses from the DB database the information related to tourist objectives, distances between them, tourists' preferences, to build a weighted graph and the numerical values Min, Max, NrO necessary to generate spanning trees with NrO nodes and the cost in the range [Min, Max], which allow planning the objectives of a tourist circuit.

3   OpApp- Applicaton for Choosing Tourist Attractions

3.1   OpApp – Specifications

The application for entering data in the DB database related to tourists' preferences regarding the tourist objectives they want to visit can be created in several ways using web programming or mobile programming. In all cases the application must contain groups of tourist objectives, for example:

- Group 1: historical objectives
- Group 2: sports objectives
- Group 3: geographical objectives
- Group 4: special building objectives
- …

Each group will contain a list of touristic objectives specific to the group, from this group the tourist chooses the tourist objectives that he wants to visit. The tourist's preferences are stored in the DB database together with the data necessary to identify the tourist (for example, the room number or the email address).

In Fig. 2 are presented the components of OpApp application.

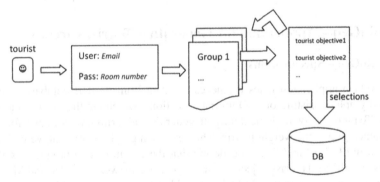

Fig. 2. Diagram of the use of the OpApp application

The groups of tourist objectives are developed one after the other in order to achieve a selection of tourist objectives in a simple, intuitive and attractive way.

3.2   OpApp – Algorithm

Next we will present the algorithm from which we start to create the OpApp application.

ALGORITHM 1: OpApp Algorithm

Step 1.The login data for the application are read in two strings: email and RoomNo

Step 2.Search the database for the data from step 1 and if they are found continue with step 3, otherwise step 1 is repeated twice more, if you continue with incorrect data twice, then the application will close

Step 3.for k =1 to Number_of_Groups do
    Print the list of tourist objectives from group k
    Make a selection of tourist objectives from group k
    for i = 1, Number_Selected_obiectiv do
        saving the ID associated to the selected tourist
        objective in an list Sel
    endfor
        endfor

Step 4.Centralized display of selected tourist attractions using Sel

Step 5.Introduction in BD of the selected tourist objectives using the Sel list

Remarks

- Number_of_Groups is the number of groups of tourist objectives
- Number_Selected_objectiv is the number of tourist objectives selected by the tourist
- Sel is the list with the IDs of the tourist objectives selected by the tourist

4   ToRoGen – Application for Generating Tourist Circuits

4.1   ToRoGen – Specifications

The ToRoGen application takes the necessary data from the DB database to build a weighted graph consisting of NrO tourist attractions, which are the most requested by tourists. To more easily implement the path generation algorithm we will use, for storing the weighted graph, the weight matrix. The notions in graph theory that we will use are presented in [3, 5, 6] and [7]. Considering that the circuit can be organized only if it contains exactly NrO tourist objectives, its total cost is between the Min and Max limits and does not exceed more than NrD times besides the same tourist objective, we obtain the components which are presented in Fig. 3 and detailed in Algorithm 2. NrO and NrD are chosen by the organizers of the excursions depending on the budget and the available time.

Using the information from the DB database related to the travel costs between the tourist objectives (coded by 1, 2,..., NrO) is obtained the matrix of costs marked with c $= (c_{ij})_{i=1,...,NrO; j=1,...,NrO}$. Each node i, i = 1, 2,..., NrO in the graph is associated with the i-th tourist objective, and c_{ij} represents the cost of travel from i to j. Particular cases: $c_{ii} = 0$, and if it is not possible to go from i to j it will be considered a very high value for c_{ij}.

Recently, a wide variety of algorithms have been created for the generation of spanning trees in the ascending order of costs, as are those presented in the papers [1, 13] and [14]. The cost of a spanning tree is the sum of the costs of its edges. Using one of these algorithms with the cost matrix c, for each spanning tree we check if it has the cost

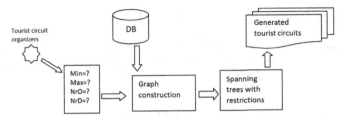

Fig. 3. Diagram of components of the OpApp application

in the range [Min, Max] and the degree of each node is at most NrD, if so we use it to store tourist circuit. In Fig. 4 we present an example of such a graph, with NrO = 6, the edges costs being written using the color red.

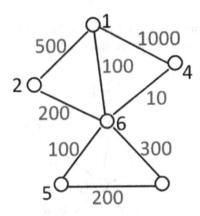

Fig. 4. Example of graph with costs of the OpApp application (Color figure online)

If we consider Min = 700, Max = 1300 si NrD = 3, then a spanning tree that verifies all of the conditions: cost in [700, 1300] and the degree of each node is at most 3 is drawn in Fig. 5.

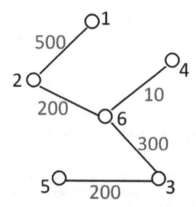

Fig. 5. Spanning tree that is not a solution generated by the OpApp application

The cost of the spanning tree in Fig. 5 is $500 + 200 + 10 + 300 + 200 = 1210$, and the node 6 has the highest degree, but is equal to 3.

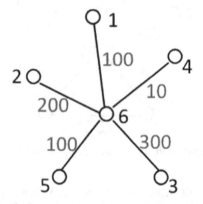

Fig. 6. Spanning tree of the OpApp application

The cost of the spanning tree in Fig. 6 is $200 + 100 + 10 + 100 + 300 = 710$. The spanning tree in Fig. 6, even though has the cost in [700, 1300], has a node with the degree 5 (node 6) and is not admissible.

4.2 ToRoGen – Algorithm

Using the notations from Sect. 4.1 we can write the following algorithm, based on generating spanning trees (noted with SpTrGen algorithm) in the order of the costs.

ALGORITHM 2: ToRoGen Algorithm

Step 1. Read Min, Max, Nr, NrO
Step 2. Read data from DB and build matrix c
Step 3.Using the algorithm SpTrGen we generate trees: T_1, T_2, ..., T_k
Step 4. for i=1 to k do
  - we calculate the maximum degree of a node from the
       spanning tree T_i in the variable MaxD
  - if Min $\leq$ cost(T_i) and cost(T_i) $\leq$ Max and MaxD $\leq$
       NrD then
      We build and save a tourist circuit
        associated to T_i spanning tree
  endif
    endfor

The algorithms for generating spanning trees presented in [1, 13] and [14] have a polynomial execution time and therefore for a maximum of 1000 tourist objectives the execution time does not exceed one second.

4.3 SpTrGen – Algorithm

In [12], P. M. Amal și K.S. Ajish Kumar presents an algorithm for generating spanning trees. This algorithm adapted to our problem is presented below.

Input.
Unoriented graph, given by n – the number of nodes, m the number of edges and m triplets of the form (i, j, cost) representing the nodes of the edges and their cost.

Output.
Spanning trees in ascending order of costs (edges and their cost).

Data structures:
c – edge cost matrix.
apm – the class for determining an spanning trees with Prim's algorithm.
tree – the class to create objects that hold partial trees through the vector vectors along with their cost.
edge – class to create objects that store edges along with their cost.
all_spanning_trees – the class that generates all spanning trees.
List_of_trees – data structure that stores the trees from which the one with minimum cost will be selected.
ST – data structure that will store spanning trees in ascending order of costs.
MST – the tree partially determined at each step of the *List_of_trees*.
MuSet – the set of graph edges that are not found in MST.

ALGORITHM 3: SpTrGen Algorithm

Step 1. Reading input data and building the cost matrix c

Step 2. Determining in *MST* a minimal cost spanning tree with Prim's algorithm and initializing *List_of_trees*, respectively *ST* with *MST*.

Step 3. *step* = 1

Step 4. As long as there are items in *List_of_trees* run

- Remove *MST* from *List_of_trees*

- For each edge [i, j] that is not in *MST* we proceed as follows:

    -we add to the MST the edge [i, j] and thus a C cycle is formed.

    -if *step* = 1 we remove from C in turn a maximum cost edge with cost less than or equal to c [i] [j] and we get new spanning trees that we add to *List_of_trees*

    - if *step* > 1 we remove from C in turn a maximum cost edge with a lower cost than c [i] [j] and we get new spanning trees that we add to *List_of_trees*

    - We determine in MST1 a tree with the lowest cost in *List_of_trees*

    step = *step* + *1*

    - *MST* = *MST1* and add *MST1* to *ST*

Step 5. Display the spanning trees in order of costs using the *ST* data structure

5 Conclusions

The model presented in this paper can be used to create web or mobile applications and is based on special results from graph theory. We are working on the implementation of this model using mobile programming in Android Studio using interfaces similar to those in [10]. We chose this option so that the tourist has at his disposal a simple mechanism for selecting the tourist objectives and the data storage will be done in SqLite.

Another implementation option is the one that uses web programming, in this case can be use PHP scripts and MySql databases and so the organizer has the advantage, because it can more easily enter the data regarding the tourist objectives. A future direction of our research involves the improving generation spanning tree algorithm by prioritizing the degree constraints.

References

1. Amal, P.M., Ajish Kumar, K.S.: An algorithm for k-th minimum spanning tree. In: Electronic Notes in Discrete Mathematics, vol. 53, pp. 343–354, Sep. (2016)
2. Bădulescu, A., Rusu, S.: The dynamics of the international tourism market. Recent developments and challenges. GeoJ. Tourism Geosites 4(2), 145–152 (2009)
3. Bălcău, C.: Combinatorică și Teoria Grafurilor, Ed. Universității din Pitești (2007)
4. Bošković, D., Saftić, D., Trošt, V.: Planning and organising touristic destinations – the example of the rural Istria cluster. In: 20th Biennial International Congress "Tourism & Hospitality Industry", Opatija, Croatia, vol. Congress Proceedings, pp. 794–807 (2010)
5. Cormen, T., Leiserson, C., Rivest, R., Stein, C.: Introduction to Alghoritms. MIT Press (2001)
6. Popescu, D.A., Ioniță, A.E.: Combinatorică si teoria grafurilor, Ed. Rhabon, Tg. Jiu (2005)
7. Popescu D.A.: Java after C++, Ed. L&S Infomat, infobits.ro (2019)

8. Donald, G.: Models in tourism planning: towards integration of theory and practice. Tour. Manage. **7**(1), 21–32 (1986)
9. Godfrey, K.B.: Towards sustainability? Tourism in the Republic of Cyprus. In: L. Harrison and Winston Husbands (ed.) Practicing Responsible Tourism: International case studies in tourism planning, policy and development, pp. 58–79. J. Wiley&Sons, New York (1996)
10. Popescu, D.A., Gosoiu, C.I., Nijloveanu, D.: Learning testing model using test generators and mobile applications. In: L2D@WSDM, pp. 41–48 (2021)
11. Ruhanen, L.: Strategic planning for local tourism destinations: an analysis of tourism, tourism and hospitality planning & development, Dec. 2004, pp. 2–39 (2004)
12. Parikshat, S.M., Koura, P., Bhagataa, A.: Silk route in the light of circuit tourism: an avenue of tourism internationalization, 5th Asia Euro Conference 2014. Procedia. Soc. Behav. Sci. **144**, 143–150 (2014)
13. Sörensen, K., Janssens, G.K.: An algorithm to generate all spanning trees of a graph in order of increasing cost. Pesqui. Oper. **25**(2005), 219–229 (2005)
14. Yamada, T., Kataoka, S., Watanabe, K.: Listing all the minimum spanning trees in an undirected graph. Int. J. Comput. Math. **87**(14), 3175–3185 (2010)

Implementation of a FHIR Specification for the Interoperability of a Remote Monitoring Platform of Patients with Vascular Diseases

Ana Vieira[1]([⊠]) [iD], Luís Conceição[1] [iD], Luiz Faria[1], Paulo Novais[2] [iD],
and Goreti Marreiros[1] [iD]

[1] GECAD – Research Group on Intelligent Engineering and Computing for Advanced
Innovation and Development, Institute of Engineering – Polytechnic of Porto, Porto, Portugal
{aavir,msc,lef,mgt}@isep.ipp.pt
[2] ALGORITMI Centre, University of Minho, Braga, Portugal
pjon@di.uminho.pt

Abstract. To address the current burdens in the healthcare of patients with vascular diseases, the Portuguese consortium of the Inno4Health project is currently developing a remote monitoring platform that aims to support the self-management of patients with vascular diseases. With the continuous remote monitoring of patients, it is intended that the platform supports both patients and health professionals. Patients will be supported through the presentation of personalized recommendations of activities to perform and health professionals will be supported in the clinical decision making through the presentation of meaningful insights. As the platform is composed by several components, including monitoring sensors, data processing modules and user applications, theressss is a need for the standardization of the data used. This work presents the implementation of a Fast Healthcare Interoperability Resources (FHIR) specification in the remote monitoring platform to ensure the standardization of the data that will be collected and exchanged between the several components of the platform. With this work, it will be possible to easily and securely exchange data, as well as integrating new monitoring sensors and user applications in the platform.

Keywords: mHealth · FHIR · Vascular diseases · Remote monitoring

1 Introduction

The healthcare of patients with vascular diseases is burdensome for both patients and national healthcare systems. These diseases, such as Intermittent Claudication, Venous Ulcers, and Diabetic Foot Ulcers, severely affect the patients' mobility [1, 2] and require frequent monitoring [3, 4]. The monitoring of patients is usually performed in clinical contexts, leaving the patient unattended while at home. This leads to a burden on patients, who frequently have to go to the hospital to be monitored and treated, and may not be able to afford the costs of the healthcare services [2]. National healthcare systems are also burdened by the healthcare of vascular diseases due to the high number of patients

A. González-Briones et al. (Eds.): PAAMS Workshops 2022, CCIS 1678, pp. 246–257, 2022.
https://doi.org/10.1007/978-3-031-18697-4_20

and the frequency of their treatments [5, 6]. To address these burdens, it has been sought the research and development of intelligent solutions that aim to support both patients and health professionals.

The international project Inno4Health[1] aims to stimulate the innovation in the continuous monitoring of the health condition and fitness of both patients and athletes. To do so, Inno4Health will develop non-invasive wearable monitoring sensors to continuously monitor patients and athletes, and a set of intelligent algorithms that will use the collected data to assess the health and fitness conditions of patients and athletes. Dashboards and mobile applications will also be developed to deliver the generated insights and relevant information to patients, athletes, physicians, and coaches. To accomplish this, Inno4Health is composed by academic and industrial partners from several countries, including Portugal. The Portuguese consortium will work within the healthcare domain of the Inno4Health project, specifically, the Portuguese partners will be focused on the healthcare of vascular diseases. The aim of the Portuguese use case is to develop a remote monitoring platform that allows the continuous monitoring and the smart coaching of patients with Intermittent Claudication, Venous Ulcers, and Diabetic Foot Ulcers. To accomplish this, non-invasive wearable sensors are being developed to allow the remote monitoring of patients and intelligent algorithms are being implemented to analyze the collected data and provide insights to both patients, through the display of personalized recommendations regarding activities to perform to improve their health condition, and health professionals, through the presentation of monitoring reports, information regarding the patient's condition, among others. The remote monitoring platform is composed by several components, such as data processing modules and smart coaching services, a mobile app for the patient, a web application for the health professionals, as well as the non-invasive wearable monitoring sensors. As this platform aims to monitor three types of vascular diseases, there will be several data formats that need to be exchanged between the components and processed by the data processing modules. Therefore, it is necessary the implementation of a data exchange standard in order to facilitate the communication of data between sensors, user applications, and data processing components.

This work explores the implementation of the data exchange standard Fast Healthcare Interoperability Resources (FHIR) in the remote monitoring platform being developed by the Portuguese consortium of the Inno4Health project. The work we present in this paper has been extended from [7] in which the architecture of the remote monitoring platform was defined. With the application of the FHIR standard in this platform it is intended to facilitate the data exchange between the monitoring sensors and applications with the rest of the platform's components, as well as to allow the easy integration of new applications or sensors into the platform.

The remainder of the paper is structured as follows. Section 2 presents the architecture of the remote monitoring platform. Section 3 presents the implementation of the FHIR specification in the remote monitoring platform, including the description of the technologies used to deploy a FHIR server, a presentation of the domain model followed in the remote monitoring platform and a presentation of the mapping of clinical concepts regarding Intermittent Claudication in the FHIR data exchange standard. In Sect. 4 conclusions are taken and future work to be performed is identified.

---

[1] Website of the Project: https://inno4health.eu.

2 Remote Monitoring Platform Architecture

Figure 1 presents the architecture of the remote monitoring platform being developed in the Portuguese use case of the Inno4Health project. The platform is composed by five main components: Monitoring Sensors, Mobile Application, Web Application, Web API, and the Data Storage.

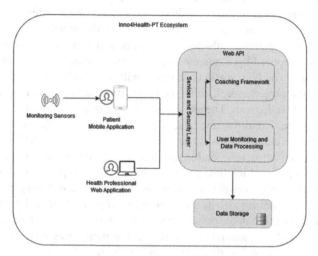

Fig. 1. Architecture of the remote monitoring platform

Monitoring Sensors will be used to continuously monitor the patient's health condition throughout the day. Two types of sensors will be used, an insole sensor and a patch. The mobile application will present to the patient information regarding activities that the patient should perform, monitoring reports, the status of the patient, among others. The web application will present information that will assist health professionals in the clinical decision making, such as monitoring reports. The main component of the platform is the Web API, composed by the Services and Security Layer, the Coaching Framework, and the User Monitoring and Data Processing component. The Services and Security Layer will expose a set of services of the platform to internal and external applications. These services include the acquisition of clinical data, presentation of insights generated by the data processing modules, among others. The User Monitoring and Data Processing will analyze the patient data collected by the monitoring sensors and will generate insights regarding the health condition. The Coaching Framework aims to perform the smart coaching of patients and will provide services such as the generation of personalized recommendations regarding behaviors to adopt, and the execution of coaching plans that the patient should follow to improve their health condition. Finally, the Data Storage will contain all data used by the platform.

3 FHIR

Even though information technologies are present in the healthcare sector and have led to the emergence of concepts such as electronic health records, there are still barriers in the data exchange between systems [8]. The interoperability in healthcare systems is often non-existent due to the complexity of mapping concepts required for the data exchange [9], leading to a need of data standards that facilitate the exchange of patient-related data between heterogeneous systems and devices. To address this, clinical data exchange standards such as Operational Data Model (ODM) [10] and FHIR [11] have emerged. FHIR is widely adopted by healthcare systems [12, 13], and presents advantages such as being easy to implement, is flexible and easily adapts to the specifications of the organizations [14]. This standard allows the interoperability of healthcare systems while ensuring the security of the data. FHIR allows the mapping of healthcare concepts into "Resources", such as the *Patient, Practitioner, Observation*, among others. The communication between systems is done through simple HTTP requests, and the data to be sent is represented in JSON or XML [14]. It should be noted that this standard presents as a disadvantage the lack of centralization, as there is a need to access several resources to have the complete information, making FHIR difficult to manage.

In the following sections related works will be explored, and the implementation of the FHIR data exchange standard in the platform, including the domain model adopted and an example of the concepts mapped regarding the monitoring of patients with Intermittent Claudication, will be presented.

3.1 Related Works

As aforementioned, FHIR is widely adopted in healthcare systems with the aim of guaranteeing their interoperability. Works such as [15–19] have been published in the literature and present the FHIR specification implemented in the healthcare systems.

In [15] a FHIR based API was developed to integrate the presented system with other applications. The authors in [16] present the implementation of the FHIR standard, including the mapping of the concepts used in the system to FHIR resources. This standard was adopted with the aim of enabling the exchange of medical records with other systems nationally. In [17] FHIR was implemented in a mobile application to enable the integration with other healthcare systems and to facilitate the interaction between patients and doctors. The authors of the work [18] propose an implementation of FHIR for maintaining maternal health records and to enable the exchange of the data. The authors note that this implementation can facilitate the analysis and evidence-based decision making. In [19] it is presented the implementation of FHIR in a microservice architecture to address common problems in healthcare systems such as scalability, and complexity. Three FHIR resources were identified by the authors, *Patient, Appointment,* and *Participant*, to represent and exchange data for scheduling appointments.

With the analysis of related works it was verified that FHIR is applied in healthcare systems with the main aim of guaranteeing the interoperability of the system, as well as addressing problems such as scalability and complexity [19]. Even though there are several works that present the implementation of the FHIR specification, it was possible to verify that most of the works do not present the implementation in detail, lacking the presentation of the domain model used in the system and the mapping of the clinical concepts used in the FHIR specification. Furthermore, there is a lack of mapping of concepts related to vascular diseases into FHIR resources.

3.2 Implementation

To guarantee the interoperability of all components of the remote monitoring platform and allow the easy integration of new sensors or applications we adopted the FHIR standard for the data exchange. To achieve this, we used HAPI FHIR[2], an open-source implementation of the FHIR specification developed in the Java programming language. It provides a flexible way to implement the FHIR standard in healthcare systems and it can be used to build client applications to fetch or store resources from a server, to build a server application to allow external applications the access of data, or it can be used to build a fully functional FHIR server with a Java Persistence API (JPA) [20]. We used HAPI FHIR to deploy a FHIR server with a JPA persistence module on the remote monitoring platform. To store the data in our server we installed a SQL Server database. This database was chosen due to being one of the most secure databases [21] and its ability to store large volumes of data. By using this server and database it is possible to store and access all the data used by the platform. Additionally, the format used to retrieve and store data will be used by all components of the platform, guaranteeing its interoperability.

Figure 2 presents the FHIR sever. In this page it is possible to check the available resources as well as the server's status.

Fig. 2. FHIR server deployed in the remote monitoring platform

By selecting one of the available resources, it is possible to view information, retrieve the update history of a certain instance, delete information, create a new instance, and update an existing instance, as can be seen by Fig. 3. It is also possible to submit a JSON regarding a specific instance of a resource to validate its format.

---

[2] Website: https://hapifhir.io.

Read an individual resource instance given its ID (and optionally a version ID to retrieve a specific version of that instance to **vread** that instance)

| ⊟ Read | ID* | | Version ID | (add for vread) |

Delete an individual instance of the resource

| 🗑 Delete | ID* |

Create an instance of the resource. Generally you do not need to specify an ID but you may force the server to use a specific ID by including one.

| ◪ Create | ID | (optional) | | Contents* | (place resource body here) |

Update an existing instance of the resource by ID.

| ◪ Update | ID* | (resource ID) | | Contents* | (place resource body here) |

Fig. 3. CRUD operations of the patient resource in the FHIR server

3.3 Domain Model

As FHIR provides the mapping of clinical concepts to over 100 resources, we identified a set of resources that would be used in the context of the Portuguese use case of the Inno4Health project. This set of resources was validated by the clinical team of the project. Figure 4 illustrates the domain model of the platform, including the FHIR resources employed, their relationships and the selected attributes.

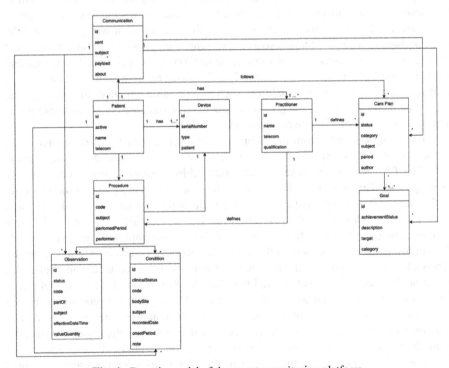

Fig. 4. Domain model of the remote monitoring platform

By analyzing the model in Fig. 4, the remote monitoring platform has resources that represent the entities of the system, the monitoring sensors, the procedures that will be performed on the patient to monitor their health condition, the clinical data collected by the sensors, and resources that represent concepts from the smart coaching services.

The remote monitoring platform has two entities: *Patient* and *Practitioner*. The *Patient* represents the patients that will be monitored, and the *Practitioner* represents the professionals who will treat the patients, whether the physicians, nurses, or caregivers. The *Patient* will have an identifier, an attribute that indicates whether the patient is active or not in the platform, the name, and contacts. The *Practitioner* will have an identifier, name, contact and qualification. The qualification indicates their role.

The *Procedure* represents medical procedures performed in the patient. These procedures will be carried out while using monitoring sensors to monitor the patient's condition. This resource will have an identifier, a code that indicates the type of procedure performed, the id of the patient, the period of time when it was performed, and the id of the device used. The *Device* resource represents the monitoring sensors, and it has an identifier, the serial number of the sensor, the type of the sensor (insole or a patch) and the identifier of the assigned patient. Regarding the monitored values that will be stored in the Data Storage of the platform, two resources were identified: *Observation* and *Condition*. The *Observation* resource represents the measurement of clinical variables of patients. One example of an *Observation* could be the measurement of steps walked by the patient. An *Observation* has an identifier, the status, the code (which identifies the variable that was measured), a reference to a procedure in which the measurement was made, a reference to the patient measured, the time where it was created, and the value registered. The *Condition* resource represents a diagnosis or a clinical event that has risen to concern, usually as a result of a medical procedure performed on the patient. Similar to the *Observation* resource, the *Condition* will have an identifier, the status, a code representing the type of condition (such as pain in one member of the body), the date when it was registered, the period of time that it lasted, the body site where it was reported, and the doctor's note regarding that condition.

Concerning concepts from the smart coaching services that will be implemented in the platform, we identified three resources: *Care Plan*, *Goal*, and *Communication*. The *Care Plan* resource represents a plan defined by the *Practitioner* to deliver care to the patient. This resource will be used to represent coaching plans in the platform, as they aim to improve the patient's health condition through the presentation of tasks to be performed during the day. A *Care Plan* has an identifier, the status (if it is in progress, completed, or failed), the category of the plan (examples of categories include the improvement of medication adherence, improvement of physical activity, among others), the assigned patient, the time period when it will be executed, and a reference to the health professional that defined the plan. A *Care Plan* will have several goals, i.e., tasks to be performed to complete the plan. These goals are represented by the *Goal* resource and will have identifier, the achievement status (completed, failed or in progress), the description of the goal, the target value, and the category of the goal. An example of a *Goal* is "walk 3000 steps during the day". Finally, the *Communication* resource will also be used in this platform. The *Communication* represents a clinical information to be shared with the patient. In the context of this work the *Communication* resource represents the personalized recommendations that will be presented to the patient. A *Communication* will have an identifier, the time when it was sent, a reference to the patient, the text that will be presented and a reference to the event that triggered the communication (such as a medical procedure, care plan executed, an exacerbation identified by the monitoring sensors, among others).

The use of these resources will allow the representation of all concepts used in the remote monitoring platform.

3.4 Code System

As mentioned in the previous section, FHIR resources such as the *Observation, Condition,* and *Device,* use an attribute "code" to identify the type of data that was measured, or the type of device used. Since different healthcare systems use different terminologies and codes to identify the clinical data stored and analyzed, FHIR provides a resource that allows the definition of codes that will be used in the system. The *CodeSystem* resource is used by FHIR to declare the existence of a code system and its key properties. Code systems allow the definition of which codes exist in the healthcare system and how they are understood in the clinical context [22].

The remote monitoring platform will have a code system that will identify the variables monitored regarding the Intermittent Claudication, Venous Ulcers and Diabetic Foot Ulcers sub-use cases. Additionally, the code system will also identify the types of monitoring sensors that are used in the patients. Figure 5 illustrates the code system defined to identify the two types of monitoring sensors used in the remote monitoring platform.

```
{
  "resourceType": "CodeSystem",
  "identifier": [
    {
      "system": "INNO-FHIR",
      "value": "example-codes"
    }
  ],
  "version": "202203",
  "name": "SensorCodes",
  "description": "This is an example code system that includes sensor codes",
  "concept": [
    {
      "code": "patch-sensor",
      "definition": "identification of patch sensor"
    },
    {
      "code": "insole-sensor",
      "definition": "identification of insole sensor"
    }
  ]
}
```

Fig. 5. JSON of a CodeSystem resource that identifies the types of monitoring sensors

It should be noted that it is possible to update the *CodeSystem* resource to identify new variables to be monitored or new monitoring sensors that were added to the remote monitoring platform.

3.5   Mapping of Intermittent Claudication Concepts

To better explain the use of the FHIR data exchange standard to represent the clinical concepts in the context of the remote monitoring platform of the Inno4Health project, in this section we illustrate the mapping of concepts regarding the monitoring of patients with Intermittent Claudication.

Figure 6 presents the concepts that are used in the monitoring of patients with Intermittent Claudication. The concepts were identified by the clinical team of the Portuguese use case of the Inno4Health project.

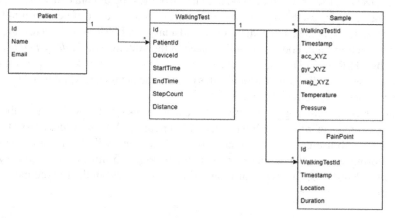

Fig. 6. Concepts regarding the monitoring of patients with Intermittent Claudication

As can be seen in Fig. 6, we have four main concepts: *Patient, WalkingTest, Sample,* and *PainPoint.* The *Patient* concept represents the patient being monitored, including their identification, name, and email. The *WalkingTest* represents a test that is performed on the patient, where they have to walk until they are physically unable to continue. With this test, it is possible to identify the distance and evaluate the performance of the patient in comparison to previous tests in order to assess their progress. Concepts associated to this test are *Sample* and *PainPoint.* A *Sample* indicates the temperature, pressure, and position of the patient in a certain timestamp. The *PainPoint* indicates whether the patient felt pain and its location.

In Fig. 7 it is presented a diagram with the mapping of the concepts presented above in the FHIR data exchange standard. It should be noted that the mapping was validated by the clinical team of the Portuguese use case of the Inno4Health project.

The *Patient* resource will represent the patient. The *WalkingTest* concept will be represented by the *Procedure* resource, as a walking test is a medical procedure to monitor the patient. Regarding the variables that will be monitored by the realization of the walking test, the *Sample* concept will be represented by the *Observation* resource, and the *PainPoint* will be represented by the *Condition* resource, as this resource specifies a condition that the patient reported as a result of a medical procedure. The *Device* resource will represent the monitoring sensor used in the monitoring of the walking test.

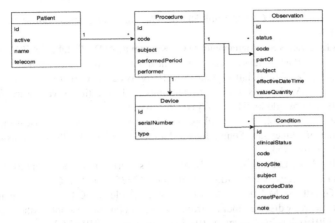

Fig. 7. Mapping of concepts regarding intermittent claudication in FHIR standard

4   Conclusions and Future Work

To address the current burdens of the healthcare of patients with vascular diseases, a remote monitoring platform that aims the self-management of patients is under development. As this platform intends to monitor three types of vascular diseases and is composed by several components for the data collection and processing, there is a need for the implementation of a data exchange standard in the platform.

In this work it is presented the implementation of a FHIR specification in the remote monitoring platform, with the aim of guaranteeing its interoperability. This work presents in detail the implementation, comprising the technologies used, the domain model adopted accompanied by the description of the clinical concepts related to vascular diseases as well as the smart coaching concepts used, and an example of the mapping of concepts into FHIR resources in the context of the monitoring of patients with Intermittent Claudication. By using this data exchange standard in the platform, it will be possible to exchange clinical data easily and securely between the monitoring sensors and the remaining components of the platform. Additionally, it will be possible to easily integrate new monitoring sensors and external applications.

As future work we intend to include the definition of codes regarding all clinical variables that will be monitored in the code system present in the FHIR server of the remote monitoring platform.

Acknowledgements. This research work was developed under the project Inno4Health (EUREKA-ITEA3: 19008; POCI-01-0247-FEDER-069523) and by National Funds through FCT (Fundação para a Ciência e a Tecnologia) under the project UIDB/00760/2020. Ana Vieira is supported by national funds through FCT PhD studentship with reference UI/BD/151115/2021.

References

1. McDermott, M.M., Guralnik, J.M., Tian, L., Ferrucci, L., Liu, K., Liao, Y., Criqui, M.H.: Baseline functional performance predicts the rate of mobility loss in persons with peripheral

arterial disease. J. Am. Coll. Cardiol. **50**(10), 974–982 (2007). https://doi.org/10.1016/j.jacc. 2007.05.030

2. Milic, D.J., Zivic, S.S., Bogdanovic, D.C., Karanovic, N.D., Golubovic, Z.V.: Risk factors related to the failure of venous leg ulcers to heal with compression treatment. J. Vasc. Surg. **49**(5), 1242–1247 (2009). https://doi.org/10.1016/j.jvs.2008.11.069

3. McDermott, M.M.: Exercise training for intermittent claudication. J. Vasc. Surg. **66**(5), 1612–1620 (2017). https://doi.org/10.1016/j.jvs.2017.05.111

4. Tummala, S., Scherbel, D.: Clinical assessment of peripheral arterial disease in the office: what do the guidelines say? Semin. Interv. Radiol. **35**(5), 365–377 (2018). https://doi.org/10. 1055/s-0038-1676453

5. Nicolaides, A.N., Labropoulos, N.: Burden and suffering in chronic venous disease. Adv. Ther. **36**(1), 1–4 (2019). https://doi.org/10.1007/s12325-019-0882-6

6. Kohn, C.G., Alberts, M.J., Peacock, W.F., Bunz, T.J., Coleman, C.I.: Cost and inpatient burden of peripheral artery disease: findings from the national inpatient sample. Atherosclerosis **286**, 142–146 (2019). https://doi.org/10.1016/j.atherosclerosis.2019.05.026

7. Vieira, A., et al.: Defining an architecture for a remote monitoring platform to support the self-management of vascular diseases. In: De La Prieta, F., El Bolock, A., Durães, D., Carneiro, J., Lopes, F., Julian, V. (eds.) PAAMS 2021. CCIS, vol. 1472, pp. 165–175. Springer, Cham (2021). https://doi.org/10.1007/978-3-030-85710-3_14

8. Nordo, A.H., et al.: Use of EHRs data for clinical research: historical progress and current applications. Learn Health Syst **3**(1), e10076–e10076 (2019). https://doi.org/10.1002/lrh2. 10076

9. Cheng, A.C., et al.: REDCap on FHIR: clinical data interoperability services. J. Biomed. Inform. **121**, 103871 (2021). https://doi.org/10.1016/j.jbi.2021.103871

10. "ODM-XML | CDISC." https://www.cdisc.org/standards/data-exchange/odm. Accessed 6 Apr 2022

11. "FHIR v4.0.1." https://www.hl7.org/fhir/. Accessed 6 Apr 2022

12. Lehne, M., Luijten, S., Imbusch, P., Thun, S.: The use of FHIR in digital health-a review of the scientific literature Stud. Health Technol. Inform. **267**, 52–58 (2019)

13. Ayaz, M., Pasha, M., Alzahrani, M., Budiarto, R., Stiawan, D.: The fast health interoperability resources (FHIR) standard: systematic literature review of implementations, applications, challenges and opportunities. JMIR Med. Inform. Rev. **9**(7), e21929 (2021). https://doi.org/ 10.2196/21929

14. "Summary - FHIR v4.0.1." https://www.hl7.org/fhir/summary.html. Accessed 6 Apr 2022

15. Kasthurirathne, S.N., Mamlin, B., Kumara, H., Grieve, G., Biondich, P.: Enabling better interoperability for healthcare: lessons in developing a standards based application programing interface for electronic medical record systems. J. Med. Syst. **39**(11), 1–8 (2015). https://doi. org/10.1007/s10916-015-0356-6

16. Baskaya, M., Yuksel, M., Erturkmen, G., Cunningham, M., Cunningham, P.: Health4Afrika-implementing HL7 FHIR based interoperability. Stud. Health Technol. Inform. **264**, 20–24 (2019)

17. Lamprinakos, G.C.: et al.: Using FHIR to develop a healthcare mobile application. In: 2014 4th International Conference on Wireless Mobile Communication and Healthcare - Transforming Healthcare Through Innovations in Mobile and Wireless Technologies (MOBIHEALTH), pp. 132–135. 3–5 Nov 2014. https://doi.org/10.1109/MOBIHEALTH.2014.7015927

18. Ismail, S., Alshmari, M., Qamar, U., Butt, W.H., Latif, K., Ahmad, H.F.: HL7 FHIR compliant data access model for maternal health information system. In: 2016 IEEE 16th International Conference on Bioinformatics and Bioengineering (BIBE), pp. 51–56. 31 Oct–2 Nov 2016 (2016). https://doi.org/10.1109/BIBE.2016.9

19. Bettoni, G.N., Camargo, T., Tavares, B., Flores, C., Santana da Silva, F.: Application of HL7 FHIR in a microservice architecture for patient navigation on registration and appointments. In: 2021 IEEE/ACM 3rd International Workshop on Software Engineering for Healthcare (SEH) (2021)
20. "HAPI FHIR - The Open Source API for Java." https://hapifhir.io. Accessed 13 April 2022
21. "SQL   Server|Microsoft."https://www.microsoft.com/pt-pt/sql-server/sql-server-2019. Accessed 18 Apr 2022
22. "CodeSystem - FHIR v4.0.1." https://www.hl7.org/fhir/codesystem.html. Accessed 14th Apr 2022

Legal Issues of the Use of Chatbot Apps for Mental Health Support

Chiara Gallese[1,2(✉)] (iD)

[1] Department of Electrical Engineering, Eindhoven University of Technology,
Eindhoven, The Netherlands
c.g.gallese.nobile@tue.nl
[2] School of Engineering, Carlo Cattaneo University - LIUC, Varese, Italy
cgallese@liuc.it

Abstract. Chatbots are increasingly used in many health care applications and are a useful tool to interact with patients without the need of human intervention. However, if not carefully built and employed, patients could face adverse effects from the interaction with these systems, especially when they are in a vulnerable state of mind. This article explores some of the legal issues regarding the use of conversational agents aimed at offering psychological support.

Keywords: Privacy · AI · Telemedicine · GDPR · Continuous learning

1 Introduction. Conversational Agents in the Mental Health Care Context

In recent years, the use of conversational agents in the health care field has increased [12,32]. For example, chatbots are used to book appointments, to provide help with panic attack management, to teach meditation exercises, to keep track of mood variations, to provide emotional support, and to manage stress [2].

Mental health care is a field in which conversational agents may have a significant role [8,11], as they are suited to provide emotional support to lonely people [6] who may feel more comfortable to talk with a chatbot app than seeking help to peers, caregivers, counselors or doctors [13]. If we look at the Android Play Store, we can find several apps that advertise their potential useful role in providing support to people with mental health problems, such as Wysa, Youper Therapy, InnerHour. Looking at the online opinions [22], these apps seems very popular, and reviews confirm their usefulness [5,26,31] and cost-effectiveness [3], although some have highlighted that their scripted dialogues may be harmful in certain circumstances [7,30][1].

---

[1] Dr. Iulia Turc has argued that more attention should be paid to their responses in case of users' suicidal ideation, see https://towardsdatascience.com/unconstrained-chatbots-condone-self-harm-e962509be2fa.

Funded by the REMIDE project, Carlo Cattaneo University - LIUC.

We selected some of the most popular chatbot apps in the Playstore[2] that were explicitly advertised as mental health help apps and that had a non-guided chat option, as free conversation poses the most privacy concerns because users can share as many personal data as they wish. Some of these apps were recently reviewed by Arfan et al. [1].

Table 1 shows data about downloads and reviews[3] of five chatbots described as tools for improving mental health.

Table 1. Apps downloads, reviews, and overall rating in Google Play Store.

Chatbot name	Downloads	Reviews	Overall rating
Replika	10 million	391.270	3.8
Wysa	1 million	118.723	4.7
Youper	1 million	49.153	4,1
InnerHour	1 million	23.448	4,6
Anima	500.000	14.572	4,1

Multiple laws and regulations apply to the domain of conversational agents in the mental health care field. Because health data are processed by the systems, GDPR applies, together with other relevant data protection laws (e.g., Convention 108+, national law), and some internal medical laws may be applicable too (e.g., regarding informed consent). When the system is employed to provide mental health aid, even if no registered professional is directly involved, the Medical Device Regulation will apply. Moreover, when the system is based

---

[2] Replika has the least positive reviews if compared to the other apps selected for this article, due to recent changes in the model and in the free services. Users stress the fact that it does not seem intelligent and the dialogue feels scripted. In addition, users report that their preferences on triggers were ignored. Wysa has the majority of its reviews with a positive feedback from users: some highlight how comfortable it is to have someone to talk about their problem "anonymously", claiming that it is better than seeking comfort from friends and family members; some claim that it has been useful to manage panic attacks and anxiety; some other say that it helps to get asleep. Negative reviews mostly focus on the fact that the conversation feels scripted, or that it is only available in English. Youper Therapy has some negative reviews due to technical issues, lack of different languages, and repetitive scripts. Positive ratings highlight the possibility of performing mindfulness exercises and the fact that it helps understanding users' feelings. InnerHour has many positive reviews as well, with only limited critical opinions from its users, who report their quick mood improvement. Anima has many positive reviews, although it also has some mixed and negative reviews. Users complaint mostly about the price and the lack of different languages. Positive reviews report that it feels as if thay were talking to a real person.

[3] Reviews are now localized and the rating may vary in different countries. Results shown are updated at the 04th of May 2022.

on Artificial Intelligence, it falls within the scope of the AI Act proposal, which classifies all medical devices as "high risk" systems. If the system is connected to a network, it is also subject to the new Data Act proposal. In addition, when the chatbot is able to sign contracts, it must comply with contractual law as well.

This article proposes to analyze the theme of the application of voice assistants to the domain of digital psychology, highlighting the critical legal issues regarding personal data protection. The second section will describe data protection principles that are relevant for the topic. In particular, the discussion will be divided into three sub-sections: one dedicated to security measures, one to automated decision making and the last one to informed consent issues. The third section, then, will describe the relevance of the Medical Device Regulation for conversational agents in psychology. The fourth section will be dedicated to the novelties introduced by the Data Act proposal. The fifth section will describe the relevance of the Data Act proposal the last one will discuss some contractual aspects.

2   Data Protection Principles Governing the Use of Conversational Agents

2.1   Data Protection by Design: Special Categories of Data

When using a chatbot app to improve their mental health, users share their health data, such as their mood variations, burnout, information about mental disability, neurodiversity, or disorders. Under the current GDPR framework in the EU, this information is considered a special category of personal data (article 9). The data collected by the chatbot are not anonymous, since each user is assigned with an unique identifier[4].

This pieces of sensitive information are stored on the cloud provided by the app producers' processors or on their proprietary servers. Due to the severe consequences occurring in case of a data breach of mental health data, a stricter legal discipline applies.

Other types of personal data are also collected, such as usage data, which may fall under the scope of the Data Act proposal (see Sect. 5).

As a measure to comply to the Privacy by Design principle, all the relevant information should be given to data subjects before they start chatting with the chatbot. However, this is not always the case: privacy policies are hidden inside links that generally users don't read [10], and only Anima responded with transparency when directly asked about the use of personal data, while Replika tried to dodge the question and gave vague answers.

---

[4] See Wysa's Privacy Policy: https://legal.wysa.io/privacy-policy. Data is only de-identified, therefore it is still considered as "pseudonymized" under the legal framework of GDPR.

2.2 Security Measures

Special categories of data must be protected with greater care than other types of data, and this means that stricter technical and organizational measures must be enacted, as provided by article 32 of GDPR[5]. Because of the large amount of health data shared with the chatbot app, security measures are a major concern [18,24].

According to the accountability principle, it is the Data Controller who is responsible and liable for the compliance to relevant data protection laws and regulations.

The first challenge that the Controller has to face is the storage of data, in particular the transfer abroad, since most cloud providers are located outside the EU, especially in the US. After the Schrems judgments invalidating all privacy agreement between the US and the EU, it is not considered secure to transfer data in that country. In fact, due to the Cloud Act, there is always a possibility that US agencies have access to European data. In addition, it might be difficult for data subjects to seek compensation and to exercise their rights in the US if data is leaked or wrongfully used by an organization in US territory; for this reason, at least standard contractual clauses should be used by the company providing the chatbot service and its data processors.

Therefore, before transferring data outside the EU, a careful transfer assessment should be carried out, and users must be informed both of the transfer itself and of the risks associated with the transfer.

Connected to the necessity of storing users' data is the risk of data breaches, which would be particularly harmful due to the sensitive information about mental issues and other private information that users often disclose to the chatbot[6].

Controllers need to perform an accurate assessment of risks and of the transfer outside the EU, taking into consideration the likelihood and impact of unauthorized or accidental destruction, loss, change, access, or disclosure of data, even if for a short period of time.

Technical measures are complemented by organizational measures, including employees training. Although it may be claimed that the content of the chat is

---

[5] First paragraph: "Taking into account the state of the art, the costs of implementation and the nature, scope, context and purposes of processing as well as the risk of varying likelihood and severity for the rights and freedoms of natural persons, the controller and the processor shall implement appropriate technical and organisational measures to ensure a level of security appropriate to the risk", and second paragraph: "In assessing the appropriate level of security account shall be taken in particular of the risks that are presented by processing, in particular from accidental or unlawful destruction, loss, alteration, unauthorised disclosure of, or access to personal data transmitted, stored or otherwise processed".

[6] In fact, many reviews point out that they feel more comfortable in disclosing their problems to a chatbot than to family and friends, meaning that certain information are kept secret even from the closest persons in their lives.

not disclosed to a human employee[7], humans do have access to servers where data are stored. In addition, data may be used for research purposes[8] or to improve the service. Therefore, there is still the risk that employees make an error or get victim of phishing and social engineering, making an effective data protection training mandatory. Recently, the Cluj Court of Appeal[9] confirmed a fine issued by the Romanian Data Protection Authority, stating that is not enough to establish internal procedures on data protection and compliance training activities, companies must also be able to prove that their employees attended the courses and understood the information provided.

2.3 ADM, Profiling, and Transparency

The transparency principle, an overarching obligation in GDPR,is translated into a series of rights provided to the data subjects when Profiling and Automated Decision Making are involved.

In GDPR, *Profiling* is the collection of aspects of an individual's personality, behavior, interests, habits, and other elements, collected in order to analyze their behavior, make predictions, or take decisions about them through an automated process (GDPR, Recital 71 and Article 22). AI systems employed to deliver psychological support in apps collect a series of personal elements from the user in order to build a profile (e.g., to provide personalized conversation and services), therefore they fall within the definition of Profiling. Automated decisions can be made without profiling and profiling can take place without automated decisions.

Automated decision making (ADM), on the other hand, is the process of taking a decision without human intervention, that produces legal effects or that has a significant impact on a person.

According to many authors [16,17,21,34], the interpretation that considers sufficient any human intervention in the decision-making process must be rejected: in fact, it would make it possible to circumvent the provisions of Article 22 GDPR by including a merely formal human intervention in the process, while the actual decision would remain that of the machine[10].

In the context of the chatbot apps, it may occur when the app decide to warn emergency services or contacts when concerned about the safety of the user, when it makes the user enter into contracts (e.g., with human therapists),

---

[7] See Wysa's Privacy Police: "No human has access to or gets to monitor or respond during your chat with the AI Coach", *ibid.*

[8] See Wysa's Privacy Policy under the "How do we handle your data when used for research purposes?" section, *ibid.*

[9] Civil Decision no. 9 of 13.04.2022, see the statement of the Romanian Data Protection Authority here: https://www.dataprotection.ro/?page=Comunicat_Presa_14_04_2022&lang=ro.

[10] This is confirmed by the Guidelines issued by Article 29 Working Party: "The controller cannot avoid the Article 22 provisions by fabricating human involvement. For example, if someone routinely applies automatically generated profiles to individuals without any actual influence on the result, this would still be a decision based solely on automated processing".

or when it decides what services are available to that specific user according to their profile and psychological peculiarities. In fact, as noted by the Guidelines on ADM, targeted advertising can have a significant effect if it uses the knowledge of the vulnerabilities of the data subjects targeted [4].

In these cases, users have the right to object, to contest the decision, and to share their point of view. As explained in paragraph 4 of Article 22, there is a general prohibition of employing ADM systems to health data, unless there is the explicit informed consent of the data subject, or the processing is necessary for reasons of "substantial public interest" or for entering into a contractual agreement, or for the performance of a contract, and at the same time there are suitable measures in place as a guarantee.

In addition to those provisions, data subjects also have the "right of explanation", which means that they have the right to have information about the rationale behind or the criteria relied on in reaching the decision, and about the significance and envisaged consequences of the processing of their data, as also provided by Article 10 of the Council of Europe's Convention 108+.

2.4   Informed Consent

According to the privacy framework in Europe, users' explicit consent is necessary to process their mental health data. Controllers, that is the companies producing the chatbots, need to be able to demonstrate that users gave a free consent, but also that they agree to each purpose individually[11].

In the case of the chatbot apps, a separate opt-in box must be provided, for example, for the consent regarding the processing of health data that are not necessary to enter into a contract, for the use of the conversation to train the AI model, and for the re-use of the chat messages for research purposes, including publications.

3   The Medical Device Regulation (MDR)

Devices employed to perform telemedicine services are subject to the MDR and must therefore undergo the procedure provided by law. In addition, even if the chatbot app does not provide mental health support by human psychologists,

---

[11] As noted by the EDBP guidelines, "Pursuant to Article 5(1)(b) GDPR, obtaining valid consent is always preceded by the determination of a specific, explicit and legitimate purpose for the intended processing activity. The need for specific consent in combination with the notion of purpose limitation in Article 5(1)(b) functions as a safeguard against the gradual widening or blurring of purposes for which data is processed, after a data subject has agreed to the initial collection of the data. This phenomenon, also known as function creep, is a risk for data subjects, as it may result in unanticipated use of personal data by the controller or by third parties and in loss of data subject control", and "controllers should provide specific information with each separate consent request about the data that are processed for each purpose, in order to make data subjects aware of the impact of the different choices they have".

they may still fall within the scope of the regulation depending on the state intended use and the way they are advertised [20].

The intended use of the app is a key factor in assessing whether the MDR is applicable and companies providing those apps must carefully review the definition of medical devices provided for in the relevant legislation. Whereas well-being apps that support users with meditation, sleep, mood tracking, and stress relief, are generally not considered medical devices [14], apps that address mental illnesses, claim to improve mental conditions, or provide consultations with certified mental health professionals, fall within the scope of the regulation and need to comply with the relevant obligations, including those related to safety and security.

4   The AI Act Proposal (AIA)

The AI Act proposal classify medical devices as high risk systems[12]. When a chatbot fall within the scope of the MDR, it also needs to comply with the requirements of the new regulation, that will be enacted in the next few years, such as having a risk management system in place, drawing appropriate data governance practices, keeping technical documentation and records, enacting transparency measures and provide information to users, providing for human oversight measures, ensuring accuracy, robustness and cybersecurity, having a quality management system in place, undergoing a conformity assessment and providing a way to automatically generate logs.

5   The Data Act Proposal

Conversational agents are explicitly mentioned[13] in the new proposal published by the European Commission on the 23rd of February 2022, although the definition only apply to "software that can process demands, tasks or questions including based on audio, written input, gestures or motions, and based on those demands, tasks or questions provides access their own and third party services or control their own and third party devices"[14].

The new regulation will grant users with the right to access to the data generated by the chatbot (personal and non-personal) and the right to portability of that data to third parties. Companies will therefore need to provide for appropriate means to comply with the new requirements set out at the EU level.

---

[12] The explanatory memorandum of the AIA notes that "The regulation follows a risk-based approach, differentiating between uses of AI that create (i) an unacceptable risk, (ii) a high risk, and (iii) low or minimal risk". Available at https://eur-lex.europa.eu/legal-content/EN/TXT/HTML/?uri=CELEX:52021PC0206&from=EN.

[13] See Article 7: "Where this Regulation refers to products or related services, such reference shall also be understood to include virtual assistants, insofar as they are used to access or control a product or related service".

[14] Recital 22 contains an explanation about the scope of the Regulation regarding virtual assistants and it also gives a hint about the relevance of chatbot apps.

6   Contractual Liability

Chatbots available in the Play Store are qualified as a service (free or paid) offered to the general public of that specific country. Therefore, their term and conditions qualify as "adhesion contract", serving many parties (users) with homogeneous transactions. Although they generally do not vary according to the nationality of the user, contractual law and in particular consumer law may be very different depending on the jurisdiction where the download was made, even when the contract (unilaterally) specifies the choice of law[15].

In addition, contracts concluded by the chatbot automatically or upon request (e.g., renewal of subscription plans, purchasing of additional services, booking individual therapy with trained psychologists) should also comply with the applicable laws and regulations, as their validity and legal qualification [28] may depend on national case law and different *jus poenitendi* time-frame may apply.

7   The Protection of Vulnerable Patients: Legal Issues

Although their mental state does not necessarily impair the ability to make decisions, users with mental conditions are considered particularly vulnerable. Consequently, particular care should be used when selling them services or influencing their behavior. Legal and ethical principles should be applied at the highest standards. However, although there is research about implementing ethical rules in chatbots [9,15,19,23,25,27,29,33], a gap in science has been identified in the literature regarding legal requirements [24].

From a legal point of view, companies targeting vulnerable users may face liability if the chatbot causes negative effects on users' mental health or if their vulnerabilities are unfairly exploited to induce addiction and the purchase of paid services.

8   Conclusion

Due to the multiple legal and ethical issues arising with the increase of the popularity of chatbots aimed to offer psychological support, more research is needed to assess the potential adverse effects on users and consequent liability that may arise if the system is not carefully designed in compliance with existing laws and ethical guidelines.

References

1. Ahmed, A., et al.: A review of mobile chatbot apps for anxiety and depression and their self-care features. Comput. Methods Programs Biomed. Update **1**, 100012 (2021)

---

[15] The legal classification may differ as well: some authors have qualified those terms as mere juridical acts instead of contracts.

2. Alhasani, M., Mulchandani, D., Oyebode, O., Baghaei, N., Orji, R.: A systematic and comparative review of behavior change strategies in stress management apps: opportunities for improvement. Front. Public Health **10** (2022)
3. de Almeida, R.S., da Silva, T.: AI chatbots in mental health: are we there yet? In: Digital Therapies in Psychosocial Rehabilitation and Mental Health, pp. 226–243 (2022)
4. Article 29 Data Protection Working Party: Guidelines on automated individual decision-making and profiling for the purposes of regulation 2016/679. **1**, WP215 (2017)
5. Callejas, Z., Griol, D.: Conversational agents for mental health and wellbeing. In: Lopez-Soto, T. (ed.) Dialog Systems. LAR, vol. 22, pp. 219–244. Springer, Cham (2021). https://doi.org/10.1007/978-3-030-61438-6_11
6. Corbett, C.F., Wright, P.J., Jones, K., Parmer, M.: Voice-activated virtual home assistant use and social isolation and loneliness among older adults: mini review. Front. Public Health **9** (2021)
7. Denecke, K., Schmid, N., Nüssli, S., et al.: Implementation of cognitive behavioral therapy in e-mental health apps: literature review. J. Med. Internet Res. **24**(3), e27791 (2022)
8. Denecke, K., Vaaheesan, S., Arulnathan, A.: A mental health chatbot for regulating emotions (SERMO)-concept and usability test. IEEE Trans. Emerg. Topics Comput. **9**(3), 1170–1182 (2020)
9. Dyoub, A., Costantini, S., Lisi, F.A.: An approach towards ethical chatbots in customer service. In: AIRO@ AI* IA (2019)
10. Elshout, M., Elsen, M., Leenheer, J., Loos, M., Luzak, J., et al.: Study on consumers' attitudes towards terms and conditions (T&CS) (2016)
11. Fitzpatrick, K.K., Darcy, A., Vierhile, M.: Delivering cognitive behavior therapy to young adults with symptoms of depression and anxiety using a fully automated conversational agent (Woebot): a randomized controlled trial. JMIR Mental Health **4**(2), e7785 (2017)
12. Gaffney, H., Mansell, W., Tai, S., et al.: Conversational agents in the treatment of mental health problems: mixed-method systematic review. JMIR Mental Health **6**(10), e14166 (2019)
13. Gamble, A.: Artificial intelligence and mobile apps for mental healthcare: a social informatics perspective. Aslib J. Inf. Manage. **72**(4), 509–523 (2020)
14. Gerke, S., Minssen, T., Cohen, G.: Ethical and legal challenges of artificial intelligence-driven healthcare. In: Artificial Intelligence in Healthcare, pp. 295–336. Elsevier (2020)
15. Goirand, M., Austin, E., Clay-Williams, R.: Implementing ethics in healthcare AI-based applications: a scoping review. Sci. Eng. Ethics **27**(5), 1–53 (2021). https://doi.org/10.1007/s11948-021-00336-3
16. Guarda, P., Petrucci, L.: Quando l'intelligenza artificiale parla: assistenti vocali e sanità digitale alla luce del nuovo regolamento generale in materia di protezione dei dati. BioLaw J.-Rivista di BioDiritto **2**, 425–446 (2020)
17. Hänold, S.: Profiling and automated decision-making: legal implications and short-comings. In: Corrales, M., Fenwick, M., Forgó, N. (eds.) Robotics, AI and the Future of Law. PLBI, pp. 123–153. Springer, Singapore (2018). https://doi.org/10.1007/978-981-13-2874-9_6
18. Hasal, M., Nowaková, J., Ahmed Saghair, K., Abdulla, H., Snášel, V., Ogiela, L.: Chatbots: security, privacy, data protection, and social aspects. Concurr. Comput. Pract. Exp. **33**(19), e6426 (2021)

19. Kretzschmar, K., Tyroll, H., Pavarini, G., Manzini, A., Singh, I., Group, N.Y.P.A.: Can your phone be your therapist? Young people's ethical perspectives on the use of fully automated conversational agents (chatbots) in mental health support. Biomed. Inform. Insights **11**, 1178222619829083 (2019)

20. Ludvigsen, K., Nagaraja, S., Angela, D.: When is software a medical device? Understanding and determining the "intention" and requirements for software as a medical device in European union law. Eur. J. Risk Regul. **13**(1), 78–93 (2022)

21. Malgieri, G., Comandé, G.: Why a right to legibility of automated decision-making exists in the general data protection regulation. International Data Privacy Law (2017)

22. Malik, T., Ambrose, A.J., Sinha, C., et al.: Evaluating user feedback for an artificial intelligence-enabled, cognitive behavioral therapy-based mental health app (Wysa): qualitative thematic analysis. JMIR Hum. Factors **9**(2), e35668 (2022)

23. Martinez-Martin, N.: Trusting the bot: addressing the ethical challenges of consumer digital mental health therapy. In: Developments in Neuroethics and Bioethics, vol. 3, pp. 63–91. Elsevier (2020)

24. May, R., Denecke, K.: Security, privacy, and healthcare-related conversational agents: a scoping review. Inform. Health Soc. Care **47**(2), 194–210 (2021)

25. Möllmann, N.R., Mirbabaie, M., Stieglitz, S.: Is it alright to use artificial intelligence in digital health? A systematic literature review on ethical considerations. Health Inform. J. **27**(4), 14604582211052392 (2021)

26. Myers, A., Chesebrough, L., Hu, R., Turchioe, M.R., Pathak, J., Creber, R.M.: Evaluating commercially available mobile apps for depression self-management. In: AMIA Annual Symposium Proceedings, vol. 2020, p. 906. American Medical Informatics Association (2020)

27. Parviainen, J., Rantala, J.: Chatbot breakthrough in the 2020s? An ethical reflection on the trend of automated consultations in health care. Med. Health Care Philos. **25**(1), 61–71 (2022). https://doi.org/10.1007/s11019-021-10049-w

28. Ricci, F.: Libertà e responsabilità nei contratti telematici. Studi in onore di Giuseppe Benedetti **3**, 1593–1609 (2007)

29. Ruane, E., Birhane, A., Ventresque, A.: Conversational AI: social and ethical considerations. In: AICS, pp. 104–115 (2019)

30. Sedlakova, J., Trachsel, M.: Conversational artificial intelligence in psychotherapy: a new therapeutic tool or agent? Am. J. Bioeth. 1–10 (2022)

31. Sweeney, C., et al.: Can chatbots help support a person's mental health? Perceptions and views from mental healthcare professionals and experts. ACM Trans. Comput. Educ. **2**(3), 1–15 (2021)

32. Vaidyam, A.N., Wisniewski, H., Halamka, J.D., Kashavan, M.S., Torous, J.B.: Chatbots and conversational agents in mental health: a review of the psychiatric landscape. Can. J. Psychiatry **64**(7), 456–464 (2019)

33. Vanderlyn, L., Weber, G., Neumann, M., Väth, D., Meyer, S., Vu, N.T.: "It seemed like an annoying woman": on the perception and ethical considerations of affective language in text-based conversational agents. In: Proceedings of the 25th Conference on Computational Natural Language Learning, pp. 44–57 (2021)

34. Veale, M., Edwards, L.: Clarity, surprises, and further questions in the article 29 working party draft guidance on automated decision-making and profiling. Comput. Law Secur. Rev. **34**(2), 398–404 (2018)

A Hybrid Model to Classify Physical Activity Profiles

Vítor Crista[1]([⊠]) [iD], Diogo Martinho[1] [iD], Jorge Meira[1] [iD], João Carneiro[1] [iD],
Juan Corchado[2] [iD], and Goreti Marreiros[1] [iD]

[1] Research Group on Intelligent Engineering and Computing for Advanced Innovation and
Development (GECAD), Institute of Engineering, Polytechnic of Porto, Porto, Portugal
{vvrpc,diepm,janme,jrc,mgt}@isep.ipp.pt
[2] BISITE Digital Innovation Hub, University of Salamanca, Edifício Multiusos, Salamanca,
Spain
corchado@usal.es

Abstract. Diabetes is a chronic disease characterized by high blood glucose levels. This condition has a strong impact on the heart, eyes, and even kidneys, leading to several long-term health problems. It is estimated that about 422 million people live with this condition and over 1.5 million deaths per year are related to diabetes. Although there is no cure for diabetes, it can still be prevented or in the worst case managed, by implementing a healthy lifestyle, where exercising is a priority. One of the most basic ways to exercise is by walking. Although simple, it can be helpful to reduce blood sugar levels. The first step toward the right lifestyle for the diabetic patient is to maintain an active routine and improve it every day. Therefore, it is important to create an environment where the person can be motivated to be healthier and at the same time be supported to do so. Additionally, it is needed to consider that every person is different and therefore the support provided for each diabetic patient must be personalized according to his/her capabilities and necessities. In this paper, using a dataset of user activity, more specifically the daily walking data of different users, the focus was to define a machine learning model, capable of identifying distinct groups of users, to find their favorite routines related to physical activity data. To reach the proposed goal, a classification model with 95,6% prediction accuracy was produced. The resulting hybrid model, using temporal predictors, such as period of day and weekday, could identify 13 clusters that describe 13 different profiles of users according to 31 generated rules.

Keywords: Classification model · Decision tree · Diabetes · Hierarchical clustering · Machine learning · Physical activity

1 Introduction

Considering the rise of the population with diabetes, mostly due to the elevated levels of a sedentary lifestyle, which is becoming increasingly evident today, it becomes fundamental to encourage the population to adopt healthier lifestyles that comprise the practice of physical exercise. In this context, it is essential to establish techniques that can motivate users to achieve physical-related goals, that when done correctly can be one of the most effective ways to prevent diabetes. Otherwise, and in cases where the patient has already been diagnosed with diabetes, the practice of physical exercise can prevent associated complications, and control blood sugar levels [1]. Current literature tells us that physical exercise stimulates the production of insulin and facilitates its transport to the cells. When exercising, there is a tendency to increase the use of glucose by the muscles, and, as such, blood glucose will tend to decrease.[1]

Given the high rate of the sedentary lifestyle of a large part of the world population, it was sought that this paper focus on a form of exercise that can be performed easily by most people, which is the walking exercise [2]. This type of exercise can help those who are trying to make physical activity part of their daily lives, and at the same time not forget those who already practice physical exercise daily.

Additionally, with the growth of mobile and sensor technologies, there are now limitless ways to collect user data from their daily activities and also from the surrounding environment [3–9] and also to allow more personalized interactions with the user [10, 11].

The work here presented is part of the FoodFriend project, which consists of a healthcare solution, which has the main goal to help people with type 2 diabetes to develop improved healthy habits, eat better and practice more exercise. In general, the purpose is to coach and motivate users to reach their goals, using gamification techniques, and provide a personalized interaction between the user and the system. It is important to mention that food is also a fundamental part of the prevention and control of diabetes [12], however, and since the FoodFriend app also allows connection with fitness services, such as Google Fit and Huawei Health, it is possible to monitor various metrics, such as the number of daily steps performed by the user. Once this data is provided by the users, it can be used in conjunction with different machine learning techniques, to identify divergent profiles of users based on physical activity data. By doing so, it will be possible to create and provide personalized feedback to each user of the app based on their capabilities and interests.

Regarding the adopted methodology, it was analyzed the Fitbit dataset, from the Kaggle website,[2] consists of the steps taken by 33 users. This dataset was first pre-processed and then applied a hybrid clustering model (using hierarchical clustering and decision tree algorithm) to find the optimized number of user groups and corresponding rules that characterize them.

In terms of data credibility, it was possible to verify that the sample was small, thus not being representative of the major population. Additionally, it still had missing information about users, such as age, gender, and nationality, among others which could have been used to better describe the obtained groups of users. Despite this, the results obtained with this data were still truly relevant and adequate to describe correctly different profiles of physical activity, as a first approach, and the same process can then be applied as more data is collected within the FoodFriend project and its users.

The rest of the paper is organized in the following order: Sect. 2 explains the clustering analysis performed together with the architecture considered. In Sect. 3, we explain in depth the hierarchical clustering analysis undertaken to find the most adequate method to split the data. In Sect. 4, we applied clustering validation to identify the optimal

---

[1] https://apdp.pt/diabetes/tratamento/exercicio-fisico.

[2] https://www.kaggle.com/datasets/arashnic/fitbit.

number of clusters. In Sect. 5, we present the classification model, to describe each cluster discovered. Finally, some conclusions are taken in Sect. 6, along with the work to be done hereafter.

2   Clustering Analysis

In this paper, clustering analysis of the Fitbit database was performed.[3] As such, we defined a machine learning model combining clustering division and classification. To do so, a hybrid model consisting of two different clustering models was defined, one for hierarchical clustering and the other for classification. Figure 1 represents the architecture that was used for the model, and the main steps of each phase of the clustering process are described in the following sections.

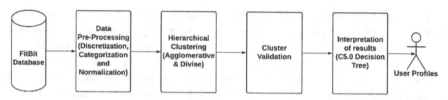

Fig. 1. Architecture of the model

2.1 Data Description

This model was developed with the help of the database obtained through the Kaggle website, a dataset based on the activity data of different users. This dataset includes 33 Fitbit users who consented the use of their tracker data. The Fitbit dataset includes several files regarding various aspects of user activity, such as sleep quality, minutes active, weight logs, and most important, steps activity data. The data has a focus on the daily steps, and offer different recorded timeframes of the same date, regarding minutes, hours, and days. Since the goal was to predict and find clustering based upon not only the day of the week but also the period within the day, the most suitable timeframe was the hourly one. In this case, each row represents an entry of a specific user on a specific hour, and the steps done in that hour, with a total of 22099 observations regarding the 33 distinct users. Using an hour-based dataset allows to transform it into daily entries, which can be done by applying different pre-processing techniques, such as discretization, among others that will be explained in the next section. In terms of features, the dataset was quite simple, only having the user id, the data, the time of the entry, and the total steps done in that time. Regarding limitations, this dataset has a lack of information about the user, such as gender and age, as mentioned previously.

---

[3] https://www.kaggle.com/datasets/arashnic/fitbit.

2.2 Data Pre-processing

The dataset was represented in hours, and every observation represents the total steps done by a user in a particular hour. The first step, the pre-processing of data, was performed to do a discretize the data in the hour format. With this process, it is possible to reduce the number of values for a given continuous attribute by dividing the range of the attribute into intervals [13]. In this case, is a suitable technique because with this was possible to create features regarding different periods within a day, and use those features to generate more interesting clusters. For this, we considered the morning, afternoon, and night intervals. The morning starts at 6 am and ends at 12 am, the afternoon period starts at 12 am and ends at 7 pm and finally, the night goes from 7 pm to 6 am. Since there was no information about the users regarding time zones, these intervals were used across all samples. After this step, the data was grouped into a dataset with a total of 934 observations and 4 different variables, total steps, morning steps, afternoon steps, and night steps. After a quick analysis, 12 NAs were spotted and have been removed from the total sample, as these records represent a small portion of the dataset. The next step was to proceed with a categorization of the weekday. To do so, it was also necessary to group all samples according to the corresponding day of the week. Finally, it was done a normalization of the dataset to reduce data inconsistencies. So, after the preprocessing, there was a dataset with a total of 922 observations with an average of around 27 entries per user.

3 Hierarchical Clustering

Hierarchical clustering is a technique to identify distinct groups within a dataset. This method is like k-means clustering, however, it has a particularity in which is not required to specify the number of clusters, instead, the number can be visually accessible through the help of a graph called dendrogram [14].

To proceed with the hierarchical clustering, first, it was necessary to generate the dissimilarity matrix. To do so, the most usual metric applied is the Euclidean distance, but, because the dataset is composed of mixed data, numerical and categorical, the Gower distance was chosen since is capable of handling both types of data [15]. After measuring the dissimilarity matrix, the hierarchical clustering can be applied using either divisive or agglomerative clustering. The agglomerative clustering starts with multiple clusters, and it pairs the clusters and successively merges until there is only one cluster left. On the other hand, divisive clustering is the reverse, it starts with only one cluster and proceeds by splitting clusters recursively until individual data have been split into singleton clusters [16].

Since there are different options and even agglomerative clustering has different methods to choose from, it is particularly important to pick the most suitable approach, and for that, it was used a metric called clustering coefficient. This coefficient shows the strength of the clustering structure. Values closer to 1 represent a more balanced clustering structure, on the other hand, values closer to 0 suggest less well-formed clusters, so it is important to find the approach where the coefficient is at its highest.[4]

---

[4] https://bradleyboehmke.github.io/HOML/.

In the case of the agglomerative clustering, there are several different methods to choose from, with different coefficients, on the other hand, divisive clustering does not have a specific method. The resulting coefficients of each different approach are presented in Table 1.

Table 1. Clustering coefficients

Coefficient	Clustering type
0.9533403	Agglomerative single
0.9910034	Agglomerative complete
0.9839920	Agglomerative average
0.9992280	Agglomerative ward
0.9900518	Divisive

From the table above the best approach to agglomerative clustering is with the ward method and Fig. 2 and Fig. 3 report the dendrogram of the ward method and the divisive clustering to visually compare them.

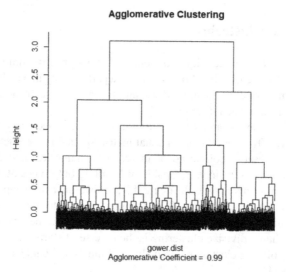

Fig. 2. Agglomerative clustering dendrogram

From the two figures, it is clear that the divisive clustering dendrogram is inconsistent in terms of the way it groups the data. On the other hand, agglomerative clustering in Fig. 2 is much clear and it is easy to see how clusters are being divided. With these results, agglomerative clustering using the ward method was considered for the rest of the clustering study presented in this work.

Divisive Clustering

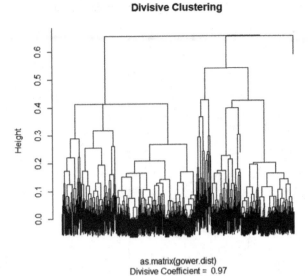

as.matrix(gower.dist)
Divisive Coefficient = 0.97

Fig. 3. Divisive clustering dendrogram

4 Cluster Validation

Although agglomerative clustering dendrogram is visually more pleasant, there is no real access to the optimal number of clusters, and this is something necessary to identify, even before proceeding to the classification model. To find the optimal number of clusters, there are many different techniques, the one used was the silhouette method. Ranging from -1 to 1, the silhouette method consists of finding how close each point in one specific cluster is to the points in the neighboring clusters thus providing a way to find the optimal number of clusters [17]. Figure 4 represents the plot of the silhouette method.

There are three different areas where there are significant bends. First at 6 clusters, then at 8 clusters, and finally at 13 clusters. Although 13 clusters seem to have the least bend of the three, it was found later, by doing the classification model, that 6 and 8 clusters do not give very conclusive results and with 13 we were able to obtain more relations between the features.

5 Classification Model

Once the number of clusters was found, it is time to address their classification using the C5.0 Decision-Tree algorithm. This algorithm measures which of the analyzed variables affects more in the division of each instance of the clusters. To avoid overfitting or underfitting the decision model, it was used a technique of cross-validation where the data is split into training data and testing data, and the ratio used was 75% for training and the remaining 25% for testing the model afterward. It was done iteratively, and the more times the model runs, the more accurate it becomes. So the optimal number of folds was 10, which produces a model with remarkably high accuracy. As can be seen, in Fig. 5,

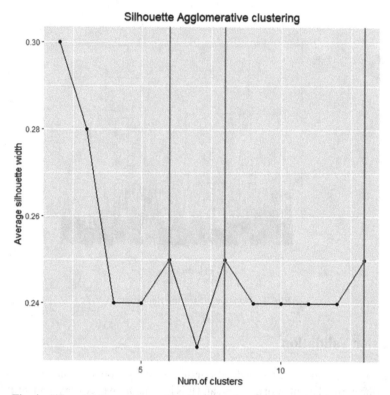

Fig. 4. Silhouette for agglomerative clustering (bends observed at 6, 8, and 13)

the model performed very well, with the most iteration performed with a 100% accuracy. The worst performed accuracy was in iteration 5 with 75% and the second-worst was in iteration 8 with 95%. The most well-performed iteration among the 10 done, was the first, with only a 1.8% error.

5.1 Interpretation of Results

This section describes the results presented in Table 2, where there are the rules that characterize the 13 different clusters, for iteration 1. Cluster 1 represents users that prefer walking at the beginning of the week, more precisely, Monday and Tuesday. Cluster 2 also denotes users that walk in the early week, but for this profile, users are quite active in the afternoon and not so much in the morning and night. For cluster 3, users also like the beginning of the week to do their walking routine and they are less active in the morning and night. Cluster 4 is quite different from the previous ones because users prefer not only the beginning but also the middle of the week, but overall they are not active at all, being the day with the least walking activity, the Wednesday with 1675 steps. Cluster 5 is the ideal profile, which people should follow. Every rule that characterizes this cluster has at least 12.000 walking steps, which by far exceeds the minimum number required to start improving their health. This cluster also covers

Table 2. Classification rules

Rule	Cluster	Conditions
1	1	NightSteps > 3539, Weekday = [Monday, Tuesday]
2	2	TotalSteps > 8382, AfternoonSteps ≤ 12204, NightSteps ≤ 3539, Weekday = [Monday, Tuesday]
3	2	TotalSteps > 6805, MorningSteps ≤ 2445, NightSteps ≤ 3539, Weekday = [Monday, Tuesday]
4	2	MorningSteps > 3382, AfternoonSteps ≤ 12204, NightSteps ≤ 3539, Weekday = Tuesday
5	3	TotalSteps > 1551, TotalSteps ≤ 6805, NightSteps ≤ 3539, Weekday = [Monday, Tuesday]
6	3	TotalSteps ≤ 8382, MorningSteps > 2445, Weekday = [Monday, Tuesday]
7	4	TotalSteps ≤ 1551, Weekday = [Monday, Tuesday]
8	4	TotalSteps ≤ 3365, AfternoonSteps ≤ 710, Weekday = Thursday
9	4	TotalSteps ≤ 1675, Weekday = Wednesday
10	5	AfternoonSteps > 14435, Weekday = [Friday, Thursday, Wednesday]
11	5	AfternoonSteps > 12204, Weekday = [Monday, Tuesday]
12	5	TotalSteps > 12957, NightSteps ≤ 5552, Weekday = Wednesday
13	6	TotalSteps > 1675, TotalSteps ≤ 12957, NightSteps ≤ 5552, Weekday = Wednesday
14	7	TotalSteps > 7303, AfternoonSteps ≤ 8374, NightSteps ≤ 4470, Weekday = [Friday, Thursday]
15	7	TotalSteps > 12957, MorningSteps > 7028, Weekday = Wednesday
16	7	TotalSteps ≤ 7303, AfternoonSteps > 3537, Weekday = Friday
17	8	NightSteps > 4470, Weekday = [Friday, Thursday]
18	8	NightSteps > 6322, Weekday = [Friday, Saturday, Sunday, Thursday, Wednesday]
19	8	NightSteps > 4850, Weekday = [Friday, Saturday, Sunday, Thursday, Wednesday]
20	9	TotalSteps ≤ 7303, AfternoonSteps > 710, AfternoonSteps ≤ 3537, Weekday = [Friday, Thursday]
21	9	TotalSteps ≤ 7303, AfternoonSteps > 710, Weekday = Thursday
22	9	TotalSteps > 3365, AfternoonSteps ≤ 710, Weekday = [Friday, Thursday]
23	10	AfternoonSteps > 6871, NightSteps ≤ 6322, Weekday = [Saturday, Sunday]
24	10	AfternoonSteps > 8374, AfternoonSteps ≤ 14435, NightSteps ≤ 4470, Weekday = [Friday, Thursday]

(continued)

Table 2. (*continued*)

Rule	Cluster	Conditions
25	10	TotalSteps > 10081, NightSteps ≤ 4850, Weekday = Saturday
26	11	TotalSteps ≤ 4188, Weekday = Sunday
27	11	TotalSteps ≤ 2283, Weekday = [Saturday, Sunday]
28	11	TotalSteps ≤ 3365, AfternoonSteps ≤ 710, Weekday = Friday
29	12	TotalSteps > 4188, TotalSteps ≤ 10081, Weekday = Saturday
30	12	TotalSteps > 2283, TotalSteps ≤ 10081, Weekday = Saturday
31	13	TotalSteps > 4188, AfternoonSteps ≤ 6871, NightSteps ≤ 6322, Weekday = Sunday

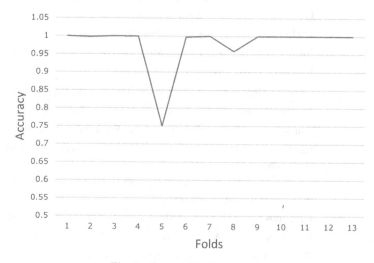

Fig. 5. Cross-validation analysis

all week, being the end of the week more active than the beginning. Beyond this, there is also a particularity, which is in the middle of the week, more precisely Wednesday, users do less walking at the night. Cluster 6 is only composed of one rule, to nominate, users prefer walking in the middle of the week. Cluster 7, is characterized by users that are more active through the morning, in the middle of the week (Wednesday), and less active through the afternoon, at the end of the week (Friday). The cluster 8 represents users that like walking mostly at the end of the week and weekend, and prefer doing it at the night, although they are not highly active with only half of the 10.000 recommended steps. Cluster 9 represents people that enjoy walking on Thursday and Friday, but are not so active. Cluster 10 is about users that are fairly active and prefer walking in the afternoon. Cluster 11, in its turn, represents users that prefer the weekend and are not regularly active, especially during the afternoon. Cluster 12 is about users that are fairly active on Saturdays. Finally, cluster 13 represents users somewhat active, although not doing the 10.000 recommend steps, and that prefer late time Sundays.

6 Conclusions and Future Work

The sedentary lifestyle of the population has increased over the years and brings with it several health complications, and diabetes is one of them. To face this, and to create possibilities for users to improve their health by themselves, it is important to figure out a way to better interact with the user, because every person is unique and has his routine and tastes. The machine learning model built and presented in this paper opens a possibility to find out what are those routines and tastes and group them into a profile. Once the profile is discovered, there is a more personalized way to communicate to the users, for example with feedback messages. As mentioned, a database composed of 33 users was used to train the model and the results consist of 13 different clusters or profiles. The results generated from the clusters show that users seem not to be highly active. Only one cluster, cluster 5, represents active users, surpassing the 10.000 recommend daily steps.

In conclusion, this study was considered successful, thus being a model with a prominent level of reliability, with 95,6% accuracy. This study was relevant because this model allows building a personalized way of interacting with a user.

As was mentioned before, the dataset used for this paper has some limitations, like the number of users involved in the study, and the lack of information about them. So, in future work, the next logical step is to apply this approach to the data collected from the users of the FoodFriend app. The sample needs to be significant, and therefore the study should be applied to a maximum of people, of different ages and genders, to understand if there are significant differences when it comes to physical activity and people who fall into distinct categories. In addition, this process could also be applied to other metrics and not only in walking. Walking is one of the many things that a person can do in their daily life, so the considered study could be more generalized to other contexts, even to understand other healthy habits such as food intake to obtain nutritional profiles.

Acknowledgments. This research work was developed under the project Food Friend – "Autonomous and easy-to-use tool for monitoring of personal food intake and personalised feedback" (ITEA 18032), co-financed by the North Regional Operational Program (NORTE 2020) under the Portugal 2020 and the European Regional Development Fund (ERDF), with the reference NORTE-01-0247-FEDER-047381 and by National Funds through FCT (Fundação para a Ciência e a Tecnologia) under the project UI/DB/00760/2020.

References

1. De Feo, P., et al.: Exercise and diabetes. Acta Biomed. **77**, 14–17 (2006)
2. Morris, J.N., Hardman, A.E.: Walking to health. Sports Med. **23**, 306–332 (1997)
3. Alshutayria, A., et al.: An interactive mobile application to request the help of the nearest first aider by the injured: the design and implementation of an interactive mobile application to request the help of the nearest first aider by the injured. Adv. Distrib. Comput. Artif. Intell. J. **10**(1), 15–32 (2021). https://doi.org/10.14201/ADCAIJ20211011532

4. Nakahara, T., et al.: Mobile device-based speech enhancement system using lip-reading. In: Dong, Y., Herrera-Viedma, E., Matsui, K., Omatsu, S., Briones, A.G., González, S.R. (eds.) DCAI 2020. AISC, vol. 1237, pp. 159–167. Springer, Cham (2021). https://doi.org/10.1007/978-3-030-53036-5_17

5. Rathod, Y.A., Kotwal, C.B., Pandya, S.D., Sondagar, D.R.: An access control and authorization model with open stack cloud for smart grid. Adv. Distrib. Comput. Artif. Intell. J. **9**, 69–87 (2020)

6. de Oliveira, M., Teixeira, R., Sousa, R., Tavares Gonçalves, E.J.: An agent-based simulation to explore communication in a system to control urban traffic with smart traffic lights. Adv. Distrib. Comput. Artif. Intell. J. **10**(3), 209–225 (2021)

7. Khan, R., Siddiqui, S., Rastogi, A.: Crime detection using sentiment analysis. Adv. Distrib. Comput. Artif. Intell. J. **10**(3), 281–291 (2021)

8. Carlei, V., Adamo, G., Ustenko, O., Barybina, V.: Stacking generalization via machine learning for trend detection in financial time series. In: Bucciarelli, E., Chen, S.-H., Corchado, J.M., Javier, P.D. (eds.) DECON 2020. SCI, vol. 990, pp. 159–166. Springer, Cham (2021). https://doi.org/10.1007/978-3-030-75583-6_16

9. Carlei, V., Terzi, S., Giordani, F., Adamo, G.: Portfolio management via empirical asset pricing powered by machine learning. In: Bucciarelli, E., Chen, S.-H., Corchado, J.M., Javier, P.D. (eds.) DECON 2020. SCI, vol. 990, pp. 121–129. Springer, Cham (2021). https://doi.org/10.1007/978-3-030-75583-6_12

10. Márquez-Sáncheza, S., Mora-Simonb, S., Herrera-Santosa, J., Roncerod, A.O., Rodríguez, J.M.C.: Intelligent Dolls and robots for the treatment of elderly people with dementia. Adv. Distrib. Comput. Artif. Intell. J. **9**, 99–112 (2020)

11. Basarslan, M.S., Kayaalp, F.: Sentiment analysis with machine learning methods on social media. Adv. Distrib. Comput. Artif. Intell. J. **9**(3), 5–15 (2020). https://doi.org/10.14201/ADCAIJ202093515

12. Povey, R.C., Clark-Carter, D.: Diabetes and healthy eating. Adv. Distrib. Comput. Artif. Intell. J. **33**, 931–959 (2007)

13. Liu, H., Hussain, F., Tan, C.L., Dash, M.: Discretization: an enabling technique. Data Min. Knowl. Discov. **6**, 393–423 (2002)

14. Nielsen, F.: Hierarchical clustering. In: Nielsen, F. (ed.) Introduction to HPC with MPI for Data Science, pp. 195–211. Springer International Publishing, Cham (2016). https://doi.org/10.1007/978-3-319-21903-5_8

15. Gagolewski, M., Bartoszuk, M., Cena, A.: A new, fast, and outlier-resistant hierarchical clustering algorithm. Inf. Sci. **363**, 8–23 (2016)

16. Roux, M.: A comparative study of divisive and agglomerative hierarchical clustering algorithms. J. Classif. **35**(2), 345–366 (2018). https://doi.org/10.1007/s00357-018-9259-9

17. Sai Krishna, T., Yesu Babu, A., Kiran Kumar, R.: Determination of optimal clusters for a non-hierarchical clustering paradigm K-means algorithm. In: Proceedings of International Conference on Computational Intelligence and Data Engineering, pp. 301–316. Springer (2018)

Workshop on Multi-Agent Based Applications for Modern Energy Markets, Smart Grids and Future Power Systems (MASGES)

Workshop on Multi-Agent Based Applications for Modern Energy Markets, Smart Grids and Future Power Systems (MASGES)

Future power systems will probably be characterized by very large penetrations of renewables (towards 100%) and support the operation of wholesale markets (e.g., day-ahead and balancing markets) together with local markets. Electricity markets are a complex and evolving reality, meaning that researchers are lacking insight into numerous open problems that are being raised (e.g., the need of new market designs to manage the variability and uncertainty of the increasing levels of renewable generation). Also, future power systems will integrate a large number of distributed energy resources and new players. Smart grids are intrinsically linked to the challenges raised by new power systems and are expected to improve in efficiency and effectiveness, while ensuring reliability and a secure delivery of electricity to end-users. They should be capable of autonomously and intelligently configuring themselves to make the most efficient use of the available resources, to be robust to different kinds of failures and energy production deviations, and to be extendable and adaptable in face of the rapidly changing technologies and requirements.

The focus of this workshop is on the modeling and simulation of modern power systems, supporting electricity markets capable of integrating large levels of variable renewable energy, and also the existence of emerging technologies, such as distributed generation, demand response, energy storage, smart homes, and electric vehicles.

Organization

Organizing Committee

Fernando Lopes	National Laboratory of Energy and Geology, Portugal
Zita Vale	Polytechnic Institute of Porto, Portugal

Program Committee

Nick Bassiliades	Aristotle University of Thessaloniki, Greece
Olivier Boissier	Mines Saint-Étienne, France
Miguel Carmona	University of Alcala, Spain
Helder Coelho	Universidade de Lisboa, Portugal
António Couto	National Laboratory of Energy and Geology, Portugal
Christian Derksen	University Duisburg-Essen, Germany
Frank Dignum	Utrecht University, The Netherlands
Alberto Fernández	Universidad Rey Juan Carlos, Spain
Massimiliano Giacomin	University of Brescia, Italy
Nikos Hatziargyriou	National Technical University of Athens, Greece
Koen Hindriks	Delft University of Technology, The Netherlands
Wojtek Jamroga	Clausthal University of Technology, Germany
Souhila Kaci	Artois University, France
Ivana Kockar	University of Strathclyde, UK
Matthias Klusch	DFKI, Germany
Fernando Lezama	Polytechnic Institute of Porto, Portugal
Morten Lind	Technical University of Denmark, Denmark
Fernando Lopes	National Laboratory of Energy and Geology, Portugal
Zheng Ma	University of Southern Denmark, Denmark
Pavlos Moraitis	Paris Cité University, France
Jörg Müller	Clausthal University of Technology, Germany
Emmanouil Rigas	Aristotle University of Thessaloniki, Greece
Juan A. Rodríguez-Aguilar	IIIA-CSIC, Spain
Murat Sensoy	University of Aberdeen, UK
Tiago Pinto	Polytechnic Institute of Porto, Portugal
Alexander Pokahr	University of Hamburg, Germany

Impact Assessment of Simultaneous Deployment of Electric Vehicle and Solar Energy Sources in Unbalanced Distribution Network

Sasmita Tripathy[1]([⊠]), Sriparna Roy Ghatak[1], Parimal Acharjee[2], and Fernando Lopes[3]

[1] School of Electrical Engineering, KIIT University, Bhubaneswar, India
{2081095,sghatakfel}@kiit.ac.in
[2] School of Electrical Engineering, NIT, Durgapur, India
parimal.acharjee@ee.nitdgp.ac.in
[3] LNEG-National Laboratory of Energy and Geology, Lisbon, Portugal
fernando.lopes@lneg.pt

Abstract. Due to rising pollution, countries across the world are concentrating towards Electrification in transportation sector. To meet the increasing charging demand of vehicles, integration of clean and green solar renewable sources in distribution network ia a viable option. In this paper, the impact of assimilating plug in hybrid electric vehicle (PHEVs) with solar panel in the distribution network in terms of all the technical factors such as voltage profile, line loss, voltage unbalance are analysed. Taking into account the uncertainty of PHEV load, the 24 h power demand curve of PHEVs is developed. The modelling of photovoltaic (PV) is done in OpenDSS software. The hourly load flow for unbalanced distribution system is performed in OpenDSS software interfaced with MATLAB. Highly unbalanced IEEE 13 bus system is choosen as the test network to perform the research work. The performance parameters are studied for different penetration levels of PHEVs with PV in the existing system. It is observed that with the injection of PV in the existing grid consisting of PHEVs and commercial load, voltage profile improves, voltage unbalance and the system loss reduces. Further it was also observed from the result that deployment of PV resulted in enhancement of penetration level of PHEV in the distribution network.

Keywords: Plug in hybrid electric vehicle · Probability density function · Photovoltaic · Voltage profile · Voltage unbalance factor

1 Introduction

In order to reduce the greenhouse gas emission and people's dependency on fossil fuel, electric vehicles are developed rapidly in the transportation sector as an alternative to internal combustion engine vehicles [1]. PHEVs have large battery pack and they are charged by either electric outlet like on a car park, at home, or by means of on-board electricity generation. As PHEVs consume large amount of electrical energy, so this increased demand of electricity may cause voltage drop, voltage unbalance condition or increased power losses in the system [2]. In the construction of smart energy city, a commercial building microgrid containing EVs and a solar energy system will play an important role.

To meet the additional demand of existing grid due to PHEV load and to improve the environmental condition, PV module is integrated with the system [3]. As a renewable and clean energy, solar renewable energy can be produced anywhere, including the urban areas for EV applications. Therefore, the joint allocation of PV with EV charging station is considered to reduce the greenhouse gas emission, meet the daytime charging demand and reduce the dependence on the power grid. The rising EV industry suggests a potential of zero emissions when they are powered by solar energy. If these high charging loads are charged by fossil fuel power plants, then they will have adverse effects on the environment. Therefore, it is important to charge these EVs through solar energy as much as possible [4]. However in many previous literature papers analysis of voltage unbalance condition is not being considered because it gives negative impacts on the electrical grid system [5].

In [6, 7], the voltage profile of the system integrated with EV load in distribution system was studied considering static load model. However dynamic EV load model considering time variation is more practical and realistic than static EV load models those are independent of time. Analysing, the impact performance of EV without considering the hourly load variation and in balanced system may lead to incorrect results [8, 9]. In [10, 11], the deterministic approach was considered for PHEV loads modelling in which exact data are taken from the historical datasheet without considering the uncertainty parameters. To analyze the impacts of EV in the distribution system, estimated PHEV load curve gives more appropriate result than the deterministic load curve of EV for 24 h.

Considering the above fact in this paper an effective planning model is developed which will enable safe and secured integration of PHEV with PV system in the unbalanced distribution network. To develop a realistic PHEV load model considering uncertainty, in this paper, around 40,000 vehicle trips are taken from NHTS datasheet. Here level 2 charger (6.6 kW) is considered for charging the PHEV in the commercial building. Considering practical condition such as solar irradiance and atmospheric temperature, the PV model is developed in the present research work. Also in this paper, the benefit of solar renewable source in maintaining voltage profile and voltage unbalance factor of the unbalanced distribution system in the presence of charging stations is studied and analyzed. To build a practical planning model along with PHEV a 24 h commercial load curve is considered in this paper.

In order to analyze the impacts of simultaneous allocation of PHEVs and solar energy source in IEEE 13 bus system, all the technical parameters such as voltage profile, voltage unbalance factor and system loss are considered. The load flow of the system with commercial load, PHEVs and PV is done considering their time varying characteristics. If the system parameters are not within the permissible limits, then the system may collapse. So it becomes essential to evaluate these parameters with incorporation of PHEV and solar renewable energy source. Moreover the performance parameters are also analyzed for different penetration level of PHEVs with PV in the existing system. From the literature [12, 13], it was observed that simultaneous allocation PV and capacitor in a single bus improves the system performance. Therefore considering this fact the buses having capacitors are chosen for the incorporation of PV panels.

The main contributions of this paper are as follows.

1. Considering the uncertainty parameters like trip miles and trip end time, the PDF, SOC and energy required by PHEVs are evaluated and realistic power demand curve is developed.
2. PV modelling is done and it is integrated in the test system.
3. The performance parameters such as voltage profile, voltage unbalance factor and active power loss are evaluated and compared for different penetration level of PHEVs with PV in the existing network containing commercial load.

The rest of the paper is organized as follows. Uncertainty behaviour of PHEV daily load and PV modelling will be presented in Sect. 2. Section 3 will describe the system parameters i.e. system power loss, voltage profile and voltage unbalance factor. Then methodology with proposed flowchart will be presented in Sect. 4. Results and discussions will be described in Sect. 5 and at last the conclusion will be represented in Sect. 6.

2 PHEV Load and PV Modelling

In this section, the detail modeling of PHEV load and PV are explained.

2.1 PHEV Modelling

To assess the impacts of PHEV on the distribution network, historical data i.e. transportation data is required. NHTS 2001 (National Household Travel Survey) [14] which is sponsored by U.S. Department of Transportation gives the complete data about travel and transportation in the United States. This NHTS datasheet comprises of data like house ID number, vehicle ID number, trip miles, trip end time, trip start time, type of vehicle, person ID number, weekdays, weekends etc. in [14]. In the NHTS datasheet, four types of PHEVs are identified i.e. automobile/car/wagon, Van (mini, cargo and passenger), Sports utility vehicle and Pickup Truck. Hence there is different battery capacity for 4 different vehicle types given in [14]. Here the daily driven distance is considered as the sum of all trips of the day. In this paper, uncertainty analysis of PHEV is done, therefore to generate the estimated PHEV load profile for 24 h probability density function is considered. To develop estimated PHEV load curve, the probability density function (PDF), state of charge (SOC), energy consumption and power demand are evaluated by considering uncertainties i.e. trip miles and trip end time.

Probability Density Function

About 40,000 vehicle trips are studied to develop PDF. The probability density functions are used to estimate the SOC of vehicle and also used to model the behavior of trip miles of each vehicle. The PDFs for each vehicle are calculated by the Gaussian Distribution Formula explained [15] in the following equation.

$$f_d(x) = \frac{1}{d\sigma_d\sqrt{2\pi}} \exp[-\frac{(\ln d - \mu_d)^2}{2\sigma_d^2}]$$

(1)

where σ_d = Standard deviation, μ_d = Mean and D = Distance driven by each vehicle.

State of Charge (SOC)

Initial SOC is one of the stochastic factor which is determined by using battery capacity and trip miles. In this paper, it is assumed that the EV owners will recharge their vehicles as soon as they finish their last trip. Under this assumption, we conclude that the ending time of the last travelling is considered as the starting time to charge. All EVs having initial SOC are assumed to be integrated with the distribution system. Here SOC is calculated by following equation.

$$SOC = \begin{cases} 100.\left(\frac{x-d}{x}\right), & d \le x \\ 0, & d > x \end{cases}$$

(2)

where x = All Electric Range (AER) of the PHEV i.e. 30 as referred [16]. Then proportional energy needed (PEN) is the total energy required to fully charge the EV. PEN of each PHEV is calculated by following equation,

$$PEN = 100 - SOC$$

(3)

In this paper, the four types of PHEVs with their battery capacity i.e. Compact Sedan (9.765 KWh), Mid-size Sedan (10.815 KWh), Mid-size SUV (13.125 KWh) and Full-size SUV (15.225) are mapped with the vehicle types. The energy consumption for each vehicle is calculated as follows. Where BC = Battery Capacity of PHEV

$$E_R = PEN \times BC$$

(4)

Charging Level

To calculate the charging duration time for PHEV, the charging level is required which is explained by the following equation.

$$\tau_{ch} = \frac{E_R}{CL}.$$

(5)

Here the standard outlets of 110 V/15 A (Single phase, 1.44 KW) and 240 V/30 A (Three phase, 7.2 KW) are labeled as normal and fast charging level respectively. These two charging levels are presented by EPRI and SAE J1772 standards, both are applicable in U.S. [16, 17]. By using the charging duration time, the power demand of each PHEV for 24 h is estimated.

2.2 PV Modelling

A PV module converts energy from the sun into electrical form depending upon the incident radiation on the module surface. By injecting PV module in the distribution system, system loss will reduce and voltage profile will improve. Here PV system model [13] is a combined model consisting of PV array and PV inverter for the distribution system impact analysis. It appears the same to the circuit model as a generator or storage device according to the function of active power. The maximum output power is extracted from a PV module, by controlling through MPPT controller. Here the active power is a function of the irradiance, temperature, and rated power at the maximum power point.

3 Performance Parameters

3.1 Voltage Profile

Voltage profile is a serious issue in power system network. To maintain the voltage stability, the voltage profile of the system should be within the permissible limits. The limit of voltage variation in between 0.9–1.1 pu is declared as the statutory limits of voltage profile at the consumers' terminals [18]. Whenever there is a change in the load of the system, the voltage profile changes in the distribution system. With the rapid increase of electricity loads, the power demand increases day by day, so the voltage at the consumer premises falls.

3.2 Voltage Unbalance Condition

In a three-phase system, voltage unbalance is a condition in which the three-phase voltages differ in amplitude or are displaced from their normal 120° phase relationship, or both [18]. The degree of unbalance is usually defined by the ratio of the negative sequence to positive sequence voltage component as follows.

$$\%VUF = \frac{negative\ sequence\ voltage}{positive\ sequence\ voltage} \times 100 \tag{6}$$

Like voltage drop, voltage unbalance factor causes motor damage, damage of electrical appliances etc. In this paper, the range of voltage unbalance factor should be in between 2%–3% taken as statutory limits of the system.

3.3 Active Power Loss

The increase of inductive loads like electric furnace, induction motors in the system leads to poor power factor as they draw reactive power. So the active loss of the system increases. As the radial distribution networks have high R/X ratio, so the system loss increases. The system loss is calculated for hourly basis after the dynamic load flow is done.

4 Methodology

The methodology adopted in this paper to get the result is explained in the above Fig. 1. Different data such as arrival time, trip miles, battery capacity and vehicle type are extracted from NHTS datasheet. By using these data, the pdf, SOC and the estimated power demand are evaluated and the probabilistic load curve of PHEV load for 24 h is developed and PV modelling is done. This 24 h load curve of PHEV load and PV renewable energy source are integrated with the existing unbalanced system to assess the impacts on the system.

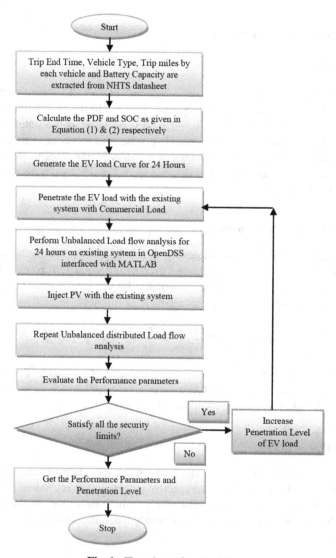

Fig. 1. Flowchart of methodology

Here the dynamic load flow of the existing system integrated with PHEV load is done and the different technical parameters are evaluated for analysis. The PV is incorporated with the system at different penetration of PHEVs and the system parameters i.e. system power loss, hourly voltage profile and voltage unbalance condition are evaluated and studied. If all the technical parameters are within the security limit, then the penetration level of PHEV load with size and location of PV system is obtained otherwise the process continues to get the best result.

5 Results and Discussion

In this paper, an unbalanced test system i.e. IEEE 13 bus system [19] is taken for analysis. It is a small system which operates at 4.16 kV. In addition, it has one source, one regulator, a number of short unbalanced transmission lines and shunt cpapcitors at the bus no. 611 and 675. The bus no. 650 is considered as bus no.1. Similarly bus no. 633, 634, 671, 645, 646, 692, 675, 611, 652, 632, 680 and 684 are taken as no. 2 to no. 13 respectively. MATLAB-OpenDSS interface is taken for unblanced load flow for 24 h. OpenDSS is an electric power distribution system simulator (DSS) which is basically a open source software [20]. This software is mainly suitable for unbalanced load flow and modifications can easily be done. As discussed earlier, probabilistic daily load curve of PHEV is generated by extracting the data from NHTS using Gaussian distribution formula. After integtrating the PHEV load curve in the system having commercial load, the above mentioned system parameters are assessed and analyzed for penetration levels of PHEV load. PV of 25 KW is injected at bus no. 611.

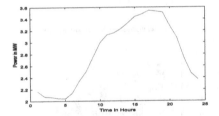

Fig. 2. Commercial load curve for 24 h

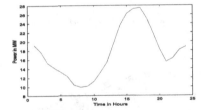

Fig. 3. Probabilistic curve of PHEV load

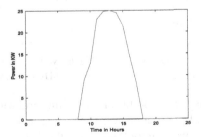

Fig. 4. PV curve

Practically the load at the bus can't be only PHEV load, so for real life analysis the combination of PHEV load and commercial load is taken. Figure 2 shows that the maximum active power of the system only with commercial load is 3.5 MW at 4 pm. Figure 3 demonstartes that the maximum power of probabilistic load curve of PHEV is 27.9 MW at 4 pm. If this probabilistic PHEV load curve will combine with the system with commercial load, then the load of the system is very high as it is the 100% penetration of PHEV load at each bus with commercial load for every hour. As we know, the voltage profile drops and the loss increases because of higher load on the system, so for analyzing the impacts on the system with the PHEV load, 10% of PHEV load is penetrated in the system with commercial load at first. Then the penetration level of PHEV load is increased for the comparision of results. The performance parameters i.e. voltage profile, voltage unbalace factor and the active loss of the system are observed and analysed.

To reduce the impacts of green house gas effects, solar panels are injected into the system. Therefore the impacts of simultaneously allocation of solar and PHEV load in the unbalanced system are assessed. Figure 4 represents the PV curve of solar output power on hourly basis from 9 am then reaches its maximum at 12 o'clock. Again it decreases to zero at 5 pm as the temperature falls. So the peak hour is in between 9 am to 5 pm and it becomes maximum at 1 pm.

5.1 Voltage Profile

It is observed from Table 1, the voltage profile lies in between 0.96–1.06 pu for 10% pentration of PHEV load with commercial load. Further it is observed that with the placement of PV module of size 25 kW at bus no. 611 in the existing system, the voltage profile improves and the range is in between 0.98–1.07 pu.

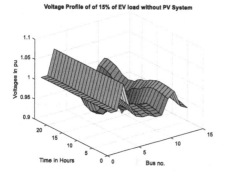
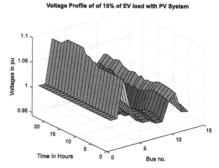

Fig. 5. Voltage Profile of the system with 15% of PHEV load without PV

Fig. 6. Voltage Profile of the system with 15% of PHEV load with PV

Figure 5 represents the voltage profile of the existing grid with commercial load with 15% of PHEV load for 24 h at different bus. The voltage at bus no. 650, source bus, 634 and 633 the voltage maintains 1 pu for through out the day. Here also the voltage at the bus no. 611, 675, 645 and 692 lies in between 0.9–0.96 pu during peak hours i.e. from 9 am to 5 pm and for remaining hours, it lies 1–1.06 pu. It shows that the voltage profile satisfies the security limit. After placing PV module in the existing system, the voltage at the bus no. 611, 675, 645 and 692 improves and the range is in between 0.95–1.08

pu as shown in Fig. 6. At the peak hours where the voltage is low, the voltage profile improves from 0.9 to 0.95 by adding PV system. Other than these buses, the voltage remains same as in case of 15% of PHEV load without solar system.

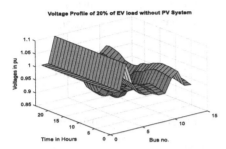

Fig. 7. Voltage profile of the system with 20% of PHEV load without PV

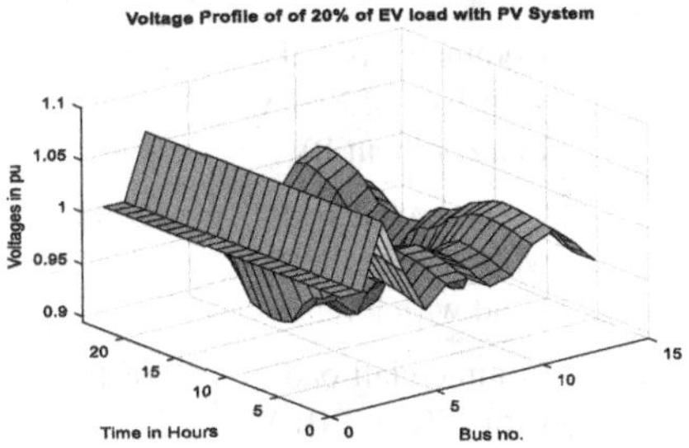

Fig. 8. Voltage profile of the system with 20% of PHEV load with PV

As shown in Fig. 7, the voltage profile of the sytsem with commercial load with 20% of PHEV ranges in between 0.85–1.1 pu. This range violates the security limit. The voltage remains low i.e. 0.85 during peak hours at the bus no. 675, 611, 645 and 692. Therefore the 20% of PHEV load with the commercial load can't be penetrated into the system. In this system if PV system is integrated, then the voltage profile improves and the range is within the security limits i.e. 0.9–1.1 p.u. The voltage at the bus no. 675,611, 652 and 692 increases from 0.85 p.u to 0.9 p.u by incorporating PV system as observed in Fig. 8.

5.2 Real Power Loss

From Table 1, it is observed that by increasing the penetration level, the daily real power loss increases. But by injecting solar panel into the system, the daily system loss decreases slightly. 5 solar panels of 5 KW each size at the bus no. 611 are incorporated with the system. As capacitor is present at bus no 611, the loss decreases, and the voltage profile improves due to the combination of capacitor and PV in the system.

5.3 Voltage Unbalance Factor (VUF)

Figure 9 represents the graph of the voltage unbalance condition for 24 h at different buses without PV. Further it is observed that at bus no. 675, the VUF is maximum. Therefore, in this paper further study of the VUF at bus no. 675 for hourly basis is evaluated for 15% and 20% of PHEV load with and without PV.

The voltage unbalance condition for 15% and 20% penetration level of PHEV load with commercial load and with PV system is observed in Fig. 10 and Fig. 11. During the peak hours i.e. from 9 am to 5 pm, the voltage unbalance condition increases and reaches its maximum and gradually decreases. It is shown from Fig. 10 that for 15% of penetration level of PHEV load, this value gradually increases as load increases and reaches its peak at 2.5%, after that it decreases as load decreases. Due to the presence

Table 1. Total real loss, maximum and minimum voltage at different penetration level of PHEV with PV

Sl. No	Different combination	Daily system loss (in MW)	Maximum voltage (in pu)	Minimum voltage (in pu)
1	CommercialLoad with 10% of PHEV Load without PV	2.3568	1.062327	0.968305
2	CommercialLoad with 10% of PHEV Load with PV	2.2484	1.082289	0.976963
3	CommercialLoad with 15% of PHEV Load without PV	7.6841	1.062142	0.917592
4	CommercialLoad with 15% of PHEV Load with PV	6.7038	1.099468	0.956324
5	CommercialLoad with 20% of PHEV Load without PV	11.5794	1.061855	0.858416
6	CommercialLoad with 20% of PHEV Load with PV	10.1535	1.099501	0.903348

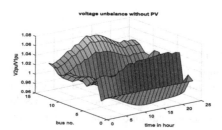

Fig. 9. Voltage unbalance condition versus different buses

of solar panel at bus no. 611, the voltage unbalance factor improves from 2.5% to 2.2% during the hours i.e. from 9 am to 5 pm.

At 20% penetration level in the existing system consisting of commercial load the value rises to 4.3% which is beyond the security limit as shown in Fig. 11. Due to the presence of PV system in the existing grid, the VUF improves means its value decreases to 3% which is within the limit.

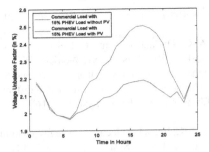

Fig. 10. VUF of the System with 15% of PHEV with & without PV

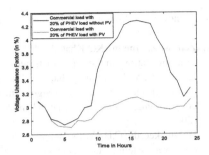

Fig. 11. VUF System with 20% of PHEV with & without PV

6 Conclusion

The simultaneous allocation of PHEV load and solar renewable energy source is considered to improve the system performance and to reduce environmental emission in this present paper. The estimated demand curve of PHEV load is incorporated with the existing IEEE-13 bus system with commercial load to study and analyze the impacts on distribution systems with different penetration levels. After incorporating PV module in the grid, the system performance such as voltage profile, VUF and system loss improves. For 20% penetration level of PHEV, the voltage profile lies in between 0.85–1.1 pu which violates the security constraints. But it is observed that the voltage profile remains in between 0.9–1.1 pu for 20% of PHEV load with PV which satisfies the security limit. Another major technical index is voltage unbalance, the maximum VUF is 2.5% and 4.3% for 15% and 20% of PHEV without PV module respectively. The maximum VUF becomes 2.2% and 3% for the system with 15% and 20% of PHEV load with PV module respectively. Hence it is observed that the voltage unbalance factor reduces when there is assimilation of PV in the distribution network. For the present work it is observed that without solar panels only 15% of total PHEV loads can be safely integrated in the network. But the penetration level increases to 20% when solar panels are integrated as it is observed from the results. Therefore it can be concluded that joint allocation of PV and PHEV enables higher penetration of PHEV in the distribution network.

In future, different strategies of smart charging can be adopted for integration of PHEVs with PV into the system to improve the penetration level of PHEV load.

References

1. Cazzola, P., Gorner, M., Schuitmaker, R., Maroney, E.: Global EV Outlook 2017. In: Int. Energy Agency (IEA), Paris, French, Tech. Rep., pp. 1–71 (2017)
2. Pieltain Fernandez, L., Gomez San Roman, T., Cossent, R., Mateo Domingo, C., Frías, P.: Assessment of the impact of plug-in electric vehicles on distribution networks. IEEE Trans. Power Syst. **26**(1), 206–213 (2011)
3. Turan, M.T., Ates, Y., Erdinc, O., Gokalp, E., Catalão, J.P.S.: Effect of electric vehicle parking lots equipped with roof mounted photovoltaic panels on the distribution network. Int. J. Electr. Power Energy Syst. **109**, 283–289 (2019)

4. Ajanovic, A.: Promoting environmentally benign electric vehicles. Energy Procedia **57**, 807–816 (2014)
5. Zeb, M.Z., Imran, K., Khattak, A., Janjua, A.K.: Optimal placement of electric vehicle charging stations in the active distribution network. IEEE Access **8**, 68124–68134 (2020)
6. Kongjeena, Y., Bhumkittipicha, K., Mithulananthan, N., Amiri, I.S., Yupapin, P.: A modified backward and forward sweep algorithm for microgrid load flow analysis under different electric vehicle load mathematical models. Elsevier Electr. Power Syst. Res. **168**, 46–54 (2019)
7. Dharmakeerthi, C.H., Mithulananthan, N., Saha, T.K.: Impact of electric vehicle fast charging on power system voltage stability. Int. J. Electr. Power Energy Syst. **57**, 241–249 (2014)
8. Kongjeen, Y., Bhumkittipich, K.: Impact of plug-in electric vehicles integrated into power distribution system based on voltage-dependent power flow analysis. Energies **11**(6), 1571 (2018)
9. Cheng, S., Gao, P.-F.: Optimal allocation of charging stations for electric vehicles in the distribution system. In: IEEE 3rd International Conference on Intelligent Green Building and Smart Grid (IGBSG), pp. 1–5 (2018)
10. Lin, S., He, Z., Zang, T., Qian, Q.: Impact of plug-in hybrid electric vehicles on distribution systems, power system technology (POWERCON). In: IEEE International Conference on Power System Technology, pp. 1–5 (2010)
11. Shafie, S., Firuzabad, M.F., Rastegar, M.: Investigating the impacts of plug-in hybrid electric vehicles on power distribution systems. IEEE Trans. Smart Grid **4**(3), 1351–1360 (2013)
12. Ghatak, S.R., Basu, D., Acharjee, P.: Voltage profile improvement and loss reduction using optimal allocation of SVC. In: 2015 IEEE India Conference (INDICON), pp. 1–6 (2015)
13. Mohanty, S., Tripathy, S., Ghatak, S.R., Mohapatra, A.: Impact assessment of PV penetration on unbalanced distribution network with dynamic load condition. In: 2nd International Conference on Power Electronics & IoT Applications in Renewable Energy and its Control (PARC), pp. 1–6 (2022)
14. National Household Travel Survey. http://nhts.ornl.gov
15. Xinwen, N., Lo, K.: A methodology to model daily charging load in the EV charging stations based on Monte Carlo simulation. In: IEEE International Conference on Smart Grid and Clean Energy Technologies (ICSGCE), pp.125–130 (2020)
16. Darabi, Z., Ferdowsi, M.: Extracting probability distribution functions applicable for PHEVs charging load profile. IEEE Trans. Sustain. Energy **2**(4), 501–508 (2011)
17. Morrow, K., Karner, D., Francefort, J.: U.S. Department of Energy Vehicle Technologies Program—Advanced Vehicle Testing Activity — Plug-in Hybrid Electric Vehicle Charging Infrastructure Review, Final report INL/EXT-08-15058, Idaho National Laboratory (INL) (2008)
18. Roy Ghatak, S., Sannigrahi, S., Acharjee, P.: Multiobjective framework for optimal integration of solar energy source in three-phase unbalanced distribution network. IEEE Trans. Ind. Appl. **56**(3), 3068–3078 (2020)
19. Nanchian, S., Majumdar, A., Pal, B.C.: Three phase state estimation using hybrid particle swarm optimization. In: IEEE Power and Energy Society General Meeting (PESGM), Boston, MA, USA (2016)
20. Dugan, R.: OpenDSS Circuit Solution Technique. EPRI, Palo Alto, CA, USA (2017)

Strategic Bidding of Retailers in Wholesale Energy Markets: A Model Using Hybrid Forecast Methods

Hugo Algarvio[✉] and Fernando Lopes

LNEG–National Laboratory of Energy and Geology,
Est. Paço do Lumiar 22, Lisbon, Portugal
{hugo.algarvio,fernando.lopes}@lneg.pt

Abstract. The liberalization of the electricity sector brought wholesale and retail competition to electricity markets. In the retail sector, different retailers compete to sign bilateral contracts with consumers. Typically, retailers consider high premiums to cover their potential risks when acquiring energy in wholesale markets. This paper proposes a model for strategic bidding of retailers in wholesale markets. The model includes several hybrid forecast methods, namely a multivariate time series for long-term prediction of electricity prices and consumption, a historical meteorological comparison of consumption to day-ahead forecast, and short-run trends for intra-day forecast of consumption. The paper also presents a case study where retailers with different risk attitudes submit bids to the spot market to satisfy their consumers. The results show that bidding to short-term markets leads to lower forecast errors than bidding to medium- and long-term markets. Furthermore, retailers with large and varied portfolios of customers may have lower forecast errors than retailers with small portfolios of customers.

Keywords: Electricity markets · Retailer entities · Strategic bidding · Risk management · Forecast methods · Portfolios of consumers

1 Introduction

The deregulation of the electricity industry brings competition to the energy supply in both wholesale and retail sectors [1]. Market entities can trade electricity at wholesale markets, bilateral markets and non-organised markets [2]. In wholesale markets, they can submit bids to day-ahead and intraday (sub-) markets. Real-time deviations from the schedules of balance responsible parties (BRPs) need to be managed at balancing markets [3]. BRPs may have to pay/receive the down/up balancing costs, which normally results in penalties. In bilateral markets, participants can sign standard financial and physical contracts to hedge against spot price volatility (and consumption uncertainty), reducing their risk. For non-standard agreements, they can negotiate privately the terms and conditions of bilateral contracts [4,5].

A. González-Briones et al. (Eds.): PAAMS Workshops 2022, CCIS 1678, pp. 295–305, 2022.
https://doi.org/10.1007/978-3-031-18697-4_24

Retailers can sign private bilateral contracts with end-use consumers, thus obtaining a private portfolio to manage. They usually follow a business as usual strategy, considering high risk premiums in their proposed tariffs. These risk premiums depend on the risk attitude of retailers (also known as risk preference or appetite), which can be characterized as risk-averse, risk-neutral or risk-seeking (see, e.g., [6,7]).

To avoid losses, a major issue that retailers should consider when proposing tariffs to consumers is the forecast of market prices. The dynamic of the portfolios is very dependent of the meteorological conditions, the consumption days (weekdays, holidays or weekends), and the type of consumers (residential, commercial, industrial, etc.). So, minimizing the variability of the portfolios can be a good solution to avoid high forecast errors, which can result in unbalances, and consequently in the payment of penalties. Short-run strategic bidding is often considered crucial to retailers, since bilateral transactions are usually made in the long-run (months before real-time consumption).

Ayón et al. [8] pointed out that large and varied portfolios of consumers may reduce demand forecast errors. The authors also stated that aggregations of flexible demand are beneficial to reduce demand forecast errors, increasing the return of aggregators. Wei et al. [9] presented a review of 128 forecast models for energy demand. They indicated a mean absolute percentage error (MAPE) of 10% as the threshold for highly accurate forecasts. They concluded that small-scale forecasts (e.g., small consumers) have larger errors than large-scale forecasts (e.g., large consumers). Koponen et al. [10] presented a review of 12 models to forecast short-term electricity demand. They used the models in 6 different scenarios. They concluded that the normalized root mean square error (NRMSE) of the forecasts decreases with the number of aggregated consumers. They also stated that hybrid methods should be used to compute demand forecasts.

Against this background, this paper focuses on developing a strategic bidding model for retailers participating in spot markets, aiming at reducing forecast errors, and consequently unbalances and penalties, increasing the return. The work presented here refines and extends our previous work on portfolio optimization [6,7,11], electricity markets [3], and risk management [12,13].

The remainder of the paper is structured as follows. Section 2 presents an overview of bilateral contracting, risk management and portfolio optimization. Section 3 introduces a model for strategic bidding of retailers. Section 4 presents a case study. Finally, concluding remarks are presented in Sect. 5.

2   Risk Management and Portfolio Optimization

Sellers and buyers of electricity negotiate bilateral contracts to hedge against spot price volatility. Their attitude towards risk can be classified as risk-averse, risk-neutral, and risk-seeking. They consider different utility functions according to their risk attitude [12]. Typically, they follow a risk management process involving three main phases: risk assessment, risk characterization and risk mitigation.

Retailers want to optimize the risk-return output of their portfolios by taking into account their attitude towards risk. They sign customized contracts with key consumers and select the best market options to purchase electricity. In [6], we proposed an optimization model that can be used to select key consumers for portfolios of retailers, using the aforementioned three phases of the risk management process, as well as a risk-return optimization of the portfolios and the Markowitz theory, in order to obtain the efficient frontier that optimizes the portfolios. In the first phase, retailers face the following risk factors: market price volatility and consumption uncertainty of portfolios. In the second phase, retailers can use the VaR to verify how the previous risk factors can affect their potential return. In the third phase, by adopting the optimization problem described in [6], they can obtain the point that optimizes their risk-return ratio (consisting in a share of consumers in their portfolios), considering their risk attitude and the tariffs proposed to consumers.

The Markowitz efficient frontier is obtained by considering the conditions of the markets defined in the first phase of the risk management process, the risk analysis carried out in the second phase (e.g., using VaR), and the optimized points obtained in the third phase. Retailers obtain the efficient frontier from the different efficient points (a specific point is considered efficient if no other point can surpass its result in terms of risk or return).

The electricity tariff is essentially a two-part tariff with a fixed payment for power (contracted capacity) and a price per unit of used electricity (variable fee). Both fees are divided into several parts, but the part that may give a return to retailers is the energy part [6]. So, retailers can set a return tax for each consumer, according to the sum of the risk-free (deposits) of the global markets with the risk premium. The risk premium depends on several factors (e.g., the risk associated with the market price volatility and the consumption uncertainty).

In [6], we also presented several pricing strategies to be adopted by retailers to negotiate with consumers. The strategies can be selected by considering the type of tariff (single, dual, three-rate, etc.), the equality of tariff (personalized or not), the equality of return (if every consumer gives a similar return to retailer), etc. The "Equal Return OPtimization" (EROP) strategy defines the minimum tariff that retailers may offer to consumers to receive an equal target return from each of them. The "Equal Tariff Optimization strategy at a Minimum Return" (ETOMinR) is not personalized, considering the same tariff for all consumers. Retailers compute a tariff to each consumer and select the highest one because it guarantees that them receive the minimum target return. The "Equal Tariff Optimization at a Maximum Return" (ETOMaxR) strategy is also not personalized. To guarantee a maximum target return from all consumers, retailers compute a tariff to each consumer, and the minimum tariff (between all computed) is selected, because it guarantees that retailers receive their target maximum return. The "Equal Return Tariff based on Market-Costs" (ERTMC) strategy reflects the expected costs of retailers with each consumer, considering their consumption pattern [7].

The Calinski-Harabasz (CH) criterion computes the Euclidean distance between different clusters and compares it with the internal sum of squared errors for each cluster. K-means clustering is a robust technique that minimizes the distance between each point and the centre of its respective cluster [7]. Considering the consumption profile of each consumer, and using the CH criterion, it is possible to obtain the optimal number of profiles (clusters). Furthermore, by using K-means clustering, it is possible to divide consumers by profile. Each cluster represents the consumption segment of each consumer, with a typical load profile.

Future predictions of the arithmetic cost of electricity for each consumer are computed by considering a forecast method adapted from [6]. The method consists of a Multivariate Time series (MTS) that uses the wholesale market prices of electricity, the electricity consumption, and the share of renewable energy associated with the production of electricity. Also, future predictions of the electricity consumption are computed by using an MTS forecast method adapted from [7].

Now, by considering the optimization model and the pricing strategies, it is possible to compute the expected return of retailers for long periods of time. However, retailers need to submit bids to wholesale markets based on power forecasts, which can lead to power deviations and penalties during real-time operation. The next section discusses the strategic bidding of retailers in wholesale markets, in order to reduce the errors of consumption forecasts and their effects on the final return.

3   Strategic Bidding in Wholesale Markets

Retailers can submit bids to wholesale markets or enter into bilateral agreements to acquire energy from producers and other suppliers. As BRPs, they are responsible for their deviations, meaning that their imbalances need to be compensated in balancing markets. Also, the day-ahead market (DAM) can be used to obtain/sell the need/excess of electricity. Furthermore, the intra-day market (IDM) can be used to compensate potential short-run imbalances.

Retailers select the past day, $\hat{D}$, with the minimum Euclidean distance, d, between the historical weather data of a particular past day, W_{D-i}, and the weather forecast of the target day, $\hat{W}_D$, considering one or more weather sensitive variables (e.g., humidity or ambient temperature).

$$\hat{D} = min(d(\hat{W}_D, W_{D-i})) \tag{1}$$

Retailers compute the expected consumption, $\hat{q}_{j,D}$, by getting the consumption of the past day, $q_{j,\hat{D}}$, and considering the consumption forecast of the current year, $\hat{q}_t$, as well as the consumption of the past year q_{t-1}:

$$\hat{q}_{j,D} = q_{j,\hat{D}} \frac{\hat{q}_t}{q_{t-1}} \tag{2}$$

To forecast the yearly electricity consumption, retailers use an MTS method adapted from [7]. They compute the (hourly) consumption forecast of the portfolio, $\hat{q}_{D,h}$, by considering the forecast, $\hat{q}_{j,D,h}$, of each consumer c_j for each time period h of day D:

$$\hat{q}_{D,h} = \sum_{h=1}^{H}\sum_{j=1}^{J} \hat{q}_{j,D,h} \tag{3}$$

Retailers determine the bids to submit to the DAM by considering the energy involved in the entire portfolio $q_{0,h}$. For each time period, they may consider several contracts Ct. The total quantity of electricity guaranteed through bilateral contracts is denoted as $q_{c,h}$, so that:

$$q_{0,h} = \hat{q}_{D,h} - q_{c,h} \tag{4}$$

$$q_{c,h} = \sum_{ct=1}^{Ct} q_{c_{ct},h} \tag{5}$$

For a particular time period of the day, if the quantity of electricity guaranteed through bilateral contracts is higher than the energy forecasted, $\hat{q}_{D,h}$, then retailers try to sell the excess in the intra-day market. To this end, the bids are computed by using a simple strategy: in the case of buying electricity, retailers offer the price-cap (maximum price) of the market, to guarantee that they buy the required electricity to satisfy their portfolio; otherwise, they offer the price of the bilateral contracts, to avoid economic losses.

Retailers compute the consumption forecast, $\hat{q}_{s,j,h}$, for bidding at each session of the intra-day market s, by using a method that takes into account the meteorological conditions and the short-run consumption tendency, as well as the bids submitted to the DAM and the growth-rate method for a short-run period of 1 h–7 h:

$$\hat{q}_{s,j,h} = \hat{q}_{s,j,h-1}\left(\sum_{h=1}^{H}\sum_{j=1}^{J} \frac{\hat{q}_{j,D,h}}{\hat{q}_{j,D,h-1}}\right) \tag{6}$$

This formula considers the real observed consumption of the previous time period, if it exists, or the forecast, $\hat{q}_{s,j,h-1}$. For each consumer j and time period h, it uses the bids submitted to the DAM at h (i.e., $\hat{q}_{j,D,h}$), and also at a previous time period, $\hat{q}_{j,D,h-1}$.

Retailers compute the bids to submit to each intra-day session, $q_{s,h}$, at time period, h, by considering the short-run forecast, as well as the electricity acquired through bilateral contracts, $q_{c,h}$, through the DAM, $q_{0,h}$, and in previous intra-day sessions, $q_{i,h}$:

$$q_{s,h} = \hat{q}_{j,h} - q_{c,h} - q_{0,h} - \sum_{i=1}^{s-1} q_{i,h} \tag{7}$$

They compute the imbalances for each time period, $q_{dev,h}$, by taking into account the real-time consumption of each consumer of the portfolio, $q_{j,h}$:

$$q_{dev,h} = \sum_{j=1}^{J} q_{j,h} - q_{c,h} - q_{0,h} - \sum_{s=1}^{S} q_{s,h} \tag{8}$$

Also, they compute their balance responsibility for each time period, $C_{dev,h}$, by considering their deviations, $q_{dev,h}$ and the prices of the excess, $P_{up,h}$, or the lack, $P_{down,h}$, of electricity, in cases of up or down deviations, respectively.

$$\begin{cases} C_{dev,h} = q_{dev,h} P_{up,h}, & \text{for } q_{dev,h} > 0 \\ C_{dev,h} = |q_{dev,h}| P_{down,h}, & \text{for } q_{dev,h} < 0 \end{cases} \tag{9}$$

Different bilateral contracts may have different prices for the energy. A contract ct has price, $P_{c_{ct},h}$, and the investment, I_h, of retailers is:

$$I_h = \sum_{j=1}^{J} \sum_{ct=1}^{Ct} P_{c_{ct},h} q_{c_{ct},h} + P_{0,h} q_{0,h} + \sum_{s=1}^{S} P_{s,h} q_{s,h} - C_{dev,h} \tag{10}$$

The profit per time period of retailers and the return on investment (ROI) are computed as follows:

$$R_h = \sum_{j=1}^{J} T_{j,h} q_{j,h} - \sum_{ct=1}^{Ct} P_{c_{ct},h} q_{c_{ct},h} + P_{0,h} q_{0,h} + \sum_{s=1}^{S} P_{s,h} q_{s,h} - C_{dev,h} \tag{11}$$

$$ROI = \sum_{h=1}^{H} \frac{R_h}{I_h} \tag{12}$$

The ROI is a performance indicator that allows to measure the profitability of investments.

To evaluate the performance of the forecast techniques, two different indicators, MAPE and NRMSE, are used:

$$MAPE = \frac{100\%}{H} \sum_{h=1}^{H} \left| \frac{q_h - \hat{q}_h}{q_h} \right| \tag{13}$$

$$NRMSE = 100\% \frac{\sqrt{\frac{1}{H} \sum_{h=1}^{H} (\hat{q}_h - q_h)^2}}{q_{max}} \tag{14}$$

where q_{max} is the maximum consumption per time period of the portfolio.

MAPE results are very intuitive, which makes this indicator one of the most used to measure forecasts accuracy. However, it has limitations, particularly it cannot be used with zero values and overestimates of negative errors ($\hat{q}_h > q_h$) concerning positive errors. NRMSE is used to evaluate energy forecasts. It overvalues high errors concerning low errors, which is often acceptable, due to the critical nature of the energy balance on power systems.

Table 1. Characteristics of retailers.

Retailer	Risk preference	Pricing strategy	Tariff type	Number of clients	Yearly energy (GWh)	Expected ROI (%)	VaR (%)
Ret_1	High aversion	EROP	3-rate	5	2.76	3.75	3.42
Ret_2	Moderate averse	ETOMaxR	3-rate	22	475.17	3.95	3.78
Ret_3	Small aversion	EROP	Single	13	30.46	7.54	3.99
Ret_4	Small seeking	ERTMC	3-rate	32	290.99	7.3	4.13
Ret_5	Moderate seek	ETOMinR	3-rate	13	48.58	7.79	4.19
Ret_6	High seeking	ETOMinR	3-rate	227	917.03	9.95	4.59

4   Case Study

This case study considers six computational agent retailers that want to invest in the Portuguese electricity market. The time period of the study ranges from January 1, 2012 to December 31, 2013.[1] The retailers are assumed to start operating at MIBEL in 2013, meaning that they can use real data from MIBEL. They have a target market of 312 real Portuguese consumers for their portfolios, corresponding to around 5% of the total consumption of the country [14]. Table 1 presents the main characteristics of each retailer, such as the expected ROI or VaR. The consumers are assumed to be connected to the middle voltage, so some of them are aggregations of residential and small commercial consumers. They are assumed to be divided into five segments: industrial (Ind), large commercial (LCom), aggregation of small commercials (AggSCom), aggregation of residentials (AggRES), and other aggregations.

Retailers propose customized bilateral contracts to consumers and, to satisfy their consumption needs, they acquire electricity on the wholesale market. The contracts involve either fixed single or three-rate tariffs, and variable consumption. The energy part of the tariff is the only part that can be negotiated. Retailers can offer personalized tariffs to different consumers or the same tariff to consumers inside the same consumption segment.

Retailers use an optimization model, adapted from [6], to obtain the optimized portfolios of end-use consumers, involving the Markowitz theory, pricing strategies, and risk/return objectives. To obtain the optimal portfolio for 2013, they use real market prices of 2012, updated with the forecasts for 2013, as well as real consumption from the target consumers from 2012, updated with forecasts for 2013. The forecast techniques presented in the previous section predicted a decrease in the wholesale market prices of 4.83% and an increase in consumption of 0.36%. This expected decrease in prices can be the result of an increase in the variable renewable generation with near-zero marginal costs.

---

[1] This data set can be found in an online repository: https://archive.ics.uci.edu/ml/datasets/ElectricityLoadDiagrams20112014#.

Table 2. Results of the study using real data from 2013.

Retailer	Optimal ROI (%)	Real ROI (%)	Demand variation (%)	DAM bids (%)	DAM MAPE (%)	IDM bids (%)	IDM direction (%)	IDM MAPE (%)
Ret_1	6.82	5.09	−5.43	101.88	41.96	34.02	−3.18	23.24
Ret_2	7.25	5.96	−8.76	104.91	25.15	26.74	−10.05	15.73
Ret_3	12.21	11.10	−4.84	102.96	12.63	12.97	−16.15	8.73
Ret_4	12.35	11.62	−7.50	105.22	12.15	12.20	−43.45	7.25
Ret_5	10.10	9.15	−6.75	105.05	11.94	11.85	−36.87	7.21
Ret_6	12.18	11.67	−2.22	101.02	6.68	6.58	−23.90	3.49

Retailers enter into retail competition by offering tariffs to consumers, thus obtaining a private portfolio to manage.[2] In general, the optimized portfolios only suggest a small number of consumers (but see [7]). To increase that number, different constraints in the optimization model can be considered, such as the quantity of electricity or the investment.

To determine the bids to submit to the DAM, forecasts based on the expected weather of the following day are used, considering the ambient temperature (see Eq. 1).[3] Tables 2 and 3 present the results of the case-study. The results shown in Table 2 indicate that the real returns obtained through the strategic bidding process are higher than the expected returns, because the wholesale market prices decreased around 9.2%, from 2012 to 2013. Also, the consumption needs of all portfolios decreased. Such decreases led to retailers bidding the excess quantities of energy in the day-ahead market.

Retailers that have portfolios with few consumers have higher errors in their forecasts, being the versatility and complementarity between consumers a good solution to avoid errors. While Ret_1 is the retailer with less risk, it is also the retailer with the highest forecast errors, because it is the retailer with fewer consumers. By comparing the real ROI with the optimal ROI, it is possible to verify that retailers with larger portfolios and lower forecast errors have lower differences in the ROI. Naturally, portfolios with a small number of consumers have substantial forecast errors. The forecast MAPE of Ret_6 is in line with the forecast accuracy of highly accurate forecast models from the literature, validating the proposed forecast models [9]. The DAM forecast deviations can be fixed in the intra-day market, resulting in a traded quantity significantly lower than in the DAM.

In 2013, the consumption decreases, leading retailers to trade the excess quantities of energy in the DAM (i.e., in the majority of hours, retailers sell the

---

[2] Tariffs proposed to target consumers, and their optimal and final portfolios, are presented in [15].

[3] Day-ahead forecasts of the ambient temperature consider data from the Global Forecast System at 7 a.m. (CET). Observed and forecast meteorological data can be found at: http://www.meteomanz.com/index?l=1.

Table 3. Results of the study using real data from 2013 (cont.).

Retailer	Expected ROI (%)	Real ROI (%)	IR (%)	DAM MAPE (%)	DAM NRMSE (%)	IDM MAPE (%)	IDM NRMSE (%)
Ret_1	3.75	5.09	35.73	41.96	13.16	23.24	10.41
Ret_2	3.95	5.96	50.89	25.16	14.02	15.73	7.34
Ret_3	7.54	11.10	47.21	12.63	8.25	8.73	4.54
Ret_4	7.93	11.62	46.53	12.15	8.71	7.25	4.38
Ret_5	7.79	9.15	17.59	11.94	7.67	7.21	4.36
Ret_6	9.95	11.67	17.29	6.68	5.96	3.49	2.99

excess in the intra-day market). The forecast errors of the bids submitted to the intra-day market are lower due to the use of upgraded meteorological information (such as, data closer to real-time consumption). These errors need to be fixed in balancing markets. The intrinsic variation in the ROI computes the difference between the real ROI and the expected $\hat{ROI}$, evaluating the output of retailers as follows:

$$IR = \frac{ROI - \hat{ROI}}{\hat{ROI}} \times 100 \qquad (15)$$

By analysing the IR, it is possible to verify that risk-seeking retailers have lower increases in their expected returns, which means that even with higher forecast errors, the portfolios of risk-averse retailers are more stable, leading to better outputs. Also, note that a decrease in energy consumption conducts to an excess of energy acquired in the DAM, leading to up deviations concerning real consumptions. Up deviations overvalues the MAPE, because real consumptions are lower than forecast consumptions in the majority of cases. In this way, the NRMSE can probably be a better indicator to evaluate the forecast results, by obtaining results that are independent of the deviation direction.

5   Conclusion

This article presented a simplified model for retailers trading energy in wholesale markets. The model considered three different hybrid forecast methods: a multi-variate time series for long-term prediction of electricity prices and consumption, a historical meteorological comparison of consumption to day-ahead forecasts, and a short-run trend for intraday forecasts of consumption.

Also, the article presented a case study to test the model in a simple set-ting, considering real data from Portuguese consumers and the MIBEL, for the period 2012–2013. The results confirmed that large amounts of diversified aggre-gated demands conduct to higher forecast accuracies. Risk-seeking retailers have a behaviour similar to traditional retailers, considering large portfolios with substantial risk, and high risk premiums in their tariffs. Risk-seeking retailers propose more competitive tariffs than risk-averse retailers. However, risk-averse retailers may obtain a better output from electricity markets, even with higher demand forecast errors than risk-seeking retailers.

The main issues that retailers face in energy markets are the volatility of spot prices and the uncertainty in the energy needs of their portfolios. Accordingly, to mitigate the associated effects, they can propose more competitive tariffs to target consumers. Additionally, they can enter into bilateral contracts in the wholesale market and sign demand response contracts with consumers in retail markets.

Future work is intended to study how derivatives products, private bilateral contracts, and demand response programs can be used as risk mitigation instruments, (potentially) increasing the risk-return ratio of retailers.

Acknowledgments. This work has received funding from the EU Horizon 2020 research and innovation program under project TradeRES (grant agreement No 864276).

References

1. Algarvio, H., Lopes, F., Couto, A., Estanqueiro, A., Santana, J.: Effects of regulating the European internal market on the integration of variable renewable energy. WIREs Energy Environ. **8**(6), e346 (2019)
2. Lopes, F., Coelho, H.: Electricity Markets with Increasing Levels of Renewable Generation: Structure, Operation, Agent-based Simulation, and Emerging Designs. Springer, Cham (2018). https://doi.org/10.1007/978-3-319-74263-2
3. Algarvio, H., Lopes, F., Couto, A., Estanqueiro, A.: Participation of wind power producers in Day-ahead and balancing markets: an overview and a simulation-based study. WIREs Energy Environ. **8**(5), e343 (2019)
4. Lopes, F., Coelho, H.: Concession behaviour in automated negotiation. In: Buccafurri, F., Semeraro, G. (eds.) EC-Web 2010. LNBIP, vol. 61, pp. 184–194. Springer, Heidelberg (2010). https://doi.org/10.1007/978-3-642-15208-5_17
5. Lopes, F., Coelho, H.: Concession strategies for negotiating bilateral contracts in multi-agent electricity markets. In: 23rd Database and Expert Systems Applications (DEXA 2012), pp. 321–325, IEEE (2012)
6. Algarvio, H., Lopes, F., Sousa, J., Lagarto, J.: Multi-agent electricity markets: retailer portfolio optimization using markowitz theory. Electr. Power Syst. Res. **148**, 282–294 (2017)
7. Algarvio, H., Lopes, F.: Agent-based retail competition and portfolio optimization in liberalized electricity markets: a study involving real-world consumers. Int. J. Electr. Power Energy Syst. **137**, 107687 (2022)
8. Ayón, X., Gruber, J., Hayes, B., Usaola, J., Prodanovic, M.: An optimal day-ahead load scheduling approach based on the flexibility of aggregate demands. Appl. Energy **198**, 1–11 (2017)
9. Wei, N., Li, C., Peng, X., Zeng, F., Lu, X.: Conventional models and artificial intelligence-based models for energy consumption forecasting: a review. J. Petrol. Sci. Eng. **181**, 106187 (2019)

10. Koponen, P., Ikäheimo, J., Koskela, J., Brester, C., Niska, H.: Assessing and comparing short term load forecasting performance. Energies **13**(8), 2054 (2020)
11. Algarvio, H.: Multi-step optimization of the purchasing options of power retailers to feed their portfolios of consumers. Int. J. Electr. Power Energy Syst. **142**, 108260 (2022)
12. Algarvio, H., Lopes, F.: Risk management and bilateral contracts in multi-agent electricity markets. In: Corchado, J.M., et al. (eds.) PAAMS 2014. CCIS, vol. 430, pp. 297–308. Springer, Cham (2014). https://doi.org/10.1007/978-3-319-07767-3_27
13. Lopes, F., Algarvio, H., Santana, J.: Agent-based simulation of electricity markets: risk management and contracts for difference. In: Alonso-Betanzos, A., et al. (eds.) Agent-Based Modeling of Sustainable Behaviors. UCS, pp. 207–225. Springer, Cham (2017). https://doi.org/10.1007/978-3-319-46331-5_10
14. Rodrigues, F., Trindade, A.: Load forecasting through functional clustering and ensemble learning. Knowl. Inform. Syst. **57**(1), 229–244 (2018). https://doi.org/10.1007/s10115-018-1169-y
15. Algarvio, H.: Retailers' Portfolio of Consumers. Harvard Dataverse, V2 (2021). https://doi.org/10.7910/DVN/WFQ5V0. Accessed on 3 June 2022

Approximate Time-Series Data Aggregation Using Grouping Nodes in Peer to Peer Network

Saptadi Nugroho[1,2(✉)], Christian Schindelhauer[1], and Andreas Christ[2]

[1] Albert-Ludwigs-Universität Freiburg,
Georges-Koehler-Allee 51, 79110 Freiburg, Germany
{snugroho,schindel}@informatik.uni-freiburg.de
[2] Offenburg University of Applied Sciences,
Badstraße 24, 77652 Offenburg, Germany
{saptadi.nugroho,christ}@hs-offenburg.de

Abstract. We consider the local group of agents for exchanging the time-series data value and computing the approximation of the mean value of all agents. An agent represented by a node knows all local neighbor nodes in the same group. The node has the contact information of other nodes in other groups. The nodes interact with each other in synchronous rounds to exchange the updated time-series data value using the random call communication model. The amount of data exchanged between agent-based sensors in the local group network affects the accuracy of the aggregation function results. At each time step, the agent-based sensor can update the input data value and send the updated data value to the group head node. The group head node sends the updated data value to all group members in the same group. Grouping nodes in peer-to-peer networks show an improvement in Mean Squared Error (MSE).

Keywords: Agent based sensor · Time series data · Approximation · Random call model · Peer to peer network

1 Introduction

In the energy market transactions, the prosumer and the consumer agents can communicate using a peer to peer network to exchange information about energy demand and availability. The energy market transactions based on a distribution network can balance the energy supply and demand [1]. In the peer to peer market, the prosumer and the consumer agents can perform the negotiation directly to match the energy demand and supply under the energy trading [2]. The agent-based sensors can produce time-series data values x_t updated over an indefinite time. A software agent uses time-series data values from agent-based sensors as input data. The updated data values are exchanged by agents in r rounds at each time t for computing an aggregation function [3].

© The Author(s), under exclusive license to Springer Nature Switzerland AG 2022
A. González-Briones et al. (Eds.): PAAMS Workshops 2022, CCIS 1678, pp. 306–312, 2022.
https://doi.org/10.1007/978-3-031-18697-4_25

The local community group for exchanging energy and information can be developed based on peer to peer approach in energy markets [1]. The agent-based sensors can be grouped to coordinate energy transactions with other agent-based sensors between the local distribution networks. The rapid growth of agent-based sensors in the network may become an issue in the aggregation process involving all agent-based sensors in the network. Therefore, the approximation of aggregation time-series data value involving a few nodes in the local community group is sufficient.

Contribution. In this paper, we propose the concept of data aggregation, which approximates the mean value of the nodes that have been grouped by using the Push and Pull communications of R. Karp et al. [4] in a peer to peer network. The nodes use the hashing function [5] to determine the group. We observe the message complexity, time complexity, and accuracy of the result of time-series data aggregation.

2   Related Work

The push and the pull random phone calls are the communication model proposed by R. Karp et al. [4]. In the push communication model, each caller node u chooses a callee node v randomly from V in the communication graph $G_t = (V, E_t \subseteq V \times V)$ to send the message. In the pull communication model, each callee node v replies to the caller node u, which requests the node v's message. The data aggregation based on the Push-Sum protocol [6] has the convergence rate exponentially to estimate the average.

The structure of network topologies can affect the performance of the time-series data aggregation process in the peer to peer network. The nodes can collect the data values using the random-walk-based approach [7,8]. In the tree-based approach proposed by M. Bawa et al. [8], the parent nodes collect the messages from their children and send the aggregation function result to their children. The message can be exchanged between the parent nodes and the children nodes.

In the Kelips algorithm proposed by Gupta et al. [5], nodes are joined in k affinity groups. Each node knows all neighbor nodes which are in the same affinity group. In addition, every node has the contact information of other nodes lying in the other groups. The node uses the hashing function for assigning the node to a group.

3   Methods

Let a node represents an agent-based sensor that produces time-series data value of $x_t \in \mathbb{R}_0^+$. Nodes are fully connected in the communication graph G_t. Nodes use the push and pull communication protocol that occurs synchronously. Every node runs the algorithm described in Algorithm 1. In the first round, the INITIALIZATION procedure is called. The node generates the node's identity I, the group identity I_G, and the set of the group member C_m. The group head C_h

Algorithm 1. Grouping Node Algorithm

---

procedure INITIALIZATION
    Generate Node ID $I_u \leftarrow f_{hash}(ID)$
    Group Identity $I_{G_u} \leftarrow I_u$ Mod k_u
    A Group Head $C_h \leftarrow \varnothing$
    Set of Group Member $C_m \leftarrow \{(x_u, I_u, I_{G_u})\}$
    Set of Group Non Member $C_{nm} \leftarrow \varnothing$
end procedure
procedure REQUESTDATA
    if $C_h = \varnothing$ **then**
        Choose one neighbor node v randomly
    else if $C_h \neq \varnothing$ **then**
        node $v \leftarrow C_h$
    end if
    Send C_{m_u} to the node v
end procedure
procedure RESPONSEDATA
    if $I_{G_u} \neq I_{G_v}$ **then**
        Send the information about node u
    else
        Send C_{m_u} to the node v
    end if
end procedure
procedure AGGREGATE
    if $I_{G_u} == I_{G_v}$ **then**
        $C_{m_v} \leftarrow$ Set of x_v, I_v, I_{G_v} of the caller node v
        $C_{m_u} \leftarrow$ Set of x_u, I_u, I_{G_u} of the node u called by node v
        $C_{m_u} \leftarrow C_{m_u} \bigcup C_{m_v}$
        $C_h \leftarrow f_{min}(I_u)$
        $s_u \leftarrow \sum_{i \in C_{m_u}} x_i, n_u \leftarrow |C_{m_u}|$
        $f_{avg} \leftarrow \frac{s_u}{n_u}$
    else
        Update C_{nm}
    end if
end procedure

---

is set to $\varnothing$. In every round of agent communication, every agent will exchange the set of group member C_m, consisting of the local measurement value x, agent identity I, and agent group identity I_G. The node will calculate the approximate value of the mean $f_{avg} = \frac{s}{n}$.

Every node executes the REQUESTDATA procedure in every round except the first round. In the REQUESTDATA procedure, if the caller node u has no group head, $C_{h_u} = \varnothing$, then the caller node u will randomly choose one neighbor node v and send the C_{m_u} to the node v for requesting data. If the caller node u has a group head, then the caller node u will send the C_{m_u} to the group head for requesting data.

At the end of every round, nodes run the RESPONSEDATA procedure. In the RESPONSEDATA procedure, the callee node v sends the C_{m_v} to the caller node u if the caller node u and the callee node v are in the same group. If the caller node u and the callee node v are not in the same group, the callee node v sends the node's information C_{m_v}. In the AGGREGATE procedure, the nodes will do the aggregation process if they are in the same group.

4   Experimental Results

Every node retrieves the C_m from other nodes and calculates the approximate mean value of the sensor inputs. The PeerSim [9] is used to simulate the push and pull communication process. The network's mean ground truth $f_{MeanGroundTruth}$ and the nodes' approximate mean value f_{avg} are inputs for the observer to calculate the Mean Squared Error (MSE) in every round of communication.

$$f_{MSE} = \frac{1}{N} \sum_{i=1}^{N} \left(f_{MeanGroundTruth} - f_{avg_i} \right)^2 \tag{1}$$

The number of nodes N used in the experiments is 10^3 nodes. The experiment is performed 50 times. The input data value x used by every node is uniformly distributed in the range from 0 to 100. Nodes can change the input data value x every time t. The nodes communicate using the push and pull communication protocol at a time t in synchronous r rounds until the network converges to a result value of the aggregation function.

The nodes in the same group exchange the C_m and choose the C_h. At $t = 1$, the node needs some rounds r to have the same C_m and C_h, as shown in Fig. 1.

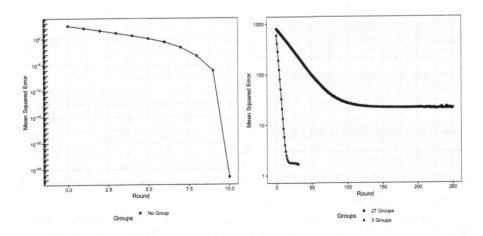

Fig. 1. The number of rounds and the MSE of grouping nodes with the uniformly distributed input data values and $N = 10^3$ at $t = 1$.

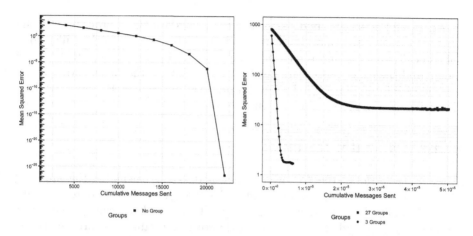

Fig. 2. The cumulative message sent and the MSE of grouping nodes with the uniformly distributed input data values and $N = 10^3$ at $t = 1$.

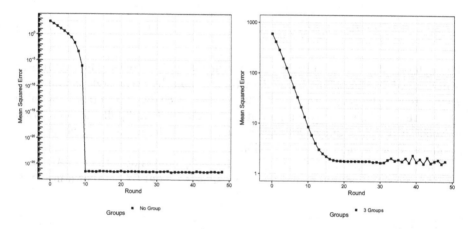

Fig. 3. The number of rounds and the MSE of grouping nodes with the uniformly distributed input data values and $N = 10^3$ at $t \geq 1$.

The greater the number of groups formed by nodes in a network using the push and pull communication protocol, the more rounds r are needed to obtain the same C_m and C_h. The cumulative number of messages sent by nodes will increase as the number of rounds increases, as shown in Fig. 2. Each node that is part of a group I_G will point to one node as the group head C_h. All nodes will have the group head C_h after some round r at $t = 1$. Each node calculates the approximate aggregation of the mean value $f_{avg} = \frac{\sum_{j \in C_m} x_j}{|C_m|}$.

The number of rounds and the number of messages needed for calculating the approximate aggregation at time $t \geq 1$ are shown in Fig. 3 and Fig. 4. At time $t = 1$, the caller node u chooses the callee node v randomly for exchanging the message C_m. The detail rounds in Fig. 3 and the detailed number of cumulative

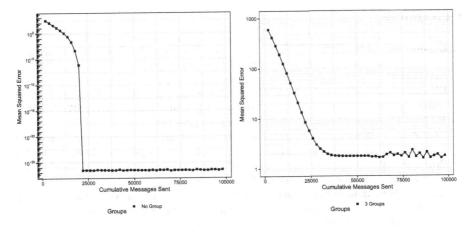

Fig. 4. The cumulative message sent and the MSE of grouping nodes with the uniformly distributed input data values and $N = 10^3$ at $t \geq 1$.

messages sent by nodes in Fig. 4 at time $t = 1$ are plotted in Fig. 1 and Fig. 2. Every time t, each node can get a new data value x_t. At time $t > 1$, all nodes u send the message to the group head C_h. The group heads C_h aggregate all messages received from the group members in C_m. Each group head C_h replies to all group members' requests by sending the C_m in the same round. Every node can calculate the approximate aggregation of the mean value f_{avg} after getting the response from the group head C_h. As shown in Fig. 3 and Fig. 4, the nodes can quickly approximate the time series data aggregation with a few number of cumulative messages sent at time $t > 1$.

5   Conclusion

We investigated the design of grouping nodes in the peer to peer network to compute the approximation of aggregation time-series data value. All nodes exchange the message C_m used as an input for the aggregation function. At $t = 1$, the node needs some round r to have the same C_m and elect the group head C_h. At time $t = 1$, the push and pull communication protocol for grouping nodes showed an exponential improvement in accuracy over the number of messages sent by nodes. At time $t > 1$, all nodes send the updated message to the group head C_h. The group heads C_h aggregate all messages sent by the group members. The group head will send the aggregation result message C_m to nodes of the group member.

Acknowledgment. This work was supported by the Indonesian Endowment Fund for Education (LPDP) scholarship program. The authors acknowledge support from Albert-Ludwigs-Universität Freiburg and Offenburg University of Applied Sciences.

References

1. Honarmand, M.E., Hosseinnezhad, V., Hayes, B., Siano, P.: Local energy trading in future distribution systems. Energies **14**, 3110 (2021). https://doi.org/10.3390/en14113110
2. Khorasany, M., Mishra, Y., Ledwich, G.: A decentralized bilateral energy trading system for peer-to-peer electricity markets. IEEE Trans. Ind. Electron. **67**(6), 4646–4657 (2020). https://doi.org/10.1109/TIE.2019.2931229
3. Nugroho, S., Weinmann, A., Schindelhauer, C., Christ, A.: Averaging emulated time-series data using approximate histograms in peer to peer networks. In: De La Prieta, F., et al. (eds.) PAAMS 2020. CCIS, vol. 1233, pp. 339–346. Springer, Cham (2020). https://doi.org/10.1007/978-3-030-51999-5_28
4. Karp, R., Schindelhauer, C., Shenker, S., Vöcking, B.: Randomized rumor spreading. In: Proceedings 41st Annual Symposium on Foundations of Computer Science, pp. 565–574. IEEE Computer Society, United States (2000)
5. Gupta, I., Birman, K., Linga, P., Demers, A., van Renesse, R.: Kelips: building an efficient and stable P2P DHT through increased memory and background overhead. In: Kaashoek, M.F., Stoica, I. (eds.) IPTPS 2003. LNCS, vol. 2735, pp. 160–169. Springer, Heidelberg (2003). https://doi.org/10.1007/978-3-540-45172-3_15
6. Kempe, D., Dobra, A., Gehrke, J.: Gossip-based computation of aggregate information. In: 2003 Proceedings of 44th Annual IEEE Symposium on Foundations of Computer Science, pp. 482–491 (2003). https://doi.org/10.1109/SFCS.2003.1238221
7. Datta, S., Kargupta, H.: Uniform data sampling from a peer-to-peer network. In: 27th International Conference on Distributed Computing Systems (ICDCS 2007), pp. 1–8 (2007). https://doi.org/10.1109/ICDCS.2007.6238553
8. Bawa, M., Garcia-Molina, H., Gionis, A., Motwani, R.: Estimating aggregates on a peer-to-peer network. Technical report TR-2003-24. Stanford University (2003). Stanford InfoLab Homepage. https://ilpubs.stanford.edu:8090/586/. Accessed 1 Apr 2021
9. Montresor, A., Jelasity, M.: PeerSim: a scalable P2P simulator. In: Proceedings of the 9th International Conference on Peer-to-Peer (P2P 2009), Seattle, WA, pp. 99–100, September 2009

Author Index

Printed in the United States
by Baker & Taylor Publisher Services